DATE DUE			

Using Discounted
Cash Flow Effectively

Using Discounted Cash Flow Effectively

Herbert E. Kroeger

DOW JONES-IRWIN
Homewood, Illinois   60430

© DOW JONES-IRWIN, 1984

This publication is designed to provide accurate and authoritative information in regard to the subject matter covered. It is sold with the understanding that the publisher is not engaged in rendering legal, accounting, or other professional service. If legal advice or other expert assistance is required, the services of a competent professional person should be sought.

From a Declaration of Principles jointly adopted by a Committee of the American Bar Association and a Committee of Publishers.

ISBN 0-87094-553-X

Library of Congress Catalog Card No. 84–70259

Printed in the United States of America

1 2 3 4 5 6 7 8 9 0 K 1 0 9 8 7 6 5 4

Dedicated to
My wife,
CAROLINE

Preface

For as long as discounted cash flow has been used in capital investments, professionals in both the business community and in academic circles have been critical of the financial criteria determined by discounted cash flow techniques. These criticisms are unwarranted and unjustifiable because there is nothing intrinsically wrong with the financial criteria, except for the manner in which they are determined. This is particularly true, for example, in the case of the discounted cash flow (DCF) rate of return.

Surely, no one can seriously quarrel with the fact that the compound interest rate is considered to be a true and realistic rate as used by banks and other lending institutions in making self-amortizing loans to outside borrowers. It is a constant-level rate used to calculate the interest factor on the unpaid balance of the loan principal, and the remainder of the periodic loan payment amounts represents repayment of the principal during the loan term.

Similarly, the DCF rate of return, as it is used by business organizations in internal loans to projects, is a constant-level rate used to calculate the profit factor on the unrecovered portion of the capital investment, and the remainder of the annual cash income on savings amounts represents recovery of the capital investment during the project's economic life.

Since the DCF rate of return is comparable to the compound interest rate and both rates are determined by the same discounted cash flow technique, one may reasonably inquire why the DCF rate of return so frequently is grossly distorted and dangerously unrealistic. The reason for this is twofold.

First, in the use of the compound interest rate, banks and other lending institutions are dealing with financial factors that are actual, such as the loan amount, the loan term, and the periodic loan payment amounts. On the other hand, in the use of the DCF rate of return, business organizations are dealing with similar financial factors, but they are estimated, such as the capital investment amount, the project's economic life, and the annual cash income or savings amounts. This *difference* in dealing strictly with estimated instead of with actual financial factors explains in part why DCF rates of return can be only as realistic as the estimates on which they are calculated are realistic, and the assumptions on which these estimates are based are plausible. Obviously, to overcome this serious problem requires that the estimates of a prospective project's capital cost, cash returns, and economic life be prepared thoroughly and intelligently by experts in particular areas.

Second, in the use of the compound interest rate, loans of banks and other lending institutions to outside borrowers invariably occur in a lump-sum amount at the zero reference point, which is immediately before the time the loans start generating periodic loan payment amounts. On the other hand, in the use of the DCF rate of return, internal loans of companies to projects may occur in a lump-sum amount at the zero reference point, or they may occur in a series of amounts extending over a period of years either before or after that point in time. This difference in the timing of the loan amounts, or capital outlays, creates another serious problem in determining realistic DCF rates of return because it requires selecting the proper rate to use for compounding and/or discounting when early or delayed capital spending occurs in prospective projects. This raises the question as to what rate to use. Should it be the rate used in the conventional DCF method that is arrived at by trial and error and is a different rate for each prospective project—no matter how outrageous and preposterous it is? Or should it be the company's opportunity cost of money rate, or its prime interest or direct borrowing rate, which in either case will mean the same rate will be used for all prospective projects?

Whether meaningful and realistic DCF rates of return will be arrived at when early or delayed capital spending occurs in prospective projects will depend on whether the proper rate is used for compounding and/or discounting the capital outlays. This means that the rate used must arrive at present values, or lump-sum amounts, at the zero reference point that will represent realistic investment bases on which to calculate the prospective projects' DCF rates of return.

This dual problem of preparing realistic estimates and selecting the proper rate for compounding and/or discounting exists when business organizations must determine: (1) how much they can afford to invest in prospective projects, (2) how much cash income or savings they have to generate, (3) how long they have to be productive, (4) what rate of return they will earn, and (5) how much companies to be acquired are worth and what price to pay for them.

Herbert E. Kroeger

Contents

Lease Fixed Assets. Factors Required to Determine the Profitability and the Liquidity of Leased Fixed Assets. How to Calculate DCF Rates of Return for Projects Involving Leased Fixed Assets: *Step Number 1. Step Number 2. Step Number 3. Step Number 4.* What Rate to Use for Discounting to Determine the Investment Equivalent. How Buy versus Lease Decisions Are Made. How to Determine the After-Tax Cost of Leasing. Why Leasing Benefits Are Illusory.

Description of Project A. Project A's DCF Rate of Return Calculated under the Conventional DCF Method. If Projects A and B Are Financed through External Sources. Profitability of Projects A and B if Financed Externally. Project A's DCF Rate of Return Calculated by the Proposed DCF Method. Determine Net Present Values (NPVs) for Alternatives I and II. Project A's DCF Rate of Return Based on Comparison of the Right Alternatives. Project A's NPV Based on Comparison of the Right Alternatives. The Actual Investment Decision Made by the Multinational Company. Similar Unwise Investment Decisions Can Be Avoided.

What Depreciation Is. How Many Depreciation Methods Are There? When the Accelerated Depreciation Methods May Be Used for Tax Purposes. How Annual Depreciation Charges Are Calculated. What the Differences in the Timing of Depreciation Charges Indicate. Proof Sum-of-the-Years'-Digits Method Is More Advantageous than Straight-Line Method for Income Tax Purposes. Why the Straight-Line Method Is Normally Used for Book Purposes. The Rationale on Which Depreciation Is Based. The Accounting Treatment and Financial Reporting of Depreciation: *Step Number 1. Step Number 2. Step Number 3. Step Number 4. Step Number 5.* How Inflation Creates Depreciation Deficiencies. Popular Misconception of How to Determine Depreciation Deficiencies. How to Recover the Full Purchasing Power of Original Investments during Inflationary Periods. Effect on Profitability When Depreciating Project C's Fixed Assets on Their Original versus Their Current-Year Replacement Cost.

Pitfalls Encountered in Estimating Prospective Projects' Capital Costs and Capital Recoveries. Pitfalls Encountered in Estimating Prospective Projects' Future Cash Income or Savings. Pitfalls in Estimating Prospective Projects' Economic Lives. Pitfalls Encountered in the Selection of the Most Economic Alternative. Pitfalls Encountered in the Consideration of Imponderables.

What "Must" Investments Are. How to Select the Least Expensive Alternative Method for a "Must" Investment. Post-Completion Audits Required for Profit-Generating and Cost-Saving Prospective Projects. Principal Obstacles Encountered in Making Post-Completion Audits of New Projects. New Profit-Generating and Cost-Saving Projects that Warrant Only Limited Post-Completion Audits. New

Profit-Generating and Cost-Saving Projects that Warrant More Elaborate Post-Completion Audits. When New Profit-Generating and Cost-Saving Projects Are Ready for Post-Completion Audits. Procedure for Conducting Post-Completion Audits for New Profit-Generating and Cost-Saving Projects: *Project D's Economic Evaluation. Project D's Post-Completion Audit which Ignores Proper Adjustment for Inflation. Project D's Post-Completion Audit Results versus Its Original Estimates.* Another Method of Proving Why Present Corporate Income Tax Laws Pertaining to Depreciation Should Be Revised. The Effects of Inflation on New Projects' Cash Flows. The Proper Index to Use for Adjusting New Projects' Cash Flows for Inflation. The Problem of Depreciation Deficiencies—What Can Be Done about It.

Chapter 1

When to Use Discounted Cash Flow _____

Capital investments of business organizations generally involve these basic financial factors: the investment amount or capital cost, the annual cash income or savings amounts, the economic or productive life, the rate of return or profitability indicator, and the payout period or liquidity barometer.

The most powerful and effective financial criteria for determining *(a)* how much a company considered for acquisition is worth or how much a company can afford to invest in a project or venture, *(b)* how much cash income or savings a project must generate, *(c)* how long a project must be productive, and *(d)* how high a rate of return a project is expected to earn, are those developed and arrived at by various discounted cash flow (DCF) techniques.

Discounted cash flow has been around for a number of decades—particularly the discounted cash flow (DCF) rate of return. This financial yardstick has been used widely over the years to assist top management in making important capital investment decisions.

The application of discounted cash flow that has gained considerable prominence in recent years is the one that enables companies to determine how much a company considered for acquisition is worth. This is confirmed by an article titled "The Cash-Flow Takeover Formula," which appeared in *Business Week* on December 18, 1978, and states in part that

> Financial experts estimate that as many as half of the big companies now active in making acquisitions are relying heavily on DCF, compared with only a handful during the merger wave of the late 1960s, when purchase prices were commonly figured on earnings per share. Companies traditionally use DCF to gauge the returns they expect from internal capital investments in such things as plant and

1

equipment. Until recently, DCF has not been commonly used, however, in evaluating the worth of an entire company to be acquired and in fixing a purchase price.

The entire spectrum of capital investments in new projects or ventures by companies may be divided into four separate and distinct phases, each requiring special types of economic studies, analyses, or evaluations, such as (1) feasibility studies, (2) economic evaluations, (3) post-completion audits, and (4) analyses assessing the impact profits from new projects or ventures are having on the company's overall profitability. These economic studies, analyses, and evaluations and their functions, which normally are prepared in the above order, may be described briefly as follows.

Feasibility studies. When an idea for a prospective project that promises to generate additional profits or cost savings first comes to its originator, or sponsor, the company's first step usually is to have a feasibility study made. A feasibility study is a preliminary study prepared specifically for the purpose of ascertaining whether a proposed undertaking is feasible, has merit, and, based upon the study's findings, should be pursued further or abandoned.

To enable top management to make this determination, the following financial criteria normally are prepared in a feasibility study: (1) how much money the company can afford to invest in the project; (2) how much cash income or savings the project must generate; (3) how long the project must be productive; (4) what rate of return the project must yield commensurate with the risk involved; and (5) how rapidly the project will recover the invested capital. These financial criteria will then serve as guidelines and will be compared to the sponsor's rough, initial estimates of the prospective project's capital cost, cash returns, economic life, rate of return, and payout period. The comparison will make it possible for top management to make an intelligent decision as to whether the proposed venture should be pursued further or dropped.

Economic evaluations. If the feasibility study discloses that the prospective project shows a strong possibility of yielding an attractive rate of return and rapidly recovering its capital investment, then the second step is to prepare a more precise and comprehensive economic evaluation of the prospective project. This more formal economic evaluation may be defined as a detailed, up-to-date, and extensive project investment analysis. It is especially prepared for the purpose of developing more accurate, realistic, and reliable financial criteria that will assist top management in the decision-making process.

These financial criteria include the rate of return, which measures the prospective project's profitability, and the payout period, which measures its liquidity, i.e., how rapidly the project's capital investment will be recovered. The financial criteria are calculated on the most accurate, up-to-date, and realistic estimates of the prospective project's capital cost, cash income or savings, and economic life. These estimates in turn are based not only on the most plausible assumptions as to what is most likely going to occur during the prospective project's economic life but also on the most economic alternative courses of action available to management. These financial criteria, along with any recommendations as well as any imponderables that cannot be reduced to numbers and therefore will not be reflected in these financial criteria, will enable top management to make a sound investment decision on the acceptance or the rejection of the prospective project.

Post-completion audits. After the capital investment for a *new* project has been on the company's books for a reasonable length of time, depending on the size and economic life of the new project, the third step should be to make a post-completion audit of the new project. The purpose of this post-completion audit is to determine whether or not the *new* project's actual performance measures up to the original forecast of the *prospective* project.

If the results of the post-completion audit reveal that the actual performance is subnormal and, moreover, that this trend is expected to continue with the result that the project probably will fail to earn an acceptable rate of return on its capital investment, the company's management then will be able to exercise one of two alternate courses of action.

Management may decide to invest additional funds in the project, providing further studies indicate these funds will improve the project's future performances so that it will yield an acceptable rate of return on its total capital investment. Or if the additional studies indicate that this course of action will be unproductive and therefore inadvisable, the company's management may then choose to abandon the project, investing the proceeds from the disposition of its assets into other more profitable ventures.

In this manner, post-completion audits of new projects fulfill their purpose of not saddling companies with unprofitable ventures that otherwise may have a negative effect on the company's future overall profitability.

Unfortunately, it is highly questionable that many companies presently are making post-completion audits of new projects because of the complexity of this task and the lack of information available on this subject. Conceivably, this failure of conducting post-completion audits of new projects can be costly to companies when they are obliged to continue carrying unprofitable projects on their books for prolonged periods of time.

Analyses of new projects' impact on companies' overall profitability. Since capital investments in new projects are made by companies primarily for the purpose of enhancing their future overall profitability, one of top management's major concerns is to ascertain whether this objective has been achieved. Hence, the fourth and final step in the evaluations of capital investments in new projects is to make a study assessing the impact capital investments in new projects made during recent years have on the current overall profitability of the business.

This type of financial analysis is becoming increasingly more important because more and more environmental legislation and other governmental restrictions are responsible for funneling larger proportions of company funds into "must" projects that generate no additional profits or cost savings. As time goes on, this fact unquestionably will have a more serious offsetting effect on the impact that a company's total capital investments in new projects will have on its future overall profitability.

Like post-completion audits of new projects, it is also questionable that many companies—if any—are presently making this type of financial analysis, which intends to assess the impact that capital investments in new projects are having on their future overall profitability. One reason for not making this type of financial analysis is that the work involved in preparing it is extremely complex because of the necessary inflation adjustments in the company's profit and loss and balance sheet figures. Another reason is that the rates of return used for *(a)* measuring the *prospective* project's profitability for investment decision-making purposes and *(b)* measuring the *new* project's impact on the company's overall profitability are neither comparable nor compatible. Also, very little information—if any—is available on this vital subject. For example, *current value accounting*—a method that attempts to put profit and loss and balance sheet figures in comparable current-year dollars by making adjustments for inflation as well as for other factors responsible for the appreciation of assets, liabilities, and stockholders equity—is still in the talking stage by professional accountants, economists, and financial analysts.

In conclusion, various discounted cash flow (DCF) techniques are the most realistic, reliable, and effective financial criteria for determining *(a)* the feasibility and the merit of prospective projects in phase 1; *(b)* their profitability, liquidity, and acceptability in phase 2; *(c)* their actual performance versus their original forecast in phase 3; and *(d)* their impact on business organizations' future overall profitability in phase 4.

Chapter 2

Fundamentals of Discounted Cash Flow _____

$\mathbf{T}$he most realistic and effective profitability indicator is the discounted cash flow (DCF) rate of return, provided it is arrived at by the proper application of the DCF concept. Whether the DCF rate of return determined under the conventional DCF method is arrived at by the proper application of the DCF concept and, therefore, results in a realistic and reliable DCF rate of return perhaps is judged best by a comparison of the DCF rates of return and the net present values (NPVs) for two mutually exclusive projects such as those illustrated in Table 43, page 111. The DCF rate of return for Project A in Table 43 is 50 percent compared to the 25.18 percent for Project B. This substantial difference in these two DCF rates of return would seem to indicate that Project A is more profitable and therefore preferable over Project B.

However, the exact opposite is true when the NPVs arrived at under the conventional NPV method are used as the financial criteria for making the proper selection of these same two projects (see Table 45, page 114). The NPV for Project B is $29,429 compared to the $11,032 for Project A. This indicates that contrary to the projects' DCF rates of return, according to their NPVs, Project B is more profitable and therefore preferable over Project A, instead of the other way around. Both sets of these profitability indicators—the DCF rates of return and the NPVs—cannot possibly be correct because they arrive at conflicting results and therefore lead to confusing choices. Obviously, something must be wrong with one or possibly both of these conventional methods for determining DCF rates of return and NPVs.

Even though discounted cash flow has been around for a long time, there apparently continues to be a great deal of misunderstanding as well as lack of understanding surrounding the proper determination and use of the DCF

5

rate of return in the decision-making process. To clear up these misunderstandings and eliminate the lack of understanding, a thorough and comprehensive knowledge of the fundamentals of discounted cash flow is a prerequuisite.

Since the DCF rate of return is the foremost and certainly by far the most frequently and widely used financial criterion determined by one of these DCF techniques, it is discussed first. This discussion explains *(a)* where the DCF rate of return originated, *(b)* what it is, *(c)* why it is called by that name, and *(d)* on what theory it is applied by companies to proposed capital investments in prospective projects.

Where the DCF Rate of Return Originated

The DCF concept, as it is applied to the cash flows of prospective investment proposals by companies, is based on discounting and compounding techniques borrowed from the banking community. Lending institutions use these techniques principally for determining *(a)* the cash loan amounts for commercial paper and *(b)* the periodic constant-level loan payment amounts for self-amortizing bank loans.

What It Is

The DCF rate of return, which is widely used by companies for measuring the profitability of prospective investment proposals, is a financial yardstick that is identical with the compound interest rate, which is commonly used by banks and other lending institutions for calculating interest charges on mortgage and other self-amortizing bank loans. They both are constant-level rates used to calculate the periodic profit or interest amounts on the unrecovered portion or unpaid balance of business investments or bank loans, respectively, that are outstanding at the start of each accounting period during the project's economic life or the bank loan's term. Similar to the compound interest rate used in bank loans, the DCF rate of return used in business investments reflects both the capital recovery and the timing of the cash flows to and from the prospective project.

Why It Is Called by That Name

The DCF rate of return derives its name from the discounting technique by which it is determined under the conventional DCF method. In the conventional method, the zero reference point normally is the point in time when the first cash outlay for the prospective project is expected to occur. All the prospective project's forecasted cash outlay and cash income or savings amounts are then netted and discounted back to that point in time. As will be noted later in this book, the term *DCF rate of return* may be somewhat of a misnomer because both the discounting and the compounding techniques may have to be used. Both techniques will have to be used if the zero reference point is the point in time when the prospective project first starts generating cash income or savings instead of the point in time when its first cash outlay is expected to occur in situations where portions of the prospective project's cash outlays are expected to occur either before or after the zero reference point.

On What Theory It Is Applied

The DCF concept is applied to prospective investment proposals on the theory that treasurer's departments of companies perform functions similar to those performed by banks and other lending institutions. One of these functions is that monies are loaned to prospective projects in much the same manner that monies are loaned by banks and other lending institutions to prospective outside borrowers. Obviously, the analogy here is that monies are loaned by a company's treasurer's department to a prospective project on the same basic principle that monies are loaned by banks and other lending institutions to outside borrowers. In other words, monies committed by companies to prospective projects are expected to yield acceptable rates of return commensurate with the risks involved. Based on this rationale, companies use the DCF rate of return as a profitability indicator in the decision-making process of prospective capital investment proposals. However, this premise leads to improper applications of the DCF concept whenever DCF rates of return are determined in capital investment situations in which portions of the capital outlays are expected to occur either before or after the time that prospective projects are expected to start generating cash income or savings.

A thorough and comprehensive understanding of the fundamentals of discounted cash flow also includes a knowledge of *(a)* what interest is, *(b)* how interest is calculated, *(c)* how the simple interest rate differs from the compound interest rate, *(d)* what compounding and discounting techniques mean, and *(e)* how these two techniques differ from one another.

Interest Expense and Interest Income

It is an indisputable fact that money has a time value. The term *interest expense* therefore refers to the charge that is levied by lenders against borrowers for monies loaned to them for specific time periods at specified interest rates. Contrariwise, the term *interest income* refers to the income that accrues to lenders for monies loaned by them to borrowers for specific time periods at specified interest rates.

Simple Interest Rate

This is an interest rate that is calculated on the original principal amount during the loan term (see Table 1). In Table 1, the interest rate is assumed to be 12 percent per annum. Note that the constant-level 12 percent annual interest amounts are calculated on the original $1 principal amount that is on

TABLE 1

Simple Interest Rate

(1)	(2)	(3)	(4)	(5)
		Interest Earned at 12% and Paid Out to Depositor		
	Principal at Start			Principal at End
Year	of Year	Annual	Cumulative	of Year
1	$1.0000	$0.1200	$0.1200	$1.0000
2	1.0000	0.1200	0.2400	1.0000
3	1.0000	0.1200	0.3600	1.0000
4	1.0000	0.1200	0.4800	1.0000
5	1.0000	0.1200	0.6000	1.0000
Total		$0.6000		

deposit in the bank at the start of each year during the five-year loan term. This simple interest rate assumes that the 12 cents annual interest amounts are paid out by the bank to the depositor at the end of each year. Note also that at this 12 percent simple interest rate the depositor is earning total interest of 60 cents on the original $1 principal amount on deposit in the bank at the start of each year during the five-year loan term.

Compound Interest Rate

This is an interest rate that is calculated on the original principal amount plus the accumulated interest amounts during the loan term. In other words, the interest is compounded periodically (see Table 2). The compound interest rate in Table 2 is assumed to be 12 percent and is compounded annually. Note that the variable annual interest amounts, ranging from 12 cents in year 1 to 18.88 cents in year 5, are calculated on the original $1 principal amount plus the accumulated interest amounts on deposit in the bank at the start of each

TABLE 2

Compound Interest Rate

(1)	(2)	(3)	(4)	(5)
		Interest Earned at 12% and Retained by Bank		
	Start			Principal at End
Year	of Year	Annual	Cumulative	of Year
1	$1.0000	$0.1200	$0.1200	$1.1200
2	1.1200	0.1344	0.2544	1.2544
3	1.2544	0.1505	0.4049	1.4049
4	1.4049	0.1686	0.5735	1.5735
5	1.5735	0.1888	0.7623	1.7623
Total		$0.7623		

year. It is assumed that the annual interest amounts are retained by the bank and are added to the depositor's principal amount on deposit at the end of each year. Note also that the total interest amount earned at the 12 percent compound interest rate is 76.23 cents compared to the 60 cents total interest amount earned at the 12 percent simple interest rate. Obviously, the 16.23 cents difference in the total interest amount is attributable to the interest earned annually on the accumulated interest amounts during the five-year loan term.

From Table 2 we may conclude that $1 invested at the beginning of year 1 and compounded annually at the 12 percent compound interest rate will grow to $1.7623 at the end of year 5. This conclusion leads us to our next subject, which is the compounding technique.

Compounding Technique

Compounding refers to the technique of determining the future value of money that is to be spent or received at some future point in time when money is worth a specific interest or profit rate. Future values of $1 are available for easy reference in future value tables. The future values in these tables generally are arranged horizontally on the page by interest rates and vertically on the page by years. A facsimile of a future value table is shown in Table 3. This table shows the future values of $1 compounded annually at the

TABLE 3

Future Value Table Facsimile

(1)	(2)
Year	Future Value of $1 at 12%
0	1.0000
1	1.1200
2	1.2544
3	1.4049
4	1.5735
5	1.7623

TABLE 4

Compounding Technique

(1)	(2)	(3)	(4)
Year	Principal at Start of Year 100%	Annual Interest at 12%	Principal at End of Year 112%
1	$1.0000	$0.1200	$1.1200
2	1.1200	0.1344	1.2544
3	1.2544	0.1505	1.4049
4	1.4049	0.1686	1.5735
5	1.5735	0.1888	1.7623

12 percent compound interest rate for time periods ranging up to five years. Generally, future value tables give easy access to future values of $1 for interest rates and time periods ranging from fractions of 1 percent and 1 year up to 100 percent and 50 years.

The compounding technique is shown in Table 4. As indicated by the downward pointing of the arrow from year 1 to year 5 on the right side of the table, the information in this table shows that compounding proceeds from the present to some future point in time. For example, let us assume that the principal at the start of each year is 100 percent. The annual compound interest rate is 12 percent, and therefore the principal at the end of each year, or the beginning of the next year, is 112 percent. Consequently, when the principal at the start of the year is multiplied by 112 percent, the product represents the principal at the end of that year, or the beginning of the next year. Note that in Table 4, the series of principal amounts at the end of each year is identical with the series of future values of $1 at the 12 percent compound interest rate shown in the future value table facsimile in Table 3. This simplified example shows how the future values of $1 shown in future value tables are arrived at by the compounding technique. The calculation of the future values of $1 may be reduced to this mathematical formula: $AN = P(1 + r)^n$. In this formula, AN represents the amount, P represents the principal, r represents the rate (expressed as a decimal), and n represents the number of years.

Discounting Technique

Discounting is the opposite of compounding. The term *discounting* refers to the technique of determining the present value of money that is to be spent or received at some future point in time when money is worth a specific interest or profit rate.

Present values of $1 are also available for easy reference in present value tables. The present values in these tables generally are arranged in a manner similar to the future values in future value tables, i.e., the present values of $1 are shown horizontally across the page by interest rates and vertically down the page by years. Present values of $1 also are available in present value tables for interest rates and time periods ranging from fractions of 1 percent and 1 year to 100 percent and 50 years.

A facsimile of a typical present value table is shown in Table 5. This table shows the present values of $1 discounted annually at the 12 percent interest rate for periods up to five years. These present values indicate that if money is worth 12 percent, the present value of $1 to be spent or received at the end of year 1 is 89.29 cents, the present value of $1 to be spent or received at the end of year 2 is 79.72 cents, and the present value of $1 to be spent or received at the end of year 5 is 56.74 cents.

The discounting technique used to arrive at the present values in Table 5 is shown in Table 6. Since discounting is the opposite of compounding, discounting proceeds from some future point in time back to the present time. This is shown by the upward pointing arrow from the year 5 to the year 1 on the left side of Table 6. To illustrate the discounting technique, let us assume that the principal at the end of the year is 112 percent. The annual compound interest rate is 12 percent, and therefore the principal at the start of the year or at the end of the previous year is 100 percent. Now, working in reverse, when the principal at the end of the year is divided by 112 percent, the

	TABLE 5

Present Value
Table Facsimile

(1)	(2)
	Present Value of $1 at 12%
Year	
0	1.0000
1	.8929
2	.7972
3	.7118
4	.6355
5	.5674

			TABLE 6

Discounting Technique

(1)	(2)	(3)	(4)
Year	*Principal at Start of Year 100%*	*Annual Interest at 12%*	*Principal at End of Year 112%*
1	$0.5674	$0.0681	$0.6355
2	0.6355	0.0763	0.7118
3	0.7118	0.0854	0.7972
4	0.7972	0.0957	0.8929
5	0.8929	0.1071	1.0000

quotient represents the principal at the start of that year, or the end of the previous year. Note that when this procedure is worked from the year 5 back to the year 1, a series of principal amounts at the start of each year, or at the end of the previous year, is obtained that is identical (in reverse order) with the series of present values of $1 at the 12 percent compound interest rate shown in Table 5. This simplified illustration shows how the present values of $1 in the present value table are arrived at by the discounting technique. The calculation of the present values of $1 may be reduced to this mathematical formula: $P = AN/(1 + r)^n$. As in the formula for compounding, P represents the principal, AN represents the amount, r represents the rate (expressed as a decimal), and n represents the number of years. It should be noted at this point that since discounting is the opposite of compounding, the present value of $1 to be spent or to be received at the end of year 5 is 56.74 cents at the start of year 1 because this amount invested at that point in time at the 12 percent interest rate and compounded annually for five years will be worth $1 at the end of year 5.

Chapter 3

How to Apply Various Discounting Techniques in the Banking and the Business Community _____

The application of various discounting techniques by the banking and the business community in bank loan and business investment situations, respectively, is predicated on the mathematical premise that when three financial factors are known in bank loan or business investment situations, the fourth unknown financial factor can be solved mathematically. These unknown factors include:

> The bank loan or project investment amount.
> The constant-level bank loan payment or project cash income or savings amount.
> The bank loan's specified compound interest rate or the prospective project's estimated DCF rate of return.
> The bank loan's term or the prospective project's economic life.

The procedures for determining these unknown factors are discussed in this chapter.

Determine Bank Loan or Project Investment Amount

Generally, the unknown bank loan amount must be solved mathematically only when commercial paper is assigned to banks or other lending institutions and they must determine the cash loan amount that the assignor is entitled to receive when money is worth a specified interest rate. On the other hand, the project investment amount generally must be solved mathematically only when companies must determine how much money they can afford to invest in prospective projects if they are to earn the predetermined minimum acceptable DCF rates of return commensurate with the risks involved.

To make it feasible to solve for the unknown bank loan or project investment amount, these three financial factors must be known or carefully estimated:

1. The periodic bank loan payment or project cash income or savings amounts.
2. The bank loan's specified compound interest rate or the prospective project's predetermined minimum acceptable DCF rate of return.
3. The bank loan's term or the prospective project's economic life.

Table 7 shows how the unknown bank loan or project investment amount is solved mathematically. It is assumed that the annual bank loan payment or project cash income or savings amounts range from $1.12 in the year 1 to $1.7623 in year 5, the bank loan's specified compound interest rate or the prospective project's predetermined minimum acceptable DCF rate of return is 12 percent, and the bank loan's term or the prospective project's economic life is five years. To determine the unknown bank loan or project investment amount, it is necessary to multiply the annual bank loan payment or project cash income or savings amounts by the present value factors for the 12 percent specified compound interest rate, or the 12 percent predetermined minimum acceptable DCF earnings rate for the bank loan's five-year term or the project's five-year life. The resultant $5 total present value represents the bank loan amount the assignor of the commercial paper is entitled to receive from the bank, or the investment amount the company can afford to invest in the prospective project, based on the above-mentioned three known financial factors.

The future values of $1 at the 12 percent rate for the five-year period shown in Table 3 were chosen purposely to represent the annual bank loan payment or project cash income or savings amounts in Table 7. Likewise, the 12 percent rate and the five-year period were chosen intentionally to represent the bank loan's specified compound interest rate or the prospective project's predetermined minimum acceptable DCF rate of return and the bank loan's term or the project's economic life, respectively. This was done so that by using both the future and the present values of $1 at the 12 percent rate and for the five-year period, it would be possible to highlight these two significant facts simultaneously; namely, that discounting is the opposite of compounding; and that this procedure, as illustrated in Table 7, mathematically solves for the unknown bank loan or project investment amount.

In Table 7, note that when the series of annual bank loan payment or project cash income or savings amounts, which are identical with the future value factors of $1 at the 12 percent rate and for the five-year period shown in Table 3, are multiplied by the present value factors at the 12 percent rate for the five-year period shown in Table 5, the resultant present values are $1 for each year This proves that discounting is the opposite of compounding be-

TABLE 7

Determine Bank Loan or Project Investment Amount When Three Factors Are Known (see Note)

(1)	(2)	(3)	(4)
Year	Bank Loan Payment or Project Cash Income Amounts	Present Value Factor at 12%	Present Value
1	$1.1200	.8929	$1.0000
2	1.2544	.7972	1.0000
3	1.4049	.7118	1.0000
4	1.5735	.6355	1.0000
5	1.7623	.5674	1.0000
Total	$7.1151		$5.0000

Note: The three known factors are:
1. The annual bank loan payment or the annual project cash income amounts.
2. The bank's specified interest rate or the project's predetermined DCF earnings rate.
3. The bank loan's term or the project's estimated productive life.

cause the discounting procedure reverses the effects of the compounding procedure.

Note also in Table 7 that when the bank loan's specified compound interest rate or the prospective project's predetermined minimum acceptable DCF rate of return is 12 percent, the future value of $1 to be repaid or recovered at the end of year 1 is $1.12, the future value of $1 to be repaid or recovered at the end of year 2 is $1.2544, and the future value of $1 to be repaid or recovered at the end of year 5 is $1.7623. This means that when (a) the bank loan's specified compound interest rate or the prospective project's predetermined minimum acceptable DCF rate of return is 12 percent, (b) the bank loan's term or the prospective project's economic life is five years, and (c) the pattern of the bank loan's cash payment amounts or the prospective project's cash income or savings amounts range from $1.12 in year 1 to $1.7623 in year 5, then the unknown bank loan or prospective project's investment amount is determined by multiplying the annual bank loan payment or project cash income or savings amounts shown in Column 2 by the present value factors for the 12 percent compound interest rate or the 12 percent predetermined minimum acceptable DCF earnings rate in Column 3. The resultant $5 total present value represents the amount the bank can afford to loan the assignor of the commercial paper or the company can afford to invest in the prospective project. This also proves that the procedure shown in Table 7 determines the bank loan's principal amount or the prospective project's investment amount when (a) the annual bank loan payments or project cash income or savings amounts, (b) the bank's specified compound interest rate or the prospective project's predetermined minimum acceptable DCF rate of return, and *(c)* the bank loan's term or the prospective project's economic life are known.

In connection with the above-mentioned procedure, it also should be noted that discounting has the effect of eliminating from the stream of annual bank loan payment or project cash income or savings amounts the annual interest or profit factor equal to the bank loan's specified compound interest rate or the prospective project's predetermined minimum acceptable earnings rate at which it is discounted. Hence, the remainder, or the total present value of this stream of annual bank loan payment or project cash income or savings amounts, represents the bank loan or the project investment amount, respectively.

Table 8 shows proof that $5 is the correct bank loan or project investment amount for the example in Table 7. When the stream of annual bank loan

TABLE 8

Proof That Bank Loan or Project Investment Amount Is $5 as Determined in Table 7

(1) Year	(2) Bank Loan Payment or Project Cash Income Amounts	(3) Bank Loan or Project Investment Principal Start of Year	(4) Annual Interest or Earnings at 12%	(5) Repayment of Principal	(6) Bank Loan or Project Investment Principal End of Year
1	$1.1200	$5.0000	$0.6000	$0.5200	$4.4800
2	1.2544	4.4800	0.5376	0.7168	3.7632
3	1.5059	3.7632	0.4516	0.9533	2.8099
4	1.5735	2.8099	0.3372	1.2363	1.5736
5	1.7623	1.5736	0.1887	1.5736	–0–
Total	$7.1151		$2.1151	$5.0000	

payment or project cash income or savings amounts ranges from $1.1200 in the year 1 to $1.7623 in the year 5, as shown in Column 2 of Table 8, this stream is sufficient for the $5 bank loan or project investment amount to be repaid in addition to the bank earning the 12 percent specified interest rate or the company earning the 12 percent DCF rate of return on the unpaid portion of the bank loan or the project investment amount outstanding at the start of each year. A modification of this technique makes it adaptable for determining the worth of companies considered for acquisition or merger. This is discussed in greater detail in Chapter 16 because of its importance due to the effects of inflation on a company's books.

Determine Bank Loan Payment or Project Cash Income or Savings Amount

This financial factor normally is solved mathematically by banks and other lending institutions when they must determine the periodic constant-level bank loan payment amount to be paid by the outside borrower during the bank loan's term. This periodic bank loan payment amount must be sufficient to repay the bank loan's principal in addition to yielding interest at the specified interest rate on the unpaid bank loan balance outstanding at the start of each accounting period. Banks and other lending institutions generally have booklets to which they refer for the periodic bank loan payment amounts when making self-amortizing commercial and mortgage loans. These booklets contain monthly bank loan payment amounts that are arranged horizontally across the page by years and vertically down the page by principal amounts. Normally, these monthly bank loan payment amounts are for principal amounts ranging from $100 to $50,000, loan terms ranging from 1 year to 50 years, and interest rates ranging from 7 percent to 20 percent.

On the other hand, companies normally are required to solve for this unknown financial factor only when they must know the stream of annual constant-level project cash income or savings amounts required to be generated by the prospective project. Likewise, this annual project cash income or savings amount must be sufficient to recover the estimated project investment amount in addition to earning the minimum acceptable DCF rate of return predetermined by top management.

Table 9 shows how the annual constant-level bank loan payment or project cash income or savings amount, which is required to be received or gener-

TABLE 9

Determine Annual Constant-Level Bank Loan Payment or Project Cash Income Amount When Three Factors are Known (see Note)

(1) Year	(2) Bank Loan Payment or Project Cash Income Amounts	(3) Present Value Factor at 12%	(4) Present Value
1	$1.3870	.8929	$1.2385
2	1.3870	.7972	1.1057
3	1.3870	.7118	0.9873
4	1.3870	.6355	0.8814
5	1.3870	.5674	0.7870
Total	$6.9350	3.6048	$5.0000

Note: The three known factors are:
1. The bank loan or the project investment amount.
2. The bank's specified interest rate or the project's predetermined DCF earnings rate.
3. The bank loan's term or the project's estimated productive life.

ated during the bank loan's term or the prospective project's economic life, is solved mathematically when these three factors are known: *(a)* the bank loan or prospective project investment amount, *(b)* the bank loan's specified interest rate or the prospective project's predetermined minimum acceptable DCF rate of return, and *(c)* the bank loan's term or the prospective project's economic life.

As shown in Table 9, the unknown annual constant-level bank loan payment or project cash income or savings amount is determined by dividing the $5 bank loan or project investment amount by the 3.6048 total present value factors for the five-year period at the 12 percent rate. The five-year period and the 12 percent rate, of course, represent the bank loan's term or the prospective project's economic life and the bank loan's specified interest rate or the prospective project's predetermined minimum acceptable DCF rate of return. Note in Column 2 that the stream of annual constant-level bank loan payment or project cash income or savings amounts required to be received from the outside borrower or generated by the prospective project during the five-year bank loan term or project life is $1.3870.

Table 10 shows proof that $1.3870 is the correct annual constant-level bank loan payment or project cash income or savings amount for the example

TABLE 10

Proof that Annual Constant-Level Bank Loan Payment or Project Cash Income Amount Is $1.3870 as Determined in Table 9

(1)	(2)	(3)	(4)	(5)	(6)
Year	Bank Loan Payment or Project Cash Income Amounts	Bank Loan or Project Investment Principal Start of Year	Annual Interest or Earnings at 12%	Repayment of Principal	Bank Loan or Project Investment Principal End of Year
1	$1.3870	$5.0000	$0.6000	$0.7870	$4.2130
2	1.3870	4.2130	0.5055	0.8815	3.3315
3	1.3870	3.3315	0.3997	0.9873	2.3442
4	1.3870	2.3442	0.2813	1.1057	1.2385
5	1.3870	1.2385	0.1485	1.2385	–0–
Total	$6.9350		$1.9350	$5.0000	

in Table 9. Table 10 shows that the $1.3870 annual constant-level bank loan payment or project cash income or savings amount (Column 2) is sufficient to recover the $5 bank loan or project investment amount (Column 5) in addition to earning 12 percent interest or profit (Column 4) on the unrecovered portion of the bank loan or project investment balance outstanding at the start of each year (Column 3) during the five-year bank loan's term or prospective project's economic life.

Determine Prospective Project's DCF Rate of Return or Bank Loan's Interest Rate

The DCF rate of return invariably is the unknown financial factor in a company's economic evaluation of proposed capital investments in prospective projects in which cash outlays, cash returns, and economic lives are forecasted and therefore are presumed to be known factors. DCF rates of return must be determined for prospective projects because top management must know whether the projects will earn DCF rates of return that promise to be at least equal to or exceed the predetermined minimum acceptable DCF rates of return commensurate with the risks involved. It may be well to point out here that companies use the DCF rate of return not only as a profitability indicator but also as a project selection device in the investment decision-making process.

Contrary to the DCF rate of return, which invariably is an unknown financial factor, the bank's interest rate for various types of bank loans and commercial paper is always specified and a known factor. In banking transactions, either the constant-level bank loan payment amount or the bank loan principal amount are the unknown financial factors required to be solved mathematically in processing bank loans or commercial paper.

The prospective project's DCF rate of return or the bank loan's interest rate (if the latter were unknown) can be solved mathematically when the known factors are: *(a)* the project investment or the bank loan amount, *(b)* the stream of project cash income or savings or bank loan payment amounts, and *(c)* the prospective project's economic life or the term of the bank loan.

Table 11 shows how to determine a prospective project's DCF rate of return or a bank loan's interest rate (if the latter were unknown). In Table 11, it is assumed that the three known financial factors are identical with those in Table 7 with the exception of the flow of the annual project cash income or savings or bank loan payment amounts, which is assumed to be in reverse order compared to Table 7. Since cash is returned faster in the example in Table 11 than in the example in Table 7, it follows that the unrecovered balances of the project investment or the bank loan amount outstanding at the start of each year are lower in Table 12 than in Table 8. Consequently, since all other financial factors are equal in both situations, it also follows that the DCF rate of return or the interest rate for the prospective project or the bank loan in Table 12 is higher compared to the DCF rate of return or the interest rate for the prospective project or the bank loan in Table 8.

The 14.269 percent DCF rate of return or interest rate (if the latter were unknown) for the prospective project or the bank loan in Table 11 is determined by finding a rate by trial and error in the present value table that discounts the stream of annual project cash income or savings or bank loan payment amounts totaling $7.1151 down to a total present value equal to the $5 project investment or bank loan amount at the zero reference point. The rate that does this is the prospective project's DCF rate of return or the bank loan's interest rate. Since present value factors are shown only for whole rates in most present value tables, it usually becomes necessary to interpolate be-

TABLE 11

Determine Project's Estimated DCF Earnings Rate or Bank Loan's Compound Interest Rate (see Note)

(1)	(2)	(3)	(4)	(5)	(6)	(7)
Year	Project Investment or Bank Loan Amount	Project Cash Income or Bank Loan Payment Amounts	Present Value Factor at 14%	Present Value	Present Value Factor at 15%	Present Value
0	$5.0000					
1		$1.7623	.8772	$1.5459	.8696	$1.5325
2		1.5735	.7695	1.2108	.7561	1.1897
3		1.4049	.6750	0.9483	.6575	0.9237
4		1.2544	.5921	0.7427	.5718	0.7173
5		1.1200	.5194	0.5817	.4972	0.5569
Total	$5.0000	$7.1151		$5.0294		$4.9201

Interpolation

Present value of total project cash income or bank loan
payment amounts at 14 percent $\quad = \$5.0294$ $\left.\right]$ $\$0.0294$

Project investment or bank loan amount $\quad = \$5.0000$ $\qquad$ $\$0.1093$

Present value of total project cash income or bank loan
payment amounts at 15 percent $\quad = \$4.9201$

$$\$0.0294 \div \$0.1093 = 0.269\% + 14\% = \boxed{14.269\%}$$

Note: The following three factors are known:
  1. The project investment or the bank loan amount.
  2. The annual project cash income or bank loan payment amounts.
  3. The project's estimated productive life or the bank loan's term.

tween two whole percentage rates to arrive at the precise DCF rate of return or interest rate if the latter is an unknown factor. For example, in Table 11 the stream of annual project cash income or savings or bank loan payment amounts in Column 3, which total $7.1151, discounts down to a total present value of $5.0294 at the 14 percent rate as shown in Column 5. This is $0.0294 higher than the $5 project investment or bank loan amount at the zero reference point in Column 2. The same stream of annual project cash income or savings or bank loan payment amounts discounts down to a total present value of $4.9201 at the 15 percent rate as shown in Column 7. This is $0.0799 lower than the $5 project investment or bank loan amount at the zero reference point in Column 2. Consequently, the precise DCF rate of return or interest rate for the prospective project or the bank loan lies between the 14 percent and the 15 percent rate and therefore must be obtained by interpolating between these two rates.

It was pointed out previously that discounting has the effect of eliminating from the stream of project cash income or savings or bank loan payment amounts the profit or interest factor equal to the rate at which it is discounted.

In the example in Table 11, the stream of annual project cash income or savings or bank loan payment amounts totaling $7.1151 discounts down to a total present value equal to the $5 project investment or bank loan amount at the zero reference point at the 14.296 percent rate. Hence, this rate is the precise DCF rate of return or interest rate for the prospective project or the bank loan shown in Table 11.

Table 12 shows the proof that 14.269 percent is the precise DCF rate of return or interest rate for the prospective project or the bank loan based on

TABLE 12

Proof that Project's Estimated DCF Earnings Rate or Bank Loan's Compound Interest Rate Is 14.269 Percent as Determined in Table 11

(1)	(2)	(3)	(4)	(5)	(6)
Year	Project Cash Income or Bank Loan Payment Amounts	Project Investment or Bank Loan Balance Start of Year	Annual Earnings or Interest at 14.269%	Repayment of Principal	Project Investment or Bank Loan Balance End of Year
1	$1.7623	$5.0000	$0.7133	$1.0490	$3.9510
2	1.5735	3.9510	0.5636	1.0099	2.9411
3	1.4049	2.9411	0.4195	0.9854	1.9557
4	1.2544	1.9557	0.2790	0.9754	0.9803
5	1.1200	0.9803	0.1397	0.9803	–0–
Total	$7.1151		$2.1151	$5.0000	

the three known financial factors in the example in Table 11. This proof is evidenced by the fact that the company or bank is earning a 14.269 percent DCF rate of return or interest rate on the unpaid balance of the $5 project investment or bank loan amount outstanding at the start of each year, in addition to recovering the original $5 project investment or bank loan amount during the five-year prospective project's economic life or the bank's loan term. Contrariwise, the prospective project is paying the company's treasurer's department 14.269 percent profit, or the outside borrower is paying the bank 14.269 percent interest on the unpaid balance of the project investment or the bank loan amount outstanding at the start of each year in addition to repaying the original $5 project investment or bank loan amount during the five-year project life or the bank loan term. As pointed out previously, since money is returned faster and, therefore, the unrecovered balances of the $5 project investment or bank loan amount outstanding at the start of each year are lower for the prospective project or the bank loan shown in Table 12 compared to those for the prospective project or the bank loan shown in Table 8, the DCF rate of return or the interest rate for the prospective project or the bank loan shown in Table 12 is 2.269 percent higher than the DCF rate of return or the interest rate for the prospective project or the bank loan shown in Table 8.

Determine Prospective Project's Economic Life or Bank Loan's Term

The economic life of prospective projects is solved mathematically only on relatively rare occasions by companies. It generally becomes necessary to solve for this financial factor when preliminary feasibility studies are made and companies must determine how long prospective projects must be productive in order to yield at least the predetermined minimum acceptable DCF rates of return. To enable companies to determine the length of time prospective projects must be productive, the sponsors must first estimate the prospective projects' investment amount and their annual cash income or savings amounts and predetermine the minimum acceptable DCF rates of return commensurate with the risks involved.

The bank loan term invariably is a known factor in bank loan transactions either because banks or other lending institutions specify the length of time for which certain types of loans will be granted or because prospective borrowers specify the length of time for which bank loans are needed. Hence, under normal circumstances, banks and other lending institutions are never required to solve for this financial factor mathematically.

The procedure for determining the required economic life of a prospective project involves finding a time period by trial and error in the present value table under the interest rate column equivalent to the prospective project's predetermined minimum DCF rate of return for which the present value factors within that time period discount the series of annual project cash income or savings amounts down to a total present value equal to the project investment amount at the zero reference point. The time period under the proper interest rate column in the present value table that does this represents the prospective project's required economic life. Similar to the procedure for calculating DCF rates of return, this procedure uses interpolation to arrive at the precise economic life because the prospective project's cash income or savings amounts generally are forecasted on an annual basis and present value tables show present value factors only for whole years. Thus, interpolation between two successive years is necessary to arrive at the precise time period that a prospective project must be productive.

Table 13 shows how long a project that is expected to cost $5, generate $1.25 annual cash income or savings, and yield a 12 percent DCF rate of return must be productive. This is determined by discounting the stream of $1.25 annual cash income or savings amounts at the 12 percent rate until a total present value equal to the $5 capital cost at the zero reference point is arrived at. Table 13 shows that at the end of the fifth year, the total present value is equal to $4.506, which is $0.494 below the $5 capital cost at the zero reference point; whereas the total present value at the end of the sixth year is $5.139, which is $0.139 in excess of the $5 capital cost at the zero reference point. This means that the number of years the project has to be productive

TABLE 13

Determine How Long Project Costing $5 and Generating $1.25 Annual Cash Income Must Be Productive to Yield a 12 Percent DCF Rate of Return

(1)	(2)	(3)	(4)	(5)	(6)
	Project Investment Amount	Project Cash Income Amounts	Present Value Factor at 12%	Total Present Value	
Year				Annual	Cumulative
0	$5.00				
1		$1.25	.8929	$1.116	$1.116
2		1.25	.7972	0.997	2.113
3		1.25	.7118	0.890	3.003
4		1.25	.6355	0.794	3.797
5		1.25	.5674	0.709	4.506
6		1.25	.5066	0.633	5.139
Total	$5.00	$7.50		$5.139	

Interpolation

Total present value at 5 years = $4.506 ⎤
Project investment or bank loan amount = $5.000 ⎦ 0.494 ⎤
Total Present value at 6 years = $5.139 ⎦ 0.633

$$\frac{0.494}{0.633} = 0.78 + 5 = \underline{\underline{5.78 \text{ years}}}$$

lies between five and six years. By interpolation, this proves to be 5.78 years. This means that during the sixth year the project has to generate only $0.975 ($1.25 × 0.78 years) in order to yield a 12 percent DCF rate of return during the 5.78 years.

To prove that a project expected to cost $5, generate a stream of $1.25 annual cash income or savings amounts, and yield a 12 percent DCF rate of return must be productive for 5.78 years, it is necessary to show that the stream of annual cash income or savings amounts totaling $7.225 discounts down to a total present value equal to the $5 capital cost at the zero reference point at the 12 percent rate (see Table 14). This can be proved further by showing that the prospective project will earn 12 percent profit on the unrecovered portion of the project investment outstanding at the start of each year in addition to recovering the $5 capital cost during the 5.78-year period (see Table 15).

In the preparation of preliminary feasibility studies to determine whether proposed projects are feasible and have merit, thus enabling sponsors to decide whether the proposed projects should be pursued further or dropped, several or possibly all four of the above-mentioned financial criteria—the capital cost, the cash returns, the economic life, and the DCF rate of return—may have to be determined by the applicable DCF techniques. These financial criteria, of course, are calculated on rough, preliminary estimates.

TABLE 14

Proof that Project Costing $5, Generating $1.25 Annual Cash Income, and Having a 5.78-Year Economic Life Will Yield Expected 12 Percent DCF Rate of Return

(1) Year	(2) Project Investment Amount	(3) Project Cash Income Amounts	(4) Present Value Factor at 12%	(5) Total Present Value
0	$5.000	—		
1		$1.25	.8929	$1.116
2		1.25	.7972	0.997
3		1.25	.7118	0.890
4		1.25	.6355	0.794
5		1.25	.5674	0.709
6		0.975*	.5066	0.494
Total	$5.000	$7.225		$5.000

* $1.25 × 0.78 years = $0.975.

TABLE 15

Proof that Project Costing $5, Generating $1.25 Annual Cash Income, and Expecting to Yield 12 Percent DCF Rate of Return Will Have to Be Productive 5.78 Years

(1) Year	(2) Project Cash Income Amounts	(3) Project Investment Balance Start of Year	(4) Profit at 12%	(5) Capital Recovery	(6) Project Investment Balance End of Year
1	$1.25	$5.00	$0.60	$0.65	$4.35
2	1.25	4.35	0.52	0.73	3.62
3	1.25	3.62	0.43	0.82	2.80
4	1.25	2.80	0.34	0.91	1.80
5	1.25	1.89	0.23	1.02	0.87
6	0.975	0.87	0.105	0.87	–0–
Total	$7.225		$2.225	$5.00	

On the other hand, in the preparation of final economic evaluations to determine the profitability and the acceptability of proposed projects, which will enable top management decide whether they should be accepted or rejected, only the DCF rate of return generally is determined by the applicable DCF technique. This financial criterion, of course, is calculated on the most plausible assumptions and the most accurate, reliable, and up-to-date estimates.

Chapter 4

Average Annual Earnings Rate of Return Compared to DCF Rate of Return

A comparison of the DCF rate of return and the average annual earnings rate of return is perhaps the most effective way of inducing companies, whose management is either unfamiliar with the DCF rate of return or finds its calculations too complex and cumbersome, to switch to and adopt the more sophisticated DCF rate of return, which is by far a more realistic profitability indicator and reliable project selection device than the average annual earnings rate of return.

It was pointed out earlier that the DCF rate of return used by companies for evaluating and selecting prospective projects is identical with the compound interest rate used by banks and other lending institutions for computing interest charges and discounting commercial paper. The illustrations in the preceding chapter prove that the financial tools developed by the four different discounting techniques are the most realistic, reliable, and effective financial tools for companies to use in prospective project evaluations, providing they are used in situations similar to those in which the compound interest rate is used by banks and other lending institutions. There is no question, for example, that the DCF rate of return is actually the only true measurement device for assessing the profitability of a company's capital investments compared to other profit indicators such as the average annual earnings rate of return and the year-to-year book rate of return. Before we compare the DCF rate of return to the average annual earnings rate of return, let us first establish *(a)* what the average annual earnings rate of return is, *(b)* why it is still being used, *(c)* how it is determined, and *(d)* why it fails to reflect the capital recovery and the timing of the cash flows to and from projects.

What the Average Annual Earnings Rate of Return Is

The average annual earnings rate of return is a much less sophisticated financial criterion than the DCF rate of return. Nevertheless, it is still being used by some companies as a profitability indicator and project selection device in proposed capital investments in new projects. However, it has become apparent that since the introduction of the DCF rate of return several decades ago, this financial yardstick has fallen into disfavor because of its glaring shortcomings. Consequently, it is being used much less frequently by financial analysts today.

Why It Is Still Used

Despite the apparent superiority of the DCF rate of return, the average annual earnings rate of return is still being used by some financial analysts largely because they are *(a)* unacquainted with the DCF rate of return; *(b)* unfamiliar with its proper use and true meaning; *(c)* finding the DCF rate of return calculation cumbersome and time consuming; or *(d)* distrustful of its soundness and reliability as a profitability indicator and project selection device, particularly in capital investment situations in which portions of the cash outlays of prospective projects are expected to occur over a period of years either before or after the time the projects are expected to start generating cash income or savings.

How It Is Determined

Table 16 shows how to determine the average annual earnings rate of return, which involves averaging the prospective project's total profits generated during its economic life. This is accomplished by dividing the prospective project's total forecasted profits by the number of years of its estimated economic life. The resultant average annual profit amount is then divided by the pro-

TABLE 16

Determine Average Annual Earnings or Interest Rate for Project or Bank Loan Shown in Table 9*

Total project cash income or bank loan amounts during the five-year period	= $6.9350
Project investment or bank loan amount at the start of year 1	= 5.0000
Total project earnings or bank loan interest during the five-year period	= $1.9350
Average annual project earnings or bank loan interest during the five-year period	= $0.3870
Project's average annual earnings rate or bank loan's average annual interest rate	= 7.74%

* In Table 9, the annual project cash income or bank loan payment amounts are at a constant-level rate.

spective project's forecasted total investment amount. The quotient represents the prospective project's average annual earnings rate of return. The forecasted total profits in this formula, of course, represent the excess of the prospective project's total cash inflow over its total cash outflow. Note that in Table 16, the average annual earnings rate of return is 7.74 percent compared to the 12 percent DCF rate of return shown for the same prospective project in Table 9.

It Fails to Reflect the Prospective Project's Capital Recovery

The 4.26 percent difference between the average annual earnings rate of return and the 12 percent DCF rate of return arrived at for the same prospective project by the DCF method is due to the failure of the average annual earnings rate of return to reflect the prospective project's capital recovery during its five-year economic life. This is one of the major shortcomings of the average annual earnings rate of return as shown in Tables 16 and 17.

TABLE 17

Proof that 7.74 Percent Average Annual Earnings or Interest Rate Determined in Table 16 Fails to Reflect Repayment of Project's Investment or Bank Loan's Principal*

(1)	(2)	(3)	(4)	(5)	(6)
Year	Project Cash Income or Bank Loan Payment Amounts	Project Investment or Bank Loan Balance Start of Year	Average Annual Earnings or Interest at 7.74%	Repayment of Principal	Project Investment or Bank Loan Balance End of Year
1	$1.3870	$5.0000	$0.3870	–0–	$5.0000
2	1.3870	5.0000	0.3870	–0–	5.0000
3	1.3870	5.0000	0.3870	–0–	5.0000
4	1.3870	5.0000	0.3870	–0–	5.0000
5	1.3870	5.0000	0.3870	–0–	5.0000
Total	$6.9350	$5.0000	$1.9350		$5.0000

* As shown in Table 10, the project's estimated DCF earnings rate or the bank loan's specified compound interest rate is 12 percent in this particular situation.

To emphasize how unrealistic and unreliable the average annual earnings rate of return is as a profitability indicator and project selection device, the three known financial factors in Tables 16 and 17, which are identical with those in Tables 9 and 10, will be considered in subsequent examples as pertaining to either a prospective business investment or a prospective bank loan. Consequently, the calculated rate arrived at under the average annual earnings or interest rate method will represent either the prospective project's average annual earnings rate of return or the bank loan's average annual interest rate. This analogy is made despite the realization that banks and other lending institutions under no conceivable circumstances would ever consider calculating average annual interest rates for bank loans similar to those calculated for the hypothetical bank loans in Tables 16 and 18, because such interest rates would be absolutely meaningless, misleading, and absurd.

Table 17 shows the proof that the average annual earnings or interest rate completely ignores the capital recovery, or repayment of the $5 business investment or bank loan amount, during the five-year project life or bank loan term. Note that the 7.74 percent average annual earnings or interest rate is calculated erroneously on the $5 initial project investment or bank loan amount as representing the balance outstanding at the start of each year instead of on the actual balance outstanding at the start of each year, which ranges from $5 at the start of year 1 to $1.2385 at the start of year 5, as shown in Table 10.

The manner in which the average annual earnings or interest rate is calculated clearly implies that the company's project or the bank's outside borrower is paying and, contrariwise, the company or the bank is receiving, constant-level annual cash income or bank loan payment amounts of only $0.3870 instead of $1.3870. Since the 7.74 percent average annual earnings or interest rate fails to reflect the repayment of the $5 business investment or bank loan amount during the five-year project life or bank loan term, this rate obviously is seriously understated and unrealistic.

As mentioned previously, it isn't only inconceivable that banks or other lending institutions would ever calculate average annual interest rates, but it is equally inconceivable that they, as in this example, would ever contend that the outside borrower is paying only 7.74 percent instead of 12 percent interest or, contrariwise, that the bank is earning only 7.74 percent instead of 12 percent interest on the $5 bank loan shown in Tables 10 and 17. There isn't an outside borrower that wouldn't be fully aware of the fact that in this particular situation he is actually paying $1.3870 and not $0.3870 annually to the bank and that the former amount includes both repayment of principal plus interest on the unpaid bank loan balance outstanding at the start of each year. Hence, the unpaid balance outstanding at the start of each year on which he is required to pay interest would not be $5, as shown in Table 17, but would range from $5 at the start of year 1 to $1.2385 at the start of year 5, as shown in Table 10. Consequently, the true interest rate the outside borrower is paying and the bank is earning on this $5 bank loan is 12 percent and not 7.74 percent.

The same rationale that applies to the 7.74 percent average annual interest rate for the bank loan applies equally to the 7.74 percent average annual earnings rate of return for the prospective project in this example. Obviously, the 7.74 percent average annual earnings rate of return is equally as meaningless, misleading, and absurd as the 7.74 percent average annual interest rate because the prospective project is forecasted to generate annual cash income or savings of $1.3870 and not $0.3870 and therefore the $1.3870 annual cash income or savings amount includes both capital recovery and profit on the unrecovered project investment balance at the start of each year. Hence, the unrecovered portion of the prospective project's total investment amount outstanding at the start of each year is not $5, as shown in Table 17, but it also declines and ranges from $5 at the start of year 1 to $1.2385 at the start of year 5, as shown in Table 10. This is indisputable evidence that the company is earning 12 percent on the unrecovered portion of the project investment amount outstanding at the start of each year and not 7.74 percent, which is based on the $5 initial investment amount and therefore fails to take into account the portions of the total project investment amount that are recovered during the prospective project's five-year economic life. Obviously, this failure of the average annual earnings rate of return to reflect the prospective project's capital recovery during its economic life invariably tends to understate and distort its profitability seriously. This defect in the average annual earnings rate of return could lead companies to reject profitable prospective projects, which otherwise would be acceptable if their top management were to consider this financial criterion a sound profitability indicator and a reliable project selection device.

It Fails to Reflect the Timing of the Prospective Project's Cash Flows

In addition to failing to reflect a prospective project's capital recovery, another equally critical shortcoming of the average annual earnings rate of return is that it doesn't recognize the timing of the cash flows to and from prospective projects. Tables 18 and 19 show this defect. Again, for the pur-

TABLE 18

*Determine Average Annual Earnings or Interest Rate for Project or Bank Loan Shown in Tables 7 and 11**

Total project cash income or bank loan payment amounts during the five-year period	= $7.1151
Project investment or bank loan amount at the start of year 1	= 5.0000
Total project earnings or bank loan interest during the five-year period	= $2.1151
Average annual project earnings or bank loan interest during the five-year period	= $0.42302
Project's average annual earnings rate or bank loan's average annual interest rate	= 8.46%

* In Tables 7 and 11, the annual project cash income or bank loan payment amounts are at increasing and decreasing rates, respectively.

pose of highlighting how unrealistic and unreliable the average annual earnings rate of return is as a profit measurement and project selection device, the financial factors in Tables 18 and 19, which are identical with those in Tables 7 and 8 and Tables 11 and 12, will be considered as pertaining either to

TABLE 19

Proof that 8.46 Percent Average Annual Earnings or Interest Rate Determined in Table 18 Fails to Reflect Timing of Project's Cash Income or Bank Loan's Payment Amounts*

(1)	(2)	(3)	(4)	(5)	(6)	(7)
	Project Cash Income or Bank Loan Payment Amounts		*Project Investment or Bank*	*Average Annual Earnings or Interest*		*Project Investment or Bank*
			Loan Balance	*at* 8.46%	*Repayment of*	*Loan Balance*
Year	*Increasing Flow*	*Decreasing Flow*	*Start of Year*		*Principal*	*End of Year*
1	$1.1200	$1.7623	$5.0000	$0.4230	–0–	$5.0000
ʼ2	1.2544	1.5735	5.0000	0.4230	–0–	5.0000
3	1.4049	1.4049	5.0000	0.4230	–0–	5.0000
4	1.5735	1.2544	5.0000	0.4230	–0–	5.0000
5	1.7623	1.1200	5.0000	0.4230	–0–	5.0000
Total	$7.1151	$7.1151	$5.0000	$2.1151		$5.0000

* As shown in Tables 8 and 12, the prospective project's estimated DCF earnings rates or the bank loan's specified compound interest rates are 12 percent and 14.269 percent when the annual project cash income or bank loan payment amounts are at increasing and decreasing rates, respectively.

prospective projects or bank loans. Consequently, the rates calculated for them will represent either the prospective project's average annual earnings rates of return or the bank loan's average annual interest rates.

To illustrate that average annual earnings or interest rates fail to reflect the timing of prospective projects' or bank loans' cash flows, the two prospective projects or bank loans shown in Tables 7 and 8 and 11 and 12, in which all the financial factors except the timing of the cash flows are identical, are chosen as examples. The annual project cash income or savings or bank loan payment amounts are at an increasing rate and therefore are returning slower for the prospective project or bank loan shown in Tables 7 and 8, while they are at a decreasing rate and therefore are returning faster for the prospective project or bank loan shown in Tables 11 and 12.

Despite the fact that money is returned faster for the prospective project or the bank loan shown in Tables 11 and 12 than it is for the prospective project or the bank loan shown in Tables 7 and 8, the 8.46 percent average annual earnings rate of return or interest rate is identical for both prospective projects or bank loans as shown in Table 18. You will note in this table that this defect in the average annual earnings rate of return or interest rate of failing to reflect the timing of the cash flows is attributable to the fact that the $2.1151 total project earnings or bank loan interest amounts are identical for these two prospective projects or bank loans. Consequently, when these two identical total earnings or interest amounts are averaged over the identical five-year project economic lives or bank loan terms, the $0.42302 average annual project earnings or bank loan interest amounts are also identical for these two prospective projects or bank loans. This means that when the identical $0.42302 average annual earnings or interest amounts are equated to the identical $5 initial business investment or bank loan principal amounts, this results in identical 8.46 percent average annual earnings rates of return or interest rates for the two prospective projects or bank loans shown in Tables 7 and 8 and Tables 11 and 12.

Now let us examine the logic of the average annual interest rate. It shouldn't be too difficult to visualize that when two self-amortizing bank loans, such as shown in Tables 7 and 8 and Tables 11 and 12, call for identical $5 bank loan principal amounts, identical $7.1151 total bank loan payment amounts, and identical five-year loan terms, but in which the timing of the annual bank loan payment amounts for the bank loan in Tables 11 and 12 is faster than the timing of the annual bank loan payment amounts for the bank loan in Tables 7 and 8, that the interest rate specified for the bank loan in Tables 11 and 12 must be higher than the one specified for the bank loan in Tables 7 and 8. The reason for this should be quite obvious. Inasmuch as the bank loan shown in Tables 11 and 12 is repaid more rapidly than the one shown in Tables 7 and 8, the unpaid bank loan balance outstanding at the start of each year for the bank loan in Tables 11 and 12, naturally, is lower, ranging from $5 at the start of year 1 to $0.9803 at the start of year 5, than that for the bank loan shown in Tables 7 and 8, which ranges from $5 at the start of year 1 to $1.5736 at the start of year 5. Hence, the interest rate specified for the bank loan shown in Tables 11 and 12, which is repaid faster, is 2.269 percent higher than the 12 percent interest rate specified for the bank loan shown in Tables 7 and 8, which is repaid slower—all other financial factors being equal in these two bank loans.

Contrariwise, the bank is earning a 2.269 percent higher interest rate on the bank loan shown in Tables 11 and 12, which is repaid faster, than the 12 percent interest rate it is earning on the bank loan shown in Tables 7 and 8, which is repaid more slowly—all other financial factors being equal in these two bank loan transactions.

It also shouldn't be too difficult to realize that it would be dishonest, fallacious, and absurd for the bank to assert that the two outside borrowers are both paying a 8.46 percent interest rate on their respective bank loans shown in Tables 7 and 8 and Tables 11 and 12. As shown in Tables 8 and 12, the outside borrowers are paying interest at the rate of 12 percent and 14.269 percent and, contrariwise, the bank is earning interest at the rate of 12 percent and 14.269 percent on the two bank loans shown in Tables 7 and 8 and Tables 11 and 12, respectively. In other words, 12 percent and 14.269 percent are the true interest rates specified for these two self-amortizing loans made by the bank to the two outside borrowers.

The same rationale, of course, applies to the average annual earnings rate of return. Since the identical 8.46 percent average annual earnings rate of return for the two prospective projects shown in Tables 7 and 8 and Tables 11 and 12, also fail to reflect the timing of their cash flows, they are equally as dishonest, fallacious, and absurd as the 8.46 percent average annual interest rates for the two bank loans shown in these four tables. Consequently, the true DCF rates of return for the two prospective projects shown in Tables 7 and 8 and Tables 11 and 12 that reflect the timing of the cash flows are 12 percent and 14.269 percent, respectively.

The timing of cash flows to and from prospective projects is so critical that prospective projects earning larger total profit amounts could be less profitable than projects earning lower total profit amounts but whose cash is returned more rapidly during their economic lives.

The failure of the average annual earnings rate of return or interest rate to reflect the timing of the cash flows of prospective projects or bank loans is shown even more vividly in Table 19. You will note that despite the difference in the timing of the $7.1151 total project cash income or savings or bank loan payment amounts for the two prospective projects or bank loans shown in Columns 2 and 3, the 8.46 percent average annual earnings rates of return or interest rates for these two prospective projects or bank loans are identical. Now let us refer to Tables 8 and 12 and note that the unrecovered portions of the project investment amount or the unpaid balances of the bank loan principal amount outstanding at the start of each year are lower for the prospective project or bank loan shown in Table 12, in which cash is returned faster, compared to the unrecovered portions for the prospective project or bank loan shown in Table 8, in which cash is returned slower. It should be noted further in these two tables that since the $7.1151 total project cash income or bank loan payment amounts and the five-year economic lives or loan terms of the company or the bank respectively are identical in both situations, it naturally follows that the earnings or interest rate must be higher for the prospective project or bank loan in which cash is returned faster compared to the earnings or interest rate for the prospective project or bank loan in which cash is returned slower. This is proven by the 14.269 percent DCF rate of return or interest rate for the prospective project or bank loan in Table 12, which reflects the faster cash return, and the lower 12 percent DCF rate of return or interest rate for the prospective project or bank loan in Table 8, which reflects the slower cash return. Obviously, the 2.269 percent difference in these two DCF rates of return or interest rates reflects the difference in the timing of the cash flows of the two prospective projects or bank loans, whereas the identical 8.46 percent average annual earnings rates of return or interest rates for these two prospective projects or bank loans fail to reflect the difference in their cash flow time patterns.

It should be apparent from the illustrations in the above-mentioned tables that the failure of the average annual earnings rate of return to reflect the capital recovery and the timing of the cash flows to and from prospective projects makes this a most unrealistic profit indicator and unreliable project selection device. The use of this financial criterion could lead to serious unsound investment decisions that could affect a company's overall profitability adversely for many years—particularly in the case of investment decisions involving long-term investments that generally are irreversible. The failure of the average annual earnings rate of return to reflect the capital recoveries of prospective projects during their economic lives has a tendency to understate their earnings rates. Hence, the use of the average annual earnings rate of return as a profitability indicator could lead to the rejection of profitable prospective projects. For example, according to the 7.74 percent average annual earnings rate of return, the two prospective projects in Tables 7 and 8 and Tables 11 and 12 are both equally unacceptable if we assume that the minimum acceptable rate of return predetermined for these two prospective projects is 10 percent. This proves that if the average annual earnings rate of return is used as a financial criterion in the investment decision-making process, this would result in the rejection of both of these profitable prospective projects shown in Tables 7 and 8 and Tables 11 and 12 when according to their DCF rates of return they are both acceptable because they are yielding 12 percent and 14.269 percent, respectively.

Furthermore, the use of the average annual earnings rate of return also could lead to the adoption of less profitable prospective projects because of its failure to reflect the difference in the time patterns of cash flows to and from prospective projects. For example, let us assume that a choice has to be made by top management between the two mutually exclusive prospective projects shown in Tables 7 and 8 and Tables 11 and 12. According to their identical 8.46 percent average annual earnings rates of return, these two prospective projects appear to be equally attractive. However, according to their actual 12 percent and 14.269 percent DCF rates of return as a result of reflecting (*a*) the difference in the timing of their cash flows and (*b*) their capital recovery, the prospective project shown in Tables 11 and 12 is more attractive than the one shown in Tables 7 and 8. This proves that if the average annual earnings rate of return is used in the investment decision-making process, it could lead to the adoption of the less profitable prospective project shown in Tables 7 and 8.

To avoid such unwise and costly investment decisions, it would be most advantageous for companies now using the average annual earnings rate of return as a profitability indicator and project selection device to convert to the DCF rate of return, which apparently is far more realistic, reliable, and effective. This switch from the average annual earnings rate of return to the DCF rate of return, which would tend to channel available funds into the most profitable projects, would be highly beneficial not only to companies but also to the nation's economy as a whole.

Chapter 5

Year-to-Year Book Rate of Return Compared to DCF Rate of Return

$\mathbf{T}$he year-to-year book rate of return is not a financial criterion that is designed to be used by companies in the evaluation and the selection of prospective projects. Nevertheless, it will be compared to the DCF rate of return in this book for the purpose of determining whether it is compatible with the DCF rate of return.

What the Year-to-Year Book Rate Is

The year-to-year book rate of return is a financial yardstick used primarily for measuring management's effective and economic utilization of a company's total assets, i.e., for measuring overall profitability. It ordinarily isn't used by companies for appraising management's efficient utilization of a single capital asset as shown in the example in Table 20. The year-to-year book rates of return shown in Table 20 were calculated only for the purpose of comparing them to the DCF rate of return that was calculated for this capital asset prior to its acquisition.

When It Is Used

While the DCF rate of return is used principally before capital assets are acquired and thus serves decision-making management in determining their profitability and acceptability, the year-to-year book rate of return is used almost exclusively after capital assets are acquired and thus serves operating management in measuring their effective utilization after they have been in use for some time.

TABLE 20

Determine Year-to-Year Book Rate of Return or Year-to-Year Interest Rate for Project or Bank Loan in Table 12

(1) Year	(2) Project Cash Income or Bank Loan Payment Amounts	(3) Recovery of Project Investment or Repayment of Bank Loan	(4) Project's Profits or Bank Loan Interest	(5) Initial Project Investment or Initial Bank Loan Amount	(6) Year-to-Year Book Rate of Return or Year-to-Year Interest Rate	(7) Unrecovered Project Investment or Unpaid Bank Loan Principal Start of Year	(8) Year-to-Year Book Rate of Return or Year-to-Year Interest Rate	(9) Average Unrecovered Project Investment or Unpaid Bank Loan Principal during Year	(10) Year-to-Year Book Rate of Return or Year-to-Year Interest Rates
Example 1: Recovery of Project Investment or Bank Loan Based on the Straight-Line Method									
1	$1.7623	$1.0000	$ 0.7623	$5.0000	15.25%	$5.0000	15.25%	$4.5000	16.94%
2	1.5735	1.0000	0.5735	5.0000	11.47	4.0000	14.34	3.5000	16.39
3	1.4049	1.0000	0.4049	5.0000	8.10	3.0000	13.50	2.5000	16.20
4	1.2544	1.0000	0.2544	5.0000	5.09	2.0000	12.72	1.5000	16.96
5	1.1200	1.0000	0.1200	5.0000	2.40	1.0000	12.00	0.5000	24.00
Total	$7.1151	$5.0000	$ 2.1151						
Example 2: Recovery of Project Investment or Repayment of Bank Loan Based on the Double-Declining-Balance Method*									
1	$1.7623	$2.0000	$(0.2377)	$5.0000	(4.75)%	$5.0000	(4.75)%	$4.0000	(5.94)%
2	1.5735	1.2000	0.3735	5.0000	7.47	3.0000	12.45	2.4000	15.56
3	1.4049	0.6000	0.8049	5.0000	16.10	1.8000	44.72	1.5000	53.66
4	1.2544	0.6000	0.6544	5.0000	13.09	1.2000	54.53	0.9000	72.71
5	1.1200	0.6000	0.5200	5.0000	10.40	0.6000	86.67	0.3000	173.33
Total	$7.1151	$5.0000	$ 2.1151						

* Switching to the straight-line method in the third year.

How It Is Determined

The year-to-year book rate of return is determined by dividing the company's annual net income amount, after depreciation and income taxes, by the book value of the total assets employed in its operations. The year-to-year book rate of return arrived at under this procedure depends entirely on the depreciation method and the investment base chosen by companies for this calculation. Some of the depreciation methods companies may choose to use for this purpose include the straight-line method, the double-declining-balance method, or the sum-of-the-years'-digits method. However, it is almost invariably more advantageous for companies to use either the sum-of-the-years'-digits method or the double-declining-balance method for tax purposes and to use the straight-line method for book purposes. On the other hand, some of the book values companies may choose as their investment base include *(a)* the first cost or undepreciated book value of their total assets at the start of each year, *(b)* the depreciated book value of their total assets at the start of each year, or *(c)* the average depreciated book value of their total assets during each year. The book value of the total assets used as the investment base in the year-to-year book rate of return calculation includes both the book value of the company's total current and total fixed assets. The procedure for the year-to-year book rate of return calculation is shown in Table 20. The year-to-year book rates of return shown in Table 20 are on a before-tax basis in order to make them comparable with the 14.269 percent DCF rate of return shown for this capital asset in Tables 11 and 12 which also is on a before-tax basis.

Why It Is Unrealistic

Solely for the purpose of highlighting the absurdity and the ineffectiveness of the year-to-year book rate of return as a sound profitability indicator of the effective utilization of a company's total assets, the financial data in Table 20, which are identical with those in Tables 11 and 12, should be examined again as pertaining to either a business investment in a capital asset or a bank loan to an outside borrower.

It will be proven next that the year-to-year book rates of return, like the year-to-year interest rates, are unrealistic, meaningless, and misleading as profitability indicators of a company's investments in capital assets, primarily because the year-to-year book rates of return can be anything a company wants them to be. This is because of the number of different combinations of depreciation methods and investment bases that a company can choose from in calculating year-to-year book rates of return.

As explained earlier, the DCF concept is applied on the premise that a company's treasurer's department lends money to new projects in much the same manner that a bank lends money to outside borrowers and, moreover, that the DCF rate of return is comparable to the compound interest rate.

It is logical to deduce from this premise that the $5 loan made by the company's treasurer's department to the new project, or by the bank to the outside borrower, which returns $7.1151 cash income or savings or interest income, respectively, yields a 14.269 percent DCF rate of return to the company, or a 14.269 percent interest rate to the bank. Moreover, this 14.269 percent DCF rate of return or interest rate represents the true earnings rate on the company's unrecovered portion of its $5 capital investment during the project's five-year life, or on the bank's unpaid balance of its $5 loan during the outside borrower's five-year term.

However, the $5 loan made by the company to the new project is treated entirely differently on the company's books than the $5 loan made by the bank to the outside borrower is treated on the bank's books. This difference in the accounting treatment of loans made by a bank to outside borrowers versus those made internally by a company's treasurer's department to new projects is the prime reason for the lack of understanding on the part of top management of the fundamental differences between the DCF rate of return and the year-to-year book rate of return and their proper applications.

In bank loan transactions, the interest amount is computed first at the specified interest rate on the unpaid balance of the principal at the start of each accounting period, and the remainder of the periodic loan payment amount represents the amortization, or repayment, of principal. The accounting treatment of bank loans on the books of banks or other lending institutions follows this compound interest procedure.

The DCF rate of return naturally works the same way because it is identical with the compound interest rate. The profit amount is computed first on the unrecovered portion of the capital investment at the start of each accounting period, and the remainder of the periodic cash income or savings amount represents amortization, or capital recovery. However, it must be borne in mind that the DCF rate of return is used only as a financial yardstick in guiding management in its decision-making process before the acceptance of new projects. Consequently, the DCF procedure doesn't enter into the accepted accounting treatment of new projects' capital assets on the company's books.

Once new projects are accepted and their capital assets are acquired and recorded on the company's books, their accepted accounting treatment from that point on is the exact opposite of that described for bank loans. The depreciation charge, or capital recovery, of the capital assets is computed first on their original cost, usually at a constant-level rate for book purposes, and the remainder of the periodic cash income or savings amount generated by the assets represents their profit. The examples in Tables 12 and 20 prove, incontrovertibly, that the DCF rate of return and the year-to-year book rate of return are diametrically opposed to one another and therefore are incompatible.

As shown in Table 20, as many as nine—and possibly even more—different series of year-to-year book rates of return could be calculated for the new project's capital asset shown in Table 12, depending on which one of the three depreciation methods—straight-line, double-declining balance, or sum-of-the-years'-digits—and which one of three investment bases—initial capital investment, unrecovered capital investment at the start of each year, or average unrecovered capital investment during each year—are chosen by the company for these year-to-year book rates of return calculations.

Six different series of year-to-year book rates of return for this new project's capital asset are shown in Table 20. When the straight-line method is chosen for book purposes—which it generally is—then the year-to-year book rates of return for this capital asset range from 15.25 percent in the first year to 2.40 percent in the fifth year calculated on the initial capital investment, from 15.25 percent in the first year to 12.00 percent in the fifth year calculated on the unrecovered capital investment at the start of each year, and from 16.94 percent in the first year to 24.00 percent in the fifth year calculated on the average unrecovered capital investment during each year.

On the other hand, when the double-declining-balance method is chosen for book purposes—which it generally is not, but it well could be—then the year-to-year book rates of return for this new project's capital asset range from (4.75) percent in the first year to 10.40 percent in the fifth year calculated on the initial capital investment, from (4.75) percent in the first year to 86.67 percent in the fifth year calculated on the unrecovered capital investment at the start of each year, and from (5.94) percent in the first year to 173.33 percent in the fifth year calculated on the average unrecovered capital investment during each year.

If the sum-of-the-years'-digits method is chosen by the company for book purposes, then similar year-to-year book rates of return for this new project's capital asset would be even more erratic and absurd than those arrived at when the straight-line or the double-declining-balance methods are chosen.

It is inconceivable and absurd to believe that the bank would think of calculating year-to-year interest rates for this bank loan similar to the year-to-year book rates of return calculated for this business investment and then contend, for example, that the outside borrower is paying and, contrariwise, the bank is earning annual interest rates on this $5 loan ranging from 16.94 percent in the first year to 24.00 percent in the fifth year on the average unpaid principal balance during each year, when in reality the interest specified for this $5 loan and paid by the outside borrower and, contrariwise, earned by the bank is 14.269 percent on the unpaid principal balance outstanding at the start of each accounting period. We may conclude from Tables 12 and 20 that whether a loan is made by a bank or other lending institution to an outside borrower, or internally by a company's treasurer's department to a new project, the same rationale applies in both financial situations. The bank loan's specified (compound) interest rate and the comparable project's DCF rate of return represent the bank's and the company's true earnings rate, respectively. Likewise, the company's year-to-year book rates of return for its capital investment in the new project are in reality as arbitrary, unrealistic, and absurd as the comparable year-to-year interest rates would be for the bank's loan to its outside borrower if such annual interest rates were computed by the bank.

The purpose of comparing the DCF rate of return to the year-to-year rate of return is not so much to prove that the latter is arbitrary, unrealistic, and actually absurd because it can be anything companies want it to be, but rather to prove that these two rates of return, or profitability indicators, are diametrically opposed to one another and therefore are incompatible. This means it will be virtually impossible for companies to assess the effect recent capital investments in new projects is having on their overall profitability.

Why the Year-to-Year Book Rate of Return Is Incompatible with the DCF Rate of Return

The primary financial objective for the addition of new and the replacement of antiquated and inefficient capital assets is to increase a company's sales volume and improve its operating efficiency and thereby enhance its future overall profitability. To determine whether companies have achieved this financial objective, they must be able to assess the impact recent capital investments in new projects are having on their overall profitability. This determination poses a most complex and vexing problem when a company's investment decisions for the acquisition of new capital assets are based on the DCF rate of return, while after their acquisition their effective utilization by management is based on the year-to-year book rate of return. The reason for this is because these two rates of return, as pointed out previously, are diametrically opposed to one another and therefore they are completely incompatible and irreconcilable. Unfortunately, this problem is not as yet too well recognized and understood either by a company's financial analysts or its decision-making management.

As explained earlier in this book, the DCF rate of return used by companies is a constant-level earnings rate that is identical with the compound interest rate used by banks and other lending institutions. Consequently, it accurately measures the anticipated profitability of prospective projects during their economic lives, predicated, of course, on carefully forecasted financial factors. In the application of the DCF rate of return, the annual profit factor included in the forecasted annual cash income or savings amount of prospective projects is determined first by multiplying the unrecovered portion of their investment amount at the start of each year by their calculated constant-level DCF rate of return. The remainder of the forecasted annual cash income amount of the prospective projects represents the annual capital recovery amount that, according to this procedure, is recovered at a variable rate during their economic lives.

Diametrically opposed to the DCF rate of return is the year-to-year book rate of return. This is a variable earnings rate that neither realistically measures the profitability nor the effective utilization of a company's capital assets for the simple reason that it may be anything companies want it to be, depending on the capital recovery (depreciation) method and the investment base they elect to choose for the year-to-year book rate of return calculation.

Contrary to the application of the DCF rate of return, in the application of the year-to-year book rate of return, the annual capital recovery (depreciation) amount is determined first by multiplying the original cost of the capital assets by the constant-level depreciation rate of the straight-line method, which is most widely used for book purposes. The remainder of the annual cash income or savings amount of the capital assets represents the annual profit amount that is then related to one of a number of different investment bases that the companies have chosen for the year-to-year book rate of return calculation. This procedure obviously results in making the year-to-year book rate of return not only a variable earnings rate but also *any* earnings rate companies want it to be during the economic lives of the capital assets.

In other words, in the application of the DCF rate of return, similar to that of the compound interest rate, the annual profit amount is determined first by multiplying the unrecovered portion of the investment amount of the capital assets at the start of each year by their constant-level DCF rate of return, and the remainder of their annual cash income or savings amount represents the annual depreciation (capital recovery) amount that is recovered at variable rates during their economic lives. It is imperative to understand that in determining the year-to-year book rate of return the exact opposite takes place, if we are to understand *why* the DCF rate of return and the year-to-year book rate of return are diametrically opposed to one another and therefore incompatible. Under this procedure, the annual depreciation (capital recovery) amount is determined first by multiplying the original cost or depreciated book value of the capital assets at the start of each year by the fixed depreciation (capital recovery) rate of the depreciation method arbitrarily chosen by companies for book purposes. The remainder of the annual cash income or savings amount of the capital assets represents the annual profit amount that, when related to an arbitrarily chosen investment base, results in variable year-to-year book rates of return during the economic lives of the capital assets.

These detailed descriptions of the DCF and the year-to-year book rates of return should make it clear that the year-to-year book rate of return is not only an unrealistic, meaningless, and misleading financial yardstick for assessing the profitability of capital assets but it also is incompatible with the DCF rate of return because it is diametrically opposed to it. Hence, it is virtually impossible for top management to gauge with any degree of accuracy the impact newly acquired capital assets are having on a company's overall profitability when investment decisions for the acquisition of new capital assets are based on the DCF rate of return, while an assessment of their effective utilization after their acquisition is based on the year-to-year book rate of return.

It should be clear at this point that there is nothing inherently wrong with the DCF rate of return per se when it is applied by companies in situations similar to those in which the compound interest rate is applied by banks and other lending institutions. It also should be evident by now that the DCF rate of return is the only true profitability indicator of a company's capital investments compared to the average annual earnings rate of return and the year-to-year book rate of return, inasmuch as it is the only financial criterion that accurately reflects both the capital recovery and the timing of cash flows of business investments, providing the DCF concept is applied properly. Consequently, we may conclude from the above assertions that if in certain situations unrealistic DCF rates of return are arrived at, the fault must lie with the manner in which the DCF concept is applied in those situations rather than with the DCF rate of return per se.

Chapter 6

Basic Difference between Application of Discounted Cash Flow Concept and Compound Interest Principle

To thoroughly understand the proper application of the DCF concept and the effective use of the DCF rate of return, it is absolutely essential to have a comprehensive knowledge of the basic differences between the DCF concept and the compound interest principle.

There are two basic differences between the application of the DCF concept by companies and the application of the compound interest principle by banks and other lending institutions that must be recognized and understood by financial analysts and decision-making management. They must realize first that all the known financial factors involved in the appraisal of prospective self-amortizing bank loans or commercial paper to be discounted by banks and other lending institutions invariably are actual, whereas all the so-called known financial factors involved in the evaluation of prospective projects by companies invariably are estimated. They also must be aware of the fact that generally different unknown financial factors are required to be solved mathematically by banks and other lending institutions than are required to be solved mathematically by companies.

Actual Known Financial Factors in the Compound Interest Rate Application

In the application of the compound interest rate involving self-amortizing bank loans, the *bank loan principal amount* always represents the actual cash amount the outside borrower needs or desires to borrow or the bank is willing to loan for the particular type of loan; the *loan term* always represents the actual length of time for which the outside borrower is requesting the bank loan or the bank is willing to grant the particular type of loan; the *specified interest rate* always represents the actual interest rate that will be charged to the outside borrower and, contrariwise, that will be earned by the bank, depending on the type of loan and the risk involved; and finally, the *bank loan repayment amount* always represents the actual periodic constant-level cash payment amount the outside borrower is committed to make to the bank during the bank loan term to repay the bank loan principal amount in addition to paying the interest at the specified interest rate on the unpaid balance outstanding at the start of each accounting period. As a general rule, the above financial factors are stipulated in the bank loan agreements; and, consequently, they represent the actual contractual obligations between the bank and the outside borrower. This means that the bank is always assured of earning the predetermined interest rate specified for the particular type of loan unless, of course, the outside borrower defaults or is lax in making his periodic bank loan payments on time during the bank loan term.

Unknown Factors Solved Mathematically by Banks

The unknown financial factor most commonly solved mathematically by banks and other lending institutions is the periodic bank loan payment amount for self-amortizing bank loans. However, in reality, these periodic constant-level bank loan payment amounts are predetermined and arranged in tables for various bank loan principal amounts, bank loan terms, specified interest rates, and compounding periods as a matter of expediency.

Another unknown financial factor, but one that is required to be solved much less frequently, is the bank loan principal amount. This unknown factor is solved for exclusively in situations in which commercial paper is assigned to and required to be discounted by banks and other lending institutions to determine assignors' loan amounts.

Selection of Proper Alternatives by Banks

In the evaluation of prospective bank loans, the banks and other lending institutions generally must consider only two alternate courses of action, namely, whether to grant the loans or whether to disallow them. Normally, this decision depends on whether the outside borrower's credit ratings are satisfactory or unsatisfactory. In other words, the selection of the proper alternatives in prospective bank loan transactions is a relatively simple one, as it usually is restricted to deciding whether to do something versus doing nothing.

Estimated Known Financial Factors in the DCF Rate of Return Applications

Contrary to the known financial factors in the application of the compound interest rate, which invariably are actual, the known financial factors in the application of the DCF rate of return, such as the total cash outlay amounts, the annual cash income amounts, the timing of the cash flows to and from prospective projects, and the length of time they will be productive, invariably are estimated. Furthermore, these estimated financial factors generally are based on various sets of assumptions that certain events will take place during the economic lives of the prospective projects. Consequently, it follows that DCF rates of return calculated for prospective projects will only be as realistic and reliable as the estimates and the assumptions on which they are based are plausible and valid.

To preclude the possibility of making an unwise investment decision, it should be mandatory for the sponsor of a major prospective project, which involves substantial capital outlays, to make a number of different estimates and to prepare a series of different DCF rates of return and payout periods for the major prospective project, predicated on various sets of assumptions. For example, one DCF rate of return and payout period may be calculated on the most optimistic set of assumptions as to what may occur, another DCF rate of return and payout period may be calculated on the most pessimistic set of assumptions as to what may occur, and finally, a DCF rate of return and payout period may be calculated on a set of assumptions based on what is most likely to occur during the prospective project's economic life. This series of different DCF rates of return and payout periods will give top management a range of financial criteria on which to base its investment decision with respect to the major prospective project which, because of its size, could have a marked effect on the company's overall profitability for years to come.

Unknown Factors Solved Mathematically by Companies

The unknown financial factors most commonly solved mathematically by companies in the economic evaluations of prospective projects are their earnings rate and payout period. The amount of money companies can afford to expend for prospective projects, the cash returns they have to generate, and the length of time they have to be productive to yield acceptable DCF rates of return commensurate with the risks involved generally have to be solved mathematically only in preliminary feasibility studies for proposed capital investments.

Selection of Proper Alternatives by Companies

In cases where monies are to be loaned to prospective projects by a company's treasurer's department, generally the alternate courses of action available to management regarding the objectives to be attained by such prospective projects are numerous in every instance. Hence, to maximize profits, it is imperative that top management, through the process of elimination and the comparison of the two most advantageous alternatives, choose the most economic course of action that is open with respect to each prospective project.

The Effective Use of the DCF Rate of Return

Although the DCF rate of return is identical with the compound interest rate, the roles they play in the economic evaluation of proposed capital investments or bank loans are quite different. The compound interest rate is always specified by banks and is used to indicate the interest rate outside borrowers are expected to pay under the bank loan agreements. The compound interest rate is never used as a financial criterion in the decision-making process of prospective bank loans. Decisions as to whether prospective bank loans should be granted or denied invariably are dependent on the outside borrower's credit rating, i.e., whether it is satisfactory or unsatisfactory.

On the other hand, the primary function of the DCF rate of return is to serve top management as a financial criterion in the decision-making process. Standards, or minimum acceptable DCF rates of return, generally, are predetermined by top management for various types of projects based on the inherent risks involved in them. When the estimated DCF rates of return calculated for prospective projects meet or exceed these predetermined minimum acceptable DCF rates of return, prospective projects normally are considered acceptable for adoption by top management.

However, in the effective use of the DCF rate of return, it is essential that top management bear in mind at all times these salient facts concerning this financial criterion: (1) DCF rates of return are calculated on estimates of the cash outlays, cash returns, and economic lives of the prospective projects. These estimates are predicated on various assumptions made by the prospective projects' sponsors. Hence, DCF rates of return calculated for prospective projects are only as realistic and reliable as the assumptions on which they are based are plausible and valid. (2) DCF rates of return usually do not reflect certain imponderables, such as the political climate of foreign countries, the threat of nationalization of companies within the industry by a foreign country's government, the probability of expropriation of a company's assets by a foreign country's government, etc. Conceivably, these imponderables could have a profound negative influence on the acceptability of prospective projects, despite the attractive DCF rates of return shown in their economic evaluations. Imponderables, like the above mentioned, normally cannot be reduced to meaningful figures. As a result, these imponderables can neither be comprehended in the estimates of the cash outlays, cash returns, and economic lives of the prospective projects, nor can they be reflected in the projects' DCF rates of return. This means that in the effective use of DCF rates of return, proper mental allowances must be made for and serious consideration must be given to the likely impact such imponderables could have on the success or the failure of prospective projects. (3) DCF rates of return must be based on a comparison of the two most economic alternatives in each case when numerous courses of action are available to management with respect to individual new project proposals. This comparison of the proper alternatives in each case, arrived at by a process of elimination, will assure companies of (*a*) making the right investment decisions, (*b*) channeling their available funds into the most profitable ventures, and *(c)* maximizing their overall future profitability. (4) DCF rates of return unquestionably depend as much on the soundness of the techniques by which they are calculated as on the plausibility and the validity of the estimates and the selection of the right alternative to qualify as realistic profitability indicators and reliable project selection devices.

Application of DCF Concept

As mentioned repeatedly, the DCF rate of return is comparable to the compound interest rate; and, moreover, the DCF concept is applied on the premise that money is loaned by treasurer's departments of companies to prospective projects in much the same manner that money is loaned by banks and other lending institutions to outside borrowers. Based on this rationale, it seems only natural that companies would tend to apply the DCF concept in internal loans to prospective projects in a manner similar to that in which banks and other lending institutions apply the compound interest principle in loans to outside borrowers.

For example, in loans made by banks to outside borrowers, the earnings rates realized on them by the banks, contrariwise, represent the interest rates charged to the outside borrowers for such loans. Similarly, in internal loans made by companies to prospective projects, the earnings rates realized on them by the companies, contrariwise, are considered to represent the interest rates charged to the prospective projects for such internal loans. This is the pivotal point in the proper application of the DCF concept by companies; namely, that these rates, which represent prospective projects' calculated DCF rates of return that are equal to or exceed their predetermined minimum acceptable DCF rates of return, are considered to be the appropriate rates instead of the company's direct borrowing rate for discounting or compounding the capital outlays in the DCF rate of return calculations under the conventional DCF method. This, naturally, implies that these interest rates charged for internal loans to prospective projects are considered to be the company's cost of money. Consequently, these interest rates are used for compounding or discounting portions of the capital outlays that are expected to occur either before or after the time prospective projects are expected to start generating cash income or savings. Since these interest rates, which must be at least equal to or exceed prospective projects' predetermined minimum acceptable DCF rates of return, are almost invariably considerably higher than the company's current direct borrowing rate, the resultant alternate lump-sum investment amounts at the start of prospective projects' economic lives as well as their calculated DCF rates of return are practically without exception grossly distorted.

This leads us to the problem of what interest rate should be considered as the company's cost of money in its proper application of the DCF concept apropos to the proper application of the compound interest principle by a bank or other lending institution.

Chapter 7

Alternate Use Value of Money versus Cost of Financing

$\mathbf{T}$he crux of the proper application of the DCF concept in determining DCF rates of return is to know what rate to use for compounding or discounting capital outlays expected to occur over a period of years either before or after the time prospective projects are expected to start generating cash income or savings. Should companies use their alternate use value of money rate or their direct borrowing rate? Which one of these two rates represents their "cost of money" and is the appropriate rate to use for compounding or discounting capital outlays that are spread over a period of years in DCF rate of return calculations? To know which rate to use for compounding or discounting in these situations requires that a company's financial analysts be able to distinguish between the alternate use value of money and the direct borrowing rate, as well as between their respective usage. To understand their basic differences and to know when to use them is extremely vital because most of the major prospective projects of companies usually involve large capital outlays. Therefore, large projects ordinarily entail prolonged construction periods during which substantial portions of their sizable capital outlays frequently are expected to occur either before or after the time such major prospective projects are expected to start generating cash income or savings.

The principal reason for improper applications of the DCF concept may be ascribed to the confusion and the misunderstanding that exist in the minds of so many business executives, financial analysts, engineers, economists, and others about the term *cost of money*. Improper applications of the DCF concept take place primarily *(a)* when cash outlays are estimated to occur either before or after the time prospective projects are expected to start generating cash income or savings; *(b)* when salvage or residual values for both nondepreciable and depreciable fixed assets are involved during and at the end of prospective projects' estimated economic lives; and *(c)* when capital outlay, capital recovery, and cash income or savings dollars are commingled and netted in prospective projects' cash flows.

What Cost of Money Means

The term *cost of money* in most instances is used indiscriminately by the above-mentioned professionals without being specific as to just what they mean by the usage of this term. At times the term *cost of money,* as it is used by them, seems to denote what money is worth to companies in the sense of what money will earn for them when it is put to work in prospective projects or ventures. In other words, when the term *cost of money* is used in this sense, it appears to refer to the earnings rate or rates at which companies presume their available funds can be put to work in prospective projects.

At other times the usage of the term *cost of money* seems to suggest the rate companies are willing to pay for the use of money. In other words, when the term *cost of money* is used in this sense, it refers to the interest rate companies are willing to pay banks or other lending institutions for the use of money. This rate is commonly referred to as a company's direct borrowing rate or prime interest rate.

In proper applications of the DCF concept it is essential for financial analysts to be able to distinguish between the "alternate use value of money," which is expressed in terms of the earnings rate or rates at which top management presumes it can invest money in prospective projects, and the "cost of financing," which is expressed in terms of the interest rate companies are willing to pay banks and other lending institutions for the use of money for investment or other purposes.

What the Alternate Use Value of Money Means

The term *alternate use value of money* refers to what money is worth to companies. This term most likely originated as a result of the great variety of projects with varying degrees of risk that companies can choose to invest their available funds. Consequently, companies have as many alternate use value of money rates as they have predetermined minimum acceptable earnings rates for the many different types or classes of projects. These "predetermined minimum acceptable earnings rates" or "alternate use value of money rates" may vary widely depending on the elements of risk involved in the various types or classes of projects. This situation, which exists predominantly in large companies, apparently has given rise to the term *alternate use value of money.* In other words, the *alternate use value of money* indicates the alternate uses or choices companies have of investing their available funds in various types and classes of projects that command different rates of return predetermined for them depending on the risks involved.

It should be made clear at this point that since the *alternate use value of money* is expressed in terms of earnings rates, it naturally follows that a company's standards, that is, its predetermined minimum acceptable earnings rates for different projects involving various elements of risk, must be expressed in the form of DCF rates of return. This is necessary if companies use the DCF rate of return as their profitability indicator and project selection device on which to base their investment decisions for prospective projects.

Methods of Financing Prospective Projects

There are at least three different methods by which companies can finance the acquisition of fixed assets of prospective projects. Companies can acquire fixed assets with equity money, debt money, or lease money. The major problems that arise with the proper applications of the DCF concept are largely attributable to the fact that all too many businessmen consider it to be a financing method only when payments for new fixed assets are made with debt money borrowed from outside sources such as banks and other lending institutions. Businessmen fail to recognize and understand that payments made for new fixed assets with equity (company) money or lease money, likewise, are bona fide financing methods. This is borne out by Webster's *New American Dictionary* which defines the verb *finance* as "to manage, financially; to provide funds for." This definition doesn't state that the funds to provide for the acquisition of new fixed assets necessarily must come from outside sources. Why payments made for new fixed assets with equity (company) money or lease (rental) money, as a general rule, are not considered financing methods, probably, is due to the following reasons.

Payments made with equity money are probably not considered as a method of financing because when individuals purchase, for example, new automobiles and pay cash for them with their own money, they are considered not to be financing the purchases of their new automobiles. On the other hand, when individuals purchase new automobiles, pay only the required down payment with their own money, and then pay the remainder of the purchase price with money borrowed from banks or other lending institutions, they are considered to be financing the purchases of their new automobiles. The rationale of individuals not having financed the purchases of their new automobiles when they have paid cash for them with their own money apparently has carried over to companies who likewise are considered not to have financed purchases of new fixed assets when they have paid for them with their own (equity) money. This rationale is fallacious, particularly when it is applied to companies.

Leasing usually is not considered a financing method primarily because companies acquire fixed assets without the benefit of ownership, pay for their use in the form of lease rentals, and the latter are treated on the company's books as regular operating expenses instead of as financing charges. The fact that the acquisition of leased fixed assets is never recorded on the company's books probably is another reason why leasing is not considered a financing method by many businessmen. This is true despite the fact that usually the lease rentals of a fixed asset during its useful life will exceed the bank loan payments of the same fixed asset because the interest rate in lease rentals normally is higher than the company's prime interest rate.

Cost of Financing

The cost of financing prospective projects is the company's direct borrowing rate, which is commonly known as the prime interest rate and represents the rate companies are willing to pay banks or other lending institutions for the use of money.

The crux of the problem of improper applications of the DCF concept in determining DCF rates of return lies in the confusion created by the indiscriminate use of the term *cost of money.* Judging from the descriptive nomenclature, one would assume that the term *cost of money* would be synonymous with the term *cost of financing,* i.e., the interest rate companies are willing to pay banks and other lending institutions for the use of money. Unfortunately, this term isn't used in this sense in many instances. When *cost of money* is used by businessmen, they more often than not have in mind the company's alternate use value of money, i.e., the earnings rate companies presume they can realize from investments in one type of project as opposed to that from investments in another type of project. This confusing and improper usage of *cost of money* probably is due to the analogy and the premise on which the DCF concept is applied in the economic evaluation of prospective projects.

As explained earlier, money is presumed to be loaned by treasurer's departments of companies to prospective projects in much the same manner that money is loaned by banks and other lending institutions to outside borrowers. To carry this analogy one step further, it likewise is presumed that the interest rates charged by banks to outside borrowers, conversely, represents the earnings rates (before operating expenses) realized by banks on the monies loaned to outside borrowers. Based on the same rationale, a great many businessmen obviously presume that the earnings rates realized from investments in prospective projects represent the interest rates charged by treasurer's departments of companies for the monies loaned to such prospective projects. This, in all probability, is how the confusion and the misuse of *cost of money* arose.

Factors to Consider in Determining the Rate to Be Used for Compounding and Discounting

In determining the rate to be used for compounding or discounting the capital outlays and capital recoveries of prospective projects, the following basic principles must be thoroughly understood and kept foremost in mind.

- The higher the rate at which one compounds a stream of cash outlays to some future point in time, the higher will be the future value at that point in time. Contrariwise, the lower the rate at which one compounds a stream of cash outlays to some future point in time, the lower will be the future value at that point in time.
- The higher the rate at which one discounts a stream of cash outlays back from some future point in time, the lower will be the present value at the zero reference point. Contrariwise, the lower the rate at which one discounts a stream of cash outlays back from some future point in time, the higher will be the present value at the zero reference point.
- The zero reference point may represent either the point in time when prospective projects are expected to start generating cash income or savings or when their first capital outlay is expected to occur.
- At whatever rate one compounds a stream of cash outlays to some future point in time, an interest factor equal to the rate at which one is compounding is added to the lump-sum amount, or future value, at that future point in time, or zero reference point.
- Contrariwise, at whatever rate one discounts a stream of cash outlays back from some future point in time, an interest factor equal to the rate at which one is discounting is excluded from the lump-sum amount, or present value, at the zero reference point.
- The capital cost and the capital recovery dollars must never be commingled and netted with the cash income or savings dollars in economic evaluations of prospective projects, as this procedure inevitably leads to compounding or discounting these two different types of dollars at the same rate and, consequently, results in unrealistic DCF rates of return.
- The alternate lump-sum capital cost, which represents a higher future value at the zero reference point, to be acceptable in lieu of a series of cash outlays expected to occur during a period of years before that point in time must include an interest factor at a rate that the company sponsoring the prospective project is willing to pay for the use of money.
- On the other hand, the alternate lump-sum capital cost, which represents a lower present value at the zero reference point, to be acceptable in lieu of a series of cash outlays expected to occur during a period of years after that point in time must exclude an interest factor at a rate that the suppliers and the contractors of the company sponsoring the prospective project are willing to pay for the use of money.

What Rate to Use for Compounding or Discounting Capital Outlays and Capital Recoveries

The rate to use for compounding or discounting prospective projects' capital outlays when they are expected to occur during a period of years either before or after the zero reference point is the prime interest rate at which companies sponsoring the prospective projects or their suppliers and contractors can borrow money from banks and other lending institutions. This, presumably, is the interest rate companies are willing to pay for the use of money. Hence, this interest rate may be defined as representing the *cost of money* or *cost of financing* of the companies or their suppliers and contractors.

When the series of cash outlays for a prospective project, which is expected to occur during a period of years either before or after the zero reference point, is compounded or discounted at the company's or its suppliers' and contractors' direct borrowing rate of, say, 10 percent, the resultant future value or present value at the zero reference point represents the prospective project's true investment base. The DCF rate of return calculated on this true investment base will be realistic and, therefore, lead to a sound investment decision.

On the other hand, when the "cost of money" concept—which in DCF rate of return calculations can only mean the "cost of financing" or the interest rate at which the company can borrow money and is willing to pay for its use—is confused with the "alternate use value of money" concept—which means what money is worth to the company in terms of the earnings rate at which the company presumably can invest money, and the earnings rate is used for compounding or discounting the prospective project's series of cash outlays—then the investment base arrived at the zero reference point will be seriously distorted. This will result in an unrealistic DCF rate of return and could lead to an unsound investment decision.

For instance, when a series of cash outlays for a prospective project, which is expected to occur during a period of years before the zero reference point, is compounded at the prospective project's estimated 15 percent DCF earnings rate, instead of at the company's 10 percent direct borrowing rate, then the resultant lump-sum investment base at the zero reference point will be grossly overstated. This means that the DCF rate of return calculated on this overstated investment base will be seriously understated, which could lead to the rejection of an otherwise profitable prospective new project.

On the other hand, when a series of cash outlays for a prospective project, which is expected to occur during a period of years after the zero reference point is discounted at the prospective project's estimated 15 percent DCF earnings rate instead of at the company's 10 percent direct borrowing rate, then the resultant lump-sum investment base at the zero reference point will be grossly understated. This means that the DCF rate of return calculated on this understated investment base will be seriously overstated, which could lead to the acceptance of an otherwise unprofitable prospective project.

The above examples typify how the confusion and the misunderstanding as to what rate represents the company's *cost of money* can lead to the selection of an improper rate for compounding and/or discounting a series of capital outlays that are expected to occur either before or after the time prospective projects are expected to start generating cash income or savings. This, in turn, can lead to unrealistic DCF rates of return and consequently to unwise and costly investment decisions.

Proper Method of Calculating DCF Rates of Return Important

The proper application of the DCF concept that will result in realistic DCF rates of return and reliable project selection devices, thus avoiding unwise and costly investment decisions, is equally as important as making realistic estimates based on plausible and valid assumptions of the capital cost, the capital recovery, the annual cash income or savings, and the economic life of prospective projects.

When a company's direct borrowing rate is used for compounding or discounting a prospective project's cash outlays of which portions are expected to occur either before or after the time the project starts generating cash income or savings, which is usually the zero reference point, there should be consistency in arriving at sound lump-sum investment bases at the zero reference point under the following three financing methods:

1. *Equity financing.* Effect is given to the timing of the cash outlays by compounding them down to the zero reference point at the company's direct borrowing rate when they are expected to occur before that point in time, and by discounting them back to the zero reference point at that rate when they are expected to occur after that point in time. This procedure results in larger lump-sum investment bases at the zero reference point and lower DCF rates of return for prospective projects when their cash outlays are expected to occur before the zero reference point, and, contrariwise, results in lower lump-sum investment bases at the zero reference point and higher DCF rates of return for prospective projects when their cash outlays are expected to occur after the zero reference point.

2. *Debt financing.* When the periodic bank loan payments are discounted back to the zero reference point at a company's direct borrowing rate, the present value at that point in time will be equal to the prospective project's purchase price, or cost of acquisition.

3. *Lease financing.* When the periodic lease rentals, after excluding from them all items incidental to ownership, are discounted back to the zero reference point, the present value at that point in time will exceed the prospective project's purchase price, or cost of acquisition, if the interest factor in the lease rental is higher than the company's direct borrowing rate. Contrariwise, the present value at the zero reference point will be lower than the prospective project's purchase price, or cost of acquisition, if the interest factor in the lease rental is lower than the company's direct borrowing rate. Since the interest factor in lease rentals generally is higher than a company's direct borrowing rate, the present value, or lump-sum investment base at the zero reference point, normally is higher than a prospective project's purchase price, or cost of acquisition. Consequently, the DCF rates of return generally are lower when prospective projects are leased than when they are purchased and equity or debt financed.

It is interesting to note further that computed under these three financing methods, the lump-sum investment bases at the zero reference point are amounts that companies would be willing to pay or their suppliers, contractors, and lessors would be willing to accept at that point in time in lieu of a series of cash payments during a period of years either before or after the zero reference point. This is a sound and valid criterion for judging whether the DCF concept in the determination of DCF rates of return for prospective projects is properly or improperly applied.

Chapter 8

Application of DCF Concept Compared to Application of Compound Interest Principle

$\mathbf{I}$t has been established that the DCF rate of return is identical with the compound interest rate; that it is applied on the theory that treasurer's departments of companies loan monies to prospective projects in a similar manner that banks and other lending institutions loan monies to outside borrowers; that there is nothing inherently wrong with the DCF rate of return per se, providing it is applied by companies in situations similar to those in which the compound interest rate is applied by banks and other lending institutions; and finally, that if unrealistic DCF rates of return are arrived at, this problem must be attributable to an improper application of the DCF concept in the method by which DCF rates of return are calculated.

It also was stated that unrealistic DCF rates of return are arrived at primarily when portions of capital outlays of prospective projects are expected to occur during a period of years either before or after the time they are expected to start generating cash income or savings. These situations, which are primarily responsible for the improper application of the DCF concept by companies, never occur in the application of the compound interest principle by banks and other lending institutions.

Application of DCF Concept versus Compound Interest Principle

To understand why banks and other lending institutions are never called upon to loan money to outside borrowers under similar conditions that treasurer's departments of companies frequently are called upon to loan money to prospective projects either before or after the time they start generating cash income or savings, these two premises must be accepted by the reader: (1) Banks and other lending institutions are never willing to loan money interest free to outside borrowers for any period of time; and contrariwise, outside borrowers are never able to borrow money interest free from banks and other lending institutions for any period of time. (2) Banks and other lending institutions are never able to earn or receive interest from outside borrowers on loans that haven't as yet been made to them; and contrariwise, outside borrowers are never willing to pay interest to banks and other lending institutions on loans that haven't as yet been received by them. In other words, self-amortizing bank loans, which involve the compound interest rate, invariably start generating periodic bank loan payment amounts, including repayment of principal and interest, immediately after the bank loan principal amounts are turned over to outside borrowers by banks or other lending institutions. This means that in bank loan transactions, *(a)* the bank loan principal is always in the form of one lump-sum amount and never in series of amounts, *(b)* the zero reference point is always the point in time when this lump-sum bank loan principal amount is turned over to the outside borrower, and *(c)* the series of periodic bank loan payment amounts that, according to the loan agreement, is committed to be made by the outside borrower during the bank loan term, always starts immediately after the zero reference point, i.e., the point in time when the loan was made. These three conditions invariably are prevalent in bank loan transactions and the proper application of the compound interest principle in self-amortizing loans by banks and other lending institutions.

It is important to bear in mind at this point that when an outside borrower's cash requirements extend over a period of years, this type of multiple bank loan situation normally is handled by banks and other lending institutions in the form of a series of separate self-amortizing bank loans instead of a single self-amortizing bank loan. This means that in this type of multiple bank loan situation there invariably will be *(a)* a separate bank loan principal amount; *(b)* a separate series of periodic bank loan payment amounts applicable to and identifiable with each bank loan principal amount; *(c)* a separate and possibly a different compound interest rate for each self-amortizing bank loan in the series; *(d)* a separate bank loan term; and *(e)* a separate zero reference point, i.e., the point in time the loan is made. This also means that in this type of multiple bank loan situation there will never be any intermingling and netting by the bank or other lending institution of the cash outflow and the cash inflow to and from the outside borrower, because the cash outflow always occurs in a lump-sum amount at the zero reference point, which is just before the time the self-amortizing bank loan starts generating bank loan payment amounts. If the DCF concept were always applied by companies under conditions identical with those under which the compound interest principle is applied by banks and other lending institutions, the DCF rates of return arrived at would consistently be realistic profitability indicators and reliable project selection devices in all proposed investment situations.

The Crux of the Problem

The contention that the DCF concept is applied on the premise that money is loaned to prospective projects by treasurer's departments of companies in a similar manner that money is loaned to outside borrowers by banks and other lending institutions is valid only insofar as both types of loans are expected to yield acceptable earnings or interest rates commensurate with the risks involved. In all other respects, this contention is invalid.

There is no doubt that in more instances than is commonly realized by top management, money is loaned to prospective projects under quite different conditions than those under which money is loaned to outside borrowers by banks and other lending institutions. This is particularly true in the majority of large companies' prospective projects, which require huge capital outlays during extended construction periods either before or after the time they start generating cash income or savings. For example, in the petroleum industry it is quite common for treasurer's departments of petroleum companies to loan hundreds of millions of dollars to prospective refining or marketing projects before or after the time they are expected to start generating cash income or savings. In prospective petroleum refining projects, for example, a number of years, generally, are required for the construction of a new refinery or chemical plant. As a result, huge sums of money normally are expended during this protracted construction period before the new refinery or chemical plant goes into operation and starts generating cash income or savings. Conversely, it also is quite common for treasurer's departments of petroleum companies to loan millions of dollars to prospective petroleum marketing projects during prolonged expansion periods after the time they start generating additional cash income.

It is inconceivable that banks and other lending institutions would ever be faced with similar situations where they would be obliged to loan money interest free to outside borrowers for extended periods before starting to receive regular periodic bank loan payment amounts or, contrariwise, where they would start receiving regular payment amounts long before money is actually loaned to outside borrowers.

The reason unrealistic DCF rates of return are arrived at when portions of capital outlays of prospective projects occur either before or after the time they start generating cash income is due to the following condition. When the DCF concept is improperly applied in DCF rate of return calculations, an interest rate is automatically charged to prospective projects, which neither the companies sponsoring them nor the suppliers and contractors supplying the materials and labor are willing to pay for the use of money compared to the interest rate at which both the companies and their suppliers and contractors presumably can borrow money from banks or other lending institutions.

Improper Application of the DCF Concept

The serious distortions of DCF rates of return arrived at due to the improper application of the DCF concept in situations where portions of a prospective project's total capital outlays occur before, at, or after the time the project starts generating cash income or savings is shown in Table 21. All the financial factors pertaining to this prospective project, namely, the $100,000 total capital outlays, the $199,250 total project cash income or savings, the $99,250 total profit, and the 10-year economic life, are identical in the four cases. Only the timing of the prospective project's capital outlays is varied in each case. In Case 1, $90,000, or 90 percent, of the total capital outlays occur during the three-year period before the zero reference point, and the remaining $10,000, or 10 percent, occur at the zero reference point. In Case 2, the entire $100,000, or 100 percent, of the total capital outlays occur at the zero reference point. In Case 3, $10,000, or 10 percent, of the total capital outlays occur at the zero reference point and the remaining $90,000, or 90 percent, occur during the three-year period after the zero reference point. In Case 4, $10,000, or 10 percent, of the total capital outlays occur at the zero reference point and the remaining $90,000, or 90 percent, occur during the nine-year period after the zero reference point. The zero reference point in all four cases represents the point in time when this prospective project is expected to start generating cash income or savings. Despite the fact that this prospective project's $100,000 total capital outlays, its $199,250 total cash income or savings, and its 10-year economic life are identical in all four cases, the prospective project's DCF rate of return arrived at as a result of the improper application of the DCF concept ranges from 9.9 percent in Case 1, in which the timing of its $100,000 total capital outlays is least advantageous, to 99.3 percent in Case 4, in which it is most advantageous. In other words, the substantial differences in this prospective project's DCF rates of return, ranging from 9.9 percent in Case 1, to 15.0 percent in Case 2, to 33.5 percent in Case 3, and to 99.3 percent in Case 4, are attributable solely to the differences in the timing of the project's $100,000 total capital outlays in the four cases.

It should be noted in Table 21 that only in Case 2 are the conditions, under which the $100,000 expected to be loaned to this prospective project by the company's treasurer's department, identical with those under which money normally is loaned to outside borrowers by banks and other lending institutions. This is because in Case 2, the $100,000 total capital outlays are expected to occur in a lump-sum amount at the zero reference point, which is the point in time immediately before this prospective project is expected to start generating cash income or savings. Hence, the 15.0 percent DCF rate of return in Case 2, which is arrived at as a result of the proper application of the DCF concept, may be assumed to be the realistic profitability indicator and the reliable project selection device for this prospective project in this particular situation.

It should be noted further in Table 21 that in Cases 1, 3, and 4, the conditions under which the $100,000 are loaned to this prospective project by the company's treasurer's department during a period of years aren't only quite dissimilar but they are actually contrary to the conditions under which money normally is loaned to outside borrowers by banks and other lending institutions. Hence, the 9.9 percent, 33.5 percent, and 99.3 percent DCF rates of return, which are arrived at as a result of the improper application of the DCF concept in Cases 1, 3, and 4, respectively, may be suspected of being unrealistic profitability indicators and unrealiable project selection devices for this prospective project in these three situations. This is a valid assumption because, as explained previously, in these three situations an interest rate equal to the prospective project's 9.9 percent, 33.5 percent, and 99.3 percent DCF earnings rate is automatically assigned to portions of its total capital outlays in Cases 1, 3, and 4, respectively. These rates are substantially lower or higher than the 12 percent prime interest rate at which the company sponsoring this prospective project and its suppliers and contractors are assumed to be able to borrow money and willing to pay for its use.

It should be noted still further in Table 21 that this prospective project's economic advantage in Case 2 over Case 1 is measured in terms of the interest savings for the use of $50,000 for three years, $25,000 for two years, and $15,000 for one year in Case 1 as opposed to Case 2; while this prospective project's economic advantage in Case 3 and Case 4 over Case 2 is measured in terms of the interest savings for the use of $15,000 for one year, $25,000 for two years, and $50,000 for three years in Case 3 as opposed to Case 2; and for

Distorted and Unrealistic DCF Rates of Return Are Arrived at under Conventional DCF Method When Portions of Project's Capital Outlays Occur before or after Zero Reference Point*

(1)	(2)	(3)	(4)	(5)	(6)
	Portions of the Project's Capital Outlays† Occur				Project's Cash Income in Cases 1 to 4
	Before Year 0 in	At Year 0 in	After Year 0		
			In	In	
Year	Case 1	Case 2	Case 3	Case 4	
3	$ (50,000)	—	—	—	—
2	(25,000)	—	—	—	—
1	(15,000)	—	—	—	—
0	(10,000)	$(100,000)	$ (10,000)	$ (10,000)	—
1			(15,000)	(10,000)	$ 19,925
2			(25,000)	(10,000)	19,925
3			(50,000)	(10,000)	19,925
4				(10,000)	19,925
5				(10,000)	19,925
6				(10,000)	19,925
7				(10,000)	19,925
8				(10,000)	19,925
9				(10,000)	19,925
10				—	19,925
Total	$(100,000)	$(100,000)	$(100,000)	$(100,000)	$199,250
DCF Rate of Return...					

* The zero reference point is the year 0 which represents the point in time when the project starts generating cash income.

† Capital outlays and bank payments in parentheses.

the use of $10,000 for one year, $10,000 for two years, $10,000 for three years, and ---- $10,000 for nine years in Case 4, as opposed to Case 2. These economic advantages in the form of interest savings solely due to the timing of this project's $100,000 cash outlays must be measured in terms of the company's and its suppliers' and contractors' direct borrowing rate that they, presumably, are willing to pay for the use of money. These economic advantages in terms of interest savings should be reflected in this project's DCF rates of return in these three cases at the 12 percent prime interest rate, which the company and its suppliers and contractors are presumed to be willing to pay for the use of money, and not at the 9.9 percent, 33.5 percent, and 99.3 percent DCF earnings rates at which portions of this prospective project's $100,000 cash outlays are compounded or discounted. This proves that the economic disadvantage in terms of the interest expense in Case 1 compared to Case 2 is understated. On the other hand, the economic advantage in terms of the interest savings in Cases 3 and 4 compared to Case 2 is overstated. This indicates that the 9.9 percent, 33.5 percent, and 99.3 percent DCF rates of return for this prospective project in Cases 1, 3, and 4, respectively, more than likely are unrealistic profitability indicators and unreliable project selection devices as arrived at under the conventional DCF method.

TABLE 21

(7)	(8)	(9)	(10)	(11)	(12)	(13)	(14)
					Memo: Bank Financing the Project in Case 2		
					Bank Loan and Bank	*Present Value Factor*	*Present*
	The Project's Net Cash Flow in						
Case 1	*Case 2*	*Case 3*	*Case 4*	*Year*	*Payments†*	*at 12%*	*Value*
$(50,000)	—	—	—		—	—	—
(25,000)	—	—	—		—	—	—
(15,000)	—	—	—		—	—	—
(10,000)	$(100,000)	$(10,000)	$(10,000)		$ 100,000		
19,925	19,925	4,925	9,925	1	(17,698)	.8929	$ 15,803
19,925	19,925	(5,075)	9,925	2	(17,698)	.7972	14,109
19,925	19,925	(30,075)	9,925	3	(17,698)	.7118	12,597
19,925	19,925	19,925	9,925	4	(17,698)	.6355	11,247
19,925	19,925	19,925	9,925	5	(17,698)	.5674	10,043
19,925	19,925	19,925	9,925	6	(17,698)	.5066	8,966
19,925	19,925	19,925	9,925	7	(17,698)	.4523	8,005
19,925	19,925	19,925	9,925	8	(17,698)	.4039	7,148
19,925	19,925	19,925	9,925	9	(17,698)	.3606	6,383
19,925	19,925	19,925	19,925	10	(17,698)	.3220	5,699
$ 99,250	$ 99,250	$ 99,250	$ 99,250	Total	$(176,980)		$100,000
9.9%	15.0%	33.5%	99.3%	Interest	$ (76,980)		

Chapter 9

DCF Concept Improperly Applied in Conventional DCF Method ——————————

The DCF concept is improperly applied in the conventional DCF method in certain investment situations—particularly in those in which portions of total capital outlays of prospective projects are expected to occur either before or after the time they are expected to start generating cash income or savings. This is a serious problem that must be resolved for these reasons. (1) These investment situations occur predominately in major prospective projects that, due to their size, generally require large capital outlays during prolonged periods of construction or business expansion. (2) The strong possibility that the grossly distorted, unrealistic DCF rates of return arrived at by the conventional DCF method in these situations may lead to the acceptance of unprofitable major projects and the rejection of profitable projects, with the result that the future overall profitability of companies may be affected adversely for years to come. (3) Investment decisions involving major projects generally are irreversible. This means that for years to come companies may have to live with unprofitable major projects that were accepted, as well as do without the benefits of profitable projects that were rejected, as a result of irreversible, unwise investment decisions that stemmed from distorted and unrealistic DCF rates of return. To better understand the seriousness of this problem, what causes it, and how it can best be resolved, it may be helpful to recapitulate briefly some of the things that have been discussed thus far about the application of the DCF concept in DCF rate of return calculations and determine to what extent they are true or false and lead to a correct or an incorrect method for calculating DCF rates of return.

Recapitulation of Some of the Things Discussed Thus Far

Some of the things discussed thus far pertaining to the application of the DCF concept in DCF rate of return calculations include the following contentions: (1) The DCF rate of return is comparable to the compound interest rate. This is true. (2) The DCF concept and its application are borrowed from the banking community. It is true that the DCF concept is borrowed from the banking community. However, its application by companies in certain situations differs from that by banks and other lending institutions. (3) The DCF concept is applied by companies on the premise that their treasurer's departments make loans internally to prospective projects in a similar manner that loans are made by banks and other lending institutions to outside borrowers. This is true only in situations in which total capital outlays of prospective projects are expected to occur at the zero reference point, which is immediately before the time they are expected to start generating cash income or savings. (4) Similar to bank loan transactions in which the earnings rate on loans made to outside borrowers represents the interest rate charged to them and therefore is the rate used by banks and other lending institutions for discounting and compounding, so likewise in capital investment transactions the earnings rate on loans made internally to prospective projects represents the interest rate charged to them and therefore is presumed to be the rate companies use for discounting or compounding. This is only partially true because this single rate doesn't apply to capital outlays expected to occur during prolonged periods of years either before or after the time prospective projects are expected to start generating cash income or savings. The rate that must be used for discounting and compounding the capital outlays in these situations is the interest rate at which companies and their suppliers and contractors are able to borrow money from banks or other lending institutions and are willing to pay for its use. Failure to heed this important exception, which is so prevalent in high-cost, long-life projects, could result in grossly distorted alternate lump-sum investment amounts at the zero reference point and consequently in unrealistic DCF rates of return that could lead to unwise and costly investment decisions. The latter in turn could affect a company's future overall profitability adversely for many years.

Problem Encountered in Application of DCF Concept

The DCF rates of return arrived at by the conventional DCF method in the above investment situations, which are present whenever money is loaned to prospective projects during extended periods either before or after the time they are expected to start generating cash income or savings, are shown most dramatically in Table 21. Similar situations, of course, are never present in self-amortizing bank loan transactions in which the compound interest rate is used. This is true because banks or other lending institutions never loan money for extended periods before the time outside borrowers start making bank loan payments on self-amortizing bank loans and, conversely, because banks or other lending institutions never receive bank loan payments for extended periods before the time they have loaned money to outside borrowers. In self-amortizing bank loans, the periodic bank loan payments, including repayment of principal and interest, always commence immediately after the money is loaned by banks or other lending institutions to outside borrowers. The four investment situations in which money is expected to be loaned to the prospective project in Table 21 shows that the conventional DCF method arrives at realistic DCF rates of return only when money is loaned internally to prospective projects in situations similar to those in which money is loaned by banks or other lending institutions to outside borrowers, and that the conventional DCF method arrives at distorted and unrealistic DCF rates of return when money is loaned internally to prospective projects in dissimilar situations that never present themselves in bank loan transactions.

It should be noted that all financial factors—the $100,000 estimated total capital outlays, the $19,925 estimated annual cash income or savings, and the 10-year estimated economic life—are identical in the four investment situations for this prospective project. Only the timing of the $100,000 estimated total capital outlays varies widely in the four investment situations in Cases 1 to 4.

It should be noted also that only in Case 2 is the manner or situation in which the estimated $100,000 is expected to be loaned to the prospective project similar to that in which banks or other lending institutions loan money to outside borrowers, i.e., the entire $100,000 is expected to be loaned immediately before the time the prospective project is expected to start generating cash income or savings.

If we assume that the $100,000, instead of representing an internal loan by a company to a prospective project, represents a $100,000 bank loan to an outside borrower, the $19,925 represents the annual bank loan payment amount and the 10-year period represents the loan term, then by discounting this stream of annual bank loan payment amounts by trial and error at various rates, we find that it discounts down to a total present value equal to the $100,000 bank loan principal at the 15 percent rate. This means the bank is earning 15 percent interest and, contrariwise, the outside borrower is paying 15 percent interest on this $100,000 bank loan.

Similarly, if we assume the $100,000 represents an internal loan made by a company to this prospective project, then the DCF rate of return is 15 percent because the $100,000 is loaned to the prospective project in a manner similar to that in which money is loaned by banks and other lending institutions to outside borrowers. Moreover, the DCF rate of return is comparable to the compound interest rate, and both rates are determined by the same procedure in this type of loan or investment situation in Case 2.

On the other hand, in Case 1, 90 percent of the $100,000 is expected to be loaned by the company to the prospective project during a three-year period before the time it is expected to start generating cash income or savings; while in Cases 3 and 4, 90 percent of the $100,000 is expected to be loaned to the prospective project during a three- and a nine-year period after that point in time.

Since money has a time value, these time intervals during which substantial portions of the $100,000 are expected to be loaned to this prospective project in Cases 1, 3, and 4 poses a serious problem. It raises the question as to what time value of money—the company's alternate use value of money rate or its direct borrowing rate—should be used for compounding or discounting the prospective project's early or delayed capital outlays. The conventional DCF method doesn't address itself to this problem. It doesn't distinguish between investment and income dollars as proven by the fact that capital outlay, capital recovery, and cash income dollars of prospective projects are netted in DCF rate of return calculations by the conventional DCF method.

The DCF Concept Improperly Applied in Conventional DCF Method

As explained earlier, it is reasonable to assume that the investment situations in which total capital outlays of prospective projects occur during prolonged periods of years either before or after the time they start generating cash income or savings generally are those that require large capital outlays and extended periods of construction or business expansion. It is primarily in these two types of investment situations that the DCF concept is improperly applied in the conventional DCF method as described below.

- The zero reference point chosen in the DCF rate of return calculation may be either the point in time when *(a)* the first capital expenditure is made for prospective projects or *(b)* prospective projects start generating cash income or savings.
- The capital outlay, the capital recovery, and the cash income or savings dollars of prospective projects are commingled and netted in the DCF rate of return calculations. Since there is no distinction made between these different dollars, this results in compounding or discounting them at the same rate.
- The DCF rate of return for prospective projects is determined by one of the following two procedures depending on which one of the two zero reference points is chosen: (1) A rate is found by trial and error in the present value table that discounts the prospective project's net cash flow back to a total present value equal to zero. This procedure is used when the zero reference point represents the point in time when the first capital expenditure is expected to be made for the prospective project. (2) An identical rate is found, by trial and error in the future value and the present value tables that compounds the prospective project's capital outlays occurring before the zero reference point forward and discounts its net cash flow occurring after the zero reference point back to the latter point in time to identical present values that cancel out to zero. This procedure is used when the zero reference point is the point in time when the prospective project is expected to start generating cash income or savings. Under the above two procedures, the rate that compounds and/or discounts the prospective project's cash outflows and

cash inflows to identical present values that cancel out to zero is the prospective project's DCF rate of return. Also, the same time value of money equal to the prospective project's calculated DCF earnings rate is automatically assigned to its capital outlay, capital recovery, and cash income or savings dollars. This rate, almost invariably, is substantially higher than the interest rate at which the company and its suppliers and contractors are able to borrow money and are willing to pay for its use. Consequently, compounding or discounting its capital outlays at this unrealistically high rate, for example, will overstate the prospective project's alternate lump-sum investment amount at the zero reference point, and thus understate its DCF rate of return, when portions of its total capital outlays occur before the time the prospective project is expected to start generating cash income or savings.

The results of the improper application of the DCF concept in the conventional DCF method are exemplified most vividly by the DCF rates of return arrived at by the conventional DCF method in the four different investment situations (Case 1 through Case 4) for the prospective project in Table 21.

As explained earlier, only in Case 2, in which the company's $100,000 internal loan to this prospective project is made in a similar manner that loans are made by banks and other lending institutions to outside borrowers, is the 15 percent arrived at by the conventional DCF method a realistic DCF rate of return.

The differences between the 15 percent DCF rate of return in Case 2 and those in Cases 1, 3, and 4 due to the different timing of the prospective project's capital outlays must reflect the differences in the interest costs or savings that must be based on an interest rate that the company and its suppliers and contractors are willing to pay for the use of money. This is their current direct borrowing rate, which is assumed to be 12 percent.

In Case 1, in which 90 percent, or $90,000, of the total capital outlays are expected to occur during a three-year period before the time the prospective project is expected to start generating cash income or savings, the prospective project's DCF rate of return arrived at by the conventional DCF method is 9.9 percent. This DCF rate of return is understated and unrealistic because compared to the 15 percent DCF rate of return in Case 2, the disadvantage in the form of interest cost, due to early capital spending, is understated because it is based on the prospective project's 9.9 percent DCF earnings rate instead of on the company's and its suppliers' and contractors' 12 percent current direct borrowing rate.

In the investment situations in Cases 3 and 4, the opposite is true. In Cases 3 and 4, in which 90 percent, or $90,000, of the total capital outlays are expected to occur during a three-year and nine-year period after the time the prospective project is expected to start generating cash income or savings, the DCF rates of return arrived at by the conventional DCF method are 33.5 percent and 99.3 percent, respectively. These two DCF rates of return are grossly overstated and unrealistic because compared to the 15 percent DCF rate of return in Case 2, the advantage of interest savings, due to delayed capital spending, is grossly overstated because the interest savings are based on the prospective project's 33.5 percent and 99.3 percent DCF earnings rates instead of on the company's and its suppliers' and contractors' 12 percent current direct borrowing rate.

Proof DCF Concept Is Improperly Applied in Conventional DCF Method

It has been established that unrealistic DCF rates of return are arrived at by the conventional DCF method when portions of the total capital outlays of prospective projects occur either before or after the time they are expected to start generating cash income or savings. From a close scrutiny of the examples in Table 21, it was concluded that *(a)* the 9.9 percent DCF rate of return for the prospective project in Case 1 is understated and unrealistic because it is determined in an investment or loan situation dissimilar to those in which the compound interest rate is determined and used by banks and other lending institutions, and *(b)* the 15.0 percent DCF rate of return for this prospective project in Case 2 is realistic because it is determined in an investment or loan situation similar to those in which the compound interest rate is determined and used by banks and other lending institutions.

Table 22 proves that the 9.9 percent DCF rate of return arrived at by the conventional DCF method in Case 1 is identical whether the zero reference point is the point in time *(a)* when the first capital expenditure for the prospective project is expected to occur or *(b)* when the prospective project is expected to start generating cash income or savings. If the zero reference point is the point in time when the first capital expenditure is expected to occur, then the discounting technique is used exclusively to determine the 9.9 percent DCF rate of return by the conventional DCF method. On the other hand, if the zero reference point is the point in time when the prospective project is expected to start generating cash income or savings, then both the compounding and the discounting techniques are used to determine the 9.9 percent DCF rate of return by the conventional DCF method.

The importance of the examples in Table 22 is to prove that the 9.9 percent DCF rate of return arrived at by the conventional DCF method is calculated on an alternate lump-sum investment amount of $123,050 (obtained by interpolation) at the zero reference point, and that this alternate lump-sum investment amount includes a 9.9 percent interest factor. It is logical and reasonable to conclude that if the company's suppliers and contractors have to pay interest at a 12 percent rate to borrow money, they naturally would be unwilling to accept $123,050 at the zero reference point, which includes interest at only a 9.9 percent rate, in lieu of $50,000 three years prior, $25,000 two years prior, $15,000 one year prior, and $10,000 at that point in time. Since the $123,050 alternate lump-sum investment amount at the zero reference point is an unacceptable one, it follows that the 9.9

Case 1: Proof that Under Conventional DCF Method a Time Value of Money Equal to Project's 9.9 Percent Estimated DCF Earnings Rate Is Assigned to Its Capital Outlays Resulting in a Distorted 9.9 Percent DCF Rate of Return*

(1)	(2)	(3)	(4)	(5)	(6)
			DCF Rate of Return Calculation		
Year	Project's Capital Outlays† and Cash Income	Present Value Factor at 9%	Present Value	Present Value Factor at 10%	Present Value

The zero reference point represents the point in time when the project's first capital outlay is made in year 0.

0	$ (50,000)	1.0000	$(50,000)	1.0000	$(50,000)
1	(25,000)	.9174	(22,935)	.9091	(22,728)
2	(15,000)	.8417	(12,626)	.8264	(12,396)
3	(10,000)	.7722	(7.722)	.7513	(7.513)
Total capital outlays	(100,000)		(93,283)		(92,637)
4	19,925	.7084	14,115	.6830	13,609
5	19,925	.6499	12,949	.6209	12,371
6	19,925	.5963	11,881	.5645	11,248
7	19,925	.5470	10,899	.5132	10,226
8	19,925	.5019	10,000	.4665	9,295
9	19,925	.4604	9,173	.4241	8,450
10	19,925	.4224	8,416	.3855	7,681
11	19,925	.3875	7,721	.3505	6,984
12	19,925	.3555	7,083	.3186	6,348
13	19,925	.3262	6,500	.2897	5,772
Total cash income	199,250		98,737		91,984
Total profit	$ 99,250		$ 5,454		$ (653)

DCF rate of return is 9.9%.

* When portions of these capital outlays occur before the time the project starts generating cash income.
† Capital outlays in parentheses.

percent DCF rate of return calculated on this unrealistic investment base is also unrealistic.

It is obvious that the investment opportunity in Case 1, in which the major portion of the $100,000 total capital outlays is expected to occur during the three-year period before the time the prospective project is expected to start generating cash income or savings, is less attractive than the investment opportunity in Case 2, in which the entire $100,000 capital outlays are expected to occur immediately before that point in time. The question then arises, "How much less attractive is the investment opportunity in Case 1 compared to that in Case 2?" The 9.9 percent DCF rate of return arrived at by the conventional DCF method indicates that the investment opportunity in Case 1 is 5.1 percent (15.0 percent − 9.9 percent) less advantageous than the one in

TABLE 22

(7)	(8)	(9)	(10)	(11)	(12)
			DCF Rate of Return Calculation		
Year	Project's Capital Outlays† and Cash Income	Future or Present Value Factor at 9%	Future or Present Value	Future or Present Value Factor at 10%	Future or Present Value

The zero reference point represents the point in time when the project starts generating cash income in year 0.

3	$ (50,000)	1.2950	$ (64,750)	1.3310	$ (66,550)
2	(25,000)	1.1881	(29,703)	1.2100	(30,250)
1	(15,000)	1.0900	(16,350)	1.1000	(16,500)
0	(10,000)	1.0000	(10,000)	1.0000	(10,000)
Total capital outlays	(100,000)		(120,803)		(123,300)
1	19,925	.9174	18,279	.9091	18,114
2	19,925	.8417	16,771	.8264	16,466
3	19,925	.7722	15,386	.7513	14,970
4	19,925	.7084	14,115	.6830	13,609
5	19,925	.6499	12,949	.6209	12,371
6	19,925	.5963	11,881	.5645	11,248
7	19,925	.5470	10,899	.5132	10,226
8	19,925	.5019	10,000	.4665	9,295
9	19,925	4604	9,173	.4241	8,450
10	19,925	.4224	8,416	.3855	7,681
Total cash income	199,250		127,869		122,430
Total profit	$ 99,250		$ 7,066		$ (870)

DCF rate of return is 9.9%.

Case 2. However, a closer examination of the examples in Tables 21 and 22 reveals *(a)* that all the financial factors, except the timing of the $100,000 total capital outlays, are identical in Cases 1 and 2; and *(b)* that the 9.9 percent DCF rate of return for the prospective project in Case 1 is calculated on an understated and unrealistic investment base of $123,050, which represents an amount the company's suppliers and contractors would be unwilling to accept at the zero reference point, in lieu of $100,000 during a three-year period before that point in time. Hence, the above-mentioned 5.1 percent economic disadvantage in Case 1 vis-à-vis Case 2 is excessive and unrealistic. This proves that the answer to the question of how much less attractive the investment opportunity in Case 1 is compared to that in Case 2 can be measured only in terms of the DCF rate of return that is calculated on the alternate lump-sum

Case 4: Proof that Under Conventional DCF Method a Time Value of Money Equal to Project's 99.26 Percent Estimated DCF Earnings Rate Is Assigned to Its Capital Outlays Resulting in a Distorted 99.26 Percent DCF Rate of Return*

	(1)	(2)	(3)	(4)	(5)	(6)	(7)
		DCF Rate of Return Calculation under Procedure 1				**DCF Rate of Return**	
Year	Project's Net Cash Flow	Present Value Factor at 99.26%	Present Value of Project's Net Cash Flow	Project's Capital Outlays†	Present Value Factor at 99.26%	Present Value of Project's Capital Outlays†
0	$(10,000)	1.0000	$(10,000)	$ (10,000)	1.0000	$(10,000)
1	9,925	.5019	4,981	(10,000)	.5019	(5,019)
2	9,925	.2519	2,500	(10,000)	.2519	(2,519)
3	9,925	.1264	1,255	(10,000)	.1264	(1,264)
4	9,925	.0634	630	(10,000)	.0634	(634)
5	9,925	.0318	316	(10,000)	.0318	(318)
6	9,925	.0160	158	(10,000)	.0160	(160)
7	9,925	.0080	80	(10,000)	.0080	(80)
8	9,925	.0040	40	(10,000)	.0040	(40)
9	9,925	.0020	20	(10,000)	.0020	(20)
10	19,925	.0010	20	—	.0010	—
Total	$ 99,250		$ –0–	$(100,000)		$(20,054)

DCF rate of return is 99.26%.   DCF Rate of return is 99.26%.

* When portions of these capital outlays occur subsequent to the time the project starts generating cash income.
    † Capital outlays in parentheses.

payment amount at the zero reference point that is acceptable to the company's suppliers and contractors in Case 1, in lieu of the series of annual payment amounts totaling $100,000 during the three-year period before that point in time.

The three procedures shown in Table 23 for arriving at the 99.26 percent DCF rate of return by the conventional DCF method is for the prospective project shown under Case 4 in Table 21. Furthermore, all the financial factors in Case 4 are identical with those for this prospective project in Case 2, except for the timing of the $100,000 total capital outlays.

The purpose of the examples in Table 23 is to prove *(a)* that under the conventional DCF method, an interest rate equal to the prospective project's 99.26 percent calculated DCF earnings rate is used for discounting its capital outlays; *(b)* that discounting the capital outlays at this exhorbitant interest rate results in a grossly understated alternate lump-sum investment amount at the

TABLE 23

(8)	(9)	(10)	(11)	(12)	(13)	(14)
					DCF Rate of Return Calculation under Procedure 3	
Calculation under Procedure 2						
		Present Value of Project's				*Present Value of Project's*
Project's Cash Income	*Present Value Factor at 99.26%*	*Cash Income*	*Net Cash Flow*	*Project's Net Cash Flow*	*Present Value Factor at 99.26%*	*Net Cash Flow*
$ —	1.0000	$ —	$(10,000)	$ (20,054)‡	1.0000	$(20,054)
19,925	.5019	10,000	4,981	19,925	.5019	10,000
19,925	.2519	5,019	2,500	19,925	.2519	5,019
19,925	.1264	2,519	1,255	19,925	.1264	2,519
19,925	.0634	1,264	630	19,925	.0634	1,264
19,925	.0318	634	316	19,925	.0318	634
19,925	.0160	318	158	19,925	.0160	318
19,925	.0080	160	80	19,925	.0080	160
19,925	.0040	80	40	19,925	.0040	80
19,925	.0020	40	20	19,925	.0020	40
19,925	.0010	20	20	19,925	.0010	20
$199,250		$20,054	$ –0–	$179,196§		$ –0–

DCF rate of return is 99.26%.

‡ Total of Column 7.
§ The $79,946 difference in the total profits ($179,196 − $99,250), shown under procedure 3 compared to those shown under procedures 1 and 2, is attributable solely to the difference between the project's total actual capital outlays and their total present values ($100,000 − $20,054). This indicates that the project is credited with profits of $79,946 that are expected to be earned in other projects due to the late capital spending in this project as shown in Table 24.

zero reference point; and *(c)* that calculating the DCF rate of return on this highly understated and distorted investment base at the zero reference point results in a seriously overstated and unrealistic DCF rate of return for this prospective project in this investment situation in Case 4. To prove this, the prospective project's 99.26 percent DCF rate of return in Case 4 is calculated by three different procedures. First, it is calculated by discounting the prospective project's net cash flow down to a total present value that is equal to zero. Second, it is calculated by discounting the prospective project's cash outlays and its cash income or savings amounts separately down to identical present values that cancel out to zero. Third, it is calculated by discounting the stream of cash income or savings amounts down to a total present value equal to the alternate lump-sum investment amount at the zero reference point, in lieu of the series of capital outlays totaling $100,000 during the 10-year period.

Table 23 shows that *(a)* in procedure 1, the 99.26 percent rate discounts the prospective project's net cash flow totaling $99,250 down to a total present value that is equal to zero; *(b)* in procedure 2, the 99.26 percent rate discounts the prospective project's cash outlays and cash returns separately down to identical present values of $20,054 that cancel out to zero; and *(c)* in procedure 3, the 99.26 percent rate discounts the prospective project's stream of cash income or savings amounts down to a total present value equal to the $20,054 alternate lump-sum investment amount at the zero reference point. The 99.26 percent DCF rate of return arrived at by these three procedures prove that under the conventional DCF method, this DCF rate of return is calculated on an alternate lump-sum investment amount of $20,054 at the zero reference point, which represents an amount the company's suppliers and contractors would be unwilling to accept at that point in time, in lieu of a series of payments totaling $100,000 during a 9-year period, because they would be paying interest in the amount of $79,946 at a 99.26 percent rate when they can borrow money at a 12 percent interest rate. Consequently, these three DCF rate of return calculations under the conventional DCF method prove that the 99.26 percent DCF rate of return for this prospective project in the investment situation in Case 4 is seriously overstated and unrealistic.

What the 99.26 Percent DCF Rate of Return Implies

If this prospective project were to be accepted and justified in terms of the 99.26 percent DCF rate of return, which is calculated on the $20,054 highly understated and unrealistic alternate lump-sum investment amount at the zero reference point, this would imply, as shown in Table 24, that management would be seeking approval for only $20,054 at that point in time, and that the remaining $79,946 would be expected to be obtained from profits earned at the same 99.26 percent on the investment amounts made available due to the delayed spending during the nine-year period. To presume that the company could earn profits at the rate of 99.26 percent on the funds made available due to the delayed spending is tantamount to professing that the company's alternate use value of money rate is 99.26 percent. Accepting the prospective project on this premise would be most unrealistic and unwise.

There is no denying that due to the delayed capital spending, the investment opportunity of this prospective project in Case 4 is economically more advantageous than the one in Case 2. However, as proven in Table 24, it simply isn't plausible for the DCF rate of return to increase from 15.0 percent in Case 2 to 99.26 percent in Case 4 merely because of the difference in the timing of the prospective project's $100,000 total capital outlays when the company's and its suppliers' and contractors' direct borrowing rate is only 12 percent. The question then arises, "What is the true and realistic DCF rate of return for this prospective project in Case 4 and how much more advantageous, economically, is the investment opportunity in Case 4 compared to that in Case 2?" The answer to this question will be found in Chapter 10.

TABLE 24

Case 4: Proof that Justification of Project's $100,000 Capital Outlays during Nine-Year Period in Terms of a 99.26 Percent DCF Earnings Rate Infers that Management Approval for Only $20,054 Instead of $100,000 Is Sought at Zero Reference Point*

(1)	(2)	(3)	(4)	(5)
			Total	
		Profits	Funds	
	Investment	Earned	Available	This
	Principal	in Other	for This	Project's
	Available	Projects	Project	Capital
Year	Start of Year	at 99.26%	End of Year	Outlays†
0	$20,054	$ —	$20,054	$ (10,000)
1	10,054	9,980	20,034	(10,000)
2	10,034	9,960	19,994	(10,000)
3	9,994	9,920	19,914	(10,000)
4	9,914	9,841	19,755	(10,000)
5	9,755	9,683	19,438	(10,000)
6	9,438	9,368	18,806	(10,000)
7	8,806	8,741	17,547	(10,000)
8	7,547	7,491	15,038	(10,000)
9	5,038	4,962	10,000	(10,000)
Total	$ –0–	$79,946	$ –0–	$(100,000)

* The remaining $79,946 will be obtained from profits earned in other projects at a 99.26 percent earnings rate due to this project's delayed capital spending.
† Capital outlays in parentheses.

Treatment of Depreciation Charges in Conventional DCF Method

In the conventional DCF method, the prospective project's annual depreciation charges are calculated on the actual capital cost of its fixed assets, while the project's DCF rate of return is calculated on the alternate lump-sum investment amount at the zero reference point. This investment base, which is arrived at by compounding or discounting at rates that normally are substantially lower or higher than the company's direct borrowing rate, is either considerably higher or lower than the actual capital outlays for the fixed assets when portions of these capital outlays are expected to occur either before or after the time the prospective project is expected to start generating cash income.

For example, Table 25 shows that the annual depreciation charges for the prospective project in Case 1, Table 21, are calculated on the fixed assets' $100,000 total capital cost, thus limiting the total depreciation charges to that amount. On the other hand, Table 22 shows that the 9.9 percent DCF rate of return for this prospective project in Case 1 is calculated on the substantially higher $123,050 alternate lump-sum investment amount at the zero reference point, which includes a 9.9 percent interest factor. This interest rate the company's suppliers and contractors unquestionably would be unwilling to

TABLE 25

Calculation of Cash Income after Taxes for Project Shown on Tables 21 to 23 in which Only Timing of Cash Outlays Is Varied

(1)	(2)	(3)	(4)	(5)	(6)
	Project's Cash Income before Taxes	Depreciation Charges*†	Taxable Income	Income Taxes	Project's Cash Income after Taxes
Year					

Under the Conventional DCF Method for Cases 1 to 4

Year					
1	$ 18,030	$ 18,180	$ (150)	$ (75)	$ 19,925
2	24,210	16,360	7,850	3,975	19,925
3	28,800	14,550	14,250	7,125	19,925
4	32,100	12,730	19,370	9,685	19,925
5	34,376	10,910	23,466	11,733	19,925
6	35,832	9,090	26,742	13,371	19,925
7	34,012	7,270	26,742	13,371	19,925
8	32,192	5,450	26,742	13,371	19,925
9	30,382	3,640	26,742	13,371	19,925
10	28,566	1,820	26,746	13,373	19,925
Total	$298,500	$100,000	$198,500	$ 99,250	$199,250

Under the Proposed DCF Method for Case 1

Year					
1	$ 18,030	$ 23,344	$ (5,314)	$ (2,657)	$ 20,687
2	24,210	21,007	3,203	1,602	22,608
3	28,800	18,683	10,117	5,059	23,741
4	32,100	16,346	15,754	7,877	24,223
5	34,376	14,009	20,367	10,184	24,192
6	35,832	11,672	24,160	12,080	23,752
7	34,012	9,335	24,677	12,338	21,674
8	32,192	6,998	25,194	12,597	19,595
9	30,382	4,674	25,708	12,854	17,528
10	28,566	2,337	26,229	13,114	15,452
Total	$298,500	$128,405	$170,095	$ 85,048	$213,452

Under the Proposed DCF Method for Case 4

Year					
1	$ 18,030	$ 11,505	$ 6,525	$ 3,263	$ 14,767
2	24,210	10,353	13,857	6,928	17,282
3	28,800	9,208	19,592	9,796	19,004
4	32,100	8,056	24,044	12,022	20,078
5	34,376	6,904	27,472	13,736	20,640
6	35,832	5,752	30,080	15,040	20,792
7	34,012	4,601	29,411	14,706	19,306
8	32,192	3,449	28,743	14,371	17,821
9	30,382	2,303	28,079	14,039	16,343
10	28,566	1,151	27,415	13,708	14,858
Total	$298,500	$ 63,282	$235,218	$117,609	$180,891

* Under the conventional DCF method, the depreciation charges are computed on the project's actual total capital outlays occurring during a period of years; whereas under the proposed DCF method, they are computed on the project's alternate lump-sum payment amount at the zero reference point.

† The depreciation charges are computed by the sum-of-the-years'-digits method under the conventional DCF method.

accept for the use of money if they have to pay 12 percent interest to borrow money from banks and other lending institutions. Hence, for this prospective project in Case 1, limiting the total depreciation charges to the $100,000 total capital outlays for its fixed assets while calculating its DCF rate of return on the substantially higher investment base of $123,050 at the zero reference point has the dual effect of seriously understating the 9.9 percent DCF rate of return. Obviously, under the conventional DCF method, the procedures for calculating the annual depreciation charges of the fixed assets and the DCF rates of return for prospective projects are highly incongruous, insofar as the calculations in these procedures are based on two different investment bases.

The incongruity of the procedures for calculating annual depreciation charges of fixed assets and DCF rates of return of prospective projects under the conventional DCF method is even more vividly highlighted when portions of the total capital outlays of prospective projects are expected to occur during a period of years after the time they start generating cash income or savings. For example, Table 25 shows that under the improper application of the DCF concept, the annual depreciation charges of the fixed assets are calculated on its $100,000 total capital outlays, thus benefiting the prospective project in Case 4 to the extent of $100,000 on the basis of its total depreciation charges, while its 99.3 percent DCF rate of return is calculated on the substantially lower and highly distorted $20,054 alternate lump-sum investment amount at the zero reference point. As explained earlier, this is an amount the company's suppliers and contractors, unquestionably, would be unwilling to accept at that point in time, in lieu of the series of annual cash payments aggregating $100,000 during the nine-year period after the zero reference point. The reason for their unwillingness to accept this alternate lump-sum investment amount at that point in time is that this would mean they would be paying interest at the rate of 99.3 percent during the nine-year period when they could borrow money at a 12 percent interest rate from banks and other lending institutions. Obviously, these incongruous and illogical procedures of calculating their fixed assets' annual depreciation charges on the $100,000 total capital cost during the nine-year period subsequent to the zero reference point, and then calculating the prospective project's DCF rate of return on the substantially lower $20,054 alternate lump-sum investment amount at the zero reference point, has the dual effect of grossly overstating the 99.3 percent DCF rate of return for this prospective project in Case 4 under the conventional DCF method.

Treatment of Residual Values in Conventional DCF Method

The treatment of residual values for the capital recoveries of fixed assets and working capital under the conventional DCF method, likewise, is illogical and unrealistic. The principal reason for this is that residual values for capital recoveries usually are discounted at rates that are either substantially lower or higher than the interest rate companies are willing to pay for the use of money. This is attributable to the fact that under the conventional DCF method no distinction is made between capital outlay, capital recovery, and cash income or savings dollars; and as a result, they are commingled and netted in the cash inflows of prospective projects, and thus are automatically discounted at their calculated DCF earnings rates. For example, Table 26 shows that the $50,000 capital recovery for land at the end of 20 years in

TABLE 26

Treatment of Residual Value under the Conventional DCF Method

| | | DCF Rate of Returns | | |
| | End of | 10% | 15% | 20% |
Item	*Year*	*Project 1*	*Project 2*	*Project 3*
Residual value for land	20	$50,000	$50,000	$50,000
Present value factor at 10%, 15%, and 20%, respectively	20	.1486	.0611	.0261
Present value at the zero reference point	–0–	7,430	3,055	1,305
Interest expense for 20 years		$42,570	$46,945	$48,695

Projects 1, 2, and 3 is automatically discounted at their respective 10 percent, 15 percent, and 20 percent calculated DCF earnings rates. This results in substantially different present values for the capital recovery and interest cost for tieing up the same amount of cash, $50,000, in land for 20 years in these three projects. These present values of the $50,000 capital recovery for the land and the consequent interest cost arrived at under the conventional DCF method are absolutely unrealistic. To be realistic, the present value of the $50,000 capital recovery as well as the applicable interest cost must be identical in each one of the three projects regardless of their DCF earnings rates. The present value of the $50,000 capital recovery in each project must be equivalent to the amount the company would be willing to accept and, contrariwise, the bank would be willing to pay at the zero reference point for the $50,000 at the end of the 20th year. This means the present value at the zero reference point of the $50,000 capital recovery for land at the end of the 20th year must reflect the interest rate the company would be willing to pay for the use of money and, contrariwise, the bank would be willing to loan money. Surely, the company would be most unwilling to pay an interest rate for the use of money equal to the 15 percent and the 20 percent DCF earnings rates on their investments in Projects 2 and 3, respectively. Conversely, neither would the bank be willing to pay an amount at the zero reference point for $50,000 at the end of the 20th year, as in Project 1 for instance, that is based on a 10 percent interest rate, if its prime interest rate to the company is 12 percent. This treatment of residual values under the conventional DCF method could lead to the rejection of profitable prospective projects due to the understated present values of capital recoveries at the zero reference point, particularly in cases where capital recoveries for nondepreciable and depreciable fixed assets are substantial and the DCF rates of return arrived at by this method are high.

Chapter 10

Proper Application of the DCF Concept Requisite in Effective DCF Method _____

$\mathbf{T}$he proper application of the DCF concept is absolutely essential in developing an effective DCF method that will produce DCF rates of return that will be realistic profitability indicators and reliable project selection devices, thus serving as effective guides in the decision-making process of proposed capital investments in new projects or ventures.

How to Resolve the Problem of Distorted DCF Rates of Return in Certain Investment Situations

Companies can satisfactorily resolve the problem of arriving at distorted DCF rates of return due to the improper application of the DCF concept in the conventional DCF method in situations *(a)* where portions of capital outlays of prospective projects are expected to occur during a period of years either before or after the time they are expected to start generating cash income or savings and *(b)* where substantial residual or salvage values are involved. This can be accomplished by companies simulating conditions in the application of the DCF concept comparable to those in which the compound interest principle is applied by banks and other lending institutions. In investment situations in which portions of capital outlays of prospective projects are expected to occur during a period of years either before or after the time they are expected to start generating cash income or savings, this will require developing an alternate lump-sum payment amount at the start of their economic lives that will be acceptable to companies or their suppliers and contractors at that point in time, in lieu of a series of payments either before or after that point in time. To be acceptable to companies or their suppliers and contractors, this alternate lump-sum payment amount at this point in time must be based on an interest rate that is equal to their direct borrowing rate which, of course, is the interest rate they are willing to pay for the use of money.

The Rationale of the Alternate Lump-Sum Payment Amount

It has been established that due to the improper application of the DCF concept in the conventional DCF method, a time value of money equal to the calculated DCF earnings rate of prospective projects is automatically assigned (*a*) to portions of their total capital outlays that occur either before or after the time they are expected to start generating cash income and (*b*) to their capital recoveries. This is true because the conventional DCF method makes no distinction between capital outlay, capital recovery, and cash income or savings dollars, which results in widely different time values of money being automatically assigned to portions of prospective projects' total capital outlays and capital recoveries, depending on the widely different DCF earnings rates arrived at by the conventional DCF method.

The rationale the alternate lump-sum payment or investment amount at the zero reference point is based on is illustrated by the debt financing of the prospective project shown in Table 21. The right side of Table 21 shows that when this prospective project's $100,000 total capital outlay, which is expected to occur at the zero reference point in Case 2, is bank financed at the company's 12 percent current direct borrowing rate, the annual bank loan payment amounts during the 10-year loan term will be $17,698. When this stream of $17,698 annual bank loan payment amounts totaling $176,980 is discounted at the company's 12 percent current direct borrowing rate, it discounts down to a total present value equal to the prospective project's $100,000 total capital outlay at the zero reference point. From the results obtained by discounting the prospective project's stream of annual bank loan payment amounts, the following conclusions may be drawn: (1) The prospective project's DCF rate of return in Case 2 may be calculated on its $100,000 total capital outlay amount, which in this investment situation is expected to occur at the zero reference point, and thus arrive at the 15 percent DCF rate of return. (2) The DCF rate of return also may be calculated on the prospective project's stream of annual bank loan payment amounts totaling $176,980 by discounting it at the company's and its suppliers' and contractors' 12 percent current direct borrowing rate, which will produce the same $100,000 total present value or alternate lump-sum payment amount at the zero reference point and, consequently, arrive at the same 15 percent DCF rate of return. (3) Conversely, this proves that the company's suppliers and contractors may choose to accept either a $100,000 lump-sum payment amount at the zero reference point or a series of $17,698 annual payment amounts during the 10-year period after that point in time. Either method of payment is equivalent to receiving a $100,000 lump-sum payment amount at the zero reference point. All the company's suppliers and contractors have to do is exercise their option and discount the notes covering these future annual payment amounts at their 12 percent current direct borrowing rate. This will net them $100,000 from the bank at the zero reference point.

Whether the acquisition of a prospective project is internally equity financed or externally debt financed, the rationale and the procedure for developing the alternate lump-sum payment or investment amount at the zero reference point, on which the DCF rate of return will be calculated, are identical in investment situations in which a portion of the prospective project's total capital outlays is expected to occur either before or after the zero reference point. If a portion of the capital outlays is expected to occur before the zero reference point, then this series of early capital outlays must be compounded forward to the zero reference point at the company's and its suppliers' and contractors' current direct borrowing rate. On the other hand, if a portion of the total outlays is expected to occur after the zero reference point, then this series of future capital outlays must be discounted back to the zero reference point at the company's and its suppliers' and contractors' current direct borrowing rate. In either case, the resultant total present value will represent the alternate lump-sum payment amount that will be acceptable to the company and its suppliers and contractors at the zero reference point, in lieu of a series of annual payment amounts either before or after that point in time. Consequently, this alternate lump-sum payment or investment amount will represent the appropriate investment base at the zero reference point on which to calculate the prospective project's DCF rate of return and expect it to be a realistic profitability indicator and reliable project selection device that will lead to a sound and wise investment decision.

The investment situations in Cases 1 and 4 for the prospective project in Table 21, in which 90 percent, or $90,000, of its total capital outlays is expected to occur during a three-year period before the zero reference point and a nine-year period after that point in time, respectively, are prime examples of how (a) unrealistic DCF rates of return are arrived at by the improper application of the DCF concept and (b) realistic DCF rates of return are arrived at by the proper application of the DCF concept.

The 9.9 Percent versus the 11.0 Percent DCF Rate of Return in Case 1

As shown in Table 22, the 9.9 percent DCF rate of return arrived at by the conventional DCF method for this project in Case 1 is unrealistic for two reasons. First, the DCF rate of return is calculated on an alternate lump-sum payment or investment amount of $123,050 at the zero reference point, which is unacceptable to the company's suppliers and contractors because it includes an interest factor of only 9.9 percent, while the current interest rate at banks and other lending institutions is 12 percent. Hence, the $123,050 alternate lump-sum payment or investment amount at the zero reference point, on which the 9.9 percent DCF rate of return is calculated, is understated. Second, the cash returns also are understated because the project's annual depreciation charges are calculated on and limited to its fixed assets'

$100,000 capital cost. This improper application of the DCF concept has a dual effect of distorting the 9.9 percent DCF rate of return in Case 1.

These two defects are eliminated by the proper application of the DCF concept under the proposed DCF method as shown in Tables 25 and 27. First,

TABLE 27

*Case 1: Proof that Under Proposed DCF Method a Time Value of Money Equal to Company's 12 Percent Current Direct Borrowing Rate Is Assigned to Project's Capital Outlays Resulting in a Realistic 11.04 Percent Instead of a Distorted 9.9 Percent DCF Rate of Return**

| | | Investment Base Calculation at the Zero Reference Point | | | DCF Rate of Return Calculation | | | |
| | Project's Capital Outlays† | Compound Factor at 12% | Future Value | Project's Cash Income | Present Value Factor at 11% | Present Value | Present Value Factor at 12% | Present Value |
Year								
3	$ (50,000)	1.4049	$ (70,245)	—	—	—	—	—
2	(25,000)	1.2544	(31,360)	—	—	—	—	—
1	(15,000)	1.1200	(16,800)	—	—	—	—	—
0	(10,000)	1.0000	(10,000)	—	—	—	—	—
1	—	—	—	$ 20,687	.9009	$ 18,637	.8929	$ 18,471
2	—	—	—	22,608	.8116	18,349	.7972	18,023
3	—	—	—	23,741	.7312	17,359	.7118	16,899
4	—	—	—	24,223	.6587	15,956	.6355	15,394
5	—	—	—	24,192	.5935	14,358	.5674	13,727
6	—	—	—	23,752	.5346	12,698	.5066	12,033
7	—	—	—	21,674	.4817	10,440	.4523	9,803
8	—	—	—	19,595	.4339	8,502	.4039	7,914
9	—	—	—	17,528	.3909	6,852	.3606	6,321
10	—	—	—	15,452	.3522	5,442	.3220	4,976
Total	$(100,000)		$(128,405)	$213,452		$128,593		$123,561

DCF rate of return is 11.04%.

* When portions of these capital outlays occur prior to the time the project starts generating cash income.
† Capital outlays in parentheses.

the series of cash outlays totaling $90,000, which are expected to occur during the three-year period before the zero reference point, is compounded at the company's suppliers' and contractors' 12 percent current direct borrowing rate. Hence, the resultant $128,405 alternate lump-sum payment amount at the zero reference point is acceptable to its suppliers and contractors, and consequently it is the appropriate investment base on which to calculate the project's DCF rate of return. Second, the project's cash returns are not understated because its depreciation charges, as shown in Table 25, instead of being calculated on the fixed assets' $100,000 actual capital outlays, are calculated on the $128,405 alternate lump-sum payment or investment amount at the zero reference point on which the project's DCF rate of return is calculated. This eliminates both the inconsistency and the distortion in the conventional

DCF method of calculating the project's DCF rate of return on one investment base, the $123,050 alternate lump-sum payment or investment amount, and calculating its depreciation charges on another investment base, the fixed assets' $100,000 actual capital outlays. The elimination of these two defects by the proper application of the DCF concept results in a realistic DCF rate of return of 11.04 percent for this project in Case 1 as shown in Table 27.

The 99.26 Percent versus the 25.09 Percent DCF Rate of Return in Case 4

As shown in Table 23, the 99.26 percent DCF rate of return arrived at by the conventional DCF method for this project in Case 4, in which 90 percent, or $90,000, of the total capital outlays is expected to occur during the nine-year period after the zero reference point, is far more seriously distorted and unrealistic than the 9.9 percent DCF rate of return arrived at by the conventional DCF method for this project in Case 1, in which the same percentage of its total capital outlays is expected to occur during the three-year period before the zero reference point. This distortion, likewise, is attributable to the same improper application of the DCF concept in the conventional DCF method.

The 99.26 percent DCF rate of return arrived at for this project in Case 4 is calculated on the $20,054 alternate lump-sum payment or investment amount at the zero reference point, which amount would be totally unacceptable to the company's suppliers and contractors, in lieu of $10,000 at the zero reference point and $90,000 in a series of constant-level annual payments during a nine-year period after that point in time. Expecting the suppliers and contractors to accept a $20,054 lump-sum payment amount at the zero reference point assumes that they would be willing to pay interest in the amount of $79,946 at a 99.26 percent rate when in reality they can borrow money currently from their banks at a 12 percent interest rate and therefore pay interest in the amount of only $36,718, as shown in Table 28. This unquestionably would be a highly unrealistic assumption, thus making the $20,054 alternate lump-sum payment amount at the zero reference point an unrealistic investment base on which to calculate this prospective project's DCF rate of return in Case 4.

Table 28 shows that at the 12 percent current direct borrowing rate, $53,282 deposited by the company's suppliers and contractors in their banks at the zero reference point will yield $10,000 each year during the nine-year period after that point in time and, contrariwise, that the series of notes covering the $10,000 annual payment amounts during the nine-year period discounted at their 12 percent direct borrowing rate will yield the suppliers and contractors $53,282 at the zero reference point. In other words, Table 29 proves that $63,282 at the zero reference point—$10,000 plus the $53,282 lump-sum amount in lieu of a series of $10,000 annual payment amounts during the nine-year period after that point in time—would be acceptable to the suppliers and contractors, whose current direct borrowing rate is 12 per-

TABLE 28

Proof that $53,282 Deposited in Bank at Zero Reference Point at 12 Percent Will Yield $10,000 Each Year for Next Nine Years Making $63,282 the Project's True Investment Base

Year	Principal Beginning of Year	Annual Bank Loan Payments	Interest at 12%	Amortization	Principal End of Year	Present Values at 12%	Compounded Value Factor at 12%	Yield End of Year
1	$53,282	$10,000	$ 6,394	$ 3,606	$49,676	$ 8,929	1.120	$10,000
2	49,676	10,000	5,961	4,039	45,637	7,972	1.254	10,000
3	45,637	10,000	5,476	4,524	41,113	7,118	1.405	10,000
4	41,113	10,000	4,934	5,066	36,047	6,355	1.574	10,000
5	36,047	10,000	4,326	5,674	30,373	5,674	1.762	10,000
6	30,373	10,000	3,645	6,355	24,018	5,066	1.974	10,000
7	24,018	10,000	2,882	7,118	16,900	4,523	2.211	10,000
8	16,900	10,000	2,028	7,922	8,928	4,039	2.476	10,000
9	8,928	10,000	1,072	8,928	–0–	3,606	2.773	10,000
Total		$90,000	$36,718	$53,282		$53,282		$90,000

TABLE 29

Case 4: Proof that under Proposed DCF Method a Time Value of Money Equal to Company's 12 Percent Current Direct Borrowing Rate Is Assigned to Its Capital Outlays* Resulting in Realistic 25.09 Percent Instead of Grossly Distorted 99.26 Percent DCF Rate of Return

(1)	(2)	(3)	(4)	(5)	(6)	(7)	(8)	(9)
		Investment Base Calculation at the Zero Reference Point			DCF Rate of Return Calculation			
Year	Project's Capital Outlays†	Present Value Factor at 12%	Present Value of Project's Capital Outlays†	Project's Cash Income	Present Value Factor at 25%	Present Value of Project's Cash Income	Present Value Factor at 26%	Present Value of Project's Cash Income
0	$ (10,000)	1.0000	$(10,000)	—	—			
1	(10,000)	.8929	(8,929)	$ 14,767	.8000	$11,814	.7937	$11,721
2	(10,000)	.7972	(7,972)	17,282	.6400	11,060	.6299	10,886
3	(10,000)	.7118	(7,118)	19,004	.5120	9,730	.4999	9,500
4	(10,000)	.6355	(6,355)	20,078	.4096	8,224	.3968	7,967
5	(10,000)	.5674	(5,674)	20,640	.3277	6,764	.3149	6,500
6	(10,000)	.5066	(5,066)	20,792	.2621	5,450	.2499	5,196
7	(10,000)	.4523	(4,523)	19,306	.2097	4,048	.1983	3,828
8	(10,000)	.4039	(4,039)	17,821	.1678	2,742	.1574	2,805
9	(10,000)	.3606	(3,606)	16,343	.1342	1,994	.1249	2,041
10	—	—	—	14,858	.1074	1,596	.0992	1,474
Total	$(100,000)		$(63,282)	$180,891		$63,422		$61,918

DCF rate of return is 25.09%.

* When portions of these capital outlays occur after the time the project starts generating cash income.
† Capital outlays in parentheses.

cent. Therefore, $63,282 represents the appropriate investment base on which to calculate this prospective project's 25.09 percent DCF rate of return in Case 4, as shown in Table 29.

Furthermore, as shown in Tables 23 and 25, under the conventional DCF method the prospective project's cash returns are seriously overstated because its depreciation charges are calculated on the $100,000 actual capital outlays, while its DCF rate of return is calculated on the $20,054 alternate lump-sum payment or investment amount at the zero reference point. This, of course, has a dual effect of seriously distorting the prospective project's DCF rate of return. This inconsistency and distortion is avoided by the proper application of the DCF concept in the proposed DCF method which calculates the depreciation charges on and limits them to the $63,252 alternate lump-sum payment or investment amount on which the 25.09 percent DCF rate of return is calculated, as shown in Table 29.

A comparison of the two sets of DCF rates of return arrived at by the conventional and the proposed DCF methods for the prospective project in Cases 1, 2, and 4, in which all the financial factors—the $100,000 capital outlays, the $199,250 cash returns, and the 10-year economic life—are identical, except the timing of the $100,000 capital outlays, confirms these facts most dramatically: (1) The conventional DCF method arrives at realistic DCF rates of return only in investment situations in which loans are expected to be made by companies to prospective projects in a similar manner that loans are made by banks and other lending institutions to outside borrowers, which means immediately before the time prospective projects are expected to start generating cash returns. This is proven by the fact that the same 15.0 percent DCF rate of return is arrived at by both the conventional and the proposed DCF methods for this prospective project in Case 2. (2) The conventional DCF method invariably arrives at distorted and unrealistic DCF rates of return in investment situations in which loans are expected to be made by companies to prospective projects either before or after the time they are expected to start generating cash returns. These types of loans represent investment or loan situations that not only are dissimilar but actually never occur in self-amortizing bank loan transactions. This is proven by the highly distorted and unrealistic 9.9 percent and the 99.3 percent DCF rates of return arrived at by the conventional DCF method compared to the true and realistic 11.0 percent and 25.09 percent DCF rates of return arrived at by the proposed DCF method for this prospective project in Cases 1 and 4, respectively. (3) Whether this project in Cases 2 and 4, for example, is equity or debt financed, the wide difference between the 99.3 percent DCF rate of return in Case 4 compared to the 15.0 percent DCF rate of return in Case 2, resulting from the difference in the timing of its $100,000 capital outlays, unquestionably is illusory and unrealistic. As explained previously, if the capital spending for this project calls for $100,000 at the zero reference point, as in Case 2, then the company's suppliers and contractors should be willing to accept either $100,000 at the zero reference point or an alternate series of constant-level annual payments, totaling $176,980, during the 10-year period before that point in time. This alternate method of payment should be acceptable because this series of future constant-level payments discounted at the bank at the 12 percent current direct borrowing rate would yield an equivalent $100,000 at the zero reference point. Similarly, if the capital spending for this prospective project calls for a $10,000 payment at the zero reference point plus a series of constant-level payments totaling $90,000 during the nine-year period after that point in time, then, conversely, the company's suppliers and contractors should be willing to accept either this method of payment or a $63,282 alternate lump-sum payment amount at the zero reference point. This alternate method of payment should be acceptable because the series of constant-level future payments totaling $90,000 discounted at the bank at the 12 percent current direct borrowing rate would yield $53,282 in addition to the $10,000 at the zero reference point. This proves, incontrovertibly, that the $100,000 in Case 2 and the $63,282 in Case 4 are the appropriate investment bases on which to calculate this prospective project's 15.0 percent DCF rate of return in Case 2 and its 25.09 percent DCF rate of return in Case 4, as they represent the payment amounts the company's suppliers and contractors would be willing to accept at the zero reference point in these two investment situations. Consequently, the 10.09 percent difference between the 25.09 percent and the 15.0 percent DCF rate of return accurately and realistically reflects this prospective project's economic advantage in Case 4 over Case 2 due to the delayed capital spending.

It should be apparent that the severity of the distortions of DCF rates of return arrived at by the improper application of the DCF concept in the conventional DCF method when portions of the total capital outlays of prospective projects are expected to occur during a period of years either before or after the time they are expected to start generating cash income or savings depends largely on these factors: (1) the size of calculated DCF earnings rates of prospective projects that are used for compounding or discounting portions of their total capital outlays expected to occur either early or late; (2) the size of total capital outlays and capital recoveries of prospective projects; and (3) the length of time during which portions of total capital outlays are expected to occur either before or after the time prospective projects are expected to start generating cash income or savings.

The compounding or discounting procedure in the conventional DCF method that arbitrarily assigns time values of money equal to prospective projects' calculated DCF earnings rates to portions of their total capital outlays, which are expected to occur either before or after the time projects are expected to start generating cash returns, is rationalized by financial analysts as being consistent with the opportunity cost of money theory. This rationalization simply doesn't stand up because the opportunity cost of money concept is just another term for the alternate use value of money concept. Hence, the opportunity cost of money rate is identical with the alternate use value of money rate. This means that similar to the alternate use value of money rate, the opportunity cost of money rate likewise is inappropriate and improper to use for (*a*) compounding or discounting portions of capital outlays of prospective projects and *(b)* discounting their capital recoveries. The term *opportunity cost of money* bears out the suspicion that there seems to exist a great deal of confusion in the minds of financial analysts as to what constitutes a company's *cost of money* with respect to what rate to use for compounding and/or discounting capital outlays and capital recoveries in the economic evaluations of prospective projects. The term, itself, seems to suggest that prospective projects' calculated DCF earnings rates, conversely, represent the interest rates charged for the funds loaned to them by treasurer's departments of companies. Hence, under the conventional DCF method, prospective projects' calculated DCF earnings rates rather than companies' current direct borrowing rates are used for compounding and/or discounting capital outlays and capital recoveries.

Treatment of Depreciation Charges in Proposed DCF Method

Under the proposed DCF method, annual depreciation charges of prospective projects will be calculated on their fixed assets' alternate lump-sum payment or investment amount at the zero reference point, which is deemed to be acceptable to companies or their suppliers and contractors at that point in time, instead of on the fixed assets' actual capital outlays, when portions of these actual capital outlays are expected to occur either before or after the zero reference point. This treatment of depreciation charges under the proposed DCF method, in which both the depreciation charges of prospective projects and their DCF rates of return are calculated on the same investment base at the zero reference point, is logical and consistent; whereas the treatment of depreciation charges under the conventional DCF method, in which both the depreciation charges of prospective projects and their DCF rates of return are calculated on two different investment bases, when portions of their capital outlays are expected to occur either before or after the zero reference point, is illogical and inconsistent.

Under the proposed DCF method, in similar capital investment situations both the annual depreciation charges of the prospective projects and their DCF rates of return are calculated on the same investment base, namely, the alternate lump-sum payment or investment amount at the zero reference point. Hence, this proper application of the DCF concept will result in arriving at realistic DCF rates of return in all such capital investment situations. For example, as shown in Table 25, the annual depreciation charges for the fixed assets for the prospective project in Table 21, under Case 1, are calculated on the $128,405 alternate lump-sum payment or investment amount at the zero reference point. This investment base includes a 12 percent interest factor and therefore represents an alternate payment amount the company would be willing to make and its suppliers and contractors would be willing to accept at that point in time for the fixed assets, in lieu of $90,000 during the three-year period before and $10,000 at the zero reference point, because the 12 percent rate represents the company's and its suppliers' and contractors' current direct borrowing rate.

In accordance with this proper application of the DCF concept, the 11.04 percent DCF rate of return arrived at for this prospective project in Case 1 is calculated on the same $128,405 alternate lump-sum payment or investment amount at the zero reference point on which its annual depreciation charges are calculated, as shown in Tables 25 and 27. Hence, the 11.04 percent DCF rate of return represents the true profitability indicator and the sound project selection device for this prospective project in Case 1.

Likewise, the annual depreciation charges for this prospective project in Case 4, as shown in Table 25, are calculated on and limited to the $63,282 alternate lump-sum payment or investment amount at the zero reference point, which excludes a 12 percent interest factor. Since this interest rate represents the company's suppliers' and contractors' current direct borrowing rate, they naturally would be willing to accept this $63,282 alternate lump-sum payment amount at the zero reference point, in lieu of $10,000 at that point in time plus the remaining $90,000 in constant-level annual payment amounts during the nine-year period after that point in time. To be logical and consistent and to arrive at a realistic DCF rate of return, the prospective project's DCF rate of return must be calculated on the same $63,282 investment base at the zero reference point. This proper application of the DCF concept for this prospective project in Case 4 is shown in Table 29.

In Table 29, the 25.09 percent DCF rate of return is calculated on the same $63,282 alternate lump-sum payment or investment amount at the zero reference point on which the annual depreciation charges are calculated. Since both the annual depreciation charges and the DCF rate of return are calculated on the same $63,282 investment base at the zero reference point, the 25.09 percent DCF rate of return is the true profitability indicator and the sound project selection device for this prospective project in Case 4.

Treatment of Residual Values in Proposed DCF Method

As discussed in Chapter 9, in economic evaluations, another factor that tends to distort prospective projects' DCF rates of return arrived at under the conventional DCF method is the treatment of residual values for the recovery of depreciable and nondepreciable fixed assets and working capital. The proper application of the DCF concept in the proposed DCF method calls for the estimated residual values for the recovery of prospective projects' depreciable and nondepreciable fixed assets and working capital to be discounted separately from their stream of cash income or savings at the company's direct borrowing rate in effect at the time the fixed assets and the working capital are expected to be acquired for or assigned to the prospective projects. This treatment of residual values is based on the rationale that the resultant present values arrived at in this manner will represent the amounts of cash the company would be willing to accept from the bank at the zero reference point if it chose to discount the future proceeds from the capital recovery of such fixed assets and working capital at that point in time.

TABLE 30

Treatment of Residual Values under the Proposed DCF Method

Item	End of Year	DCF Rate of Return		
		10% Project 1	15% Project 2	20% Project 3
Residual value for land	20	$50,000	$50,000	$50,000
Present value factor at 12%	20	.1037	.1037	.1037
Present value at the zero reference point	–0–	5,185	5,185	5,185
Interest expense for 20 years		$44,815	$44,815	$44,815

As shown in Table 30, this proper application of the DCF concept under the proposed DCF method in the treatment of residual values produces equal present values of $5,185 at the zero reference point for the $50,000 residual value for the capital recovery of land at the end of the 20th year in prospective Projects 1, 2, and 3, despite the fact that they earn widely different DCF rates of return of 10 percent, 15 percent, and 20 percent, respectively. These identical present values for the capital recovery for land in these three projects are based on the rationale that if the company's direct borrowing rate is 12 percent, it would be willing to accept and the bank would be willing to pay $5,185 at the zero reference point, in lieu of $50,000 at the end of the 20th year of the prospective project's economic life. These identical present values for the capital recovery for land also prove that the $44,815 interest expense for tying up $50,000 for land for 20 years likewise is identical for the three projects, which is logical and realistic, and this interest expense shouldn't vary even though the three prospective projects are estimated to earn widely different DCF rates of return ranging from 10 percent in Project 1, to 15 percent in Project 2, and to 20 percent in Project 3.

This concept of charging prospective projects for the use of money tied up in land at the company's current direct borrowing rate is neither a far-fetched nor startling innovation. A precedent has long been established for this concept as it has been applied for many years in sale-and-leaseback type of financial arrangements. A typical example is found in situations where petroleum companies acquire land, construct a service station building on it, sell the land and the service station building to the bank, thus recovering their entire capital cost, and then agree to lease back from the bank the land and the service station building at an agreed-upon rental in addition to buying back the land at its original cost at the end of the lease term. The latter generally coincides with the termination of the service station's economic life.

For example, as shown in Table 31, a petroleum company buys land at a cost of $50,000, constructs a service station building on it at an additional cost of $50,000, sells both the land and the service station building to the bank for $100,000, thus recovering its entire capital cost, and then agrees to lease back

TABLE 31

Annual Lease Rental Determination

Annual principal and interest payment on service station building ($50,000 ÷ 7.4694)	=	$ 6,694
Interest on land ($50,000 × 0.12)	=	6,000
Annual lease rental	=	$12,694

from the bank both the land and the service station building for 20 years at an annual rental of $12,694 in addition to buying back the land from the bank at its $50,000 original cost at the end of the 20-year lease term, which coincides with the end of the service station's 20-year economic life.

The example in Table 31 shows how the $12,694 annual lease rental in this sale-and-leaseback financial arrangement is determined. The $6,694 portion of the annual lease rental represents the repayment of the $50,000 capital cost plus interest at the 12 percent rate on the outstanding balance at the start of each year during the 20-year lease term for the service station building, while the $6,000 portion represents the annual interest at the 12 percent rate on the $50,000 capital cost for the land. Here then is a typical example where interest on money invested in nondepreciable and depreciable fixed assets is charged to prospective projects at the company's current direct borrowing rate.

The 11.04 Percent DCF Rate of Return Arrived at under Proposed DCF Method

To recapitulate, the example in Table 27 shows that the series of annual constant-level payments totaling $90,000 during the three-year period before the zero reference point is compounded at the 12 percent interest rate, which represents the company's and its suppliers' and contractors' current direct borrowing rate. Compounding this series of annual payment amounts at this interest rate means that the business organization would be willing to pay and its suppliers and contractors would be willing to accept an alternate lump-sum payment amount of $128,405 at the zero reference point, in lieu of $90,000 during the three-year period before and $10,000 at that point in time. Calculating the DCF rate of return on this $128,405 alternate lump-sum payment or investment amount at the zero reference point and, moreover, calculating the depreciation charges on the same alternate payment or investment amount proves that the 11.04 percent DCF rate of return, arrived at by the proper application of the DCF concept under the proposed DCF method, is the true profitability indicator and sound project selection device for this prospective project in Case 1. It also proves that the true economic disadvantage of investing in this prospective project in the investment situation in Case 2 as opposed to that in Case 1 is only 3.96 percent instead of 5.1 percent.

As mentioned previously, the distortions of DCF rates of return arrived at under the conventional DCF method tend to be much more pronounced and serious in investment situations in which portions of the total capital outlays are expected to occur *after* prospective projects are expected to start generating cash income and they are as frequent as when portions of the total capital outlays are expected to occur *before* that point in time. This is particularly true in the case of business expansions where major portions of total capital outlays are expected to occur during a period of years after the time they are expected to start generating cash income or savings.

The 25.09 Percent DCF Rate of Return Arrived at under Proposed DCF Method

To recapitulate, the example in Table 29, on the other hand, shows that the series of annual constant-level payment amounts totaling $90,000 during the nine-year period after the zero reference point is discounted at the 12 percent interest rate, which represents the company's and its suppliers' and contractors' current direct borrowing rate. Discounting this series of annual constant-level payment amounts at this interest rate means that the company's suppliers and contractors would be willing to accept an alternate lump-sum payment amount of $63,282 at the zero reference point, in lieu of $10,000 at that point in time plus the remaining $90,000 at annual constant-level payment amounts during the nine-year period after that point in time. Calculating the DCF rate of return on this $63,282 alternate lump-sum payment or investment amount at the zero reference point and, moreover, calculating the depreciation charges on and limiting them to the same $63,282 alternate lump-sum payment or investment amount proves that the 25.,09 percent DCF rate of return arrived at by the proper application of the DCF concept under the proposed DCF method is the true profitability indicator and sound project selection device for this prospective project in Case 4. It also proves that the true economic advantage of investing in this project in the investment situation in Case 4 as opposed to that in Case 2 is only 10.1 percent instead of 74.2 percent.

Proper Application of DCF Concept in Proposed DCF Method

What has been done in the proper application of the DCF concept in the proposed DCF method is simply to simulate conditions similar to those in which the compound interest principle is applied by banks whenever investment situations arise in which capital outlays are expected to occur during a period of years either before or after the time prospective projects are expected to start generating cash income or savings. This is achieved by determining an alternate lump-sum payment amount, by means of compounding or discounting, that will be acceptable to the company or its suppliers and contractors at the zero reference point, in lieu of a series of payments during a period of years either before or after that point in time, i.e., when prospective projects are expected to start generating cash returns. The proper application of the DCF concept in the proposed DCF method must adhere to the following conditions:

- The zero reference point must always be the point in time when prospective projects are estimated to start generating cash income or savings.
- The capital outlay and capital recovery dollars and the cash income or savings dollars must always be shown separately and compounded and/or discounted separately at different rates. They must never be commingled, netted and compounded, and/or discounted at the same rate.
- An alternate lump-sum payment or investment amount at the zero reference point must be determined when portions of the total capital outlays are expected to occur either before or after the zero reference point. This alternate lump-sum payment or investment amount at the zero reference point must be an amount that will be acceptable to the company or its suppliers and contractors, in lieu of a series of annual payment amounts (capital outlays) that are expected to occur either before or after that point in time. If the series of annual payment amounts is expected to occur before the zero reference point, it must be compounded down to that point in time. On the other hand, if it is expected to occur after the zero reference point, it must be discounted back to that point in time.
- This alternate lump-sum payment or investment amount at the zero reference point must be determined by assigning a time value of money for the total capital outlays equal to the interest rate the company or its suppliers and contractors are willing to pay for the use of money. This rate must be equivalent to the company's or its suppliers' and contractors' current direct borrowing rate.
- The alternate lump-sum payment or investment amount at the zero reference point, which is acceptable to the company or its suppliers and contractors, must be substituted at the zero reference point for the series of annual payment amounts (capital outlays) that are expected to occur either before or after that point in time.
- The annual depreciation charges must be calculated on the alternate lump-sum payment or investment amount at the zero reference point instead of on the actual capital outlays for the prospective projects' fixed assets when portions of these capital outlays are expected to occur during a period of years either before or after that point in time.
- The residual values for the recovery of depreciable and nondepreciable fixed assets and working capital in economic evaluations must be discounted at the same interest rate at which the original capital outlays for those fixed assets are compounded or discounted, which is the company's direct borrowing rate in effect at the time of the estimated acquisition or assignment of the fixed assets.

- The DCF rate of return for prospective projects must be calculated by finding an interest rate, by trial and error, in the present value table that will discount their stream of annual cash income or savings amounts down to a total present value equal to the alternate lump-sum payment or investment amount at the zero reference point. If there are expected to be residual values for the capital recovery of depreciable and nondepreciable fixed assets and working capital at the end of prospective projects' economic lives, then the investment base at the zero reference point on which the DCF rate of return will be calculated will be equivalent to the alternate lump-sum payment or investment amount at the zero reference point less the present value of the residual values for the capital recovery of the fixed assets and the working capital.

The DCF rates of return arrived at by the proper application of the DCF concept in the proposed DCF method will be realistic profit indicators and reliable project selection devices and, therefore, will lead to sound and wise investment decisions in all such capital investment situations.

Chapter 11

Application of DCF Concept and DCF Techniques in Economic Evaluations of Leased Properties

When companies must acquire new fixed assets either for the purpose of replacing worn-out fixed assets or adding new fixed assets to existing ones due to business expansion, they frequently have to choose between acquiring them by outright purchase or long-term leasing. However, in some cases, companies have no such option because some needed fixed assets, such as land, buildings, and particularly some types of machinery and equipment, can be acquired only on a lease basis.

The acquisition of new fixed assets through long-term leasing presents serious problems not only in understating the company's total assets and, contrariwise, in overstating its book profits and year-to-year book rates of return, but even more so in the economic evaluation of prospective projects. For example, if all the required fixed assets for a prospective project are acquired on a lease basis, there is no investment base on which to calculate a DCF rate of return. If only some of the required fixed assets for a prospective project are acquired on a lease basis and the rentals are included as operating expenses in the cash income flow, then the DCF rate of return for the prospective project will be seriously overstated, which could lead to an unwise and costly investment decision. The interest factor included in lease rentals is usually substantially higher than the company's current direct borrowing rate.

This chapter discusses the problems encountered in assessing the profitability of prospective projects for which the required fixed assets are acquired on a lease basis. Methods will be set forth and illustrated that will show (a) how to determine DCF rates of return for leased fixed assets comparable to those for purchased fixed assets, (b) how to determine the interest factor included in lease rentals, and (c) why owning almost invariably is more economical and advantageous than leasing.

What Is Leasing?

Webster's *New American Dictionary* defines the verb *lease* as "to let; to demise; to grant the temporary possession of (lands, tenements, or hereditaments) to another for rent reserved." According to common usage, the term *leasing* means acquiring the use of property for a period of time at an agreed rental without benefit of ownership. The party owning the property and renting it to another party is known as the lessor. The party acquiring the property and renting it from the lessor is known as the lessee.

Lease rentals frequently include cost elements incidental to ownership, such as maintenance, repairs, taxes, etc. These cost elements incidental to ownership must be extracted from lease rentals so that the lease rental for depreciable property that is used up during the lease term consists only of principal and interest, and the lease rental for nondepreciable property consists solely of interest or economic rent. Extracting the cost elements incidental to ownership from lease rentals makes lease financing comparable to debt financing in the case of depreciable and nondepreciable fixed assets.

Lease Financing versus Debt Financing

The lease financing of a depreciable and nondepreciable fixed asset is shown in Tables 32 and 34, respectively; while a comparison of the debt financing for

TABLE 32

Lease Financing a Depreciable Fixed Asset

	(1)	(2)	(3)	(4)
	Lessor's Investment Balance at Start		*Rent Payments*	
Year	of Year	Total	Principal Repayments	Interest at 15%
1	$10,000	$ 1,598	$ 98	$ 1,500
2	9,902	1,598	113	1,485
3	9,789	1,598	130	1,468
4	9,659	1,598	149	1,449
5	9,510	1,598	171	1,427
6	9,339	1,598	197	1,401
7	9,142	1,598	227	1,371
8	8,915	1,598	261	1,337
9	8,654	1,598	300	1,298
10	8,354	1,598	345	1,253
11	8,009	1,598	397	1,201
12	7,612	1,598	456	1,142
13	7,156	1,598	525	1,073
14	6,631	1,598	603	995
15	6,028	1,598	694	904
16	5,334	1,598	798	800
17	4,536	1,598	918	680
18	3,618	1,598	1,055	543
19	2,563	1,598	1,214	384
20	1,349	1,598	1,349	249
Total	$ –0–	$31,960	$10,000	$21,960

TABLE 33

Debt Financing a Depreciable or Nondepreciable Fixed Asset

	(1)	(2)	(3)	(4)
	Bank Loan Balance at Start of Year	Bank Payments		
Year		Total	Principal Repayments	Interest at 12%
1	$10,000	$ 1,339	$ 139	$ 1,200
2	9,861	1,339	156	1,183
3	9,705	1,339	174	1,165
4	9,531	1,339	195	1,144
5	9,336	1,339	219	1,120
6	9,117	1,339	245	1,094
7	8,872	1,339	274	1,065
8	8,598	1,339	307	1,032
9	8,291	1,339	344	995
10	7,947	1,339	385	954
11	7,562	1,339	432	907
12	7,130	1,339	483	856
13	6,647	1,339	541	798
14	6,106	1,339	606	733
15	5,500	1,339	679	660
16	4,821	1,339	760	579
17	4,061	1,339	852	487
18	3,209	1,339	954	385
19	2,255	1,339	1,068	271
20	1,187	1,339	1,187	152
Total		$26,780	$10,000	$16,780

the depreciable and nondepreciable fixed asset is shown in Table 33. The examples in these three tables are based on the following assumptions: (1) The depreciable and the nondepreciable fixed assets cost $10,000 each. (2) The useful life of the depreciable fixed asset is 20 years. (3) The lease terms for the depreciable and the nondepreciable fixed assets are both 20 years. (4) The lessor wants to earn 15 percent on his money. Therefore, the lessor has to charge an annual lease rental of $1,598 for the depreciable fixed asset and $1,500 for the nondepreciable fixed asset. (5) The lessee's (company's) current direct borrowing rate is 12 percent. Consequently, the annual bank loan payment is $1,339 if the depreciable or the nondepreciable fixed asset is debt financed.

Obviously, in the case of the depreciable fixed asset, lease financing is similar to debt financing because both the $1,598 annual lease rental and the $1,339 annual bank loan payment consist of repayment of principal and interest and, moreover, because the depreciable fixed asset's useful life is equal to its lease term. The total funds committed under lease financing the depreciable fixed asset is $31,960 compared to $26,780 under debt financing. The $5,180 difference, of course, is attributable to the higher interest expense ($21,960 − $16,780) of lease financing compared to debt financing.

TABLE 34

Lease Financing a Nondepreciable Fixed Asset

	(1)	(2)	(3)	(4)
	Lessor's Investment Balance at Start	Rent Payments		
Year	of Year	Total	Principal Repayments	Interest at 15%
1	$10,000	$ 1,500	—	$ 1,500
2	10,000	1,500	—	1,500
3	10,000	1,500	—	1,500
4	10,000	1,500	—	1,500
5	10,000	1,500	—	1,500
6	10,000	1,500	—	1,500
7	10,000	1,500	—	1,500
8	10,000	1,500	—	1,500
9	10,000	1,500	—	1,500
10	10,000	1,500	—	1,500
11	10,000	1,500	—	1,500
12	10,000	1,500	—	1,500
13	10,000	1,500	—	1,500
14	10,000	1,500	—	1,500
15	10,000	1,500	—	1,500
16	10,000	1,500	—	1,500
17	10,000	1,500	—	1,500
18	10,000	1,500	—	1,500
19	10,000	1,500	—	1,500
20	10,000	1,500	—	1,500
Total	$10,000	$30,000		$30,000

On the other hand, in the case of the nondepreciable fixed asset, lease financing is dissimilar from debt financing insofar as the annual lease rental consists of interest or economic rent only, because the nondepreciable fixed asset remains fully intact during the term of the lease. The annual lease rental for the nondepreciable fixed asset is $1,500 compared to the $1,339 annual bank loan payment if it is owned and debt financed. Consequently, the total funds committed for the nondepreciable fixed asset is $3,220 or 10.1 percent higher when it is leased compared to when it is owned and debt financed. Despite this dissimilarity, leasing nondepreciable fixed assets, nevertheless, is a financing device inasmuch as it involves the use of someone else's money for which interest is paid in the form of a lease rental or economic rent.

Why Debt Financing Is Preferable

Under normal circumstances, both depreciable and nondepreciable fixed assets are financed more economically through debt financing than lease financing.

Depreciable fixed assets are generally financed more economically through debt financing because (a) the interest rate in lease rentals is usually higher than the current direct borrowing rate of companies, *(b)* the timing of the tax savings is more advantageous under owning and debt financing than leasing, and *(c)* no residual value for depreciable fixed assets accrues to the companies under leasing. The more advantageous timing of the tax savings under owning and debt financing compared to leasing under normal conditions more than likely is still valid during inflationary periods because the clause providing for the escalation of lease rentals inserted in most lease contracts to protect lessors against inflation in all likelihood will compensate for the depreciation deficiencies during inflationary periods.

Since the $10,000 nondepreciable fixed asset is not used up by the lessee but remains intact during the lease term, the lessor's lease rental for the nondepreciable fixed asset more than likely would be lower than that for the $10,000 depreciable fixed asset, which is used up by the lessee during the lease term. Therefore, it is reasonable to assume that the lessor would be satisfied to limit his total interest income on the nondepreciable fixed asset to that of the depreciable fixed asset, which in this case would be approximately $22,000. This total interest amount for the nondepreciable fixed asset would be equivalent to an $1,100 annual lease rental and an 11 percent interest rate instead of a $1,500 annual lease rental and a 15 percent interest rate, as shown in Table 34. If this condition is valid—which is reasonably certain—then it would appear at first glance that nondepreciable fixed assets, such as land, are financed more economically through lease financing than debt financing. The reasons for this deceptive and erroneous conclusion are that the total funds committed for nondepreciable fixed assets are normally lower under lease financing than debt financing and that no tax benefits on depreciation accrue to companies on nondepreciable fixed assets under ownership. However, a more careful scrutiny discloses that when the lessee, or company, leases the land, it pays $22,000 just for the use of the land for the 20-year period; whereas when the company pays $26,780, or only $4,780, or 21.7 percent more, it not only has the use of the land for the 20-year period but it actually owns it, and the chances are that after 20 years the land will have appreciated in value far in excess of its $10,000 original cost. Consequently, as a general rule, it is also more advantageous to own and debt finance a nondepreciable fixed asset, such as land, than to lease it.

When It Is More Advantageous to Lease

While it is generally more costly to lease than to own and debt finance depreciable and nondepreciable fixed assets, leasing may be the recommended financing device when special circumstances produce benefits that outweigh the higher lease-financing cost. Such special circumstances could arise under the following conditions: (1) when fixed assets are subject to high obsolescence rates and therefore liable to rapid decline in market or resale value as in the case of computers and other electronic devices; (2) when fixed assets are expected to require substantial repairs by the manufacturer during their useful lives and it is believed that more efficient service will be obtained when the assets are leased instead of owned; and (3) when fixed assets have useful lives that exceed the economic life of the overall new project in which they will be used, and when their market or resale values will decline rapidly.

The above conditions, of course, assume that buy versus lease alternatives exist. This isn't always the case because all too frequently fixed assets can only be leased. When this occurs, serious problems are created in the economic evaluation of proposed new projects.

Why Owners Are Willing to Lease Fixed Assets

The reasons why owners are willing to lease but unwilling to sell fixed assets include the following: (1) Land and other fixed assets frequently are considered good hedges against inflation. (2) Owners expect to profit from market appreciation that may result from population increases or shifts. (3) Local tax laws or manufacturers' or owners' tax positions may favor leasing over selling. (4) Small businessmen often acquire fixed assets, such as land, buildings, etc., for retirement income because they are neither receiving nor entitled to pensions. (5) Building contractors acquire land and construct shopping malls, office buildings, etc., in which space is offered for lease only.

Factors Required to Determine the Profitability and the Liquidity of Leased Fixed Assets

Whether the fixed assets for a proposed new project are purchased or leased, the same four factors that enter into the DCF rate of return and the payout computations are required to be estimated by the company. As explained and illustrated previously, these four factors invariably include the following:

- The cash outlays for the project.
- The cash intakes from the project.
- The economic life of the project.
- The timing of the cash flows to and from the project.

Ordinarily, the source of the funds, i.e , whether equity, debt, or lease money is to be used to finance the proposed new project as well as the interest expense if outside capital is to be used, are not factors that are considered in the economic evaluation of proposed new projects under the conventional DCF method for these reasons.

The same principle that applies in measuring the profitability of the total assets of companies, in which interest expense is customarily added back to their net operating income, also applies in assessing the profitability of prospective projects. This means that in order to determine a prospective project's earning power, interest expense must be excluded from the cash flows.

Furthermore, the bulk of prospective projects generally is financed with equity money. Therefore, prospective projects normally are evaluated on an ex-financing (interest) cost basis in order to preclude prejudicing projects that will be financed directly with outside capital.

As shown in Table 35, the DCF rate of return is 20 percent and the payout period is 4.9 years when the fixed assets for the prospective project are ac-

TABLE 35

DCF Rate of Return Computed on the Fixed Asset's Purchase Price

Year	(1) Purchase Price and Tax Savings on Depreciation*	(2) Operating Income after Tax	(3) Project Cash Flow
0	$(10,000)†		$(10,000)†
1	457	$ 1,596	2,053
2	434	1,619	2,053
3	411	1,642	2,053
4	389	1,664	2,053
5	366	1,687	2,053
6	343	1,710	2,053
7	320	1,733	2,053
8	297	1,756	2,053
9	274	1,779	2,053
10	252	1,801	2,053
11	228	1,825	2,053
12	206	1,847	2,053
13	183	1,870	2,053
14	160	1,893	2,053
15	137	1,916	2,053
16	114	1,939	2,053
17	91	1,962	2,053
18	69	1,984	2,053
19	46	2,007	2,053
20	23	2,030	2,053
Total	$ (5,200)	$36,260	$ 31,060

DCF rate of return is 20.0%.

Payout period is 4.9 years.

* Depreciation based on sum-of-the-years'-digits method.
† Fixed asset's purchase price.

quired on a purchase basis. The economic evaluation in Table 35 is based on these assumptions:

- The total capital cost at the zero reference point for the prospective project's fixed assets on which its DCF rate of return is calculated is $10,000.
- The tax savings calculated at the company's 48 percent income tax rate on the depreciation charges arrived at by the sum-of-the-years'-digits

method range from $457 in the year 1 to $23 in the year 20 and total $5,200.

- The operating cash income after taxes (excluding depreciation) range from $1,596 in the year 1 to $2,030 in the year 20 and total $36,260.
- The cash income after taxes (including depreciation) is at an annual constant level of $2,053 and total $41,060.

It is assumed in Table 36 that the fixed assets for the prospective project are leased at an annual rental of $1,598 during the 20-year lease term or

TABLE 36

Rate of Return Computed on Fixed Asset's Lease Rental

Year	(1) Rent Payments after Tax	(2) Operating Income after Tax	(3) Project Cash Flow
0	—	—	—
1	$ (831)	$ 1,596	$ 765
2	(831)	1,619	788
3	(831)	1,642	811
4	(831)	1,664	833
5	(831)	1,687	856
6	(831)	1,710	879
7	(831)	1,733	902
8	(831)	1,756	925
9	(831)	1,779	948
10	(831)	1,801	970
11	(831)	1,825	994
12	(831)	1,847	1,016
13	(831)	1,870	1,039
14	(831)	1,893	1,062
15	(831)	1,916	1,085
16	(831)	1,939	1,108
17	(831)	1,962	1,131
18	(831)	1,984	1,153
19	(831)	2,007	1,176
20	(831)	2,030	1,199
Total	$(16,620)	$36,260	$19,640

DCF rate of return—none.

project life instead of purchased at a total cost of $10,000 at the zero reference point. A comparison of the after-tax capital cost for the use of the prospective project's fixed assets is $5,200 when they are purchased and owned compared to $16,620 when they are leased, an increase of $11,420, or 219.6 percent, in the cost of leasing over the cost of purchasing and owning the fixed assets. Since the operating cash income after taxes (excluding depreciation) is identical whether the fixed assets are purchased or leased, the $11,420 higher after-tax capital cost when they are leased instead of purchased is reflected in the comparable $11,420 reduction in the prospective project's total profits from

$31,060 when the fixed assets are purchased to $19,640 when they are leased. The above comparisons are invalid for the simple reason that the $1,598 annual lease rental includes a 15 percent interest factor because leasing is a financing device as the lessee, or company, is using the lessor's or manufacturer's money, whereas the $10,000 purchase price does not include an interest factor.

However, more important, top management of companies must have financial criteria—DCF rates of return and payout periods—for prospective projects for which the needed fixed assets are leased that are comparable to those for which the needed fixed assets are purchased and owned. This is a requisite to enable top management to lay side by side prospective projects for which some or all of the needed fixed assets are leased with those for which all of the needed fixed assets are purchased and owned, and thus enable it to make sound investment decisions on the basis of the prospective project's DCF rates of return and payout periods. To determine DCF rates of return for prospective projects for which the needed fixed assets are leased poses a number of problems: (1) The capital cost in terms of lease rentals for the use of prospective projects' fixed assets normally is spread over their entire economic lives. Consequently, there is no investment base as in the case of purchased fixed assets on which to calculate DCF rates of return. (2) The lease rentals invariably include an interest factor, whereas the fixed assets' purchase prices exclude an interest factor. (3) Lease rentals also frequently include cost elements incidental to ownership, such as taxes, maintenance, repairs, etc., whereas the capital cost for purchased fixed assets excludes such items. Consequently, to make possible the calculations of DCF rates of return and payout periods for prospective projects involving leased fixed assets comparable to those involving purchased fixed assets, it is necessary to convert the stream of future rent payments to a lump-sum investment amount at the zero reference point that excludes both the interest factor and the cost elements incidental to ownership.

How to Calculate DCF Rates of Return for Projects Involving Leased Fixed Assets

The method of determining DCF rates of return for prospective projects involving leased fixed assets comparable to those involving purchased fixed assets is shown in Tables 37, 38, and 39. This method involves the following steps.

Step Number 1

If the lease rentals include items incidental to ownership, such as taxes, maintenance, repairs, etc., they must first be excluded from the lease rentals before they are discounted. Such items should then be included in the prospective project's cash inflow as operating expenses.

TABLE 37

Computing Leased Fixed Asset's Investment Equivalent

Year	(1) Rent Payments before Tax	(2) Present Value Factor at 12%	(3) Present Value
0	—	—	—
1	$ 1,598	.8929	$ 1,427
2	1,598	.7972	1,274
3	1,598	.7118	1,137
4	1,598	.6355	1,016
5	1,598	.5674	907
6	1,598	.5066	810
7	1,598	.4523	723
8	1,598	.4039	645
9	1,598	.3606	576
10	1,598	.3220	515
11	1,598	.2875	459
12	1,598	.2567	410
13	1,598	.2292	366
14	1,598	.2046	327
15	1,598	.1827	292
16	1,598	.1631	261
17	1,598	.1456	233
18	1,598	.1300	208
19	1,598	.1161	186
20	1,598	.1037	166
Total	$31,960		$11,938

Step Number 2

The stream of annual lease rentals, which now consist of principal and interest only, must then be discounted at the lessee's, or company's, direct borrowing rate. This has the simultaneous effect of *(a)* providing a lump-sum payment amount, or investment equivalent, at the zero reference point; and *(b)* extracting from the stream of lease rentals interest equal to the lessee's, or company's, current direct borrowing rate at which it is discounted. The resultant capitalized lease rental, or investment equivalent, at the zero reference point is then used to calculate a DCF rate of return for prospective projects involving leased fixed assets that will be comparable to those involving purchased fixed assets.

This procedure is shown in Tables 37, 38, and 39. It is assumed in these tables that the prospective project's fixed assets, which can be purchased at a cost of $10,000, as shown in Table 32, also can be leased at an annual lease rental of $1,598 for 20 years. It is assumed further that the lease term is identical with the fixed asset's 20-year useful life, and that the lessee's, or company's, current direct borrowing rate is 12 percent compared with the 15

TABLE 38

Determining Amortization, or Capital Recovery, Amounts of
Leased Fixed Asset's Investment Equivalent

	(1)	(2)	(3)	(4)
Year	Investment Equivalent Balance at Start of Year	Lease Rental Payments	Amortization	Interest at 12%
0	—	—	—	—
1	$11,938	$ 1,598	$ 165	$ 1,433
2	11,773	1,598	185	1,413
3	11,588	1,598	207	1,391
4	11,381	1,598	232	1,366
5	11,149	1,598	260	1,338
6	10,889	1,598	291	1,307
7	10,598	1,598	326	1,272
8	10,272	1,598	365	1,233
9	9,907	1,598	409	1,189
10	9,498	1,598	458	1,140
11	9,040	1,598	513	1,085
12	8,527	1,598	575	1,023
13	7,952	1,598	644	954
14	7,308	1,598	721	877
15	6,587	1,598	808	790
16	5,779	1,598	905	693
17	4,874	1,598	1,013	585
18	3,861	1,598	1,135	463
19	2,726	1,598	1,271	327
20	1,455	1,598	1,455	143
Total	$ –0–	$31,960	$11,938	$20,022

percent interest factor included in the $1,598 annual lease rental. When this stream of annual lease rentals is discounted at the company's 12 percent current direct borrowing rate, the resultant $11,938 total present value represents the investment equivalent. This $11,988 investment equivalent may be defined as the bank loan amount the company could obtain at its 12 percent current direct borrowing rate if it were committed to make annual bank loan payments equal to the $1,598 annual lease rentals. It also may be defined as the alternate lump-sum payment amount the lessor, or manufacturer, would be willing to accept at the zero reference point, in lieu of a series of $1,598 annual lease rentals during the 20-year period after that point in time. The $20,022 difference between the $31,960 total lease rental commitment and the $11,938 investment equivalent represents the interest extracted from the series of annual lease rentals equal to the company's 12 percent current direct borrowing rate. The $1,938 difference between the fixed assets $10,000 purchase price and its $11,938 investment equivalent may be defined as the premium the company is obliged to pay for leasing instead of purchasing and debt financing the fixed asset. The $1,938 premium represents the present value of the 3 percent difference in the interest expense between the 15

TABLE 39

DCF Rate of Return Computed on Leased Fixed Asset's Investment Equivalent

	(1)	(2)	(3)	(4)	(5)	(6)	(7)
	Investment Equivalent and Tax Savings on	Operating Income after	Project Cash		Present Value		
Year	Amortization	Tax	Flow	Factor at 14%	Amount	Factor at 15%	Amount
0	$(11,938)	—	$(11,938)	1.0000	$(11,938)	1.0000	$(11,938)
1	79	$ 1,596	1,675	.8772	1,469	.8696	1,457
2	89	1,619	1,708	.7695	1,314	.7561	1,291
3	99	1,642	1,741	.6750	1,175	.6575	1,145
4	111	1,664	1,775	.5921	1,051	.5718	1,015
5	125	1,687	1,812	.5194	941	.4972	901
6	140	1,710	1,850	.4556	843	.4323	800
7	156	1,733	1,889	.3996	755	.3759	710
8	175	1,756	1,931	.3506	677	.3269	631
9	196	1,779	1,975	.3075	607	.2843	561
10	220	1,801	2,021	.2697	545	.2472	500
11	246	1,825	2,071	.2366	490	.2149	445
12	276	1,847	2,123	.2076	441	.1869	397
13	309	1,870	2,179	.1821	397	.1625	356
14	346	1,893	2,239	.1597	358	.1413	316
15	388	1,916	2,304	.1401	323	.1229	283
16	434	1,939	2,373	.1229	292	.1069	254
17	486	1,962	2,448	.1078	264	.0929	227
18	545	1,984	2,529	.0946	239	.0808	204
19	610	2,007	2,617	.0829	199	.0703	184
20	·698	2,030	2,728	.0728		.0611	167
Total	$ (6,210)	$36,260	$ 30,050		442		(94)

DCF rate of return is 14.8%.

Payout period is 6.7 years.

percent interest factor included in the $1,598 annual lease rental and the company's 12 percent current direct borrowing rate.

Step Number 3

The annual amortization amounts of the investment equivalent must be determined. These annual amortization amounts, as shown in Table 38, are arrived at by multiplying the investment equivalent balance at the start of each year by the company's 12 percent current direct borrowing rate and then deduct the resultant interest amounts from the annual lease rentals. If the annual lease rentals are constant-level amounts, separate computations for the annual amortization amount in Table 38 are unnecessary. The annual present value amounts in their reverse order as shown in Table 37 are identical with the annual amortization amounts shown in Table 38, except for rounding.

Table 37 is included here only to show the principle that is involved in amortizing the investment equivalent and to show the method to use for calculating the annual amortization amounts when the series of annual lease rentals are uneven during the lease term. This is usually the case in long-term leases that normally provide for an escalation of the lease rentals to protect the lessor against inflation. For the purpose of simplification, this example assumes that items incidental to ownership are not included in the annual lease rentals, and that this fixed asset has no residual value at the end of its 20-year useful life.

Step Number 4

The DCF rate of return for the leased fixed asset comparable to that for the purchased fixed asset must be determined. It is assumed that the fixed asset will earn the same stream of operating cash income after taxes (excluding depreciation) when it is leased than when it is purchased and owned. The example in Table 39 shows that when the $11,938 investment equivalent, arrived at in Table 37, and the 48 percent tax savings on the annual amortization amounts arrived at in Table 39, are substituted for the series of annual lease rentals spread over the fixed asset's 20-year lease term, the DCF rate of return arrived at for this prospective project is 14.8 percent when its fixed asset is leased compared to 20 percent when it is purchased and owned. The 5.2 percent difference in the DCF rate of return when this prospective project's fixed asset is leased compared to when it is purchased and owned is due to the $1,938 premium the company is paying for acquiring the depreciable fixed asset via the more expensive lease-financing method, and also is due to the difference in the timing of the tax benefits under owning as opposed to leasing under this method of acquisition.

What Rate to Use for Discounting to Determine the Investment Equivalent

The question as to what rate to use for discounting lease rentals to determine investment equivalents arises primarily in multinational companies that operate on a worldwide basis through foreign affiliates and branches. Should their current U.S. or their current foreign direct borrowing rate be used for discounting? Multinationals probably have as many different foreign direct borrowing rates as the number of countries they operate in. It would seem logical and advantageous to use the company's local direct borrowing rate for these reasons.

• The bulk of the prospective projects of companies, including those involving leased fixed assets, normally is approved locally. Therefore, to avoid confusion, all new investments, whether approved locally or by the parent company in the United States, should be discounted at the local direct borrowing rate.

- Lease rentals reflect the local direct borrowing or prime interest rate. Therefore, discounting at the foreign direct borrowing rate will result in investment equivalents that will be closer to the purchase prices of the depreciable fixed assets than if the parent company's U.S. direct borrowing rate were used, which may differ widely.
- The minimum acceptable earnings rates for various types of local investments will be geared to the local prime interest rate. Therefore, the DCF rates of return calculated on investment equivalents that are arrived at by discounting the lease rentals at the local direct borrowing rate will be much closer to those earnings rates the parent company is looking for in the particular foreign country.

How Buy versus Lease Decisions Are Made

The first step in evaluating prospective projects in which buy versus lease alternatives exist is to determine whether they generate sufficient profits or savings to yield acceptable DCF rates of return commensurate with the risks involved. These initial investment decisions, generally, are based on the *DCF rate of return* and the *payout period* calculated on the fixed assets' purchase prices.

If the prospective projects meet this initial test and are found to yield DCF rates of return that meet the standards predetermined for them by the company, then the second step is to determine whether the fixed assets for the prospective projects should be leased instead of purchased and owned, providing the company is interested in some form of outside lease or debt financing.

If lease financing seems desirable, then the only analysis that is needed in most instances is to determine the interest factor that is included in the lease rentals. This is accomplished by first extracting all cost elements incidental to ownership, such as taxes, maintenance, repairs, etc., from the lease rentals so that they will consist only of principal and interest and then by discounting them at various interest rates until the rate is found that discounts the series of lease rentals down to a total present value equal to the fixed asset's purchase price. The rate that does this is the interest factor included in the lease rental.

This procedure is shown in Table 40 in which it is assumed that the company has the alternative of buying a depreciable fixed asset for $10,000 or leasing it at an annual rental of $1,598 for 20 years. When the series of annual lease rentals, consisting of principal and interest only and no expenses incidental to ownership, is discounted at the 14 percent rate, the total present value is $10,583 or $583 greater than the fixed asset's $10,000 purchase price. This indicates that the interest factor included in the lease rentals still exceeds the company's 12 percent current direct borrowing rate which discounts the series of annual lease rentals down to a total present value of $11,938 as shown in Table 37. This proves that a still higher interest rate must be used for discounting. Consequently, when this series of annual lease rentals is discounted at the 15 percent rate, the resultant total present value is equal to

TABLE 40

Determining Interest Factor Included in Lease Rental for a
Depreciable Fixed Asset

Year	(1) Lease Rental before Tax	(2) Present Value Factor at 14%	(3) Present Value	(4) Present Value Factor at 15%	(5) Present Value
0	—	—	—	—	—
1	$ 1,598	.8772	$ 1,402	.8696	$ 1,390
2	1,598	.7695	1,230	.7561	1,208
3	1,598	.6750	1,079	.6575	1,051
4	1,598	.5921	946	.5718	913
5	1,598	.5194	830	.4972	794
6	1,598	.4556	728	.4323	691
7	1,598	.3996	639	.3759	601
8	1,598	.3506	560	.3269	522
9	1,598	.3075	491	.2843	454
10	1,598	.2697	431	.2472	395
11	1,598	.2366	378	.2149	343
12	1,598	.2076	332	.1869	299
13	1,598	.1821	291	.1625	260
14	1,598	.1597	255	.1413	226
15	1,598	.1401	224	.1229	196
16	1,598	.1229	196	.1069	171
17	1,598	.1078	172	.0929	148
18	1,598	.0946	151	.0808	129
19	1,598	.0829	132	.0703	112
20	1,598	.0728	116	.0611	97
Total	$31,960		$10,583		$10,000

the fixed asset's $10,000 purchase price. This means that the interest factor included in the lease rental is 15 percent or 3 percent higher than the company's current direct borrowing rate, which is assumed to be 12 percent. Therefore, it may be concluded from the analysis in Table 40 that this fixed asset should be purchased and owned instead of leased, providing depreciation is allowed as a tax deduction.

Incidentally, if as a result of discounting, the total present value arrived at had been lower than the fixed asset's $10,000 purchase price, then the interest rate at which this series of annual lease rentals was discounted would have been higher than the interest factor included in the lease rental.

As shown in Table 41, even when the interest factor included in the lease rental is identical with the company's current direct borrowing rate, owning is more economical than leasing fixed assets due to the tax advantage, providing depreciation is recognized for tax purposes. Consequently, no analysis of the after-tax cost of leasing is required to be made unless (a) the interest factor in the lease rental is lower than the company's current direct borrowing rate (which occurs rarely—if ever), or (b) special circumstances prevail that could favor leasing if lease financing isn't too much costlier than debt financing.

TABLE 41

Determining After-Tax Cost of Leasing as Opposed to Owning a Depreciable Fixed Asset

	(1)	(2)	(3)	(4)	(5)	(6)	(7)	(8)
			Purchase Price and Tax Savings*	After-Tax Cost of Leasing				
	Lease Rental					*Present Value*		
	Before Tax	*After Tax*	*on*	*Compared to*	*Factor*		*Factor*	
Year			*Depreciation*	*Owning*	*at 9%*	*Amount*	*at 10%*	*Amount*
0	—	—	$10,000	$(10,000)	1.0000	$(10,000)	1.0000	$(10,000)
1	$ 1,598	$ 831	(457)	1,288	.9174	1,182	.9091	1,171
2	1,598	831	(434)	1,265	.8417	1,065	.8264	1,045
3	1,598	831	(411)	1,242	.7722	959	.7513	933
4	1,598	831	(389)	1,220	.7084	864	.6830	833
5	1,598	831	(366)	1,197	.6499	778	.6209	743
6	1,598	831	(343)	1,174	.5963	700	.5645	663
7	1,598	831	(320)	1,151	.5470	630	.5132	591
8	1,598	831	(297)	1,128	.5019	566	.4665	526
9	1,598	831	(274)	1,105	.4604	509	.4241	469
10	1,598	831	(252)	1,083	.4224	457	.3855	417
11	1,598	831	(228)	1,059	.3875	410	.3505	371
12	1,598	831	(206)	1,037	.3555	369	.3186	330
13	1,598	831	(183)	1,014	.3262	331	.2897	294
14	1,598	831	(160)	991	.2992	297	.2633	261
15	1,598	831	(137)	968	.2745	266	.2394	232
16	1,598	831	(114)	945	.2519	238	.2176	206
17	1,598	831	(91)	922	.2311	213	.1978	182
18	1,598	831	(69)	900	.2120	191	.1799	162
19	1,598	831	(46)	877	.1945	171	.1635	143
20	1,598	831	(23)	854	.1784	152	.1486	127
Total	$31,960	$16,620	$ 5,200	$ 11,420		$ 348		$ (301)

After-tax cost of leasing is 9.54%.

* Tax savings in parentheses.

How to Determine the After-Tax Cost of Leasing

The method for determining the after-tax cost of leasing is shown in Table 41 in which all the assumptions made with respect to the fixed asset are identical with those made in Table 40. The after-tax cost of leasing this depreciable fixed asset for 20 years at an annual lease rental of $1,598 as opposed to buying it for $10,000 is $11,420, or 9.54 percent. Assuming that the company's current direct borrowing rate is 12 percent before taxes, or 6.2 percent after taxes, the depreciable fixed asset should be purchased and owned, unless the benefits that will accrue to the company as a result of leasing will exceed the 3.34 percent additional after-tax cost.

This after-tax cost of lease financing rate developed in Table 41 is commonly misinterpreted to mean that the fixed asset should be leased because the company stands to earn only 9.54 percent if it were owned compared with the 20.0 percent it might earn if the $10,000 were invested in some other

Owning and Debt Financing Is More Advantageous When Leasing Depreciable Fixed Assets Even When Interest Factor Is Identical in Lease and Debt Financing

Year	Lease Rental before Taxes	Tax Savings on Lease Rental	Lease Rental after Taxes	Bank Loan and Loan Payments	Tax Savings on Interest	Bank Loan and Loan Payments after Taxes
0	—			$ 10,000		$ 10,000
1	$ (1,598)	$ 767	$ (831)	(1,598)	$ 720	(878)
2	(1,598)	767	(831)	(1,598)	713	(885)
3	(1,598)	767	(831)	(1,598)	705	(893)
4	(1,598)	767	(831)	(1,598)	695	(903)
5	(1,598)	767	(831)	(1,598)	685	(913)
6	(1,598)	767	(831)	(1,598)	672	(926)
7	(1,598)	767	(831)	(1,598)	658	(940)
8	(1,598)	767	(831)	(1,598)	642	(956)
9	(1,598)	767	(831)	(1,598)	623	(975)
10	(1,598)	767	(831)	(1,598)	601	(997)
11	(1,598)	767	(831)	(1,598)	577	(1,021)
12	(1,598)	767	(831)	(1,598)	548	(1,050)
13	(1,598)	767	(831)	(1,598)	515	(1,083)
14	(1,598)	767	(831)	(1,598)	478	(1,120)
15	(1,598)	767	(831)	(1,598)	434	(1,164)
16	(1,598)	767	(831)	(1,598)	384	(1,214)
17	(1,598)	767	(831)	(1,598)	326	(1,272)
18	(1,598)	767	(831)	(1,598)	261	(1,337)
19	(1,598)	767	(831)	(1,598)	184	(1,414)
20	(1,598)	767	(831)	(1,598)	119	(1,479)
Total	$(31,960)	$15,340	$(16,620)	$(21,960)	$10,540	$(11,420)

fixed asset. This interpretation is incorrect because it confuses the 9.54 percent after-tax lease financing rate with the fixed asset's 20 percent DCF earnings rate based on equity financing. The 9.54 percent after-tax lease financing rate must be compared to the company's 6.2 percent after-tax direct borrowing rate to determine whether the fixed asset should be lease or debt financed if outside financing is desirable.

To avoid confusion with regard to making buy versus lease decisions, it is well to adhere to the basic principle that since leasing is merely another financing method, acquisitions of new fixed assets, under normal conditions, should be financed at the lowest financing cost. For example, why should the company pay 15 percent interest, or $1,598 annually for 20 years, to lease this depreciable fixed asset when it can borrow money at 12 percent, buy the fixed asset, and debt finance it at annual bank loan payments of only $1,339 for 20 years, and in addition enjoy the benefits of higher tax savings in the early years as well as the residual value—if any—at the end of the fixed asset's useful life.

TABLE 42

Purchase Price and Tax Savings*	Cost of Owning and Debt Financing	Net Cash Flow Owning versus Leasing	Years Invested	Compound Value Factor at 15%	Cash Generated Due to Difference† in Timing
$(10,000)	—				
457	$ (421)	410	19	14.232	$ 5,835
434	(451)	380	18	12.375	4,703
411	(482)	349	17	10.761	3,756
389	(514)	317	16	9.358	2,966
366	(547)	284	15	8.137	2,311
343	(583)	248	14	7.076	1,755
320	(620)	211	13	6.153	1,298
297	(659)	172	12	5.350	920
274	(701)	130	11	4.652	605
252	(745)	86	10	4.046	348
228	(793)	38	9	3.518	134
206	(844)	(13)	8	3.059	(40)
183	(900)	(69)	7	2.660	(184)
160	(960)	(129)	6	2.313	(298)
137	(1,027)	(196)	5	2.011	(394)
114	(1,100)	(269)	4	1.749	(470)
91	(1,181)	(350)	3	1.521	(532)
69	(1,268)	(437)	2	1.322	(578)
46	(1,368)	(537)	1	1.150	(618)
23	(1,456)	(625)	0	1.000	(625)
$ (5,200)	$(16,620)	$ –0–			$20,892

* On depreciation.
† Owning and debt financing versus leasing.

Why Leasing Benefits Are Illusory

Normally, the after-tax lease financing rate is higher than a company's after-tax current direct borrowing rate. Leasing depreciable fixed assets, nevertheless, is frequently believed to be more attractive for these reasons.

- To keep the long-term lease rental obligations or the capital cost for the use of fixed assets off the company's books. This is deemed desirable *(a)* to improve the company's overall year-to-year book rates of return based on total assets employed, total invested capital, shareholders equity, etc.; and *(b)* to enhance company's general credit standing.
- To have the lease rentals for fixed assets appear in the cash flows of prospective projects as operating expenses instead of as integral parts of their total capital cost. This, obviously, tends to yield higher and more attractive DCF rates of return for prospective projects.
- To keep the commitments of funds for new fixed assets out of the company's annual capital expenditure budget which, generally, is con-

fined to purchased fixed assets. This keeps the capital expenditure budget low, and thus makes it possible to obtain management's approval more easily.

Upon closer scrutiny, these so-called advantages are virtually nonexistent because lending institutions and investors in industrial stocks and bonds have long been accustomed to making adjustments in their economic analyses and evaluations to compensate for undisclosed financial facts before making loan or investment decisions. Therefore, the practice of not showing leased fixed assets and their related long-term rent obligations in the body of published financial reports serves no useful purpose. Likewise, showing lease rentals for component fixed assets in a prospective project's cash flows as operating expenses instead of capitalizing them and including them in their investment bases could lead to serious unwise and costly investment decisions.

Chapter 12

Improper Application of DCF Concept and Incorrect Choice of Alternatives Result in Unsound Investment Decisions _____

Profitability indicators, such as the discounted cash flow (DCF) rate of return and the net present value (NPV), are invaluable tools in aiding top management make important investment decisions. This is particularly true in large companies in which top management frequently is called upon to make investment decisions involving huge capital expenditures. Once these far-reaching investment decisions are made, they all too frequently are irreversible; and, moreover, if they are based on financial criteria that are unrealistic and misleading, then prospective projects—particularly those involving huge capital outlays—conceivably could have deleterious effects on companies' future profitability for years to come. Therefore, it is imperative that the financial criteria for prospective projects be based on realistic and reasonable estimates; that these estimates be predicated on plausible and valid assumptions; that the economic evaluations reflect comparisons of the right alternatives; and finally that the financial criteria be calculated by sound and logical economic evaluation techniques.

This chapter is devoted to an actual case history of a prospective Project A that should have been rejected instead of accepted by a multinational company's top management. The unwise and highly unprofitable investment decision made in this case was heavily influenced by an unrealistic 50.0 percent DCF rate of return that was based on a comparison of the wrong alternatives and calculated according to the conventional DCF method, which is inimical to arriving at a realistic and meaningful DCF rate of return in this particular type of investment situation because it is based on an improper application of the DCF concept.

Description of Project A

The multinational company owned a parcel of land in a foreign country that was appraised at $13 million. This land had been idle for a number of years, and the company could envision no use for the land in the forseeable future. Hence, it decided to dispose of the land, free the funds tied up in it, and channel the proceeds derived from its sale into other profit-producing ventures. However, finding a prospective buyer who was able and willing to pay $13 million for the land and assume the risk of spending additional millions of dollars for developing it posed somewhat of a problem for the multinational company. Furthermore, the political climate in the foreign country in which the land was located was not conducive to investing large sums of money on a long-term basis, and this factor was largely responsible for the multinational company's problem. However, despite this handicap, an outside developer eventually was found who was interested in *(a)* purchasing the land for $13 million, *(b)* paying for it during the five-year land development period, and *(c)* having the multinational company offering the land for sale share in the developer's profits to the extent of $6 million at the end of the five-year land development period. Several feasibility studies were made, and after a careful perusal of them, the multinational company's operating management reached the conclusion that it had these three courses of action open to it regarding the disposition of this parcel of land.

Alternative I.   The company could choose to develop the land, sell the housing units constructed thereon directly to prospective buyers, and thus enjoy the entire land development profits.

Alternative II.   The company could choose to sell the land to the outside developer and have him develop the land and sell the housing units constructed thereon directly to prospective buyers. The outside developer could then pay the company the $13 million for the land during the five-year land development period plus the agreed-upon $6 million share of the land developer's profits at the end of the land development period.

Alternative III.   The company could choose to do nothing, i.e., it could continue to hold on to the land, and thus continue to tie up the $13 million invested in it.

Project A's DCF Rate of Return Calculated under the Conventional DCF Method

The upper section of Table 43 shows that the DCF rate of return for Project A, as calculated under the conventional DCF method, is 50.0 percent. This DCF rate of return is determined on total capital outlays of $95 million and total cash returns of $119 million during Project A's five-year economic life, and it is based on the comparison of Alternative I versus Alternative III.

Under the conventional DCF method, the bulk of the $95 million total capital outlays was commingled and netted with the $119 million total operat-

TABLE 43

Distorted 50.0 Percent and the 25.18 Percent DCF Rates of Return Arrived at by Conventional DCF Method for Two Mutually Exclusive Projects A and B Due to Difference in Timing of Their $95,000 and $50,000 Capital Outlays (dollar figures in thousands)

(1)	(2)	(3)	(4)	(5)	(6)	(7)	(8)	(9)	(10)	(11)	(12)
	Project's			DCF Rate of Return Calculation under Procedure 1						DCF Rate of Return Calculation under Procedure 2	
Year	Capital Outlays*	Cash Income	Net Cash Flow	Present Value Factor at 50%	Present Value	Present Value Factor at 51%	Present Value	Year	Project's Net Cash Flow	Present Value Factor at 50%	Present Value
			Project A							**Project A**	
0	$ (2,000)	—	$ (2,000)	1.0000	$ (2,000)	1.0000	$ (2,000)	0	$(25,935)†	1.0000	$(25,935)
1	(4,000)	$ 1,000	(3,000)	.6667	(2,000)	.6623	(1,987)	1	1,000	.6667	667
2	(10,000)	9,000	(1,000)	.4444	(444)	.4386	(439)	2	9,000	.4444	4,000
3	(29,000)	30,000	1,000	.2963	296	.2904	290	3	30,000	.2963	8,889
4	(25,000)	30,000	5,000	.1975	988	.1923	962	4	30,000	.1975	5,925
5	(25,000)	49,000	24,000	.1317	3,161	.1274	3,058	5	49,000	.1317	6,454
Total	$(95,000)	$119,000	$ 24,000		$ 1		$ (116)	Total	$ 93,065		$ –0–

DCF rate of return is 50.0%.   DCF rate of return is 50.0%.

			Project B	At 25%		At 26%	
0	$(50,000)	—	$(50,000)	1.0000	$(50,000)	1.0000	$(50,000)
1		$ 1,000	1,000	.8000	800	.7937	794
2		9,000	9,000	.6400	5,760	.6299	5,669
3		30,000	30,000	.5120	15,360	.4999	14,997
4		30,000	30,000	.4096	12,288	.3968	11,904
5		49,000	49,000	.3277	16,057	.3149	15,430
Total	$(50,000)	$119,000	$ 69,000		$ 265		$ (1,206)

DCF rate of return is 25.18%.

* Capital outlays in parentheses.
† Represents the total present value of the $95,000 capital outlays, shown in Column 2, discounted at the project's estimated 50 percent earnings rate.

ing cash income. Hence, the major portion of the $95 million total capital outlays is automatically discounted at the 50.0 percent rate with the result that Project A's 50.0 percent DCF rate of return is calculated on a substantially understated investment base of $25.935 million at the zero reference point. This is shown on the extreme right side in the upper section of Table 43. Calculating Project A's DCF rate of return on this highly understated and unrealistic investment base implied that the company's suppliers and contractors were willing to accept an alternative lump-sum payment amount of $25.935 million at the zero reference point in lieu of $95 million during the five-year period after that point in time. It further implied that the company's suppliers and contractors were willing to pay $69.065 million interest at the 50 percent rate when, in actuality, they could have borrowed money at a 12 percent interest rate from banks or other lending institutions during the five-year land development period. It, obviously, is quite inconceivable that the company's suppliers and contractors would have been willing to accept $25.935 million at the zero reference point in lieu of $95 million during the five-year period after that point in time. Consequently, the 50.0 percent DCF rate of return calculated for Project A on the $25.935 million investment base at the zero reference point was grossly overstated and completely unrealistic.

In order to emphasize the extent of the distortion of Project A's 50.0 percent DCF rate of return, it will be assumed that the company had an alternate investment opportunity of generating an identical stream of cash returns aggregating $119 million in Project B during Project A's five-year land development period. However, it will be assumed further that the total capital outlays for Project B would have been only $50 million, and that this entire amount would have occurred at the zero reference point instead of part of it subsequent to that point in time. The DCF rate of return calculated for Project B under the conventional DCF method would have been 25.18 percent in this investment situation. The DCF rate of return for this hypothetical investment opportunity is illustrated in the lower section of Table 43. Since this 25.18 percent DCF rate of return for Project B is calculated under conditions that are similar to those under which the compound interest principle is applied by banks and other lending institutions, it is reasonable to assume that this 25.18 percent DCF rate of return is a realistic and true profitability indicator for Project B in this particular investment situation.

However, if the various financial factors in Projects A and B are carefully compared and scrutinized, it becomes evident that Project B must be more profitable than Project A instead of the other way around. The reason for reaching this conclusion is that while all the other financial factors are identical in both projects, the capital outlays for Project A are $45 million, or 90.0 percent higher than those for Project B. Consequently, it follows that the total profits for Project A are $45 million, or 187.5 percent, lower than those for Project B, since all other financial factors are identical in both projects. Based on the above figures, the DCF rate of return for Project A naturally has to be lower than the one for Project B. In other words, Project B must be more profitable than Project A instead of the other way around. Next, another approach to this problem will be taken in order to make certain that this is actually true.

Surely, the reader will agree that the profitability of prospective projects should be the same, whether they are financed with funds from internal or external sources. If this is so, then let us determine next if Project B is more profitable than Project A if both projects are bank financed.

If Projects A and B Are Financed through External Sources

Table 44 shows the annual bank loan payment amounts that are substituted for the actual cash outlays of $95 and $50 million for Project A and Project B, respectively, if both projects are debt financed.

TABLE 44

Bank Loans and Bank Loan Payments Required to Finance Project A's and Project B's Capital Cost of $95,000 and $50,000 (dollar figures in thousands)

(1)	(2)	(3)	(4)	(5)	(6)	(7)	(8)
			Annual Bank Payments		*Principal*		
Year	Bank Loans at Beginning of Year	Loan Terms in Number of Years	For Individual Loans	For All Loans Combined	Balance at Beginning of Year	Interest Charges at 12%	Repayment of Bank Loans
			Project A				
1	$ 6,000	5	$ 1,664	$ 1,664	$ 6,000	$ 720	$ 944
2	10,000	4	3,292	4,956	15,056	1,807	3,149
3	29,000	3	12,074	17,030	40,907	4,909	12,121
4	25,000	2	14,792	31,822	53,786	6,454	25,368
5	25,000	1	27,999	59,821	53,418	6,403	53,418
Total	$95,000			$115,293	$ –0–	$20,293	$95,000
			Project B				
1	$50,000	5	$13,870	—	$50,000	$ 6,000	$ 7,870
2	—	—	13,870	—	42,130	5,056	8,814
3	—	—	13,870	—	33,316	3,998	9,872
4	—	—	13,870	—	23,444	2,813	11,057
5	—	—	13,870	—	12,387	1,483	12,387
Total	$50,000		$69,350		$ –0–	$19,350	$50,000

As shown in the upper section of Table 44, five separate bank loans are required to finance Project A. The five separate bank loan principal amounts range from $6 million in year 1 to $25 million in year 5; the five separate bank loan terms range from 5 years for the first bank loan to 1 year for the fifth bank loan, and the annual bank loan payment amounts for the five bank loans combined range from $1.664 million in year 1 to $59.821 million in year 5. The total bank loan payments during Project A's five-year economic life amount to $115.293 million, which includes $95 million for the repayment of the five bank loan amounts and $20.293 million for the interest charges.

On the other hand, as shown in the lower section of Table 44, only one bank loan is required to finance Project B. The bank loan principal amount is $50 million, the annual bank loan payment amount is $13.87 million, and the bank loan term is five years. The total bank loan payments during Project B's five-year economic life amount to $69.35 million, which includes $50 million for the repayment of the bank loan amount and $19.35 million for the interest charges.

Profitability of Projects A and B if Financed Externally

Table 45 shows which project is more profitable, Project A or Project B, when both projects are financed through external sources. The financial factors

TABLE 45

Determine $11,032 and $29,429 NPVs after Interest Charges for Projects A and B, Showing Project B Preferable to Project A (dollar figures in thousands)

(1)	(2)	(3)	(4)	(5)	(6)	(7)	(8)	(9)
		Bank Loans to Finance		Tax Savings		Project's Net Cash Flow	NPV Calculation	
	Project's Capital	Project's Capital	Annual Bank	on Interest	Project's Cash	Including Interest	Discount Factor	Present
Year	Outlays*	Outlays*	Payments*	Charges†	Income	Charges	at 15%‡	Value
				Project A				
0	$ (2,000)	$ 2,000	—	$ —	$ —	$ —	1.0000	$ —
1	(4,000)	4,000	$ (1,664)	360	1,000	$ (304)	.8696	$ (264)
2	(10,000)	10,000	(4,956)	904	9,000	4,948	.7561	3,741
3	(29,000)	29,000	(17,030)	2,454	30,000	15,424	.6575	10,141
4	(25,000)	25,000	(31,822)	3,227	30,000	1,405	.5718	803
5	(25,000)	25,000	(59,821)	3,202	49,000	(7,619)	.4972	(3,389)
Total	$(95,000)	$95,000	$(115,293)	$10,147	$119,000	$13,854		$11,032

NPV after interest charges is $11,032.

				Project B				
0	$(50,000)	$50,000	—	$ —	$ —	$ —	1.0000	$ —
1			$ (13,870)	$ 3,000	$ 1,000	$ (9,870)	.8696	$ (8,583)
2			(13,870)	2,528	9,000	(2,342)	.7561	(1,771)
3			(13,870)	1,999	30,000	18,129	.6575	11,920
4			(13,870)	1,407	30,000	17,537	.5718	10,028
5			(13,870)	741	49,000	35,871	.4972	17,835
Total	$(50,000)	$50,000	$ (69,350)	$ 9,675	$119,000	$59,325		$29,429

NPV after interest charges is $29,429.

* Capital outlays and bank payments in parentheses.
† Table 43, Column 7 × 50 percent, which is assumed to be the company's income tax rate.
‡ The 15 percent rate used for discounting is assumed to be the company's opportunity cost of money rate.

shown for Projects A and B in Table 45 are identical with those shown for these two projects in Table 43, except that the annual bank loan payment amounts are substituted for the project's actual capital outlays and the annual tax savings on the interest charges are added to the cash flows of the two projects. The annual bank loan payment amounts, the annual tax savings on the interest charges, and the annual operating cash income or savings amounts are added together and netted, and the net cash flows for Projects A and B are then discounted at the company's assumed 15 percent opportunity cost of money rate. These net cash flows show total profits of $13.854 million and $59.325 million for Projects A and B, respectively before discounting, and NPVs of $11.032 million and $29.429 million for Projects A and B, respectively, after discounting. These total profits before discounting and their NPVs arrived at after discounting at the company's assumed 15 percent opportunity cost of money rate, prove conclusively that Project B is more profitable than Project A when both projects are bank financed.

As mentioned previously, if Project B is more profitable than Project A when both projects are financed with funds from external sources, then it follows that Project B also must be more profitable than Project A when both projects are financed with funds from internal sources. This greater profitability is evidenced by the higher DCF rate of return arrived at for Project B than the one arrived at for Project A by the proper application of the DCF concept, as shown in Table 46.

Project A's DCF Rate of Return Calculated by the Proposed DCF Method

The top section in Table 46 shows that when the DCF rate of return for Project A is calculated with the proper application of the DCF concept under the proposed DCF method, it is 17.13 percent. The bottom section shows that the 25.18 percent DCF rate of return for Project B is the same whether it is determined under the conventional or the proposed DCF method because it is calculated under conditions that are identical with those under which the compound interest principle is applied by banks and other lending institutions. The 17.13 percent DCF rate of return for Project A compared to the 25.18 percent DCF rate of return for Project B, arrived at under the proposed DCF method, confirms our findings with the NPVs arrived at in Table 45, that Project B is more profitable than Project A.

It should be noted that the financial factors for Project A shown in Table 46 are identical with those shown for this project in Table 43. It should be noted further that the difference in the calculations in Tables 43 and 46 lies solely in the methodology, i.e., in the manner in which the DCF rates of return for Projects A and B are calculated under the proper and the improper application of the DCF concept. In Table 46, the $95 million capital outlays for Project A are discounted separately at the company's 12 percent current direct borrowing rate. Under this proper application of the DCF concept, the resultant $64.259 million total present value represents the alternate lump-sum payment or investment amount at the zero reference

TABLE 46

Determine 17.13 Percent and 28.18 Percent DCF Rates of Return Arrived at by Proposed DCF Method for Projects A and B Correctly Showing Project B Preferable to Project A (dollar figures in thousands)

(1)	(2)	(3)	(4)	(5)	(6)	(7)	(8)	(9)
			Investment Base Calculation at the Zero Reference Point			DCF Rate of Return Calculation		
Year	Project's Capital Outlays*	Present Factor at 12%	Present Value of Project's Capital Outlays*	Project's Cash Income	Present Value Factor at 17%	Present Value of Project's Cash Income	Present Value Factor at 18%	Present Value of Project's Cash Income
				Project A				
0	$ (2,000)	1.0000	$ (2,000)	—	1.0000	—	1.0000	—
1	(4,000)	.8929	(3,572)	$ 1,000	.8547	$ 855	.8475	$ 848
2	(10,000)	.7972	(7,972)	9,000	.7305	6,575	.7182	6,464
3	(29,000)	.7118	(20,642)	30,000	.6244	18,732	.6086	18,258
4	(25,000)	.6355	(15,888)	30,000	.5336	16,008	.5158	15,474
5	(25,000)	.5674	(14,185)	49,000	.4561	22,349	.4371	21,418
Total	$(95,000)		$(64,259)	$119,000		$64,519		$62,462

DCF rate of return is <u>17.13%</u>.

				Project B				
					At 25%		At 26%	
0	$(50,000)	1.0000	$(50,000)	—	1.0000	—	1.0000	—
1				$ 1,000	.8000	$ 800	.7937	$ 794
2				9,000	.6400	5,760	.6299	5,669
3				30,000	.5120	15,360	.4999	14,997
4				30,000	.4096	12,288	.3968	11,904
5				49,000	.3277	16,057	.3149	15,430
Total	$(50,000)		$(50,000)	$119,000		$50,265		$48,794

DCF rate of return is <u>25.18%</u>.

* Capital outlays in parentheses.

point on which the 17.13 percent DCF rate of return for Project A is calculated.

This 17.13 percent DCF rate of return is the true profitability indicator for Project A because it is calculated on the $64.259 million alternate lump-sum payment amount at the zero reference point that the company's suppliers and contractors would be willing to accept at that point in time, in lieu of $2 million at the zero reference point and the remaining $93 million during the five-year period after that point in time. In other words, the company's suppliers and contractors are presu ned to be willing to accept $64.259 million at the zero reference point because they would be able to discount at the bank this series of future payments totaling $93 million at their 12 percent current direct borrowing rate which, presumably, is the rate they would be willing to pay for the use of money during the five-year land development period. A comparison of the NPVs and the DCF rates of return arrived at in Tables 45 and 46 proving that Project B is more profitable than Project A also bears out the contention that the profitability of prospective projects is identical whether they are financed with funds from internal or external sources.

Assuming Projects A and B are two mutually exclusive projects and the multinational company has sufficient funds for the adoption of only one of these two projects, then the investment decision based on the 50.0 percent and the 25.18 percent DCF rates of return arrived at by the conventional DCF method undoubtedly will lead to making the wrong choice. On the other hand, the investment decision based on the 17.13 percent DCF rate of return for Project A compared to the 25.18 percent DCF rate of return for Project B, both arrived at by the proposed DCF method, in all likelihood will lead to making the right choice in this investment situation.

Determine Net Present Values (NPVs) for Alternatives I and II

The problem this multinational company actually was confronted with in this investment situation did not involve the task of making the right choice between the acceptance of either Project A or Project B. As pointed out previously, Project B is purely a hypothetical project that is introduced in this chapter only for the purpose of illustrating by comparison that Project A's 50 percent DCF rate of return is distorted and unrealistic. The real problem the multinational company was concerned with in this investment situation involved the selection of the most economic alternative, that is, the most economic course of action that was available to management for the disposition of the parcel of land valued at $13 million.

It should have been obvious from the start that Alternative III, which called for doing nothing, i.e., for holding on to the undeveloped land for possible future use or sale, should have been eliminated immediately because continuing to tie up the $13 million in land for an indefinite period in the future was deemed to be too costly and therefore unacceptable. Consequently, the remaining choice was between Alternative I, which called for the company developing the land, selling the housing units constructed thereon, and thereby earning 100 percent of the land development profits, or Alternative II, which called for selling the land to the outside developer, have him develop the land and sell the housing units constructed thereon, and share part of his land development profits with the company.

The NPV calculations for Alternatives I and II are shown in Table 47. The purpose of Table 47 is to determine by means of this profitability indicator which one of these two alternatives was the most economic course of action to pursue by the company for the disposition of this $13 million parcel of land.

The net cash flows shown for Alternatives I and II in Table 47 are identical with those shown for these two alternatives in Table 50. The total net cash

TABLE 47

*Determine Project A's $10,085 and $13,563 NPVs for Alternatives
I and II Arrived at under the Conventional NPV Method (see Note; dollar
figures in thousands)*

| | | | NPV Calculation | |
| (1) | (2) | (3) | (4) | |
Year	Project's Net Cash Flow	Present Value Factor at 15%	Present Value of Project's Net Cash Flow	
		Alternative I		
0	$ (2,000)	1.0000	$ (2,000)	
1	(3,000)	.8696	(2,609)	
2	(1,000)	.7561	(756)	
3	1,000	.6575	658	
4	5,000	.5718	2,859	
5	24,000	.4972	11,933	
Total	$24,000		$10,085	

NPV for Alternative I is $10,085.

		Alternative II		
0	$ 4,000	1.0000	$ 4,000	
1	3,000	.8696	2,609	
2	2,000	.7561	1,512	
3	2,000	.6575	1,315	
4	2,000	.5718	1,144	
5	6,000	.4972	2,983	
Total	$19,000		$13,563	

NPV for Alternative II is $13,563.

Note: Alternative I—The project sponsor is to develop the land by constructing housing units on it and then sell the housing units at a profit.

versus

Alternative II—The project sponsor is to sell the undeveloped land to an outside land developer and share in the latter's housing unit development profits.

flow for Alternative I was $5 million, or 26.3 percent, higher than the $19 million total net cash flow for Alternative II. On the surface, this would have made it appear that Alternative I was more economic than Alternative II. However, when the net cash flows for Alternatives I and II were discounted at the company's predetermined 15 percent opportunity cost of money rate, the NPV for Alternative II was actually $3.47 million, or 34.5 percent, higher than the $10.085 million NPV for Alternative I. This proved, incontrovertibly, that Alternative II was the more economic course of action to pursue by the company in the disposition of this $13 million parcel of land.

TABLE 48

Determine Project A's 7.14 Percent and 7.99 Percent DCF Rates of Return Arrived at by the Conventional and the Proposed DCF Methods for Alternative I over Alternative II Showing Alternative I to Be Less Favorable than Alternative II (see Note; dollar figures in thousands)

(1)	(2)	(3)	(4)	(5)	(6)	(7)
		DCF Rate of Return Calculation under the Conventional DCF Method				
Year	Project's Net Cash Flow	Present Value Factor at 7%	Present Value of Project's Net Cash Flow	Present Value Factor at 8%	Present Value of Project's Net Cash Flow	Project's Capital Outlays*
0	$ (6,000)	1.0000	$ (6,000)	1.0000	$ (6,000)	$ (6,000)
1	(6,000)	.9346	(5,608)	.9259	(5,555)	(6,000)
2	(3,000)	.8734	(2,620)	.8573	(2,572)	(3,000)
3	(1,000)	.8163	(816)	.7938	(794)	(1,000)
4	3,000	.7629	2,289	.7350	2,205	—
5	18,000	.7130	12,834	.6806	12,251	—
Total	$ 5,000		$ 79		$ (465)	$(16,000)

DCF rate of return is 7.14%.

(8)	(9)	(10)	(11)	(12)	(13)	(14)
Investment Base Calculation at the Zero Reference Point			DCF Rate of Return Calculation under the Proper Application of the DCF Concept			
Present Value Factor at 12%†	Present Value of Project's Capital Outlays*	Project's Cash Income	Present Value Factor at 7%	Present Value of Project's Cash Income	Present Value Factor at 8%	Present Value of Project's Cash Income
1.0000	$ (6,000)	—	—	—	—	—
.8929	(5,357)	—	—	—	—	—
.7972	(2,392)	—	—	—	—	—
.7118	(712)	—	—	—	—	—
—	—	$ 3,000	.7629	$ 2,289	.7350	$ 2,205
—	—	18,000	.7130	12,834	.6806	12,251
	$(14,461)	$21,000		$15,123		$14,456

DCF rate of return is 7.99%.

Note: Alternative I—The company is to develop the land by constructing units on it and then sell the housing units at a profit.

over

Alternative II—The company is to sell the undeveloped land to an outside land developer and share in the latter's land development profits.

* Capital outlays in parentheses.
† The 12 percent rate used for discounting the project's capital outlays represents the company's current direct borrowing rate.

Since the comparison of the NPVs calculated for Alternatives I and II in Table 47 showed that Alternative I should not have been pursued because it was less economic than Alternative II, the DCF rate of return calculated on the incremental cash flow of Alternative I over Alternative II likewise should have shown that Alternative I should not have been pursued for the same reason. This should have been proven by the 7.14 percent and the 7.99 percent DCF rates of return arrived at by either the conventional and/or the proposed DCF method, respectively, in Table 48. Both of these DCF rates of return prove to be lower than the company's 15 percent opportunity cost of money rate at which the net cash flows for Alternatives I and II are discounted to arrive at their respective NPVs in Table 47.

Project A's DCF Rate of Return Based on Comparison of the Right Alternatives

As shown in Table 48, the DCF rate of return for Project A was 7.14 percent as arrived at by the conventional DCF method and 7.99 percent as arrived at by the proposed DCF method. These two DCF rates of return were calculated on the incremental cash flow of Alternative I over Alternative II. The 0.88 percent difference between these two DCF rates of return was attributable solely to the fact that under the conventional DCF method, the incremental capital outlays totaling $16 million were discounted at Project A's calculated 7.14 percent DCF earnings rate; whereas under the proposed DCF method, they were discounted at the company's 12 percent current direct borrowing rate.

It should be noted that in this case both the 7.14 percent DCF rate of return arrived at by the conventional DCF method as well as the 7.99 percent DCF rate of return arrived at by the proposed DCF method were below the company's predetermined 15 percent opportunity cost of money rate. This showed that Alternative I was less economic than Alternative II and therefore that Alternative I should have been eliminated from consideration. In other words, the $5 million incremental profit, Alternative I over Alternative II, did not yield a DCF rate of return that met the 15 percent opportunity cost of money rate, or the minimum acceptable DCF rate of return, predetermined for prospective projects by the company's top management. Consequently, Alternative II was the most economic course of action that should have been pursued by the company for the disposition of the $13 million parcel of land.

It should have been possible to arrive at the same conclusion by calculating the NPV on the incremental cash flow of Alternative I over Alternative II. This NPV should have been a negative figure to indicate that Alternative I was unacceptable.

Project A's NPV Based on Comparison of the Right Alternatives

As shown in Table 49, Project A's NPV was $(2.521) million arrived at under the conventional NPV method and $(3.796) million arrived at under the

TABLE 49

Determine Project A's ($3,796) NPV Alternative I over Alternative II Arrived at under the Conventional and the Proposed NPV Methods Showing Alternative I to Be Less Favorable (see Note; dollar figures in thousands)

(1)	(2)	(3)	(4)	(5)	(6)	(7)	(8)	(9)	(10)	(11)
		NPV Calculation under the Orthodox NPV Method			*Investment Base Calculation at the Zero Reference Point*				*NPV Calculation under the Proper NPV Method*	
									Present Value of Project's	
Year	*Project's Net Cash Flow*	*Present Value Factor at 15%*	*Present Value of Project's Net Cash Flow*	*Project's Capital Outlays**	*Present Value Factor at 12%†*	*Present Value of Project's Capital Outlays**	*Project's Cash Income*	*Present Value Factor at 15%‡*	*Cash Income*	*Net Cash Flow*
0	$(6,000)	1.0000	$(6,000)	$(6,000)	1.0000	$(6,000)	—	—	—	$(6,000)
1	(6,000)	.8696	(5,218)	(6,000)	.8929	(5,357)	—	—	—	(5,357)
2	(3,000)	.7561	(2,268)	(3,000)	.7972	(2,392)	—	—	—	(2,392)
3	(1,000)	.6575	(658)	(1,000)	.7118	(712)	—	—	—	(712)
4	3,000	.5718	1,715	—	—	—	$ 3,000	.5718	$ 1,715	1,715
5	18,000	.4972	8,950	—	—	—	18,000	.4972	8,950	8,950
Total	$ 5,000		$(2,521)	$(16,000)		$(14,461)	$21,000		$10,665	$(3,796)

NPV is $(2,521). NPV is $(3,796).

Proposed NPV Method

Note: Alternative I—The company is to develop the land by constructing housing units on it and then sell the housing units at a profit.

over

Alternative II—The company is to sell the undeveloped land to an outside land developer and share in the latter's land development profits.

* Capital outlays in parentheses.
† The 12 percent rate represents the company's current direct borrowing rate.
‡ The 15 percent rate represents the company's opportunity cost of money rate.

proposed NPV method. These two NPVs were calculated on the incremental net cash flow of Alternative I over Alternative II. The difference between these two NPVs likewise was attributable to discounting the incremental $16 million capital outlays at different rates. They were discounted at the company's predetermined 15 percent opportunity cost of money rate under the conventional NPV method and at its 12 percent current direct borrowing rate under the proposed NPV method. Since both NPVs arrived at by the two different NPV methods were negative figures, it confirmed the findings in Table 48, which showed that the two DCF rates of return, calculated on the same incremental net cash flows by two different DCF methods, were below the 15 percent opportunity cost of money rate, or minimum acceptable DCF rate of return predetermined for prospective projects. Consequently, Alternative I was the uneconomic route for the company to divest itself of the $13 million parcel of land. The two DCF rates of return and the two NPVs also substantiated that the most prominent error in this project evaluation that led to the wrong investment decision was the comparison of the wrong alternatives.

The Actual Investment Decision Made by the Multinational Company

Partly on the strength of the 50.0 percent DCF rate of return arrived at by the conventional DCF method, but more importantly as a result of the wrong comparison of Alternative I over Alternative III instead of Alternative I over Alternative II, the company's top management adopted Alternative I as the most economic course of action for divesting itself of the $13 million parcel of land for which it had no use in the foreseeable future.

As proven by the DCF rates of return in Table 48 and the NPVs in Table 49, this was an extremely unwise and costly investment decision because it was based on a profitability indicator that was seriously overstated and completely unrealistic for the following two reasons: First, because the 50.0 percent DCF rate of return was arrived at by the conventional DCF method, which discounted Project A's $95 million capital outlays at the 50.0 percent rate, its 50 percent DCF rate of return was calculated on a $25.935 million investment base at the zero reference point. This investment base, impliedly, constituted an alternate lump-sum payment amount that would have been absolutely unacceptable to the company's suppliers and contractors at that point in time, in lieu of $2 million at the zero reference point and the remaining $93 million during the five-year period subsequent to that point in time. Second, the 50.0 percent DCF rate of return calculated on the incremental net cash flow was based on a comparison of the wrong alternatives. It was calculated on the incremental net cash flow of Alternate I, which called for the company to develop the land, sell the housing units constructed thereon, and thus earn 100 percent of the total land development profits, over Alternative III, which called for doing nothing, i.e., for holding on to the land for possible future use or sale. Since Alternative III, even upon cursory examination, revealed itself to be the least economic course of action, the multinational company naturally would have had no intention of adopting it. Hence, it should have been eliminated immediately from further consideration. Alternative I should have been eliminated next based on the financial criteria determined in Tables 45 to 49.

Similar Unwise Investment Decisions Can Be Avoided

If the top management, operating departments, project sponsors, and financial analysts of companies are properly schooled in project evaluation techniques and work together as a team and supplement one another's know-how, similar unwise and costly investment decisions can easily be avoided by such combined know-how and team effort.

In this unfortunate investment situation, the wrong investment decision still could have been avoided even though the wrong alternatives were evaluated if Project A's $95 million capital outlays had been discounted at the company's 12 percent current direct borrowing rate, as called for under the proposed DCF method. As pointed out previously, this would have resulted in calculating Project A's DCF rate of return on an alternate lump-sum payment amount of $64.259 million at the zero reference point, which was an amount that would have been acceptable to the company's suppliers and contractors at that point in time because it was based on an interest rate they would have been willing to pay for the use of money. Hence, the 17.13 percent DCF rate of return calculated on this $64.259 million investment base at the zero reference point and based on the incremental net cash flow of Alternative I over Alternative III would have proven to be Project A's true profitability indicator, providing Alternative II did not exist.

Even though this 17.13 percent DCF rate of return, which was based on a comparison of the wrong alternatives and therefore was an unreliable project selection device, was still slightly higher than the company's 15 percent opportunity cost of money rate, it, nevertheless, would have been extremely unlikely that the company would have been willing to invest $76 million in addition to foregoing $13 million for the land and $6 million as its share of the outside developer's profits to earn an additional profit of only $5 million during the five-year land development period. This conclusion was based on the reasoning that the 2.13 percent margin of safety was much too small to induce the multinational company to invest such a large amount of funds in a foreign country in which the political climate was assumed not to be conducive to long-term investments.

An unwise and unprofitable investment decision more than likely would have been avoided in this investment situation also if Project A's DCF rate of return had been calculated on a comparison of the right alternatives. As indicated previously, if Project A's DCF rate of return had been calculated on the incremental net cash flow of Alternative I over Alternative II, the result would have been a 7.14 percent DCF rate of return arrived at under the conventional DCF method and a 7.99 percent DCF rate of return arrived at under the proposed DCF method. Since both of these DCF rates of return were lower than the company's 15 percent opportunity cost of money rate, Alternative I, obviously, was unacceptable as the most economic expedient for disposing of the $13 million tract of land for which the company had no use in the foreseeable future.

The above conclusions that Alternatives I and III were unacceptable and that Alternative II was the most economic route for the company to divest itself of the $13 million tract of land in the foreign country can be verified by a careful study of the net cash flows for these alternatives in Table 50. This table shows the net cash flows for Alternatives I, II, and III are $24 million, $19

TABLE 50

Determine Project A's Net Cash Flow Comparisons for Alternatives I, II, and III (see Note; dollar figures in thousands)

(1)	(2)	(3)	(4)	(5)	(6)	(7)	(8)
		I		II	III	I over II	I over III
Year	Capital Outlays*	Cash Income	Net Cash Flow	Net Cash Flow	Net Cash Flow	Net Cash Flow	Net Cash Flow
0	$ (2,000)	—	$ (2,000)	$ 4,000	–0–	$ (6,000)	$ (2,000)
1	(4,000)	$ 1,000	(3,000)	3,000	–0–	(6,000)	(3,000)
2	(10,000)	9,000	(1,000)	2,000	–0–	(3,000)	(1,000)
3	(29,000)	30,000	1,000	2,000	–0–	(1,000)	1,000
4	(25,000)	30,000	5,000	2,000	–0–	3,000	5,000
5	(25,000)	49,000	24,000	6,000	–0–	18,000	24,000
Total	$(95,000)	$119,000	$24,000	$19,000	–0–	$ 5,000	$24,000

Note: Alternative I—The company is to develop the land by constructing housing units on it and then sell the housing units at a profit.
   Alternative II—The company is to sell the undeveloped land to an outside land developer and share in the latter's land development profits.
   Alternative III—The company is to do nothing that is to say it is to hold onto the undeveloped land for future use or disposition.

* Capital outlays in parentheses.

TABLE 51

Alternative

	I	II	I over II
Cash income	$119,000	$19,000	$100,000
Cash outgo:			
Housing construction cost	(76,000)	—	(76,000)
Land value	(13,000)	—	(13,000)
Share of outside developer's profits	(6,000)	—	(6,000)
	(95,000)	—	(95,000)
Net cash income	24,000	19,000	5,000
Land value	13,000	13,000	—
Land development profit	$ 11,000	$ 6,000	$ 5,000

million, and zero, respectively. It also can be verified by a slight reconstruction of the net cash flows for Alternatives I and II as shown in Table 51.

As proven in Table 51, if the company had chosen Alternative II, it would have netted $19 million. This would have represented $13 million for the land and $6 million for its share of the outside developer's profits. By adopting Alternative II, the company would have limited its risk to $13 million. On the other hand, by adopting Alternative I, the company would have netted $24 million. However, in order to realize the additional $5 million profit during the five-year land development period, it would have had to invest an additional $76 million for the construction of the housing units. This would have increased the company's risk from $13 million to $89 million. Even if the company's top management hadn't realized or understood that this additional $5 million profit represented an unacceptable DCF rate of return of only 7.99 percent, it still could have deduced this simple truth from the information contained in Table 51—that this $5 million additional profit wasn't commensurate with the $76 million additional risk involved in Alternative II.

Chapter 13

Depreciation and Its Effect on the Profitability of Companies' Capital Investments

Depreciation is an important factor in the computation of the *DCF rate of return* and the *payout period*, which are the financial criteria most frequently used by companies in the decision-making process for the acceptance or the rejection of prospective projects. However, depreciation is an equally important factor in the computation of the *year-to-year book rate of return*, which is considered by many business executives to be the principal financial yardstick for assessing the efficient utilization of the total assets of companies.

What Depreciation Is

Webster's *New American Dictionary* defines depreciation as a "decline in value of machinery and other assets due to wear and tear, etc., a decrease in market value or purchasing power." In accounting, the annual depreciation provisions may be more precisely defined as the amounts required to amortize the net book value of fixed assets over their remaining useful lives. Inasmuch as the capital expenditures for fixed assets are incurred at the time of their acquisition and capitalized on the company's books at that time, the annual depreciation provisions, as included in the company's annual operating expenses, naturally are strictly noncash or bookkeeping transactions only.

How Many Depreciation Methods Are There?

Basically there are three different depreciation methods.[1] These include the straight-line method, the sum-of-the-years'-digits method, and the double-declining-balance method. Normally, the straight-line method is used by companies for book purposes, while the sum-of-the-years'-digits method and the double-declining-balance method are used for tax purposes. The latter two methods are commonly referred to as accelerated depreciation methods.

During periods of national emergency, such as during wartime when companies are expected to make huge capital expenditures to enable them to produce large quantities of war equipment and materials, the federal government usually accords companies a much faster write-off than the write-offs provided either under the sum-of-the-years'-digits method or the double-declining-balance method. This provision is intended to give companies immediate tax relief, and thereby provide the incentive as well as some of the necessary funds for these extraordinary large capital expenditures. However, since these special depreciation methods are relatively uncommon during normal times, they will be ignored and excluded from these discussions.

When the Accelerated Depreciation Methods May Be Used for Tax Purposes

The Internal Revenue Code of 1954 provides for the optional use of the sum-of-the-years'-digits method or the double-declining-balance method for properties, plants, and equipment acquired after December 31, 1953, provided that (1) the asset is tangible, (2) the asset has an estimated service life of three years or more, and (3) the original use of the asset began with the company after December 31, 1953.

If the double-declining-balance method is used, the Internal Revenue Code of 1954 further stipulates that the rate used under this method must not exceed twice the applicable rate used under the straight-line method. Furthermore, the adopting company must deduct an estimated salvage value from the gross investment cost before determining the depreciation rate to be used.

If the double-declining-balance method is used, the Internal Revenue Code of 1954 permits the company to switch to the straight-line method in the year in which the depreciation charge calculated on the remaining balance by the double-declining-balance method's depreciation rate is smaller than the depreciation charge calculated on the same remaining balance by the straight-line method's depreciation rate for the remaining years of the fixed asset's estimated useful life.

---

[1] To provide an incentive to induce companies to make capital investments, faster write-offs of capital assets have been provided by the Accelerated Cost Recovery System (ACRS) which was enacted into law in 1981. Since this accelerated depreciation method is applicable only to assets placed into service after 1982 and, moreover, like other accelerated capital recovery systems enacted during past wartime emergencies this one likewise is feared to be only a temporary expedient, it was not included in the discussion in this book.

How Annual Depreciation Charges Are Calculated

The procedure for calculating annual depreciation charges by the straight-line method, the sum-of-the-years'-digits method, and the double-declining-balance method are shown in Table 52.

Before annual depreciation charges can be calculated, these factors must first be estimated:

1. The fixed asset's depreciation base, which represents the cost to the company as it applies to properties, plants, and equipment. This cost includes such items as the fixed asset's invoice price, freight charges, import duties, installation costs, and other capitalized incidental expenditures.
2. The fixed asset's useful life in terms of the number of years during which it is expected to be productive. This estimate of its useful life during which the fixed asset's net cost will be depreciated, i.e., written off the books, must be submitted to, checked carefully, and then approved by the company's tax department. This is important because if the Internal Revenue Service should find the number of years estimated to represent the fixed asset's useful life unacceptable, this could adversely affect the annual depreciation charges, the operating expenses, the income tax liabilities, the book profits, the cash returns, and, consequently, the DCF rate of return, the payout period, and the year-to-year book rates of return projected for the newly acquired fixed asset.
3. The amount allowed to be depreciated during the fixed asset's estimated useful life represents the gross investment cost, including the various above-mentioned items, minus the estimated salvage value at the end of the fixed asset's useful life. For the purpose of simplification, salvage values at the end of depreciable fixed assets' estimated useful lives have been omitted from the example in all subsequent tables dealing with depreciation. In other words, it has been assumed that the fixed assets in all these examples were completely used up during their estimated useful lives and consequently they had no salvage or residual values.
4. When it is assumed that the fixed asset's estimated useful life is 20 years and that there is no salvage value at the end of the fixed asset's 20th year, the fixed asset's annual depreciation rates under the three different depreciation methods are arrived at as follows: *(a)* Under the straight-line method, the annual depreciation rate is 100 percent divided by the fixed asset's 20-year estimated useful life, which in this example is 100 percent divided by 20 years, or 5 percent per year. *(b)* Under the sum-of-the-years'-digits method, the annual depreciation rates are a series of changing fractions of which the numerator of these fractions changes each year to a number corresponding to the remaining useful life of the fixed asset, and the denominator, which remains

constant, is the sum of all the years' digits corresponding to the estimated useful life of the fixed asset. For example, when the estimated useful life of the fixed asset is 20 years, the constant denominator is $1 + 2 + 3 + 4 + 5 + \cdots + 20$ years, which is equal to a sum of 210. Consequently, the fraction or annual depreciation rate for the first year is 20/210; for the second year, 19/210; for the third year, 18/210; and for the 20th year, 1/210. To simplify the calculation of annual depreciation charges under this depreciation method, the fractions frequently are converted to decimals, which for easy reference are arranged in a table horizontally across the page by fixed assets' useful life spans and vertically down the page by individual years. For example, for fixed assets having a 20-year useful life, the annual depreciation rates, expressed in decimals, are .0952 for the first year, .0905 for the second year, .0857 for the third year, and .0048 for the 20th year. *(c)* Under the double-declining-balance method, the annual depreciation rate cannot exceed twice the depreciation rate under the straight-line method. Therefore, in the above example in which the fixed asset is assumed to have an estimated useful life of 20 years, the annual depreciation rate is 10 percent, or twice the 5 percent rate under the straight-line method. This 10 percent annual depreciation rate prevails until the 12th year, when the annual depreciation charge calculated by the double-declining-balance method is smaller than the annual depreciation charge calculated by the straight-line method on the remaining balance at the end of the 11th year. Hence, during the 12th year, the company is permitted to change from the double-declining-balance method to the straight-line method so that the annual depreciation rate becomes one ninth of the remaining balance at the end of the 11th year for each year of the remaining 9 years of the fixed asset's estimated useful life.

After the above factors have been determined, the fixed asset's annual depreciation charges can now be calculated as shown in Table 52, Columns 1 to 8.

Under the straight-line method, the constant-level 5 percent annual depreciation rate is multiplied by the fixed asset's $10,000 original cost to arrive at the $500 constant-level annual depreciation charges during the fixed asset's 20-year estimated useful life.

Under the sum-of-the-years'-digits method, the annual depreciation rates varying from 20/210, or .0952, in the first year to 1/210 or .0048, in the 20th year are multiplied by the fixed asset's $10,000 original cost to arrive at the annual depreciation charges ranging from $952 in the 1st year to $48 in the 20th year.

Under the double-declining-balance method, the constant-level 10 percent annual depreciation rate is multiplied by the individual year's declining balance until the 12th year when the $314 annual depreciation charge calculated by this method on the $3,138 remaining balance at the end of the 11th

TABLE 52

Procedures for Calculating Annual Depreciation Charges by Straight-Line, Sum-of-the-Years'-Digits, and Double-Declining-Balance Methods—Showing that Sum-of-the-Years'-Digits Method is More Advantageous for Income Tax Purposes than Other Two Depreciation Methods for Long-Life Fixed Assets

	(1)	(2)	(3)	(4)	(5)	(6)	(7)	(8)	(9)	(10)	(11)	(12)
										Present Value of Depreciation Based on Company's 15% Opportunity Cost of Money Rate		
		Straight-Line Depreciation		Sum-of-the-Years'-Digits Depreciation		Double-Declining-Balance Depreciation				Depreciation		
Year	Fixed Assets Original Cost	Rate	Amount	Rate	Amount	Rate*	Double-Declining Balance	Amount	Present Value Factor at 15%	Straight Line	Sum-of-the-Years' Digits	Double-Declining Balance
0	$10,000	—				—	$10,000		—			
1	—	5%	$ 500	.0952	$ 952	10%	9,000	$ 1,000	.8696	$ 435	$ 828	$ 870
2	—	5	500	.0905	905	10	8,100	900	.7561	378	684	680
3	—	5	500	.0857	857	10	7,290	810	.6575	329	563	533
4	—	5	500	.0810	810	10	6,561	729	.5718	286	463	417
5	—	5	500	.0762	762	10	5,905	656	.4972	249	379	326
6	—	5	500	.0714	714	10	5,314	591	.4323	216	309	255
7	—	5	500	.0667	667	10	4,783	531	.3759	188	251	200
8	—	5	500	.0619	619	10	4,305	478	.3269	163	202	156
9	—	5	500	.0571	571	10	3,874	431	.2843	142	162	126
10	—	5	500	.0524	524	10	3,487	387	.2472	124	130	96
11	—	5	500	.0476	476	10	3,138	349	.2149	107	102	75
12	—	5	500	.0429	429	(3138/9)	2,789	349	.1869	93	80	65
13	—	5	500	.0381	381	(3138/9)	2,440	349	.1625	81	62	57
14	—	5	500	.0333	333	(3138/9)	2,091	349	.1413	71	47	49
15	—	5	500	.0286	286	(3138/9)	1,742	349	.1229	61	35	43
16	—	5	500	.0238	238	(3138/9)	1,393	349	.1069	53	25	37
17	—	5	500	.0190	190	(3138/9)	1,044	349	.0929	46	18	32
18	—	5	500	.0143	143	(3138/9)	696	348	.0808	40	12	28
19	—	5	500	.0095	95	(3138/9)	348	348	.0703	35	7	24
20	—	5	500	.0048	48	(3138/9)	0	348	.0611	31	3	21
Total	$10,000	100%	$10,000	1.0000	$10,000			$10,000		$3,128	$4,362	$4,090

First 10 years' depreciation charges .... $5,000 (3); $ 7,381 (5); $ 6,513 (8)

In percent of total 20 years' depreciation charges...... 50.0%; 73.8%; 65.1%

Present value of first 10 years' depreciation charges discounted at the company's 15 percent opportunity cost of money rate $2,510 (10); $3,971 (11); $3,659 (12)

In percent of total present value of 20 years' depreciation charges........... 80.2%; 91.0%; 89.5%

* Switching from the double-declining-balance method to the straight-line method in year 12.

year is smaller than the $349 annual depreciation charge calculated on the $3,138 remaining balance at the end of that year by the straight-line method. It is during this 12th year that the company is permitted to switch from the double-declining-balance method to the straight-line method for the remaining nine years of the fixed asset's useful life. Consequently, starting with the 12th year, the $3,138 remaining balance at the end of the 11th year is depreciated at an annual rate of one ninth, which amounts to an approximate annual depreciation charge of $349 for the remaining 9 years of the fixed asset's 20 years estimated useful life.

What the Differences in the Timing of Depreciation Charges Indicate

In addition to illustrating how the annual depreciation charges are calculated by the three different depreciation methods, Table 52 also shows that of the fixed asset's total depreciation charges, $5,000 or 50 percent, $7,381 or 73.8 percent, and $6,531 or 65.3 percent occur during the first half of its 20-year useful life under the straight-line method, the sum-of-the-years'-digits method, and the double-declining-balance method, respectively.

Since the largest amount, $7,381, and the highest percentage, 73.8 percent, of the total depreciation charges that will occur during the first half of the fixed asset's 20-year estimated useful life are arrived at by the sum-of-the-years'-digits method, this is the most advantageous depreciation method to use for income tax purposes for long-life fixed assets. The reason for this, of course, is simple. This accelerated depreciation method has the effect of minimizing the company's income tax liability and, consequently, maximizing its cash returns during the early years of long-life fixed assets' estimated useful lives, and thereby enhancing the profitability of these assets. This is accentuated by the fact that when the fixed asset's annual depreciation charges arrived at by the three different depreciation methods are discounted at the company's 15 percent opportunity cost of money rate, the largest present value amount, $3,971, and the highest percentage, 91.0 percent, of the depreciation charges that will occur during the first half of the fixed asset's 20-year estimated useful life, are also those arrived at by the sum-of-the-years'-digits method.

The example in Table 53 is similar to that in Table 52, except that the $10,000 fixed asset in this case is presumed to have an estimated 4-year instead of an estimated 20-year useful life. In this example, the largest amount, $7,250, and the highest percentage, 72.5 percent, of the depreciation charges that will occur during the first half of the fixed asset's estimated four-year useful life are arrived at by the double-declining-balance method and not by the sum-of-the-years'-digits method. This proves that the double-declining-balance method is the more advantageous depreciation method to use for income tax purposes for short-life fixed assets. This fact also can be accentuated by discounting the annual depreciation charges calculated by the three depreciation methods at the company's 15 percent opportunity cost of money rate. This procedure proves that the largest amount, $6,238, and the highest

TABLE 53

Comparison of Annual Depreciation Charges Showing that Double-Declining-Balance Method Is More Advantageous for Income Tax Purposes for Short-Life Depreciable Assets than Other Two Depreciation Methods

	(1)	(2)	(3)	(4)	(5)	(6)	(7)	(8)	(9)	(10)	(11)	(12)
										Present Value of Depreciation Based on Company's 15% Opportunity Cost of Money Rate		
	Fixed Assets	Straight-Line Depreciation		Sum-of-the-Years'-Digits Depreciation		Double-Declining-Balance Depreciation			Present Value Factor at 15%	Depreciation		
Year	Original Cost	Rate	Amount	Rate	Amount	Rate*	Double-Declining Balance*	Amount		Straight Line	Sum-of-the-Years' Digits	Double-Declining Balance
0	$10,000	—	—				$10,000		—	—	—	—
1		25%	$ 2,500	.40	$ 4,000	50%	5,000	$ 5,000	.8696	$2,174	$3,478	$4,348
2		25	2,500	.30	3,000	50	2,500	2,500	.7561	1,890	2,268	1,890
3		25	2,500	.20	2,000	50	1,250	1,250	.6575	1,644	1,315	822
4		25	2,500	.10	1,000	S/L	0	1,250	.5718	1,430	572	715
Total	$10,000	100%	$10,000	1.00	$10,000			$10,000		$7,138	$7,633	$7,775

First two years' depreciation charges . . . . $ 5,000 $ 7,000 $ 7,250

In percent of total four years depreciation charges 50.0% 70.0% 72.5%

Present value of first two years' depreciation charges discounted at the company's 15% opportunity cost of money rate. $4,064 $5,746 $6,238

In percent of total present value of four years' depreciation charges 56.9% 75.3% 80.2%

* Switching from the double-declining-balance method to the straight-line method in year 4.

percentage, 80.2 percent, of the present value of the depreciation charges that will occur during the first half of the fixed asset's four-year estimated useful life are also arrived at by the double-declining-balance method and not by the sum-of-the-years'-digits method.

Proof Sum-of-the-Years'-Digits Method Is More Advantageous than Straight-Line Method for Income Tax Purposes

Comparisons of the financial criteria and the cash flows in Tables 54, 55, and 56 show that (*a*) the sum-of-the-years'-digits method is more advantageous to use for income tax purposes for long-life fixed assets than the straight-line method; (*b*) the difference in the timing of the annual cash income amounts after income taxes in tables 54 and 55 is solely due to the difference in the timing of the annual depreciation charges calculated by these two depreciation methods; and (*c*) the economic advantage of using the sum-of-the-years'-digits method for income tax purposes for long-life fixed assets is actually much greater than is indicated by the seemingly nominal 1 percent difference in the DCF rates of return and the six tenths of a year difference in the payout periods, as proven in Table 56.

The examples in Tables 54, 55, and 56 are predicated on these assumptions:

1. The cash outlay, or capital expenditure, for Project C's long-life fixed asset is $10,000.
2. The constant-level annual cash income amount after income taxes generated by Project C's fixed asset during its estimated useful life is $1,598.
3. The estimated useful life of Project C's fixed asset is 20 years.
4. The salvage, or residual, value at the end of the fixed asset's estimated 20-year life is zero, as it is expected to be completely used up and therefore is deemed to be worthless at that point in time.
5. The sum-of-the-years'-digits method is used for income tax purposes in Table 54, while the straight-line method is used for income tax purposes in Table 55.
6. The company's opportunity cost of money, or minimum acceptable DCF earnings rate, is 15 percent.

To determine the stream of annual cash income amounts before income taxes in Table 54, which is required to be generated in order to earn a 15 percent DCF rate of return after income taxes on the $10,000 capital investment in Project C's fixed asset, it is necessary to work backwards in the following manner:

1. The constant-level annual cash income amount after income taxes in Column 9 is determined by dividing the $10,000 original cost of Project C's fixed asset by 6.259, which represents the total present value factors

of $1 at the 15 percent rate for the fixed asset's 20-year estimated useful life. The resultant $1,598 represents the constant-level annual cash income amount after income taxes.

2. The annual depreciation charges for income tax purposes in Columns 4 are determined by multiplying the fixed asset's $10,000 original cost by the annual depreciation rates of the sum-of-the-years'-digits method in Column 3. The resultant annual depreciation charges range from $952 in the 1st year to $48 in the 20th year.

3. The annual profit amounts after depreciation and income taxes in Column 7 are determined by subtracting the annual depreciation charges in Column 8 from the annual cash income amounts after income taxes in Column 9. The resultant annual profit amounts after depreciation and income taxes range from $646 in the 1st year to $1,550 in the 20th year.

4. The annual income tax amounts in Column 6 are determined by multiplying the annual profit amounts after depreciation and income taxes by 48/52. The resultant annual income tax amounts range from $596 in the 1st year to $1,432 in the 20th year. The numerator of the fraction represents the company's 48 percent income tax rate, while the denominator represents 52 percent of the taxable income.

5. The annual taxable income amounts in Column 5 are determined by adding the annual income tax amounts in Column 6 back to the annual profit amounts after depreciation and income taxes in Column 7. The resultant annual taxable income amounts range from $1,242 in the 1st year to $2,982 in the 20th year.

6. The stream of annual cash income amounts before income taxes in Column 2 is determined by adding the annual depreciation charges in Column 4 back to the taxable income amounts in Column 5. The resultant annual cash income amounts before income taxes range from $2,194 in the 1st year to $3,030 in the 20th year.

When the stream of cash income amounts after income taxes, totaling $31,960 in Column 9, is discounted at the 15 percent rate, it discounts down to a total present value equal to the $10,000 cash outlay amount for Project C's fixed asset, and thus cancels out to zero at the zero reference point. As explained previously, this proves that Project C's DCF rate of return is 15 percent when the sum-of-the-years'-digits method is used for income tax purposes. Table 54 also shows that its payout period is 6.3 years when this depreciation method is used for income tax purposes.

The economic evaluation for the $10,000 capital investment in Project C's fixed asset shown in Table 55 is similar to that shown in Table 54 except that for income tax purposes the annual depreciation charges in Table 55 are calculated by the straight-line method instead of the sum-of-the-years'-digits method. This switch in depreciation methods for income tax purposes results in a change in the timing of Project C's cash income amounts after income taxes in Column 7, which now range from $1,381 in the 1st year to $1,815 in

TABLE 54

Proof that Sum-of-the-Years'-Digits Method is More Advantageous for Income Tax Purposes for Long-Life Assets—Project C's DCF Rate of Return is 15.0 Percent and Its Payout Period Is 6.3 Years

	(1)	(2)	(3)	(4)	(5)	(6)	(7)	(8)	(9)	(10)	(11)
		Cash Income before Income Taxes	Sum-of-the-Years'-Digits Depreciation		Taxable Income	Income Taxes	Profit after Depreciation and Income Taxes	Depreciation	Cash Outlay* and Cash Income after Income Taxes	Present Value	
Year	Cash Outlay*		Rate	Amount						Factor at 15%	Amount
0	$(10,000)	—	—		—	—			$(10,000)	1.0000	$(10,000)
1		$ 2,194	.0952	$ 952	$ 1,242	$ 596	$ 646	$ 952	1,598	.8696	1,390
2		2,238	.0905	905	1,333	640	693	905	1,598	.7561	1,208
3		2,282	.0857	857	1,425	684	741	857	1,598	.6575	1,051
4		2,325	.0810	810	1,515	727	788	810	1,598	.5718	914
5		2,370	.0762	762	1,608	772	836	762	1,598	.4972	795
6		2,414	.0714	714	1,700	816	884	714	1,598	.4323	691
7		2,457	.0667	667	1,790	859	931	667	1,598	.3759	601
8		2,502	.0619	619	1,883	904	979	619	1,598	.3269	522
9		2,546	.0571	571	1,975	948	1,027	571	1,598	.2843	454
10		2,589	.0524	524	2,065	991	1,074	524	1,598	.2472	395
11		2,634	.0476	476	2,158	1,036	1,122	476	1,598	.2149	343
12		2,677	.0429	429	2,248	1,079	1,169	429	1,598	.1869	299
13		2,721	.0381	381	2,340	1,123	1,217	381	1,598	.1625	260
14		2,766	.0333	333	2,433	1,168	1,265	333	1,598	.1413	226
15		2,809	.0286	286	2,523	1,211	1,312	286	1,598	.1229	196
16		2,853	.0238	238	2,615	1,255	1,360	238	1,598	.1069	171
17		2,898	.0190	190	2,708	1,300	1,408	190	1,598	.0929	148
18		2,941	.0143	143	2,798	1,343	1,455	143	1,598	.0808	129
19		2,985	.0095	95	2,890	1,387	1,503	95	1,598	.0703	112
20		3,030	.0048	48	2,982	1,432	1,550	48	1,598	.0611	95
Total	$(10,000)	$52,231	1.0000	$10,000	$42,231	$20,271	$21,960	$10,000	$ 21,960		$ —0—

DCF rate of return is 15.0%.
Pay period is 6.3 years.

* Cash outlay in parentheses.

TABLE 55

Proof that Straight-Line Method Less Advantageous for Tax Purposes for Long-Life Fixed Assets than Sum-of-the-Years'-Digits Method—Project C's DCF Rate of Return Is Only 14 Percent and Its Payout Period Is 6.9 Years

	(1)	(2)	(3)	(4)	(5)	(6)	(7)	(8)	(9)	(10)	(11)
									Present Value		
Year	Cash Outlay*	Cash Income before Income Taxes	Straight-Line Depreciation Charges	Taxable Income	Income Taxes	Profit after Depreciation and Income Taxes	Cash Outlay* and Cash Income after taxes	Factor at 14%	Amount	Factor at 13%	Amount
0	$(10,000)	—	—	—	—	—	$(10,000)	—	($10,000)	1.0000	$(10,000)
1		$ 2,194	$ 500	$ 1,694	$ 813	$ 881	1,381	.8772	1,211	.8850	1,222
2		2,238	500	1,738	834	904	1,404	.7695	1,080	.7831	1,099
3		2,282	500	1,782	855	927	1,427	.6750	963	.6930	989
4		2,325	500	1,825	876	949	1,449	.5921	858	.6133	887
5		2,370	500	1,870	898	972	1,472	.5194	765	.5428	799
6		2,414	500	1,914	919	993	1,495	.4556	681	.4803	718
7		2,457	500	1,957	939	1,018	1,518	.3996	607	.4251	645
8		2,502	500	2,002	961	1,041	1,541	.3506	540	.3762	580
9		2,546	500	2,046	982	1,064	1,564	.3075	481	.3329	521
10		2,589	500	2,089	1,003	1,086	1,586	.2697	428	.2946	467
11		2,634	500	2,134	1,024	1,110	1,610	.2366	381	.2607	420
12		2,677	500	2,177	1,045	1,132	1,632	.2076	339	.2307	377
13		2,721	500	2,221	1,066	1,155	1,655	.1821	301	.2042	338
14		2,766	500	2,266	1,088	1,178	1,678	.1597	268	.1807	303
15		2,809	500	2,309	1,108	1,201	1,701	.1401	238	.1599	272
16		2,853	500	2,353	1,129	1,224	1,724	.1229	212	.1415	244
17		2,898	500	2,398	1,151	1,247	1,747	.1078	188	.1252	219
18		2,941	500	2,441	1,172	1,269	1,769	.0946	167	.1108	196
19		2,985	500	2,485	1,193	1,292	1,792	.0829	149	.0981	176
20		3,030	500	2,530	1,215	1,316	1,815	.0728	132	.0868	158
Total	$(10,000)	$52,231	$10,000	$42,231	$20,271	$21,961	$ 21,960		$ (11)		$ (630)

DCF rate of return is 14.0%.
Payout period is 6.9 years.

* Cash outlay in parentheses.

the 20th year. Obviously, when the straight-line method is used for income tax purposes, Project C's annual cash income amounts after income taxes are returned slower during the first half and faster during the second half of the fixed asset's 20-year estimated useful life than when the sum-of-the-years'-digits method is used for income tax purposes. This change in the timing of the annual cash income amounts after income taxes has the effect of reducing Project C's DCF rate of return from 15.0 percent to 14.0 percent and increasing its payout period from 6.3 years to 6.9 years. This proves that it is less advantageous to use the straight-line method than the sum-of-the-years'-digits method for income tax purposes for long-life fixed assets.

Table 56 serves a twofold purpose: (1) to prove that when the straight-line method instead of the sum-of-the-years'-digits method is used for income tax purposes for long-life fixed assets, the 1 percent difference in Project C's DCF rate of return and the six tenths of one year's difference in its payout period is attributable solely to the difference in the timing of the annual depreciation charges calculated under these two depreciation methods; and (2) to prove that using the sum-of-the-years'-digits method instead of the straight-line method for income tax purposes for long-life fixed assets is decidedly more advantageous economically than is indicated by the DCF rates of return and payout periods arrived at for Project C in Tables 54 and 55. This is proven in Table 56 which shows that *(a)* the annual income tax savings or (losses) based on the differences in the annual depreciation charges, *(b)* the differences in the annual income tax amounts, and *(c)* the differences in the annual cash income amounts after taxes are all identical—ranging from $217 in the 1st year to ($216) in the 20th year—when the sum-of-the-years'-digits method as opposed to the straight-line method is used for income tax purposes. Thus, the difference in Project C's DCF rate of return and its payout period is attributable solely to the different depreciation methods used for income tax purposes in Tables 54 and 55.

Project C's 15.0 percent DCF rate of return when the sum-of-the-years'-digits method is used for income tax purposes compared to its 14.0 percent DCF rate of return when the straight-line method is used is somewhat deceptive insofar as this 1 percent difference in these two rates of return does not present a fair picture of the real economic advantage of using the sum-of-the-years'-digits method for income tax purposes. On the surface, this 1 percent does not appear to be a significant difference in Project C's DCF rate of return. However, when it is recognized that the company would be disinclined to let money lay idle in its cash drawers for any prolonged period of time but rather that it would be inclined to put the money to work and generate additional cash income during the remaining years of Project C's estimated economic life, a more accurate picture will be obtained of the economic advantage of the more favorable timing of Project C's annual depreciation charges as a result of using the sum-of-the-years'-digits method for income tax purposes.

This is shown in Table 56, Columns 10 to 13, which show that when the annual increases or (decreases) in Project C's annual cash income amounts

Analysis Showing that $9,678 or 44.1 Percent Additional Profits May Be Generated at Company's 15 Percent Opportunity Cost of Money Rate in Other Ventures by Using Sum-of-the-Years'-Digits Method Instead of Straight-Line Method in Project C

	(1)	(2)	(3)	(4)	(5)	(6)	(7)
	Depreciation				**Income Taxes Based on**		
Year	Straight-Line Depreciation	Sum-of-the-Years'-Digits Depreciation	Over or Under*	Income Tax Savings or Losses*	Straight-Line Depreciation	Sum-of-the-Years'-Digits Depreciation	Over or Under*
1	$ 500	$ 952	$ 452	$ 217	$ 813	$ 596	$ 217
2	500	905	405	195	835	640	195
3	500	857	357	171	855	684	171
4	500	810	310	149	876	727	149
5	500	762	262	126	898	772	126
6	500	714	214	102	918	816	102
7	500	667	167	80	939	859	80
8	500	619	119	57	961	904	57
9	500	571	71	34	982	948	34
10	500	524	24	11	1,003	991	11
11	500	476	(24)	(11)	1,025	1,036	(11)
12	500	429	(71)	(34)	1,045	1,079	(34)
13	500	381	(119)	(57)	1,066	1,123	(57)
14	500	333	(167)	(80)	1,088	1,168	(80)
15	500	286	(214)	(103)	1,108	1,211	(103)
16	500	238	(262)	(126)	1,129	1,255	(126)
17	500	190	(310)	(149)	1,151	1,300	(149)
18	500	143	(357)	(172)	1,171	1,343	(172)
19	500	95	(405)	(194)	1,193	1,387	(194)
20	500	48	(452)	(216)	1,215	1,432	(216)
Total	$10,000	$10,000	$ –0–	$ –0–	$20,271	$20,271	$ –0–

	Summary Based on			
	Straight-Line Depreciation		Sum-of-the-Year's-Digits Depreciation	
	Amount	Percent	Amount	Percent
Cash income after taxes	$31,960	—	$31,960	—
Less: Cash outlay for Project C	10,000		10,000	
Total profit from Project C	21,960	100.0	21,960	100.0
Additional profits after taxes			9,678	44.1
Total profit	$21,960	100.00	$31,638	144.1

* Figures in parentheses.

after taxes are compounded at the company's 15 percent opportunity cost of money or minimum acceptable DCF earnings rate for the remaining years of the fixed asset's 20-year estimated useful life, an additional $9,678 cash income or profit will be generated. This represents a 44.1 percent increase over Project C's $21,970 total profit, which is made possible solely due to the more

TABLE 56

(8)	(9)	(10)	(11)	(12)	(13)
Cash Income after Taxes			Additional Cash Income Due to Timing of Depreciation Charges		
Based on Straight-Line Depreciation	Based on Sum-of-the-Years'-Digits Depreciation	Over or Under*	Number of Years Compounded	Compound Factor at 15%	Amount
$ 1,381	$ 1,598	$ 217	19	14.232	$3,088
1,404	1,598	194	18	12.375	2.401
1,427	1,598	171	17	10.761	1.840
1,449	1,598	149	16	9.358	1,394
1,472	1,598	126	15	8.137	1,025
1,495	1,598	103	14	7.076	729
1,518	1,598	80	13	6.153	492
1,541	1,598	57	12	5.350	305
1,564	1,598	34	11	4.652	158
1,586	1,598	12	10	4.046	49
1,610	1,598	(12)	9	3.518	(42)
1,632	1,598	(34)	8	3.059	(104)
1,655	1,598	(57)	7	2.660	(152)
1,678	1,598	(80)	6	2.313	(185)
1,701	1,598	(103)	5	2.011	(207)
1,724	1,598	(126)	4	1.749	(220)
1,747	1,598	(149)	3	1.521	(227)
1,769	1,598	(171)	2	1.322	(226)
1,792	1,598	(194)	1	1.150	(223)
1,815	1,598	(217)	0	1.000	(217)
$31,960	$31,960	$ –0–			$9,678

favorable timing of its depreciation charges when the sum-of-the-years'-digits method is used for income tax purposes. This proves that the 1 percent higher DCF rate of return when the sum-of-the-years'-digits method is used compared to Project C's 14 percent DCF rate of return when the straight-line method is used for income tax purposes is quite deceptive and therefore fails to tell the full story. What on the surface may appear to be a somewhat insignificant economic advantage in view of the nominal 1 percent higher DCF rate of return when the sum-of-the-years'-digits method is used for income tax purposes, actually proves to be a far more significant advantage when it is realized that as a result of the funds made available for re-investment due to the more favorable timing of Project C's depreciation charges, its total profit may be increased as much as 44.1 percent.

How lucrative an economic advantage the use of the sum-of-the-years'-digits method for income tax purposes is to multinational companies may be envisioned when we bear in mind that their capital investments in plants, equipment, machinery, etc., normally amount to billions of dollars. Consequently, the additional profits these multinational companies may be able to generate because of the more favorable timing of their annual depreciation charges through the use of the above-mentioned accelerated depreciation method for income tax purposes could well amount to hundreds of millions of dollars during the companies' depreciable fixed assets' serviceable lives.

Why the Straight-Line Method Is Normally Used for Book Purposes

Before illustrating why the straight-line method is normally used for book purposes, it may be helpful to reiterate this point why the DCF rate of return and the year-to-year book rate of return are incompatible. (1) The DCF rate of return is a constant-level earnings rate during the fixed asset's useful life, while the year-to-year book rate of return is a variable earnings rate that normally increases from year to year during the fixed asset's useful life. (2) This incompatibility of these two rates of return is attributable principally to the fact that under the DCF method, the annual profit amount is calculated first at the predetermined constant-level DCF earnings rate on the unrecovered portion of the fixed asset's original cost, and the remainder of the fixed asset's annual cash income amount constitutes the annual amortization or depreciation amount. Contrariwise, under the book method, the annual depreciation or amortization amount is calculated first at a predetermined depreciation or amortization rate, depending upon the depreciation method used for book purposes, and the remainder of the fixed asset's annual cash income amount constitutes the annual profit amount. This amount is then used as the basis for calculating the fixed asset's year-to-year book rate of return on the unrecovered portion of its original cost, i.e., on its depreciated book value. This procedure, generally, tends to increase the fixed asset's year-to-year book rate of return progressively during its useful life.

Year-to-year book rates of return are calculated variously by companies either on their total assets (*a*) at the beginning of the year, (*b*) at the end of the year, or (*c*) averaged during the year. The average total assets investment base is arrived at by averaging the company's total assets carried on its books at the beginning and at the end of the year. If a nationwide survey were taken, in all likelihood it would reveal that by far the most common practice used by companies for calculating their year-to-year book rates of return is based on the average total assets employed during the year in the conduct of their business.

Table 57 serves a twofold purpose. First, it shows that under the book method, the $500 annual depreciation or amortization amounts are calculated first at the predetermined 5 percent depreciation or amortization rate on the fixed asset's $10,000 original cost in accordance with the straight-line method, and the remainder of the fixed asset's $1,598 annual cash income amounts after income taxes constitutes its $1,098 annual profit amounts. These annual profit amounts form the bases for calculating the company's year-to-year book rates of return during the fixed asset's useful life. Second, it shows that the fixed asset's year-to-year book rates of return range from 11.3 percent in the 1st year to 439.2 percent in the 20th year and from 6.8 percent in the 1st year to 6,458.3 percent in the 20th year when the sum-of-the-years'-digits method is used for income tax purposes in both series but the straight-line method is used for book purposes in the first series, while the sum-of-the-years'-digits method is used for book purposes in the second series.

These two series of year-to-year book rates of return for Project C's fixed asset are not only widely divergent as a result of the two different depreciation methods used for book purposes but even more important, they are unrealistic, illusory, and misleading compared to the 15 percent DCF rate of return which, incontrovertibly, represents the true and realistic rate of return for Project C's fixed asset, as shown in Tables 54 and 59.

Obviously, the straight-line method is the most widely accepted depreciation method used for book purposes because it produces year-to-year book rates of return that are less unrealistic and distorted than those arrived at when the sum-of-the-years'-digits method is used for book purposes.

The examples in Table 58 show comparisons of three different series of year-to-year book rates of return for Project C's fixed asset when the sum-of-the-years'-digits method is used for income tax purposes and the straight-line method, the sum-of-the years'-digits method, or the discounted cash flow method are used for book purposes. In order to make these three series of year-to-year book rates of return comparable, it is necessary to calculate them on the fixed asset's depreciated book value, or amortized investment balance, at the beginning of the year. The year-to-year book rates of return for Project C's fixed asset range from 11.0 percent in the 1st year to 219.6 percent in the 20th year when the straight-line method is used for book purposes; from 6.5 percent in the first year to 3,229.2 percent in the 20th year when the sum-of-the-years'-digits method is used for book purposes; and they are a constant-level 15 percent when the discounted cash flow method is used for book purposes.

On its far right side, Table 58 also shows the annual depreciation or amortization amounts. They are a constant-level $500 when the straight-line method is used for book purposes, and they range from $952 in the 1st year to $48 in the 20th year when the sum-of-the-years'-digits method is used for book purposes, and from $98 in the 1st year to $1,349 in the 20th year when the discounted cash flow method is used for book purposes. These annual

Comparison of Project C's Year-to-Year Book Rates of Return Calculated on Depreciated Book Value Averaged during Year When Sum-of-the-Years'-Digits Method Is Used for Tax Purposes and Straight-Line Method or Sum-of-the-Years'-Digits Method Is Used for Book Purposes

	(1)	(2)	(3)	(4)	(5)	(6)
	Original Cost and Depreciated Book Value Averaged during Year Based on				*Profit after Depreciation*	
Year	*Straight-Line Depreciation*	*Sum-of-the-Years'-Digits Depreciation*	*Cash Income before Income Taxes*	*Straight-Line Depreciation*	*but before Income Taxes*	*Income Taxes*
0	$10,000	$10,000				
1	9,750	9,524	$ 2,194	$ 500	$ 1,694	$ 596
2	9,250	8,596	2,238	500	1,738	640
3	8,750	7,715	2,282	500	1,782	684
4	8,250	6,881	2,325	500	1,825	727
5	7,750	6,095	2,370	500	1,870	772
6	7,250	5,357	2,414	500	1,914	816
7	6,750	4,667	2,457	500	1,957	859
8	6,250	4,024	2,502	500	2,002	904
9	5,750	3,429	2,546	500	2,046	948
10	5,250	2,881	2,589	500	2,089	991
11	4,750	2,381	2,634	500	2,134	1,036
12	4,250	1,929	2,677	500	2,177	1,079
13	3,750	1,524	2,721	500	2,221	1,123
14	3,250	1,167	2,766	500	2,266	1,168
15	2,750	857	2,809	500	2,309	1,211
16	2,250	595	2,853	500	2,353	1,255
17	1,750	381	2,898	500	2,398	1,300
18	1,250	215	2,941	500	2,441	1,343
19	750	96	2,985	500	2,485	1,387
20	250	24	3,030	500	2,530	1,432
Total			$52,231	$10,000	$42,231	$20,271

depreciation or amortization amounts, of course, affect both the annual profit amounts as well as the annual investment bases; hence, the wide differences in the three series of year-to-year-book rates of return for Project C's fixed asset when the three different depreciation or amortization methods are used for book purposes.

It should be noted that the annual profit amounts after income taxes are a constant-level $1,098 when the straight-line method is used for book purposes, and they range from $646 in the 1st year to $1,550 in the 20th year when the sum-of-the-years'-digits method is used for book purposes, and from $1,500 in the first year to $249 in the 20th year when the discounted cash flow method is used for book purposes. It should also be noted that when the respective annual depreciation or amortization amounts are added to the annual after-tax profit amounts under these different depreciation or amortization methods, the annual after-tax cash income amounts to a constant-level

TABLE 57

(7)	(8)	(9)	(10)	(11)	(12)
Based on Straight-Line Depreciation		**Based on Sum-of-the-Years'-Digits Depreciation**		**Reserve for Depreciation Based on**	
Book Net Income	Year-to-Year Book Rate of Return	Book Net Income	Year-to-Year Book Rate of Return	Straight-Line Depreciation	Sum-of-the-Years'-Digits Depreciation
$ 1,098	11.3%	$ 646	6.8%	$ 500	$ 952
1,098	11.9	693	8.1	1,000	1,857
1,098	12.5	741	9.6	1,500	2,714
1,098	13.3	788	11.5	2,000	3,524
1,098	14.2	836	13.7	2,500	4,286
1,098	15.1	884	16.5	3,000	5,000
1,098	16.3	931	19.9	3,500	5,667
1,098	17.6	979	24.3	4,000	6,286
1,098	19.1	1,027	30.0	4,500	6,857
1,098	20.9	1,047	36.3	5,000	7,381
1,098	23.1	1,122	47.1	5,500	7,857
1,098	25.8	1,169	60.6	6,000	8,286
1,098	29.3	1,217	79.9	6,500	8,667
1,098	33.8	1,265	108.4	7,000	9,000
1,098	39.9	1,312	153.1	7,500	9,286
1,098	48.8	1,360	228.6	8,000	9,524
1,098	62.7	1,408	369.6	8,500	9,714
1,098	87.8	1,455	676.7	9,000	9,857
1,098	146.4	1,503	1,565.6	9,500	9,952
1,098	439.2	1,550	6,458.3	10,000	10,000
$21,960		$21,960			

$1,598 in each case. As shown in Table 54, it is on this stream of annual cash income amounts that the 15 percent DCF rate of return for Project C's $10,000 fixed asset is obtained by the DCF method. As shown further in Table 58, this 15 percent DCF rate of return represents the true and realistic constant-level year-to-year-book rate of return for Project C's $10,000 fixed asset, which is neither comparable to nor compatible with the year-to-year book rates of return arrived at under the straight-line method and the sum-of-the-years'-digits method when they are used for book purposes.

As shown in Table 57, under the most widely accepted book method, the annual depreciation amount is calculated first at the predetermined depreciation rate based on the straight-line method, while the remainder of the annual cash income amount represents the annual profit amount on which the fixed asset's year-to-year book rate of return is computed, after provision is made for income taxes.

Comparison of Project C's Year-to-Year Book Rates of Return When
Sum-of-the-Years'-Digits Method Is Used for Income Tax Purposes but (A)
Straight-Line Method, (B) Sum-of-the-Years'-Digits Method and (C)
Discounted Cash Flow Method Are Used for Book Purposes

	(1)	(2)	(3)	(4)	(5)	(6)
	Under Straight-Line Method			*Under Sum-of-the-Years'-Digits Method*		
Year	*Depreciated Book Value Beginning of Year*	*Profit after Income Taxes*	*Year-to-Year Book Rate of Return*	*Depreciated Book Value Beginning of Year*	*Profit after Income Taxes*	*Year-to-Year Book Rate of Return*
1	$10,000	$ 1,098	11.0%	$10,000	$ 646	6.5%
2	9,500	1,098	11.6	9,048	693	7.7
3	9,000	1,098	12.2	8,143	741	9.1
4	8,500	1,098	12.9	7,286	788	10.8
5	8,000	1,098	13.7	6,476	836	12.9
6	7,500	1,098	14.6	5,714	884	15.5
7	7,000	1,098	15.7	5,000	931	18.6
8	6,500	1,098	16.9	4,333	979	22.6
9	6,000	1,098	18.3	3,714	1,027	27.7
10	5,500	1,098	20.0	3,143	1,047	33.3
11	5,000	1,098	22.0	2,619	1,122	42.8
12	4,500	1,098	24.4	2,143	1,169	54.5
13	4,000	1,098	27.5	1,714	1,217	71.0
14	3,500	1,098	31.4	1,333	1,265	94.9
15	3,000	1,098	36.6	1,000	1,312	131.2
16	2,500	1,098	43.9	714	1,360	190.5
17	2,000	1,098	54.9	476	1,408	295.8
18	1,500	1,098	73.2	286	1,455	508.7
19	1,000	1,098	109.8	143	1,503	1,051.0
20	500	1,098	219.6	48	1,550	3,229.2
Total	$ –0–	$21,960		$ –0–	$21,960	

The exact opposite takes place under the discounted cash flow method, as shown in Table 59. Under this method, the annual profit amounts, ranging from $1,500 in the 1st year to $249 in the 20th year, are calculated first at the 15 percent DCF earnings rate determined for Project C's $10,000 fixed asset in Table 54, while the remainder of the $1,598 constant-level cash income amounts represent the annual amortization amounts, which range from $98 in the 1st year to $1,349 in the 20th year. Under the discounted cash flow method, Project C's fixed asset earns a constant-level 15 percent profit annually on the decreasing amortized investment balance unrecovered at the beginning of each year, or a total profit of $21,960, in addition to recovering the fixed asset's $10,000 original cost during its 20-year useful life.

TABLE 58

(7)	(8)	(9)	(10)	(11)	(12)	(13)
Under Discounted Cash Flow Method			**Depreciation or Amortization under**			Cash Income
Amortized Balance Beginning of Year	Profit after Income Taxes	Year-to-Year Book Rate of Return	Straight-Line Method	Sum-of-the-Years'-Digits Method	Discounted Cash Flow Method	after Income Taxes*
$10,000	$ 1,500	15.0%	$ 500	$ 952	$ 98	$ 1,598
9,902	1,485	15.0	500	905	113	1,598
9,789	1,468	15.0	500	857	130	1,598
9,659	1,449	15.0	500	810	149	1,598
9,510	1,427	15.0	500	762	171	1,598
9,339	1,401	15.0	500	714	197	1,598
9,142	1,371	15.0	500	667	227	1,598
8,915	1,337	15.0	500	619	261	1,598
8,654	1,298	15.0	500	571	300	1,598
8,354	1,253	15.0	500	524	345	1,598
8,009	1,201	15.0	500	476	397	1,598
7,612	1,142	15.0	500	429	456	1,598
7,156	1,073	15.0	500	381	525	1,598
6,631	995	15.0	500	333	603	1,598
6,028	904	15.0	500	286	694	1,598
5,334	800	15.0	500	238	798	1,598
4,536	680	15.0	500	190	918	1,598
3,618	543	15.0	500	143	1,055	1,598
2,563	384	15.0	500	95	1,214	1,598
1,349	249	15.0	500	48	1,349	1,598
$ –0–	$21,960		$10,000	$10,000	$10,000	$31,960

Less: Capital expenditure for Project C. 10,000

Total profits for Project C $21,960

*Obtained by adding Column (2) + Column (10); Column (5) + Column (11); and Column (8) + Column (12) for the straight-line method, the sum-of-the-years'-digits method, and the discounted cash flow method, respectively.

This proves that in the same manner that monthly payment amounts on mortgage loans are handled by financial institutions in which the monthly interest amounts decrease and the monthly amortization amounts increase monthly by corresponding amounts as the unpaid balance of the mortgage loans decreases at the beginning of each month, so the annual cash income amounts derived from loans made internally by companies to their new industrial projects are handled under the discounted cash flow method. As shown in Table 59, the annual profit amounts decrease and the annual amortization amounts increase by corresponding amounts as the unrecovered portion of the project's $10,000 fixed asset investment amount decreases at the beginning of each year.

TABLE 59

Determine Project C's Annual Profit Amounts, Annual Amortization
Amounts, and Amortized Balance at Start of Year under DCF Method

	(1)	(2)	(3)	(4)
Year	Amortized Balance at Beginning of Year	Cash Income after Income Taxes	Amortization Amount	Profit after Income Taxes at 15%
1	$10,000	$ 1,598	$ 98	$ 1,500
2	9,902	1,598	113	1,485
3	9,789	1,598	130	1,468
4	9,659	1,598	149	1,449
5	9,510	1,598	171	1,427
6	9,339	1,598	197	1,401
7	9,142	1,598	227	1,371
8	8,915	1,598	261	1,337
9	8,654	1,598	300	1,298
10	8,354	1,598	345	1,253
11	8,009	1,598	397	1,201
12	7,612	1,598	456	1,142
13	7,156	1,598	525	1,073
14	6,631	1,598	603	995
15	6,028	1,598	694	904
16	5,334	1,598	798	800
17	4,536	1,598	918	680
18	3,618	1,598	1,055	543
19	2,563	1,598	1,214	384
20	1,349	1,598	1,349	249
Total	$ –0–	$31,960	$10,000	$21,960

It is this difference in how the annual profit and the amortization portions of the annual cash income or savings amounts are calculated as well as the difference in the investment base on which the year-to-year book rates of return are calculated under the orthodox and widely accepted book method and the discounted cash flow method that is responsible for making the rates arrived at under the traditional book method incompatible with the DCF rate of return, as shown in Table 58. Only the constant-level 15 percent year-to-year book rates of return arrived at under the discounted cash flow method are realistic, compatible, and consistent with the 15 percent DCF rate of return arrived at for Project C's $10,000 fixed asset by this method, as shown in Tables 54, 58, and 59.

One may well inquire why in the light of the unrealistic, distorted, and misleading year-to-year book rates of return arrived at under the orthodox and widely accepted book method it is such common practice for companies to use the straight-line method for book purposes in calculating their year-to-year book rates of return. The answer to this inquiry perhaps is as follows. First, many companies more than likely are unaware of the fact that the discounted cash flow method can be used for determining true and realistic year-to-year book rates of return. Second, as long as financial statements of companies remain unadjusted for inflation, which means that their total asset, total liability, and shareholders' equity dollars and their annual net income dollars will continue to be highly incomparable, the use of the discounted cash flow method for determining year-to-year book rates of return is both an impractical and worthless effort. Third, in the light of the far more distorted, unrealistic, and absurd year-to-year book rates of return arrived at under the book method when the sum-of-the-years'-digits method is used for book purposes, companies unquestionably consider the use of the straight-line method for book purposes the lesser of the two evils, as shown in Table 58.

The Rationale on Which Depreciation Is Based

According to orthodox accounting practices and present income tax laws, companies charge depreciation as an expense for the use of fixed assets to their business operations in amounts equal to the fixed assets' original cost less their residual, or salvage, value over their estimated useful lives—or in amounts equal to their original cost if the fixed assets are used up entirely in business operations and consequently have no residual, or salvage, value at the end of their estimated useful lives.

This procedure is predicated on the rationale that companies are entitled to charge the cost for the use of fixed assets as a regular business expense to their business operations, but that this cost must be spread more or less evenly over the fixed assets' estimated useful lives, thus enabling companies through this procedure to recover their fixed asset costs and thereby avoid paying income taxes on them. Furthermore, this procedure automatically sets up a reserve account on companies' books that theoretically provides for the necessary funds for the replacement of worn-out fixed assets at the end of their estimated useful lives. This, of course, does not imply that funds equal to the amounts shown in the reserve account have been put into companies' cash drawers and, as a result, are available for this purpose when worn-out fixed assets are imminent for replacement. The reserve account merely serves to indicate how much of original costs of the fixed assets have been recovered to date, and what their current depreciated book values are.

This rationale on which the above-mentioned depreciation procedure is based is logical and fair providing dollar values remain constant during fixed assets' estimated useful lives, which is rarely, if ever, the case. Consequently, when dollar values change as a result of inflation during fixed assets' estimated useful lives, this creates havoc with a company's overall profitability. This situation will be explained and illustrated in greater detail later on in this book.

The Accounting Treatment and Financial Reporting of Depreciation

The explanations and the examples of the accounting treatment and the financial reporting of depreciation undoubtedly will be considered rudimentary and superfluous by professional accountants. Nevertheless, they are included in this book to give nonprofessional readers who have little or no accounting background the requisite understanding of how depreciation is handled on a company's books and treated in its financial statements. This is essential in enabling nonprofessional readers to gain a much clearer and fuller understanding of the project evaluation techniques discussed in this book. These explanations and examples of the accounting and the financial reporting treatment of depreciation will comprehend all accepted accounting and financial reporting practices from the time fixed assets are acquired until the time they are retired by companies. The following assumptions are made with respect to the fixed asset in the example shown below.

1. The fixed asset's original cost is $10,000.
2. The fixed asset's estimated useful life is five years.
3. The fixed asset is completely used up in the company's normal operations, and therefore it has no salvage value at the end of its five-year useful life.
4. The fixed asset is not paid for at the time of its acquisition but at some later date.

Step Number 1

When the fixed asset is acquired, the Fixed Asset account is debited for $10,000 and the Accounts Payable account is credited for $10,000.

Fixed Asset		Accounts Payable	
(1) $10,000		(2) $10,000	(1) $10,000

This transaction records the acquisition of the fixed asset and the company's $10,000 liability to the seller for the fixed asset.

Step Number 2

When the fixed asset is paid for at a later date, the Accounts Payable account is debited for $10,000 and the Cash account is credited for $10,000.

Cash	
	(2) $10,000

This transaction records the company's $10,000 payment to the seller for the fixed asset. The company's total assets amount on its books remains unchanged as a result of the purchase of this fixed asset as the company has merely substituted on its books the $10,000 cash for the $10,000 fixed asset. Furthermore, it is important to understand and to bear in mind that if the

$10,000 fixed asset should appreciate in value due to inflation during its estimated five-year useful life, such an appreciation in value, according to accepted accounting practices, would not be recorded, or given effect to, on the company's books. The latter would continue to show the fixed asset's $10,000 original cost less the reserve for depreciation until the time of its retirement at the end of its useful life, providing it isn't disposed of at a profit or loss before that time. In the latter event, the company would incur either an income tax liability or benefit on the capital gain or loss for the difference between the fixed asset's sales price and its depreciated book value based on the accelerated depreciation method used for income tax purposes.

Step Number 3

When the fixed asset's $10,000 original cost is written off the company's books and charged to its operations during the fixed asset's estimated five-year useful life, the Depreciation Expense account is debited $2,000 and the Reserve for Depreciation account is credited for $2,000. This transaction is repeated each year during the fixed asset's estimated five-year useful life until the fixed asset's entire $10,000 original cost has been written off the company's books and charged to its business operations.

Depreciation Expense		*Reserve for Depreciation*	
(3) $2,000	(4) $2,000		(3) $2,000

The above annual transactions accomplish two purposes. In addition to writing the fixed asset's $10,000 original cost off the books by charging it to the company's operations during the fixed asset's useful life, it simultaneously sets up a reserve account for depreciation, which reveals to what extent the fixed asset's $10,000 original cost has been depreciated and what its depreciated book value is at any point in time during the fixed asset's five-year useful life.

Step Number 4

At the end of each accounting period—in this example at the end of each year—the Depreciation Expense account is closed out into the Profit and Loss account by debiting the Profit and Loss account $2,000 and crediting the Depreciation Expense account $2,000.

Profit and Loss	
(4) $2,000	

This transaction is repeated each year during the fixed asset's estimated five-year useful life. During this five-year period, these yearly transactions have the effect of reducing the company's gross profits by an amount equal to the fixed assets $10,000 original cost, thus enabling the company to recover its $10,000 investment in the fixed asset without paying income taxes on this amount.

Step Number 5

There are two ways in which companies may report fixed assets in their financial statements. One way is to show the original cost of their total fixed assets less the reserve for depreciation on the asset (left hand) side of their balance sheets as illustrated below.

Balance Sheet

Fixed asset account	$10,000
Reserve for depreciation	2,000
Depreciated book value	$ 8,000*

* At end of the first year.

This is the more common practice used by companies of showing the value of their fixed assets in their balance sheets. This method produces a lower investment base and consequently a higher year-to-year book rate of return on the depreciated value of companies' total assets.

Another way is to show the original cost of a company's total fixed assets on the asset (left-hand) side of their balance sheets and show the reserve for depreciation on the liability shareholders equity (right-hand) side of their balance sheets as shown below.

Balance Sheet

Fixed asset account	$10,000	Reserve for depreciation	$2,000

This method produces a higher investment base and therefore a lower year-to-year book rate of return on the undepreciated value of a company's total assets.

How Inflation Creates Depreciation Deficiencies

The days when a good cigar, a subway ride, or a telephone call cost only a nickel are far in the past—in fact these so-called good old days go back quite a few decades, and that is precisely how long creeping inflation has plagued our economy. Moreover, since neither federal or state corporate income tax laws nor accepted accounting principles and practices of the accounting profession recognize and make allowances for inflation, the latter presents a number of serious economic problems to the business community. The first problem that will be discussed concerns the depreciation deficiencies that arise as the replacement costs of fixed assets recorded on companies' books of account continue to rise during their estimated useful lives. This problem is shown in Tables 59–62.

The assumptions made with regard to the examples in Tables 59–62 include the following:

1. The fixed asset is acquired exclusively for Project C.
2. The fixed asset's original cost at the zero reference point, i.e., at the beginning of year 1, is $10,000.
3. The fixed asset's cost index increases at an annual rate of 10 percent from an index of 100 at the zero reference point to an index of 672.7 in the 20th year.
4. The fixed asset's $10,000 original cost at the zero reference point represents the project's total capital expenditure.

As shown in Table 61, as the fixed asset cost index increases from an index of 100 at the zero reference point to an index of 672.7 in the 20th year, the purchasing power, or value, of the fixed asset dollar declines from 100.0 cents at the zero reference point to 14.87 cents in the 20th year. Since under present corporate income tax laws, fixed assets are required to be depreciated and written off the books at their original cost during their serviceable lives, companies will recover cheap dollars of increasingly lower purchasing power and consequently fail to recover the full purchasing power of their original investments.

As shown in Table 60, when the straight-line method is used for tax purposes, the company will recover $4,258, or 42.6 percent, of its $10,000 original investment and sustain a $5,742, or 57.4 percent, depreciation deficiency; when the sum-of-the-years'-digits method is used for tax purposes, the company will recover $5,470, or 54.7 percent, of its $10,000 original investment and sustain a $4,530, or 45.3 percent, depreciation deficiency; and when the double-declining-balance method is used for tax purposes, the company will recover $5,154, or 51.5 percent, of its $10,000 original investment and sustain a $4,846, or 48.5 percent, depreciation deficiency. The examples in this table prove that companies will recover the maximum purchasing power of their original investments and, consequently, sustain the lowest depreciation deficiency when the sum-of-the-years'-digits method is used for tax purposes for long-life fixed assets during inflationary periods.

Failure to recover the full purchasing power of their original capital investments in fixed assets under present corporate income tax laws creates a twofold problem for companies. First, it results in an overstatement of the profits generated by the fixed assets due to depreciation deficiencies and consequently in overpayment of income taxes on such overstated profits. Second, it requires that companies dig into past years' profits to the extent of the losses in purchasing power during fixed assets' useful lives when they are worn out and in need of replacement. In other words, failure to recover the

TABLE 60

Comparison of Project C's Depreciation Deficiencies When Its Fixed Asset Cost Increases at an Annual Rate of 10 Percent during Its 20-Year Useful Life and the Straight-Line Method, Sum-of-the-Years'-Digits Method, or Double-Declining-Balance Method Is Used for Income Tax Purposes

	(1)	(2)	(3)	(4)	(5)	(6)	(7)
		Straight-Line Depreciation		Sum-of-the-Years'- Digits Depreciation		Double-Declining- Balance Depreciation	
	Fixed Asset Cost	*Current- Year*	*Constant*	*Current- Year*	*Constant*	*Current- Year*	*Constant*
Year	*Index*	*Dollars*	*Dollars*	*Dollars*	*Dollars*	*Dollars*	*Dollars*
0	100.0	—	—	—	—	—	—
1	110.0	$ 500	$ 455	$ 952	$ 865	$ 1,000	$ 909
2	121.0	500	413	905	748	900	744
3	133.1	500	376	857	644	810	609
4	146.4	500	342	810	553	729	498
5	161.1	500	310	762	473	656	407
6	177.2	500	282	714	403	591	333
7	194.9	500	257	667	342	531	272
8	214.4	500	233	619	289	478	223
9	235.8	500	212	571	242	431	183
10	259.4	500	193	524	202	387	149
11	285.3	500	175	476	167	349	122
12	313.8	500	159	429	137	349	111
13	345.2	500	145	381	110	349	101
14	379.7	500	132	333	88	349	92
15	417.7	500	120	286	68	349	84
16	459.5	500	109	238	52	349	76
17	505.4	500	99	190	38	349	69
18	556.0	500	90	143	26	348	63
19	611.6	500	82	95	16	348	57
20	672.7	500	74	48	7	348	52
Total depreciation		$10,000	$4,258	$10,000	$5,470	$10,000	$5,154
Percent of original cost recovered			42.6%		54.7%		51.5%
Depreciation deficiency.			$5,742		$4,530		$4,846
Percent of depreciation deficiency			57.4%		45.3%		48.5%

full purchasing power of original capital investments in fixed assets has a dual, adverse effect on the profits of companies. Therefore, it presents a serious economic problem to them that needs to be resolved through revisions in present corporate income tax laws.

Popular Misconception of How to Determine Depreciation Deficiencies

Since the professional people in the business community have long been aware of this problem, one may well ask, "Why haven't present income tax laws been revised as yet to eliminate it?" The answer to this question, perhaps, is found in the general misconception that seems to exist as to how depreciation deficiencies should be determined. This misconception is best expressed and confirmed by the following quotation from an article titled "Corporate

Profits Rise Challenged," which appeared in the *Fort Myers News-Press* on March 22, 1979.

> Inflation also can distort depreciation, a system allowing companies to shelter some income from taxes while they set aside funds to pay for new plants and machinery.
>
> The real cost of the depreciating of a firm's capital stock is the replacement cost of the buildings or equipment, economists Martin Feldstein and Lawrence Summers said in a recent report issued by the National Bureau of Economic Research.
>
> Yet for tax purposes, firms are only permitted to deduct depreciation based on the original purchase price. In inflationary periods, this may be much less than the replacement cost, they said in the private research organization report.[2]

The above statements clearly imply that depreciation deficiency represents the difference between a fixed asset's original cost at the time of its acquisition and its actual replacement cost at the end of its useful life. This misconception is cleared up in Table 61.

As shown in Table 61, as the fixed asset cost index increases from an index of 100 at the zero reference point to an index of 672.7 in the 20th year, the fixed asset replacement cost increases from $10,000 at the zero reference point to $67,270 in the 20th year. According to this popular misconception, this would make the depreciation deficiency for this fixed asset $57,270 ($67,270 − $10,000) under present income tax laws. This is preposterous for the following reason.

The $67,270 replacement cost at the end of the 20th year represents cheap dollars that have a purchasing power of only 14.87 cents. If under revised corporate income tax laws this actual replacement cost were permitted to be used for depreciating this fixed asset, the company would be recovering $67,270 in expensive dollars that range in purchasing power from 90.91 cents in the first year, to 82.64 cents in the second year, to 75.13 cents in the third year, and to 14.87 cents in the 20th year. When this stream of annual depreciation charges, expressed in current-year dollars that range from $6,404 in the first year to $323 in the 20th year and totals $67,270, is adjusted for inflation and expressed in constant dollars that are equal in purchasing power to the original investment dollars, it would amount to $36,791. In terms of purchasing power, this would mean that the company would be recovering $26,791, or 267.9 percent, in excess of the $10,000 original investment.

This would be the exact opposite of what is now taking place under present corporate income tax laws in which the $10,000 original cost, which represents expensive dollars that have a purchasing power of 100.0 cents, is recovered in cheap dollars that range in purchasing power from 90.91 cents in the first year, to 82.64 cents in the second year, to 75.13 cents in the third year, and to 14.87 cents in the 20th year. When this stream of annual depreciation charges, expressed in cheap current-year dollars and totaling $10,000, is adjusted for inflation and expressed in constant dollars that are equal in purchasing power to the original investment dollars, it amounts to $5,470. In terms of purchasing power this means that under present corporate income

---

[2] Used by permission of The Associated Press.

TABLE 61

Proof that Project C's Annual Depreciation Charges Must be Calculated on Fixed Asset's Annual Replacement Costs and Not on Its Original Cost or Its Actual Replacement Cost to Avoid Depreciation Deficiencies

Sum-of-the-Years'-Digits Depreciation Charges Calculated on the

Year	Fixed Asset Cost Index	Fixed Asset Actual Cost	Original Cost Current-Year Dollars	Original Cost Constant Dollars	Current-Year Replacement Cost Current-Year Dollars	Current-Year Replacement Cost Constant Dollars	Actual Replacement Cost Current-Year Dollars	Actual Replacement Cost Constant Dollars	Memo Depreciation Rate	Memo Purchasing Power of the Dollar
0	100.0	$10,000							—	100.0
1	110.0	11,000	$ 952	$ 865	$ 1,047	$ 952	$ 6,404	$ 5,822	.0952	90.91
2	121.0	12,100	905	748	1,095	905	6,088	5,031	.0905	82.64
3	133.1	13,310	857	644	1,141	857	5,765	4,331	.0857	75.13
4	146.4	14,640	810	553	1,186	810	5,449	3,722	.0810	68.31
5	161.1	16,110	762	473	1,228	762	5,126	3,182	.0762	61.96
6	177.2	17,720	714	403	1,265	714	4,803	2,710	.0714	56.43
7	194.9	19,490	667	342	1,300	667	4,487	2,302	.0667	51.31
8	214.4	21,440	619	289	1,327	619	4,164	1,942	.0619	46.64
9	235.8	23,580	571	242	1,346	571	3,841	1,629	.0571	42.41
10	259.4	25,940	524	202	1,359	524	3,525	1,359	.0524	38.55
11	285.3	28,530	476	167	1,358	476	3,202	1,122	.0476	35.05
12	313.8	31,380	429	137	1,346	429	2,886	920	.0429	31.87
13	345.2	34,520	381	110	1,315	381	2,563	742	.0381	28.97
14	379.7	37,970	333	88	1,264	333	2,240	590	.0333	26.34
15	417.7	41,770	286	68	1,195	286	1,924	461	.0286	23.94
16	459.5	45,950	238	52	1,094	238	1,601	348	.0238	21.76
17	505.4	50,540	190	38	960	190	1,278	253	.0190	19.79
18	556.0	55,600	143	26	795	143	962	173	.0143	17.99
19	611.6	61,160	95	16	581	95	639	104	.0095	16.35
20	672.7	67,270	48	7	323	48	323	48	.0048	14.87
Total			$10,000	5,470	$22,525	10,000	$67,270	36,791	1.0000	
Fixed asset's original cost			10,000	10,000		10,000		10,000		
Depreciation (deficiency) or surplus—dollars				$ (4,530)		$ 0		$26,791		
Depreciation (deficiency) or surplus—percent				(45.3%)		0%		267.9%		

tax laws, the company is recovering $4,530, or 45.3 percent, less than the $10,000 original investment.

If the popular misconception that depreciation deficiencies represent the difference between the original cost of fixed assets and their actual replacement cost should continue to prevail, it would seem unlikely that members of Congress would be inclined to consider making equitable and needed revisions in present corporate income tax laws that would enable companies to recover the full purchasing power of their original investments.

How to Recover the Full Purchasing Power of Original Investments during Inflationary Periods

Capital recoveries made possible through depreciation allowances should be based on the rationale that companies be permitted to recover amounts in cheap current-year dollars during inflationary periods that in terms of purchasing power are equal to the original investment dollars.

The procedure that will make this possible is shown in Table 61 which shows that when the annual depreciation charges are calculated on the fixed asset's annual replacement cost and the sum-of-the-years'-digits method is used for tax purposes, the annual depreciation charges will range from $1,047 in the first year to $323 in the 20th year and total $22,525. When this stream of annual depreciation charges, expressed in cheap current-year dollars that range in purchasing power from 90.91 cents in the 1st year to 14.87 cents in the 20th year, is adjusted for inflation and expressed in constant dollars that are equal in purchasing power to the original investment dollars, it amounts to $10,000. This proves that when the annual depreciation charges of fixed assets are calculated on their current-year replacement cost, companies will recover the full purchasing power of their original investments.

The time should be propitious for introducing legislation for the revision of present corporate income tax laws that would permit companies to depreciate fixed assets for tax purposes on their current-year replacement cost and, thereby, enable them to recover the full purchasing power of their original investments. There has been a great deal of talk throughout both the executive and legislative branch of our federal government during the last couple of years about the revitalization and the modernization of companies' plants, machinery, equipment, etc., in order to increase productivity and put companies back in a competitive position internationally, particularly in the case of major industries such as steel, auto, and others. This is expected to be achieved through investment credits, income tax reduction, relaxation of federal regulations and restrictions, decontrol of prices, etc. In view of this pervasive mood in Congress, its members should be amendable and receptive to the equitable and much needed revisions in present corporate income tax laws that would provide for full recovery of the purchasing power of companies' investments in capital assets, and thus preclude depreciation deficiencies.

For obvious reasons, this method of calculating annual depreciation charges on fixed assets' current-year replacement cost would not be feasible under the double-declining-balance method simply because the replacement cost, or investment base, for each year would change and be different so that this depreciation method would preclude the possibility of annual declining balances on which depreciation amounts could be calculated. Hence, when present corporate income tax laws are revised, the sum-of-the-year-digits' method is recommended to be used for short-life fixed assets to permit depreciating fixed assets on their current-year replacement cost.

Effect on Profitability When Depreciating Project C's Fixed Assets on Their Original versus Their Current-Year Replacement Cost

As shown in Project C's economic evaluation in Table 54, its fixed asset is expected to (a) cost $10,000, (b) generate $1,598 annual cash income, (c) have a 20-year useful life, and (d) be depreciated for tax purposes based on its $10,000 original cost by the sum-of-the-years'-digits method. Based on these

Effect Depreciation Deficiency Has on Project C's DCF Rate of Return (13.7 Percent) and Payout Period (6.7 Years) under Corporate Income Tax Laws after Adjusting for Inflation

Year	Fixed Asset Cost Index	Cash Income before Taxes Constant Dollars	Current-Year Dollars	Depreciation Charges*	Taxable Income	Income Taxes
0	100.0	—	—	—	—	—
1	110.0	$ 2,194	$ 2,413	$ 952	$ 1,461	$ 701
2	121.0	2,238	2,708	905	1,803	865
3	133.1	2,282	3,037	857	2,180	1,046
4	146.4	2,325	3,404	810	2,594	1,245
5	161.1	2,370	3,818	762	3,056	1,467
6	177.2	2,414	4,278	714	3,564	1,711
7	194.9	2,457	4,789	667	4,122	1,979
8	214.4	2,502	5,364	619	4,745	2,278
9	235.8	2,546	6,003	571	5,432	2,607
10	259.4	2,589	6,716	524	6,192	2,972
11	285.3	2,634	7,515	476	7,039	3,379
12	313.8	2,677	8,400	429	7,971	3,826
13	345.2	2,721	9,393	381	9,012	4,325
14	379.7	2,766	10,503	333	10,170	4,882
15	417.7	2,809	11,733	286	11,447	5,494
16	459.5	2,853	13,110	238	12,872	6,178
17	505.4	2,898	14,646	190	14,456	6,939
18	556.0	2,941	16,352	143	16,209	7,780
19	611.6	2,985	18,256	95	18,161	8,718
20	672.7	3,030	20,383	48	20,335	9,762
Total		$52,231	$172,821	$10,000	$162,821	$78,154

DCF rate of return is 13.7%.

Payout period is 6.7 years.

* Calculated on fixed asset's original cost as provided for in present corporate income tax laws.

estimates, Project C is expected to yield a 15.0 percent DCF rate of return and show a 6.3-year payout period. These estimates in Project C's economic evaluation ignore inflation and are expressed in constant dollars in order to avoid distortions of its financial criteria and consequently a conceivable unsound investment decision.

The example in Table 62 is based on these assumptions: (1) Project C's fixed asset cost will increase at an annual 10 percent rate from an index of 100 at the zero reference point to an index of 672.7 in the 20th year. (2) Its annual cash income will keep pace and increase at the same rate as its fixed asset's replacement cost during this 20-year period. (3) Project C's fixed asset will be depreciated by the sum-of-the-years'-digits method based on its $10,000 original cost as provided for under present corporate income laws.

If this annual 10 percent inflation rate is worked into Project C's economic evaluation, then its annual cash income before taxes will range from $2,413 in

TABLE 62

Profit after Depreciation and Taxes	Cash Outlay† and Cash Income		Present Value		Present Value	
	Current Year Dollars	Constant Dollars	Factor at 13%	Amount	Factor at 14%	Amount
—	$(10,000)	$(10,000)	1.000	$(10,000)	1.000	$(10,000)
$ 760	1,712	1,556	.8850	1,377	.8772	1,365
938	1,843	1,523	.7831	1,193	.7695	1,172
1,134	1,991	1,496	.6930	1,037	.6750	1,010
1,349	2,159	1,475	.6133	905	.5921	873
1,589	2,351	1,459	.5428	792	.5194	758
1,853	2,567	1,449	.4803	696	.4556	660
2,143	2,810	1,442	.4251	613	.3996	576
2,467	3,086	1,439	.3762	541	.3506	505
2,825	3,396	1,440	.3329	479	.3075	443
3,220	3,744	1,443	.2946	425	.2697	389
3,660	4,136	1,450	.2607	378	.2366	343
4,145	4,574	1,458	.2307	336	.2076	303
4,687	5,068	1,468	.2042	300	.1821	267
5,288	5,621	1,480	.1807	267	.1597	236
5,953	6,239	1,494	.1599	239	.1401	209
6,694	6,932	1,506	.1415	213	.1229	185
7,517	7,707	1,525	.1252	191	.1078	164
8,429	8,572	1,542	.1108	171	.0946	146
9,443	9,538	1,560	.0981	153	.0829	129
10,573	10,621	1,579	.0868	137	.0728	115
$84,667	$ 84,667	$ 19,784		$ 443		$ (152)

† Capital outlay in parentheses.

TABLE 63

Proof that Project C's 15.0 Percent DCF Rate of Return and 6.3 Payout Period Are Unaffected by Inflation under Recommended Corporate Income Laws

Year	Cash Income before Taxes Constant Dollars	Cash Income before Taxes Current-Year Dollars	Depreciation Charges*	Taxable Income	Income Taxes	Profit after Depreciation and Taxes	Cash Outlay† and Cash Income Current-Year Dollars	Cash Outlay† and Cash Income Constant Dollars	Present Value Factor at 15%	Present Value Amount
0							$(10,000)	$(10,000)	1.0000	$(10,000)
1	$ 2,194	$ 2,413	$ 1,047	$ 1,366	$ 656	$ 710	1,757	1,598	.8696	1,390
2	2,238	2,708	1,095	1,613	774	839	1,934	1,598	.7561	1,208
3	2,282	3,037	1,141	1,896	910	986	2,127	1,598	.6575	1,051
4	2,325	3,404	1,186	2,218	1,065	1,153	2,339	1,598	.5718	914
5	2,370	3,818	1,228	2,590	1,243	1,347	2,575	1,598	.4972	795
6	2,414	4,278	1,265	3,013	1,446	1,567	2,832	1,598	.4323	691
7	2,457	4,789	1,300	3,489	1,675	1,814	3,114	1,598	.3759	601
8	2,502	5,364	1,327	4,037	1,938	2,099	3,426	1,598	.3269	522
9	2,546	6,003	1,346	4,657	2,235	2,422	3,768	1,598	.2843	454
10	2,589	6,716	1,359	5,357	2,571	2,786	4,145	1,598	.2472	395
11	2,634	7,515	1,358	6,157	2,955	3,202	4,560	1,598	.2149	343
12	2,677	8,400	1,346	7,054	3,386	3,668	5,014	1,598	.1869	299
13	2,711	9,393	1,315	8,078	3,877	4,201	5,516	1,598	.1625	260
14	2,726	10,503	1,264	9,239	4,435	4,804	6,068	1,598	.1413	226
15	2,809	11,733	1,195	10,538	5,058	5,480	6,675	1,598	.1229	196
16	2,853	13,110	1,094	12,016	5,768	6,248	7,342	1,598	.1069	171
17	2,898	14,646	960	13,686	6,569	7,117	8,077	1,598	.0929	148
18	2,941	16,352	795	15,557	7,467	8,090	8,885	1,598	.0808	129
19	2,985	18,256	581	17,675	8,484	9,191	9,772	1,598	.0703	112
20	3,030	20,383	323	20,060	9,629	10,431	10,754	1,598	.0611	95
Total	$52,231	$172,821	$22,525	$150,296	$72,141	$78,155	$100,680	$ 21,960		$ –0–

DCF rate of return is 15.0%.

Payout period is 6.3 years.

* Calculated on fixed asset's current-year replacement cost as recommended in revised corporate income tax laws.
† Cash outlay in parentheses.

the 1st year to $20,383 in the 20th year and total $172,821, as adjusted for inflation and expressed in cheap current-year dollars instead of range from $2,194 in the 1st year to $3,030 in the 20th year and total $52,231, as originally estimated and expressed in expensive constant dollars.

When Project C's depreciation charges are calculated on its fixed asset's original cost, as required under present corporate income tax laws, and its annual cash income amounts after taxes, expressed in cheap current-year dollars, are adjusted for inflation and expressed in expensive constant dollars that are equal in purchasing power to its original investment dollars, then Project C's DCF rate of return will be reduced 1.3 percent (15.0 percent − 13.7 percent) and its payout period will be lengthened 0.4 (6.3 to 6.7) of a year which is attributable solely to the depreciation deficiency that will be incurred under present corporate income tax laws.

However, when Project C's depreciation charges are calculated on its fixed asset's current-year replacement cost, thus eliminating the depreciation deficiency created by present corporate income tax laws, and its annual cash income amounts after taxes are adjusted for inflation in a similar manner as in Table 62, then Project C's original forecasts of a 15.0 percent DCF rate of return and a 6.3-year payout period will remain in tact and not be affected adversely by the annual 10 percent inflation rate during its 20-year economic life. This proves that revisions in present corporate income tax laws, which would permit companies to depreciate fixed assets on their current-year replacement instead of their original cost, would prevent erosions of the cash income or savings generated by them during their useful lives. This is shown in Table 63.

Under present corporate income tax laws and conventional accounting and financial reporting practices, year-to-year book rates of return are grossly distorted during inflationary periods. This results from incurring depreciation deficiencies and comparing cheap current-year profit dollars to expensive investment dollars. This is illustrated in Table 64, which shows that Project C's year-to-year book rates of return range from 12.1 percent in the first year to 2,024.2 percent in the 20th year as a result of the 10 percent annual inflation rate compared to 11.0 percent in the first year to 219.6 percent in the 20-year based on the original forecasts, which do not reflect the 10 percent annual inflation factor, as shown in Table 58.

Table 65 serves a twofold purpose. It shows that (a) the inflation factor must not be built into the future stream of estimated cash income or savings amounts in economic evaluations of prospective projects, and (b) the stream of actual cash income or savings amounts in post-completion audits of new projects must be adjusted for inflation in order to arrive at meaningful and realistic DCF rates of return on which to base sound investment decisions and compare actual performance against original estimates.

For example, if the anticipated 10 percent inflation rate had been built into the future stream of estimated annual cash income or savings amounts in Project C's economic evaluation, then its estimated DCF rate of return would

TABLE 64

Effect of Inflation on Project C's Year-to-Year Book Rate of
Return under Present Corporate Income Tax Laws

Year	Cash Income before Taxes	Income Taxes	Depreciation	Profit after Taxes	Depreciated Book Value Start of Year	Year-to-Year Book Rate of Return
1	$ 2,413	$ 701	$ 500	$ 1,212	$10,000	12.1%
2	2,708	865	500	1,343	9,500	14.1
3	3,037	1,046	500	1,491	9,000	16.6
4	3,404	1,245	500	1,659	8,500	19.5
5	3,818	1,467	500	1,851	8,000	23.1
6	4,278	1,711	500	2,067	7,500	27.6
7	4,789	1,979	500	2,310	7,000	33.0
8	5,364	2,278	500	2,586	6,500	39.8
9	6,003	2,607	500	2,896	6,000	48.3
10	6,716	2,972	500	3,244	5,500	59.0
11	7,515	3,379	500	3,636	5,000	72.7
12	8,400	3,826	500	4,074	4,500	90.5
13	9,393	4,325	500	4,568	4,000	114.2
14	10,503	4,882	500	5,121	3,500	146.3
15	11,733	5,494	500	5,739	3,000	191.3
16	13,110	6,178	500	6,432	2,500	257.3
17	14,646	6,939	500	7,207	2,000	360.4
18	16,352	7,780	500	8,072	1,500	538.1
19	18,256	8,718	500	9,038	1,000	903.8
20	20,383	9,762	500	10,121	500	2,024.2
Total	$172,821	$78,154	$10,000	$84,667		

have been 25.1 percent instead of 15.0 percent and its payout period 5 years instead of 6.3 years, as shown in Tables 54 and 65.

If we assume that 20 percent is the minimum acceptable DCF rate of return for Project C, then it would have been found acceptable based on the 25.1 percent DCF rate of return and unacceptable based on the 15 percent DCF rate of return arrived at by correctly comparing the estimated cash income or savings dollars and the estimated investment dollars—both expressed in comparable, constant dollars of equal purchasing power. This proves that prospective projects could be made to look acceptable and lead to unwise investment decisions if a high enough inflation rate is erroneously built into their stream of estimated future annual cash income or savings amounts.

Next, let us assume that the figures in Table 65 represent the actual cash outlay and cash income or savings amounts in Project C's post-completion audit prepared at the end of its 20-year economic life. Since these dollar amounts are expressed in variable current-year dollars, ranging in purchasing power from 100.0 cents at the zero reference point to 14.87 cents in the 20th year, they need to be adjusted for inflation in order to make them comparable. Failing to do this will show that Project C realized a 25.1 percent DCF rate of return and enjoyed a 5-year payout period, when in reality it only realized a

TABLE 65

Effect of Inflation on Project C's DCF Rate of Return (25.1 Percent) and Payout Period (5 Years) under Present Corporate Income Tax Laws with No Adjustment for Inflation

Year	Cash Outlay* and Cash Income Current Dollars	Factor at 25%	Present Value Amount	Factor at 26%	Amount	Memo Purchasing Power of Dollar
0	$(10,000)	1.0000	$(10,000)	1.0000	$(10,000)	100.00
1	1,712	.8000	1,370	.7937	1,359	90.91
2	1,843	.6400	1,180	.6299	1,161	82.64
3	1,991	.5120	1,019	.4999	995	75.13
4	2,159	.4096	884	.3968	857	68.31
5	2,351	.3277	770	.3149	740	61.96
6	2,567	.2621	673	.2499	641	56.43
7	2,810	.2097	589	.1983	557	51.31
8	3,086	.1678	518	.1574	486	46.64
9	3,396	.1342	456	.1249	424	42.41
10	3,744	.1074	402	.0992	371	38.55
11	4,136	.0859	355	.0787	326	35.05
12	4,574	.0687	314	.0625	286	31.87
13	5,068	.0550	279	.0496	251	28.97
14	5,621	.0440	247	.0393	221	26.34
15	6,239	.0352	220	.0312	195	23.94
16	6,932	.0281	195	.0248	172	21.76
17	7,707	.0225	173	.0197	152	19,79
18	8,572	.0180	154	.0156	134	17.99
19	9,538	.0144	137	.0124	118	16.35
20	10,621	.0115	122	.0098	104	14.87
Total	$ 84,667		$ 57		$ (450)	

DCF rate of return is 25.1%.

Payout period is 5 years.

* Cash outlay in parentheses.

13.7 percent DCF rate of return and enjoyed a 6.7-year payout period, after proper adjustments for inflation are made, as shown in Table 62. In other words, instead of realizing a substantially higher DCF rate of return and shorter payout period, it actually realized a 1.3 percent lower DCF rate of return and a 0.4 of a year longer payout period than the 15 percent DCF rate of return and the 6.3-year payout period originally forecasted for Project C. This proves the importance of adjusting all dollar amounts in the post-completion audits of new projects for inflation, or the results of measuring actual performance against original forecasts will be grossly distorted and highly misleading.

Chapter 14

Common Pitfalls in Economic Evaluations of Prospective Projects

It has often been said that the solutions or results that come out of computers are only as sound and realistic as the data that are put into them are credible and viable. The same can be said for the various DCF techniques. The financial criteria arrived at by these DCF techniques include: (1) how profitable prospective projects are expected to be, (2) how much money companies can afford to invest in them or how much companies to be acquired are worth, (3) how much cash income or savings prospective projects must generate, and (4) how long prospective projects must be productive. These financial criteria are only as sound and realistic as the estimates of the prospective projects' capital cost, cash income or savings, economic life, and predetermined minimum acceptable DCF earnings rate and the assumptions on which they are based are realistic and plausible. In preparing these estimates for the economic evaluations of prospective projects, financial analysts may unwittingly fall prey to some subtle but common pitfalls that could result in seriously distorted and unrealistic financial criteria and consequently lead to unwise and costly investment decisions. Several of these more common pitfalls will be discussed in this chapter.

When all the factors are tied together in an effort to explain and illustrate several of the more common pitfalls that may be encountered in the economic evaluations of prospective projects, a certain amount of redundancy is unavoidable. This redundancy is justifiable because it will help the reader understand what pitfalls to look for and avoid if he bears in mind (*a*) why the DCF rate of return is the most effective profitability indicator and project selection device for prospective projects, (*b*) on what rationale the DCF concept is applied in the economic evaluations of prospective projects, and (*c*) the primary differences between the application of the discounted cash flow concept by companies and the compound interest principle by banks and other lending institutions.

Why the DCF rate of return is used as a profitability indicator for prospective projects. The services performed by banks consist primarily of lending money to outside borrowers at various interest rates, depending on the risks involved in the different types of loans. These interest rates used by the banking community in self-amortizing loans invariably are compound interest rates. This means that the interest paid by the outside borrowers and, contrariwise, the interest earned by the banks and other lending institutions on the self-amortizing loans are calculated on the unpaid balance of the loan principal outstanding at the beginning of each accounting period.

What rate could possibly be used by companies as a profitability indicator of prospective projects that will be more meaningful and effective than the DCF rate of return, which is comparable to the compound interest rate used by banks and other lending institutions who are in the business, principally, of making loans to outside borrowers? Using the DCF rate of return means that profit is paid by new projects and, contrariwise, is earned by companies on the unrecovered portion of capital investments similar to the manner interest is paid by outside borrowers and, contrariwise, is earned by banks and other lending institutions on the unpaid balance of self-amortizing loans.

Rationale on which the application of the DCF concept to industrial investments is based. Internal loans made by treasurer's departments of companies to prospective projects are considered to be made in the same manner and for the same purpose that loans are made by banks and other lending institutions to outside borrowers, namely, to earn profits or interest. This is true because bank loan payment amounts of outside borrowers and cash income or savings amounts of prospective projects are comparable insofar as they both consist of repayment of principal or recovery of capital and interest or profit. This proves not only that the DCF rate is analogous to the compound interest rate but also that the DCF concept is an application of the compound interest principle.

Basic differences in application of DCF rate of return and compound interest rate. While the DCF rate of return unquestionably is analogous to the compound interest rate, there, nevertheless, exist some basic differences between the application of the DCF concept by the business community and the compound interest principle by the banking community. These differences stem primarily from the fact that the figures in the applications for loans by banks and other lending institutions to outside borrowers invariably are *actual*; consequently, the acceptance or rejection of these loans is based on actual data. On the other hand, the figures in economic evaluations for internal loans to prospective projects by companies' treasurer's departments invariably are estimated; consequently, the acceptance or rejection of these loans is based on *estimated* data.

In loans made by financial institutions to outside borrowers, these three financial factors are always known and actual: the loan amount, the interest rate, and the loan term. From these three known and actual financial factors, financial institutions can determine the periodic bank payment amount that the outside borrowers will be obliged to pay in order to repay the principal of the loan plus the interest on the unpaid balances during the loan term. Consequently, the approval or disapproval of the loans applied for depends on the judgment of the financial institution's top management as to whether the credit ratings of the outside borrowers are satisfactory or unsatisfactory, i.e., whether or not they have the ability to pay back the principal of the loan in addition to the specified interest.

An entirely different set of circumstances exists in the case of internal loans made by treasurer's departments of companies to prospective projects. These internal loans involve unknown financial factors that must be estimated, namely, the capital cost, cash income or savings, and economic life of the prospective projects. From these three unknown and estimated financial factors, the company can determine the fourth financial factor, namely, the estimated DCF rate of return of the prospective projects. Obviously, these estimated DCF rates of return will only be as sound and realistic as the estimates of the capital cost, cash income or savings, and economic lives of the prospective projects are sound and realistic and the assumptions on which these estimates are based are plausible and viable. This proves that for the DCF rates of return of prospective projects to be effective profitability indicators and reliable project selection devices that will lead to wise and profitable investment decisions, they must be calculated on sound and realistic estimates and in accordance with the proper application of the DCF concept.

There are several other situations that only top management of companies and not financial institutions must look out for and contend with. One such situation is that in most prospective projects, companies generally have a series of alternative courses of action open to them. Companies must then prepare separate cash flow estimates for the series of alternatives and select the most economic alternative by the process of elimination. Another such situation arises when prospective projects involve imponderables that cannot be reduced to numbers and therefore their impact can neither be included in cash flow estimates nor in DCF rates of return. Companies must then prepare separate cash flow estimates based on various assumptions such as what could take place under *(a)* the most optimistic conditions, *(b)* the most pessimistic conditions, and *(c)* the most likely conditions during the economic lives of the prospective projects. This enables top management to make wise and profitable investment decisions based on what conditions in their judgment most likely will prevail during prospective projects' economic lives.

These are just two of the basic differences in the application of the DCF concept by companies compared to the application of the compound interest principle by financial institutions that normally are encountered in economic evaluations of prospective projects and could lead to unwise and costly investment decisions by top management.

Before discussing some of the more common pitfalls that may be encountered in the projections of prospective projects' capital cost, cash income or savings, and economic lives, the reader should be reminded that top management's approval of capital budgets in no way constitutes a blanket approval of the capital expenditures for all the prospective projects that are contained therein. The capital expenditure for each prospective project contained in the capital budgets must be evaluated and justified separately on its own merits. The reader should also be reminded that when in-depth feasibility studies or detailed economic evaluations of individual prospective projects are made, it isn't unusual for certain facts to come to light that may result in the automatic elimination of some of the prospective projects from the company's capital budgets. Some of these reasons for eliminating the prospective projects may include *(a)* the inability to obtain necessary permits, *(b)* changes in the zoning laws, *(c)* new or revised government rules and regulations, *(d)* the inability to purchase or lease the necessary land at a reasonable purchase price or lease rental from the owner or lessor, *(e)* the excessively high cost of construction or purchase price of new fixed assets that cannot be justified in terms of the incremental profits or savings they will generate, etc. Moreover, the proposed capital expenditures included in capital budgets of companies all too frequently fall short of the actual capital cost of prospective projects. This is sometimes true because the land and other fixed assets transferred to the prospective projects are already owned by the companies, and their capital budgets do not include the original cost or the resale value of this land or other fixed assets.

Top management's approval of a company's annual capital budget does not represent a blanket approval for all proposed capital investments for prospective projects. At best it is only an approval of how much money the company is prepared and willing to invest during the coming year in prospective projects, and in what areas of the company's operations—manufacturing, marketing, transportation, etc.,—these funds should be invested to improve the company's overall profitability by means of the additional profits or savings these prospective projects are expected to generate. If economic evaluations of prospective projects disclose that they will not meet the company's predetermined standards, i.e., the company's predetermined minimum acceptable DCF earnings rate, and therefore the prospective projects will not increase the company's overall profitability, these prospective projects are then automatically dropped from the company's capital budget.

On the other hand, it is quite customary for companies to invest funds in prospective projects that are not included in their capital budgets either because the sponsors of the projects were unaware of them or no information was available about them at the time the capital budgets were prepared. This occurs when after the preparation of the capital budgets, economic evaluations of additional prospective projects reveal that their DCF rates of return will meet or exceed the company's predetermined acceptable DCF earnings rates and thus will enhance the company's future overall profitability.

Pitfalls Encountered in Estimating Prospective Projects' Capital Costs and Capital Recoveries

The task of estimating capital costs and capital recoveries of prospective projects is a most difficult and often a time-consuming one. This is particularly true during inflationary periods when costs and prices are expected to increase rapidly and the completion of prospective projects, such as the construction of new petroleum refineries, takes as long as from four to five years before they are ready to go into operation and generate cash returns. These inflationary cycles have given rise to one of the more common pitfalls in projecting capital costs of prospective projects. This is exemplified by the rather widespread practice of financial analysts to include cost increases in the series of annual capital outlays during prolonged construction periods. This practice has the effect of injecting the inflation factor into prospective projects' economic evaluations. The reason for this practice apparently is twofold. First, capital expenditures for prospective projects are always shown in the company's annual capital budgets in current-year dollars of declining purchasing power during inflationary periods, and thus the capital budgets will include cost increases during extended construction periods. Second, financial analysts are always reluctant to show cost overruns for new projects under construction because this, in their opinion, would appear to be a poor reflection on their ability to make accurate projections of the total construction costs of prospective projects during protracted construction periods.

To be consistent, this practice of injecting the inflation factor into capital outlays of prospective projects unfortunately has led one step further and that is of injecting inflation also into their cash returns. This practice of injecting the inflation factor into projections of prospective projects' capital outlays and cash returns is an extremely precarious one insofar as the economic evaluations of prospective projects now *(a)* deal with variable dollars of widely different purchasing power, *(b)* create a situation of relating and comparing cheap cash income or savings dollars to more expensive capital investment dollars, and thereby *(c)* arrive at highly unrealistic and distorted profitability indicators and unreliable project selection devices that could lead to disasterous and costly investment decisions.

Projections of the cash outflows and cash inflows of prospective projects at all times and under all circumstances must be expressed in constant dollars that are equal in purchasing power to that of the dollar in effect at the time the economic evaluations of the projects were prepared. To assure that prospective projects will realize the DCF rates of return forecasted in their economic evaluations, companies will have to raise their prices during inflationary periods to a level that will compensate for the effects of inflation, as well as for the depreciation deficiencies. This will result in a stream of cash returns that will be equal in purchasing power to that on which the estimated DCF rates of return were determined in the economic evaluations of the prospective projects, and it is the proper way to offset the deleterious effects of inflation during prospective projects' economic lives.

Another one of the more common pitfalls in estimating capital costs and capital recoveries of prospective projects lies in the decisions that must be made as to what items to include and the costs at which they should be included. The capital recovery for land at the end of Project E's economic life, which is shown in Tables 66 and 67, is a typical example. The following assumptions are made in these two tables:

1. Project E's total capital cost comprises $30,000 of which $10,000 is for the acquisition of the land and another $20,000 is for the construction of a building thereon.
2. Project E's annual cash income is $5,947.
3. Project E's economic life is 20 years.
4. Project E's $10,000 original cost for the land is estimated to appreciate in value to $50,000 during the 20-year period as a result of population growth in the area.
5. The company's predetermined standard (DCF rate of return) for this type of project is 22 percent.

The problem involved in the economic evaluation of Project E does not involve the legitimacy of including the capital recovery for land at the end of Project E's 20-year life but rather at what value the land should be included. As shown in Table 66, when the capital recovery for land at the end of the Project E's 20-year life is included at its $10,000 estimated original cost, Project E's DCF rate of return is 20 percent.

On the other hand, as shown in Table 67, when the capital recovery for land at the end of Project E's 20-year life is included at its $50,000 estimated appreciated market value, Project E's DCF rate of return is 23.6 percent. In other words, the $40,000 difference in the capital recovery for land at the end of Project E's 20-year life not only increases its DCF rate of return from 20.0 percent to 23.6 percent but it also changes Project E from an unacceptable to an acceptable prospective project, since the acceptable DCF rate of return predetermined by management for this type of project is 22.0 percent.

The capital recovery for land at the end of Project E's 20-year life should be included at its $10,000 estimated original cost and not at its $50,000 appreciated market value at the end of 20 years for the following reasons: (1) The land actually may never appreciate in value from $10,000 to $50,000 as forecasted due to population growth. The population in that particular area actually may grow much less rapidly than anticipated, or it may even diminish as a result of a shift in population. (2) The land is not acquired for the purpose of speculation but for the purpose of putting a building thereon and operating a business on the premise. (3) If the land should appreciate in value from $10,000 to $50,000 in 20 years, this will happen in spite of this prospective

Correct Project Evaluation because Capital Recovery for Land at End of Project E's Economic Life Is Included at Original Value of Land

	(1)	(2)	(3)	(4)	(5)	(6)
	Cash Outlay* for Building and Land and Capital Recovery for Land					
		Present Value		Cash Income	Sum-of-the-	
	Cash Outlay and Capital	Factor		before	Years'-Digits	Taxable
Year	Recovery	at 12%	Amount	Income Taxes	Depreciation	Income
0	$(30,000)	1.0000	$(30,000)	—	—	—
1				$ 9,678	$ 1,905	$ 7,773
2				9,768	1,810	7,958
3				9,854	1,714	8,140
4				9,944	1,619	8,325
5				10,030	1,524	8,506
6				10,119	1,429	8,690
7				10,206	1,333	8,873
8				10,296	1,238	9,058
9				10,381	1,143	9,238
10				10,471	1,048	9,423
11				10,558	952	9,606
12				10,647	857	9,790
13				10,733	762	9,971
14				10,823	667	10,156
15				10,909	571	10,338
16				10,999	476	10,523
17				11,085	381	10,704
18				11,174	286	10,888
19				11,261	190	11,071
20				11,350	95	11,255
	10,000	.1037	1,037			
Total	$(20,000)		$(28,963)	$210,286	$20,000	$190,286

DCF rate of return is 20%.

Payout period is 5 years.

* Cash outlay in parentheses.

project and not because of it. The appreciation in land value will not be the result of this prospective project. (4) There is too much of a temptation for the sponsors who initiate prospective projects to change them from unacceptable to acceptable projects by simply including capital recoveries for land and other fixed assets at the end of their economic lives at inflated values.

As explained earlier, prospective projects' capital recoveries are discounted at the company's direct borrowing rate in effect at the time the economic evaluations of the prospective projects are prepared. In this example, the $8,963 difference between the $10,000 capital recovery at the end of

TABLE 66

(7)	(8)	(9)	(10)	(11)	(12)
	Profit after Depreciation and Income		Project Cash	Present Value	
Income Taxes	Taxes	Depreciation	Flow	Factor at 20%	Amount
—	—	—	$ (30,000)	1.0000	$(30,000)
$ 3,731	$ 4,042	$ 1,905	5,947	.8333	4,956
3,820	4,138	1,810	5,948	.6944	4,130
3,907	4,233	1,714	5,947	.5787	3,442
3,996	4,329	1,619	5,948	.4823	2,869
4,083	4,423	1,524	5,947	.4019	2,390
4,171	4,519	1,429	5,948	.3349	1,992
4,259	4,614	1,333	5,947	.2791	1,660
4,348	4,710	1,238	5,948	.2326	1,384
4,434	4,804	1,143	5,947	.1938	1,152
4,523	4,900	1,048	5,948	.1615	961
4,611	4,995	952	5,947	.1346	800
4,699	5,091	857	5,948	.1122	667
4,786	5,185	762	5,947	.0935	556
4,875	5,281	667	5,948	.0779	427
4,962	5,376	571	5,947	.0649	386
5,051	5,472	476	5,948	.0541	322
5,138	5,566	381	5,947	.0451	268
5,226	5,662	286	5,948	.0376	223
5,314	5,757	190	5,947	.0313	186
5,403	5,852	95	5,947	.0261	155
			1,037	—	1,037
$91,337	$98,949	$20,000	$ 89,986		$ –0–

Memo	
Land—original cost	$10,000
Building—original cost	20,000
Total—original cost	$30,000

the 20th year and its $1,037 present value at the zero reference point in Table 66 represents the amount of interest the company theoretically would be willing to pay at its 12 percent current direct borrowing rate for receiving $1,037 at the zero reference point in lieu of $10,000 at the end of the 20th year.

Perhaps one of the most common yet one of the most controversial of all the pitfalls in estimating total capital costs of prospective projects involves decisions as to whether fixed assets already owned by the company, and therefore requiring no additional capital outlays, should be included in the pro-

Incorrect Project Evaluation because Capital Recovery for Land at End of Project E's Economic Life Is Included at Estimated Appreciated Market Value of Land

	(1)	(2)	(3)	(4)	(5)	(6)	(7)
	Cash Outlay* for Building and Land and Capital Recovery for Land			Cash Income before Income Taxes	Sum-of-the-Years'-Digits Depreciation	Taxable Income	Income Taxes
	Cash Outlay* and Capital Recovery	Present Value					
Year		Factor at 12%	Amount				
0	$(30,000)†	1.000	$(30,000)	—	—	—	—
1				$ 9,678	$ 1,905	$ 7,773	$ 3,731
2				9,768	1,810	7,958	3,820
3				9,854	1,714	8,140	3,907
4				9,944	1,619	8,325	3,996
5				10,030	1,524	8,506	4,083
6				10,119	1,429	8,690	4,171
7				10,206	1,333	8,873	4,259
8				10,296	1,238	9,058	4,348
9				10,381	1,143	9,238	4,434
10				10,471	1,048	9,423	4,523
11				10,558	952	9,606	4,611
12				10,647	857	9,790	4,699
13				10,733	762	9,971	4,786
14				10,823	667	10,156	4,875
15				10,909	571	10,338	4,962
16				10,999	476	10,523	5,051
17				11,085	381	10,704	5,138
18				11,174	286	10,888	5,226
19				11,261	190	11,071	5,314
20				11,350	95	11,255	5,403
	50,000	.1037	5,185				
Total	$ 20,000		$(24,815)	$210,286	$20,000	$190,286	$91,337

DCF rate of return is 23.6%.

Payout period is 5.0 years.

* Cash outlay in parentheses.

† Land—original cost	$10,000
Building—original cost	20,000
Total—original cost	$30,000

spective project's total capital costs on which the project's DCF rates of return will be calculated. A typical example of this type of situation is illustrated in Tables 68 and 69, which are based on the following assumptions:

1. Prospective Project F calls for tearing down the 20-year-old building erected in Project E and constructing a new one to take its place at an estimated construction cost of $40,000.

2. The company's annual capital budget contains only the $40,000 capital

TABLE 67

(8)	(9)	(10)	(11)	(12)	(13)	(14)
Profit after Depreciation and Income Taxes	*Depreciation*	*Project Cash Flow*	*Present Value*			
			Factor at 23%	*Amount*	*Factor at 24%*	*Amount*
—	—	$ (30,000)	1.0000	$(30,000)	1.000	$(30,000)
$ 4,042	$ 1,905	5,947	.8130	4,835	.8065	4,796
4,138	1,810	5,948	.6610	3,932	.6504	3,869
4,233	1,714	5,947	.5374	3,196	.5245	3,119
4,329	1,619	5,948	.4369	2,599	.4230	2,516
4,423	1,524	5,947	.3552	2,112	.3411	2,029
4,519	1,429	5,948	.2888	1,718	.2751	1,636
4,614	1,333	5,947	.2348	1,396	.2218	1,319
4,710	1,238	5,948	.1909	1,135	.1789	1,064
4,804	1,143	5,947	.1552	923	.1443	858
4,900	1,048	5,948	.1262	751	.1164	692
4,995	952	5,947	.1026	610	.0938	558
5,091	857	5,948	.0834	496	.0757	450
5,185	762	5,947	.0678	403	.0610	363
5,281	667	5,948	.0551	328	.0492	293
5,376	571	5,947	.0448	266	.0397	236
5,472	476	5,948	.0364	217	.0320	190
5,566	381	5,947	.0296	176	.0258	153
5,662	286	5,948	.0241	143	.0208	124
5,757	190	5,947	.0196	117	.0168	100
5,852	95	5,947	.0159	95	.0135	80
		5,185	—	5,185	—	5,185
$98,949	$20,000	$ 94,134		$ 633		$ (400)

expenditure for tearing down the old building and constructing the new one.

3. The company's annual capital budget does not include any capital expenditure for land because the land for prospective Project F is already owned by the company for the past 20 years.

4. The land on which the new building in the prospective Project F will be constructed is recorded and carried on the company's books and reported in its financial statements at its $10,000 original cost.

5. However, contrary to the forecast in Project E, the land has actually appreciated in market value only from $10,000 to $30,000 instead of from $10,000 to $50,000 during the 20-year period, and it can be sold presently at this $30,000 price. In other words, the land has tripled in market value during the past 20 years.

6. Prospective Project F's annual cash income is estimated to be $8,214 compared to $5,947 for Project E 20 years earlier.

7. Its economic life is estimated to be 20 years similar to that of Project E's.

As shown in Table 68, when the present $30,000 land value is excluded from the economic evaluation, the DCF rate of return and payout period of prospective Project F are 20 percent and 4.9 years, respectively. The exclusion of the $30,000 land value from its economic evaluation is justified erroneously by some financial analysts based on this reasoning: (1) Since the land is already owned by the company, it is no part of prospective Project F's capital expenditure. (2) No capital expenditure for the acquisition of land is included in the company's annual capital budget. (3) Furthermore, no amount of cash is required or requested for the acquisition of land. (4) Since the land is recorded and carried on the company's books and reported in its financial statements only at its $10,000 original cost instead of at its $30,000 appreciated market value, the $2,267 ($8,214 − $5,947) increase in prospective Project F's cash income compared to that of Project E will increase the company's overall profitability, as will be evidenced by an increase in its year-to-year book rates of return. The rationale on which these contentions are based is absolutely fallacious because it ignores the option the company has with regard to the use or disposition of the land.

As shown in Table 69, when the land is included in the economic evaluation at its $30,000 current market value, prospective Project F's DCF rate of return is reduced from 20 percent to 10.7 percent and its payout period is increased from 4.9 years to 8.5 years. The inclusion of the $30,000 appreciated land value in prospective Project F's total capital cost in Table 69 is based on the following rationale. The company has an option of either transferring the land to Project F or of selling the land at the prevailing market price of $30,000. Since the company has decided to exercise its option in favor of transferring the land to prospective Project F instead of selling it, the company is foregoing $30,000 cash. Consequently, by transferring the land to prospective Project F and thereby foregoing $30,000 cash, the company's cost by transferring the land to this prospective project is $30,000. This obviously, makes it mandatory to include the land at its $30,000 appreciated market value in the economic evaluation as a part of prospective Project F's total capital cost.

As indicated previously, by including the $30,000 appreciated land value in the economic evaluation, not only is prospective Project F's DCF rate of return materially reduced and its payout period substantially lengthened but, even more important, the prospective Project F is changed from an acceptable to an unacceptable prospective project because the predetermined minimum

TABLE 68

Incorrect Project Evaluation Because the Current Land Value in Erection of New Building was Excluded Because Company Already Owned the Land and No Cash Requirement for Land Was Included in Company's Current-Year Budget for Project F

	(1)	(2)	(3)	(4)	(5)	(6)	(7)	(8)	(9)	(10)
									Present Value	
Year	Cash Outlay* for Building	Cash Income before Income Taxes	Sum-of-the-Years'-Digits Depreciation	Taxable Income	Income Taxes	Profit after Depreciation and Income Taxes	Depreciation	Project Cash Flow	Factor at 20%	Amount
0	$(40,000)	—	—				—	$(40,000)		$(40,000)
1		$ 12,279	$ 3,810	$ 8,469	$ 4,065	$ 4,404	$ 3,810	8,214	.8333	6,845
2		12,457	3,619	8,838	4,243	4,595	3,619	8,214	.6944	5,704
3		12,631	3,429	9,202	4,417	4,785	3,429	8,214	.5787	4,753
4		12,807	3,238	9,569	4,593	4,976	3,238	8,214	.4823	3,962
5		12,983	3,048	9,935	4,769	5,166	3,048	8,214	.4019	3,301
6		13,159	2,857	10,302	4,945	5,357	2,857	8,214	.3349	2,751
7		13,334	2,667	10,667	5,120	5,547	2,667	8,214	.2791	2,293
8		13,510	2,476	11,034	5,296	5,738	2,476	8,214	.2326	1,910
9		13,686	2,286	11,400	5,472	5,928	2,286	8,214	.1938	1,592
10		13,860	2,095	11,765	5,647	6,118	2,095	8,213	.1615	1,326
11		14,038	1,905	12,133	5,824	6,309	1,905	8,214	.1346	1,106
12		14,214	1,714	12,500	6,000	6,500	1,714	8,214	.1122	922
13		14,389	1,524	12,865	6,175	6,690	1,524	8,214	.0935	768
14		14,566	1,333	13,233	6,352	6,881	1,333	8,214	.0779	640
15		14,741	1,143	13,598	6,527	7,071	1,143	8,214	.0649	533
16		14,917	952	13,965	6,703	7,262	952	8,214	.0541	444
17		15,093	762	14,331	6,879	7,452	762	8,214	.0451	370
18		15,269	571	14,698	7,055	7,643	571	8,214	.0376	309
19		15,444	381	15,063	7,230	7,833	381	8,214	.0313	257
20		15,619	190	15,429	7,406	8,023	190	8,213	.0261	214
Total	($40,000)	$278,996	$40,000	$238,996	$114,718	$124,278	$40,000	$124,278		$ –0–

DCF rate of return is 20%.

Payout period is 4.9 years.

* Cash outlay in parentheses.

Correct Project Evaluation Because It Includes Current Market Value of Land—Thus Recognizing the Company's Alternative of Selling the Land at Its Current Market Value, and by Not Exercising This Alternative It Is Forgoing the ($30,000) Current Market Value for the Land for Project F

	(1)	(2)	(3)	(4)	(5)	(6)	(7)
	Cash Outlay* for Building and Land and Capital Recovery for Land						
	Building Cost $40,000	*Present Value*		*Cash Income before Income Taxes*	*Sum-of-the- Years'-Digits Depreciation*	*Taxable Income*	*Income Taxes*
Year	*Land Cost $30,000*	*Factor at 12%*	*Amount*				
0	$(70,000)	1.0000	$(70,000)	—	—	—	—
1				$ 12,279	$ 3,810	$ 8,469	$ 4,065
2				12,457	3,619	8,838	4,243
3				12,631	3,429	9,202	4,417
4				12,807	3,238	9,569	4,593
5				12,983	3,048	9,935	4,769
6				13,159	2,857	10,302	4,945
7				13,334	2,667	10,667	5,120
8				13,510	2,476	11,034	5,296
9				13,686	2,286	11,400	5,472
10				13,860	2,095	11,765	5,647
11				14,038	1,905	12,133	5,824
12				14,214	1,714	12,500	6,000
13				14,389	1,524	12,865	6,175
14				14,566	1,333	13,233	6,352
15				14,741	1,143	13,598	6,527
16				14,917	952	13,965	6,703
17				15,093	762	14,331	6,879
18				15,269	571	14,698	7,055
19				15,444	381	15,063	7,230
20				15,619	190	15,429	7,406
	30,000	.1037	3,111				
Total	$(40,000)		$(66,689)	$278,996	$40,000	$238,996	$114,718

DCF rate of return is 10.7%.

Payout period is 8.5 years.

* Cash outlay in parentheses.

acceptable DCF rate of return for this type of project is presumed to be 15 percent.

An important factor to consider at this point is that fixed assets are recorded and carried on the books of companies at their original costs for as long as they continue to be owned by the company, even though the current market or resale values of these fixed assets generally will have appreciated and be considerably higher, particularly if the assets have been owned by the companies for extended periods of time. This is in accordance with orthodox and accepted accounting practices. Consequently, when such fixed assets are

TABLE 69

(8)	(9)	(10)	(11)	(12)	(13)	(14)
Profit after Depreciation and Income Taxes	Depreciation	Project Cash Flow	Present Value			
			Factor at 11%	Amount	Factor at 10%	Amount
—	—	$(70,000)	—	$(70,000)	—	$(70,000)
$ 4,404	$ 3,810	8,214	.9009	7,400	.9091	7,467
4,595	3,619	8,214	.8116	6,666	.8264	6,788
4,785	3,429	8,214	.7312	6,006	.7513	6,171
4,976	3,238	8,214	.6587	5,411	.6830	5,610
5,166	3,048	8,214	.5935	4,875	.6209	5,100
5,357	2,857	8,214	.5346	4,391	.5645	4,636
5,547	2,667	8,214	.4817	3,957	.5132	4,215
5,738	2,476	8,214	.4339	3,564	.4665	3,832
5,928	2,286	8,214	.3909	3,211	.4241	3,484
6,118	2,095	8,213	.3522	2,893	.3855	3,166
6,309	1,905	8,214	.3173	2,606	.3505	2,879
6,500	1,714	8,214	.2858	2,347	.3186	2,617
6,690	1,524	8,214	.2575	2,115	.2897	2,380
6,881	1,333	8,214	.2320	1,906	.2633	2,163
7,071	1,143	8,214	.2090	1,717	.2394	1,966
7,262	952	8,214	.1883	1,546	.2176	1,787
7,452	762	8,214	.1696	1,393	.1978	1,625
7,643	571	8,214	.1528	1,255	.1799	1,478
7,833	381	8,214	.1377	1,131	.1635	1,343
8,023	190	8,213	.1240	1,018	.1486	1,220
		3,111		3,111		3,111
$124,278	$40,000	$ 97,389		$ (1,481)		$ 3,038

transferred to prospective projects, there is a tendency, more often than not, of failing to include them in their economic evaluations either at their original cost or at their current market or resale value. The reason for the reluctance to include them is that this will enhance the prospective projects' financial criteria and thereby make them acceptable when otherwise they may be unacceptable. Even when such fixed assets transferred to prospective projects are included in the economic evaluations at their current market or resale value and as a result the prospective projects show unacceptable financial criteria (DCF rates of return and payout periods), top management may still be inclined to approve the acceptance of such unprofitable prospective projects based on the rationale that the incremental profits generated by prospective projects will enhance the company's overall profitability. This is proven by the increases in the company's year-to-year book rates of return because the transferred fixed assets are carried on the company's books at their much lower original costs. Failure to include in prospective projects' economic evaluations the fixed assets transferred to the prospective projects at their current market or resale values, as well as the acceptance of prospective projects that show unacceptable financial criteria as a result of fixed assets transferred to projects at their current market or resale values instead of their substantially lower historical original costs, are conditions that are in conflict with and contrary to sound and effective project evaluation principles and techniques.

Another of the more common pitfalls in estimating capital costs of prospective projects often occurs when the prospective project is initiated in one of a company's operating departments and this operating department does not make other operating departments that are involved aware of the project, which is necessary for the project to be operative, successful, and profitable. Prospective Project G, for example, involves no less than three of the company's operating departments. Its initial economic evaluation prepared by the operating department that sponsored this new project included only the capital expenditures required to be made by its own department but not those required to be made by the other two operating departments that were also involved but were not made aware of the prospective project proposal.

We will assume that the unfortunate exclusion of the capital expenditures, capital recovery, and operating expenses of the other two operating departments from the initial economic evaluation of the prospective project was attributable to a lack of communication and coordination between the company's three operating departments that were required to play an important part in this project in order to make it viable. Prospective Project G, we will assume further, was initiated by the company's marine transportation department, but the project also affected its manufacturing and marketing departments. The project involves the conversion from conventional-size tankers to supersize tankers for the purpose of bringing about substantial savings in the company's marine transportation expenses. However, due to the enormous increase in the size of the super tankers and the huge loads of crude oil and refined petroleum products they will carry, a considerable amount of dredging near the landing docks of the company's refineries and the ocean terminals is necessitated by this changeover in the size of the company's tankers and the loads they will carry. Also additional storage tanks are required to be installed both at the refineries and the ocean terminals by the company's manufacturing and marketing department in order to enable them to receive and store the substantially larger loads of crude oil and finished petroleum products that will be transported by these super tankers.

The economic evaluations for the prospective Project G, shown in Tables 70 and 71, are based on the following assumptions:

1. The estimated capital cost for converting from the conventional size to the supersize tankers is $50 million, as forecasted by the company's marine transportation department. This estimated capital cost represents the difference between the estimated capital cost for the construction of the supersize tankers and the estimated capital recovery from the disposition of the conventional size tankers.

2. The $50 million estimated net capital cost for the conversion from the conventional size to the supersize tankers is included in the marine transportation department's initial economic evaluation as well as in its annual capital budget.

3. The estimated capital cost for the installation of the additional storage tanks needed at the company's refineries and ocean terminals is $15 million, as forecasted by its manufacturing and marketing departments.

4. The estimated capital cost for the necessary dredging near the docks of the refineries and the ocean terminals to enable the supersize tankers to dock and to load and unload their huge cargos at these manufacturing and marketing units is $5 million, as forecasted by the company's manufacturing and marketing departments.

5. Neither the $15 million estimated capital cost for the additional storage tanks nor the $5 million estimated capital cost for the required dredging near the docks of the refineries and the ocean terminals are included in the manufacturing and the marketing departments' annual capital budgets or in prospective Project G's initial economic evaluation, because neither operating department had been made aware of this prospective project at the time their annual capital budgets and the prospective project's initial economic evaluation were prepared.

6. The $5 million estimated capital cost for the dredging near the docks of the refineries and the ocean terminals are considered improvements to the land on which these manufacturing and marketing facilities are located. Therefore, it enhances the value of the land at these locations, and for this reason the $5 million estimated capital cost for the deepening of the waters near the docks of the refineries and ocean terminals is treated as capital recovery at the end of prospective Project G's 20-year economic life.

7. Prospective Project G's estimated total cash returns are $301,600,000 as shown in the initial economic evaluation in Table 70 and $305,359,000 as shown in the final economic evaluation in Table 71.

8. Prospective Project G's estimated economic life is 20 years.

9. Prospective Project G's initial economic evaluation as prepared by the company's marine transportation department and submitted to its top management for approval excludes the $15 million estimated cost for additional storage facilities, the $5 million estimated capital cost for dredging, the $5 million capital recovery for the improvements to the

land, and the additional operating expenses for the maintenance of the additional storage tanks, as shown in Table 70. These items were excluded either because the financial analysts in the company's marine transportation department, sponsors of this prospective project, simply gave no thought to the possibility that the waters around the company's refineries and ocean terminals may not be deep enough to accommodate the supersize tankers, and that the present storage facilities may not be adequate enough to receive and store the considerably larger loads; or the financial analysts simply may have assumed that the waters to the approaches to the company's refineries and ocean terminals would be deep enough and that the storage facilities at these manufacturing and marketing units would be adequate, and hence preclude the need for dredging to deepen the waters and for installing additional storage tanks.

10. Subsequent to the company's top management's review of the prospective project's initial economic evaluation, the marine transportation department was requested to prepare a new and more complete economic evaluation in cooperation with the company's manufacturing and marketing departments that would include all elements of the prospective project's capital costs, capital recoveries, operating savings, and operating expenses, as shown in Table 71.

11. The predetermined minimum acceptable DCF rate of return for this type of project is 25 percent.

When the initial economic evaluation, which showed a 30 percent DCF rate of return and a 3.3-year payout period, was presented by the company's marine transportation department to top management for approval, a series of pertinent questions were raised relative to this prospective project. The answers to some of these questions brought to light that neither the company's manufacturing nor its marketing department had been made aware of the prospective Project G, and these departments were not consulted as to whether the water near the company's refineries and ocean terminals was deep enough to accommodate the supersize tankers or the present storage facilities were adequate to receive and store the substantially larger tanker loads of crude oil and refined petroleum products.

When the company's manufacturing and marketing departments were brought into the picture, top management learned not only that an extensive amount of dredging would be necessary but also that the installation of a large number of additional storage tanks would have to be installed at both the company's refineries and ocean terminals before this prospective project could become a viable undertaking. The company's top management then ordered its marine transportation department in cooperation with its manufacturing and marketing departments to prepare and submit a new and more realistic economic evaluation for approval.

When the new economic evaluation was completed and submitted for approval, it showed a 21.7 percent DCF rate of return and a 4.5-year payout

TABLE 70

Incorrect Project Evaluation Because It Fails to Include Additional Capital Cost for Dredging Waterways and Additional Storage Facilities, Capital Recoveries for Land Improvement, and Additional Operating Expenses for Maintenance of Additional Storage Facilities for Project G
(dollar figures in the thousands)

	(1)	(2)	(3)	(4)	(5)	(6)	(7)	(8)	(9)	(10)
									Present Value	
Year	Cash Outlay* Net	Cash Income before Income Taxes	Sum-of-the-Years'-Digits Depreciation	Taxable Income	Income Taxes	Profit after Depreciation and Income Taxes	Depreciation	Project Cash Flow	Factor at 30%	Amount
0	$(50,000)†						—	$ (50,000)	1.0000	$(50,000)
1		$ 24,165	$ 5,238	$ 18,927	$ 9,085	$ 9,842	$ 5,238	15,080	.7692	11,600
2		24,407	4,976	19,431	9,327	10,104	4,976	15,080	.5917	8,923
3		24,649	4,714	19,935	9,569	10,366	4,714	15,080	.4552	6,864
4		24,890	4,452	20,438	9,810	10,628	4,452	15,080	.3501	5,280
5		25,132	4,190	20,942	10,052	10,890	4,190	15,080	.2693	4,061
6		25,373	3,929	21,444	10,293	11,151	3,929	15,080	.2072	3,125
7		25,615	3,667	21,948	10,535	11,413	3,667	15,080	.1594	2,404
8		25,857	3,405	22,452	10,777	11,675	3,405	15,080	.1226	1,849
9		26,099	3,143	22,956	11,019	11,937	3,143	15,080	.0943	1,422
10		26,341	2,881	23,460	11,261	12,199	2,881	15,080	.0725	1,093
11		26,582	2,619	23,963	11,502	12,461	2,619	15,080	.0558	841
12		26,824	2,357	24,467	11,744	12,723	2,357	15,080	.0429	647
13		27,066	2,095	24,971	11,986	12,985	2,095	15,080	.0330	498
14		27,308	1,833	25,475	12,228	13,247	1,833	15,080	.0254	383
15		27,550	1,571	25,979	12,470	13,509	1,571	15,080	.0195	294
16		27,791	1,310	26,481	12,711	13,770	1,310	15,080	.0150	226
17		28,033	1,048	26,985	12,953	14,032	1,048	15,080	.0116	175
18		28,274	786	27,488	13,194	14,294	786	15,080	.0089	134
19		28,516	524	27,992	13,436	14,556	524	15,080	.0068	102
20		28,759	262	28,497	13,679	14,818	262	15,080	.0053	79
Total	$(50,000)	$529,231	$55,000	$474,231	$227,631	$246,600	$55,000	$251,600		$ –0–

DCF rate of return is 30%.

Payout period is 3.3 years.

* Cash outlay in parentheses.
† Cash outlay for construction of super tankers $55,000,000

Capital recovery from disposition of conventional tankers   5,000,000

Net cash outlay for conversion from conventional to super tankers $50,000,000 period. This represented a 8.3 percent reduction in prospective Project G's DCF rate of return and a 1.2-year increase in its payout period. This decrease in its DCF rate of return and lengthening of its payout period, of course, were attributable to the net effect of the inclusion of the $20 million additional capital cost, the $5 million capital recovery, and the $150,000 annual operating expenses.

The two economic evaluations for this prospective project, as shown in Tables 70 and 71, emphasize the importance that nothing can be taken for granted and that every facet of a prospective project bears checking into and

Correct Project Evaluation Because It Includes Additional Capital Cost for Dredging Waterways and Additional Storage Facilities, Capital Recoveries for Land Improvement, and Additional Operating Expenses for Maintenance of Additional Storage Facilities for Project G (dollar figures in thousands)

	(1)	(2)	(3)	(4)	(5)	(6)	(7)
	Cash Outlays* and Capital Recoveries						
		Present Value		Cash Income before Income Taxes	Sum-of-the-Years'-Digits Depreciation	Taxable Income	Income Taxes
Year	Actual	Factor at 12%	Amount				
0	$(70,000)†	1.000	$(70,000)	—	—	—	—
1				$24,015‡	$ 6,190	$ 17,825	$ 8,556
2				24,257	5,881	18,376	8,820
3				24,499	5,571	18,928	9,085
4				24,740	5,262	19,478	9,349
5				24,982	4,952	20,030	9,614
6				25,223	4,643	20,580	9,878
7				25,465	4,333	21,132	10,143
8				25,707	4,024	21,683	10,408
9				25,949	3,714	22,235	10,673
10				26,191	3,405	22,786	10,937
11				26,432	3,095	23,337	11,202
12				26,674	2,786	23,888	11,466
13				26,916	2,476	24,440	11,731
14				27,158	2,167	24,991	11,996
15				27,400	1,857	25,543	12,261
16				27,641	1,548	26,093	12,525
17				27,883	1,238	26,645	12,790
18				28,124	929	27,195	13,054
19				28,366	619	27,747	13,319
20				28,609	310	28,299	13,534
	5,000	.1037	519				
Total	$(65,000)		$(69,481)	$526,231	$65,000	$461,231	$221,391

DCF rate of return is 21.7%.

Payout period is 4.5 years.

* Cash outlays in parentheses.
† Net cash outlay for conversion from conventional to super tankers (see Table 70) $50,000,000
  Cash outlay for additional storage facilities at refineries and ocean terminals   15,000,000
  Cash outlay for dreding waterways leading to refineries and ocean terminals   5,000,000
  Total cash outlays $70,000,000

‡ Additional annual maintenance expenses for all additional storage facilities $ 150,000

must be considered and evaluated carefully if unwise and costly investment decisions are to be avoided.

There, of course, are many other pitfalls encountered in estimating capital costs of prospective projects. Some of these pitfalls are encountered when determining *(a)* what fixed assets should be included in prospective projects, *(b)* at what capital costs the fixed assets should be included, and even *(c)* at what point in time during the fixed assets' economic lives they should be included.

For example, a company purchased waterfront property worth $5 million

TABLE 71

(8) Profit after Depreciation and Income Taxes	(9) Depreciation	(10) Project Cash Flow	(11) Factor at 21%	(12) Amount	(13) Factor at 22%	(14) Amount
—	—	$ (70,000)	1.0000	$(70,000)	1.0000	$(70,000)
$ 9,269	$ 6,190	15,459	.8264	12,775	.8197	12,672
9,556	5,881	15,437	.6830	10,543	.6719	10,372
9,843	5,571	15,414	.5645	8,701	.5507	8,488
10,129	5,262	15,391	.4665	7,180	.4514	6,947
10,416	4,952	15,368	.3855	5,924	.3700	5,686
10,702	4,643	15,345	.3186	4,889	.3033	4,654
10,989	4,333	15,322	.2633	4,034	.2486	3,809
11,275	4,024	15,299	.2176	3,329	.2038	3,118
11,562	3,714	15,276	.1799	2,748	.1670	2,551
11,849	3,405	15,254	.1486	2,267	.1369	2,088
12,135	3,095	15,230	.1228	1,870	.1122	1,709
12,422	2,786	15,208	.1015	1,544	.0922	1,399
12,709	2,476	15,185	.0839	1,274	.0754	1,145
12,995	2,167	15,162	.0693	1,051	.0618	937
13,282	1,857	15,139	.0573	867	.0507	768
13,568	1,548	15,116	.0474	716	.0415	627
13,855	1,238	15,093	.0391	590	.0340	514
14,141	929	15,070	.0323	487	.0279	420
14,428	619	15,047	.0267	402	.0229	345
14,715	310	15,025	.0221	332	.0187	281
		519	—	519	—	519
$239,840	$65,000	$235,359		$ 2,042		$ (951)

Present Value spans columns (11)–(14).

more than five years before it was estimated that the land would be needed for the construction of a manufacturing plant. This waterfront property was purchased far in advance of the time it was estimated to be needed because waterfront property in that particular coastal city was extremely scarce and was expected to rise rapidly in price. As it turned out later, the demand for the company's products in that particular geographical area did not reach the anticipated level that warranted the erection of a new manufacturing plant until eight years after the waterfront property had been purchased. By that time, the property had doubled in market value and could be sold for $10 million.

The company's manufacturing department's management, which initiated the prospective project for the construction of the new manufacturing plant, took the position that the waterfront property should be included in the economic evaluation at its $5 million original cost. It defended its position on the basis that the waterfront property was acquired solely for the purpose of constructing a new manufacturing plant on it and, furthermore, that it was purchased eight years ahead of the time it was needed for that purpose because waterfront property was scarce in that coastal city and the manufacturing department's management wanted to escape the substantially higher price that it anticipated would prevail at the time the land was needed some five to eight years later. On the surface, the management of the manufacturing department appears to have good reasons for taking this adamant position inasmuch as this waterfront property actually doubled in value during the eight-year period.

However, let us pursue this investment situation a little further and determine the logical capital cost for the waterfront property to be transferred to the prospective project for the construction of a new manufacturing plant.

When, in accordance with the contention of the management of the manufacturing department, the $5 million original cost is used as the capital cost for the waterfront property in the economic evaluation, the prospective project for the construction of a new manufacturing plant shows a DCF rate of return in excess of the standard or predetermined minimum acceptable DCF rate of return for this type of project. This means that on this capital cost basis, this prospective project would be a candidate for approval and acceptance by the company's top management.

On the other hand, when in accordance with sound economic and financial principles the $10 million current market, or resale, value is used as the capital cost for the waterfront property in the economic evaluation, this prospective project shows a DCF return below the standard or predetermined minimum acceptable DCF rate of return for this type of project. This, contrariwise, means that on this substantially higher capital cost basis, this prospective project would be a candidate for disapproval and rejection by the company's top management.

The rationale on which the arguments put forth by the management of the manufacturing department is based is absolutely unsound from both an economic and a financial point of view for two reasons: (1) The company has an option of either transferring the waterfront property to the prospective project for the new plant or of selling it for $10 million. Hence, by transferring the waterfront property to the prospective project for the new plant, the company is foregoing $10 million cash, which means that it is costing the company $10 million for the use of the land as a site for the new plant. (2) Assuming the company's opportunity cost of money rate is 10 percent, then by having $5 million tied up in the waterfront property for eight years, the company is foregoing $5,720,000 in profits during the eight-year period because at the 10 percent rate the $5 million will grow to $10,720,000 ($5,000,000 × 2.144) by the end of the eight-year period. In addition to foregoing these substantial profits, the company also had to pay real estate taxes on the waterfront property and, probably, some maintenance expenses during the eight-year period which could bring the total cost for the waterfront property in excess of its $10 million current market, or resale, value. Obviously, the foregoing reasons furnish convincing proof that it is sound investment practice to include the waterfront property in the prospective project's economic evaluation at the $10 million current market, or resale, value instead of at its $5 million original cost.

Another typical pitfall that may be encountered in estimating capital costs of prospective projects has to do with their timing. For example, when companies purchase land sufficient in size not only for their immediate requirements but also for future expansion, this investment situation immediately creates the problem of deciding as to what point in time during prospective projects' economic lives and at what capital costs the parcels of land acquired for future expansions should be included in the prospective projects' economic evaluations. It is assumed in the following example *(a)* that a company purchases land worth $3 million, *(b)* that two thirds of the acreage of this land is to be used immediately for the construction of a new factory, *(c)* that one third of this land is to be used for the expansion of this factory 15 years later, and *(d)* that the estimated useful life of this factory is 40 years. The additional land needed for future expansion is purchased along with that needed immediately for construction of the new factory at the beginning of the prospective project because it is feared the land will no longer be available 15 years later when it is estimated to be needed for expansion of the factory.

When the economic evaluation for the proposed construction of the new factory is prepared, the question that naturally arises is how should the land acquired for future expansion of the new factory be treated in the economic evaluation? Should the land be included at its $1 million original cost at the beginning of the prospective project, or should it be included at its estimated market, or resale, value at the time estimated for the new factory's expansion in the 15th year of its economic life?

Alternative I.   The company can choose to purchase the additional land needed for future expansion of the new factory immediately, tie up $1 million for 15 years, and not generate any profits thereon during that time period.

Alternative II.   The company can choose to postpone acquiring the additional land needed for future expansion until the 15th year, then purchase it at the prevailing market, or resale, value and invest the $1 million for 15 years in some other project to generate profits during that time period.

Assuming the company's opportunity cost of money rate is 10 percent, the $1 million invested in some other project instead of being tied up for 15 years in the additional land needed for future expansion will grow to $4,177,000 ($1,000,000 × 4.177 compound value factor) at this earnings rate by the end of the 15th year when it is needed for expansion of the new factory. This means that by tieing up the $1 million for 15 years in the additional land needed for future expansion and thus foregoing the profits that could be generated by investing the $1 million in some other project during this 15-year period, the company's cost for the additional land needed for the expansion of the new factory in the 15th year is actually $4,177,000.

Conversely, the present value at the beginning of the prospective project's economic life of the above $4,177,000 capital cost for the additional land needed for the expansion of the new factory in the 15th year is $1,000,000 ($4,177,000 × .2344 present value factor), based on the company's 10 percent opportunity cost of money rate.

What all this means is that the $1 million expended for the additional land required for the expansion of the new factory 15 years later must be included in the economic evaluation at the zero reference point, i.e., at the beginning of the prospective project's economic life and not in the 15th year of its economic life for two reasons: (1) The $1 million to be included in the economic evaluation at the zero reference point represents the present value at that point in time of the $4,177,000 capital cost for the additional land required for expansion in the 15th year of the prospective project's economic life. (2) The $1 million for the additional land is actually expended at the beginning of the prospective project's economic life and not in the 15th year of its economic life.

If the company has an option of purchasing the additional land for $1 million in the 15th year of the prospective project's economic life and then exercises its option in that year, it will be proper in the economic evaluation to include the $1 million capital cost for the land in the 15th year instead of at the beginning of its economic life. In this investment situation, the financial benefit accruing from the marked difference in the timing of the $1 million cash outlay, which now occurs 15 years later instead of at the beginning of the prospective project's economic life, naturally will have to be given effect to.

The exceedingly more favorable timing of the $1 million cash outlay will be given effect to by discounting it at the company's current 12 percent direct borrowing rate. The resultant $182,700 ($1,000,000 × .1827 present value factor) at the zero reference point will then represent the present value at that point in time of the $1 million expended for the additional land in the 15th year. As explained earlier this means that the seller of the additional land theoretically would be willing to accept $182,700 at the beginning of the prospective project's economic life in lieu of $1 million 15 years later because he would be willing to pay 12 percent for the use of money.

There are two important conditions that must be strictly observed at all times in estimating the capital costs of prospective projects. First, all future capital outlays for the expansion of prospective projects or for the replacement of component fixed assets that have shorter useful lives than the prospective projects' economic lives must be included in the economic evaluations in constant dollars, i.e., in dollars that are equal in purchasing power to that of the dollars of the initial cash outlays at the beginning of the prospective projects' economic lives. Second, in the final year of the prospective projects' economic lives, capital recoveries for nondepreciable fixed assets, such as land, must be shown separately at the identical values at which they are included at the beginning of the prospective projects' economic lives; and capital recoveries for depreciable fixed assets also must be shown separately in the economic evaluations but at their depreciated values based on the accelerated depreciation method used for income tax purposes, because the prospective projects have received the tax benefits resulting from the use of this accelerated depreciation method.

Pitfalls Encountered in Estimating Prospective Projects' Future Cash Income or Savings

While there are many pitfalls encountered in estimating capital costs of prospective projects, there are even more pitfalls encountered in estimating their future cash income or savings for several good reasons: (1) Companies have to estimate cash income or savings of prospective projects based on their incremental profits sometimes as far as 10, 20, 30, or even 40 years into the future, depending on the length of the prospective projects' economic lives. (2) Companies generally have a series of alternative courses of action available to them with respect to each prospective project, and consequently they have to prepare a series of cash returns and then by a process of elimination they must choose the most economic alternative that promises to generate maximum cash income or savings for the companies. (3) Prospective projects frequently involve some imponderables that cannot be reduced to numbers, and therefore their effect cannot be injected into the economic evaluations. However, because of the impact such imponderables could have on the success or failure of prospective projects, they somehow must be brought to the attention of top management by some other means if unwise and costly investment decisions are to be avoided.

What makes the forecasting of the streams of future cash income or savings amounts of prospective projects so critical is that in addition to recovering their capital costs, they must earn profits that will yield rates of return on their capital costs that will be at least equivalent to or exceed their predetermined standards, i.e., their minimum acceptable DCF rates of return in

Economic Evaluation of Project D Correctly Leaving Out Estimated Rate of Inflation Cash Outlays and Cash Income Expressed in Constant Dollars Not Reflecting Depreciation Deficiencies

	(1)	(2)	(3)	(4)	(5)	(6)
Year	Cash Outlay*	Cash Income before Income Taxes	Sum-of-the-Years'-Digits Depreciation Calculated on Original Cost	Taxable Income	Income Taxes	Profit after Depreciation and Income Taxes
0	$(10,000)	—	—	—	—	—
1		$ 2,500	$ 952	$ 1,548	$ 743	$ 805
2		2,500	905	1,595	766	829
3		2,500	857	1,643	789	854
4		2,500	810	1,690	811	879
5		2,500	762	1,738	834	904
6		2,500	714	1,786	857	929
7		2,500	667	1,833	880	953
8		2,500	619	1,881	903	978
9		2,500	571	1,929	926	1,003
10		2,500	524	1,976	948	1,028
11		2,500	476	2,024	972	1,052
12		2,500	429	2,071	994	1,077
13		2,500	381	2,119	1,017	1,102
14		2,500	333	2,167	1,040	1,127
15		2,500	286	2,214	1,063	1,151
16		2,500	238	2,262	1,086	1,176
17		2,500	190	2,310	1,109	1,201
18		2,500	143	2,357	1,131	1,226
19		2,500	95	2,405	1,154	1,251
20		2,500	48	2,452	1,177	1,275
Total	$(10,000)	$50,000	$10,000	$40,000	$19,200	$20,800

DCF rate of return is 15.5%.

Payout period is 5.9 years.

* Cash outlay in parentheses.

order that the company's future overall profitability will be improved. If capital investments in prospective projects fail to accomplish this, then the purpose of making them is defeated and the company's future overall profitability could worsen rather than improve.

By far the most serious and also one of the most common pitfalls usually encountered in estimating future cash income or savings amounts of prospective projects is the practice of injecting the estimated future effects of inflation into their future cash income or savings amount, thereby highly overstating future cash income or savings amounts in terms of variable cheap current-year dollars. This usually is not done deliberately in order to make prospective projects show acceptable financial criteria that otherwise would show unacceptable financial criteria and therefore would be accepted instead of

TABLE 72

(7)	(8)	(9)	(10)	(11)	(12)
	Cash Outlay* and Cash Income after		Present Value		
		Factor		Factor	
Depreciation	Income Taxes	at 15%	Amount	at 16%	Amount
—	$(10,000)	1.0000	$(10,000)	1.0000	$(10,000)
$ 952	1,757	.8676	1,528	.8621	1,515
905	1,734	.7561	1,311	.7432	1,289
857	1,711	.6575	1,125	.6407	1,096
810	1,689	.5718	966	.5523	933
762	1,666	.4972	828	.4761	793
714	1,643	.4323	710	.4104	674
667	1,620	.3759	609	.3538	573
619	1,597	.3269	522	.3050	487
571	1,574	.2843	447	.2630	414
524	1,552	.2472	384	.2267	352
476	1,528	.2149	328	.1954	299
429	1,506	.1869	281	.1685	254
381	1,483	.1625	241	.1452	215
333	1,460	.1413	206	.1352	197
286	1,437	.1229	177	.1079	155
238	1,414	.1069	151	0930	132
190	1,391	.0929	129	.0802	112
143	1,369	.0808	111	.0691	95
95	1,346	.0703	95	.0596	80
48	1,323	.0611	81	.0514	68
$10,000	$ 20,800		$ 230		$ (267)

rejected by top management. In most cases, inflation is injected into economic evaluations unwittingly and is the result of companies maintaining historical records of the selling prices of their products, which in all likelihood increased steadily during protracted inflationary periods. Consequently, future cash income amounts of prospective projects all too frequently are projected predicated on the historical inflationary movement of the selling prices of a company's products.

As shown in Table 72, the capital cost as well as the future cash income or savings amounts in this prospective project's economic evaluation must be expressed in comparable constant dollars in order to arrive at realistic and reliable financial criteria. The following assumptions are made in prospective Project D:

1. Project D's capital cost is $10,000.
2. Its annual cash income or savings amounts range from $1,757 in the first year to $1,323 in the 20th year.
3. Its economic life is 20 years.
4. Its fixed assets are completely used up during the 20 years and therefore have no salvage value at the end of that time.
5. The sum-of-the-years'-digits method is used for income tax purposes.

Based on the above assumptions, prospective Project D shows a 15.5 percent DCF rate of return and a 5.9-year payout period. These are the correct financial criteria for prospective Project D because both its capital cost

Economic Evaluation of Project D Incorrectly Injecting Estimated Rate of Inflation into Annual Cash Income Amounts Also Considered As Post-Completion Audit Incorrectly Failing to Adjust Annual Cash Income Amounts for Inflation and Reflecting Depreciation Deficiencies*

	(1)	(2)	(3)	(4)	(5)	(6)
Year	Price Index	Value or Purchasing Power of $1	Cash Income* before Income Taxes	Sum-of-the Years'-Digits Depreciation Calculated on Original Cost	Taxable Income	Income Taxes
0	100	1.000	—	—	—	—
1	108	0.926	$ 2,700	$ 952	$ 1,748	$ 839
2	116	0.862	2,900	905	1,995	958
3	124	0.806	3,100	857	2,243	1,077
4	132	0.757	3,300	810	2,490	1,195
5	140	0.714	3,500	762	2,738	1,314
6	148	0.676	3,700	714	2,986	1,433
7	156	0.641	3,900	667	3,233	1,552
8	164	0.610	4,100	619	3,481	1,671
9	172	0.581	4,300	571	3,729	1,790
10	180	0.556	4,500	524	3,976	1,908
11	188	0.532	4,700	476	4,224	2,028
12	196	0.510	4,900	429	4,471	2,146
13	204	0.490	5,100	381	4,719	2,265
14	212	0.472	5,300	333	4,967	2,384
15	220	0.455	5,500	286	5,214	2,503
16	228	0.439	5,700	238	5,462	2,622
17	236	0.424	5,900	190	5,710	2,741
18	244	0.410	6,100	143	5,957	2,859
19	252	0.397	6,300	95	6,205	2,978
20	260	0.385	6,500	48	6,452	3,097
Total			$92,000	$10,000	$82,000	$39,360

DCF rate of return is 21.7%.

Payout period is 4.9 years.

* Capital outlays are expressed in expensive zero reference point dollars. Annual cash income amounts are expressed in cheap current-year dollars.

and its stream of annual cash income or savings amounts are expressed in comparable constant dollars.

As shown in Table 73, it is assumed that due to inflation, prospective Project D's stream of future cash income or savings amounts is estimated to increase steadily at a rate of eight point annually from an index of 100 at the zero reference point to an index of 260 in the 20th year. This, of course, means that the purchasing power of the dollar is shrinking each year, and that it is declining from $1 at the beginning, to $0.385 at the end of prospective Project D's 20-year economic life. In other words, the amount of goods and services that cost $1 at the beginning of the prospective project's economic life would cost $2.60, or 2.6 times as much at the end of its economic life. When

TABLE 73

(7)	(8)	(9)	(10)	(11)	(12)	(13)
		Cash				
Profit		Outlays*†		**Present Value**		
after		and Cash				
Income		Income after	Factor		Factor	
Taxes	Depreciation	Income Taxes	at 21%	Amount	at 22%	Amount
—	—	$(10,000)	1.0000	$(10,000)	1.0000	$(10,000)
$ 909	$ 952	$ 1,861	.8664	1,612	.8197	1,525
1,037	905	1,942	.6830	1,326	.6719	1,305
1,166	857	2,023	.5645	1,142	.5507	1,114
1,295	810	2,105	.4665	982	.4514	905
1,424	762	2,186	.3855	843	.3760	809
1,553	714	2,267	.3186	722	.3033	688
1,681	667	2,348	.2633	618	.2486	584
1,810	619	2,429	.2176	529	.2038	495
1,939	571	2,510	.1799	452	.1670	419
2,068	524	2,592	.1486	385	.1369	355
2,196	476	2,672	.1228	328	.1122	300
2,325	429	2,754	.1015	280	.0920	253
2,454	381	2,835	.0839	238	.0754	214
2,583	333	2,916	.0693	202	.0618	180
2,711	286	2,997	.0573	172	.0507	152
2,840	238	3,078	.0474	146	.0415	128
2,969	190	3,159	.0391	124	.0340	107
3,098	143	3,241	.0323	105	.0279	90
3,227	95	3,322	.0267	89	.0229	76
3,355	48	3,403	.0221	75	.0187	64
$42,640	$10,000	$ 42,640		$ 370		$ (192)

† Cash outlay in parentheses.

this stream of cheap current-year cash income or savings dollars, ranging from $1,861 in the first year to $3,403 in the 20th year, is related to the expensive $10,000 capital cost dollars at the beginning of prospective Project D's economic life in determining its financial criteria, then this prospective project will show a 21.7 percent DCF rate of return and a 4.9-year payout period. However, since the annual cash income or savings amounts before income taxes shown in Table 73, Column 3, are identical in purchasing power with those shown in Table 72, Column 2, for the comparable years, the 6.2 percent higher DCF rate of return and the one year shorter payout period shown for prospective Project D in Table 73 are fictitious and illusory because they are arrived at by measuring $52,640 cheap current-year cash income or savings dollars against incomparable $10,000 expensive capital investment dollars. Similar to those in Table 72, the annual depreciation charges used for income tax purposes in Table 73 are calculated by the sum-of-the-years'-digits method on the fixed assets' $10,000 original cost, as permitted under present corporate income tax laws.

The 21.7 percent DCF rate of return and 4.9 years payout period shown in Table 73, which are highly distorted and fictitious compared to the true and realistic 15.5 percent DCF rate of return and 5.9 payout period shown in Table 72 for prospective Project D, prove that realistic and reliable DCF rates of return and payout periods for prospective projects can be arrived at only by computing them on comparable, constant capital investment and cash income dollars if sound investment decisions are to be made by top management.

The effects of future inflation must always be excluded from estimates of future capital outlay, capital recovery, and cash income or savings amounts. Failure to abide by this rule and giving effect to inflation in these estimates could result in acceptable DCF rates of return and payout periods that otherwise would be unacceptable, and thus lead to unwise and costly investment decisions.

Forecasting streams of annual cash income or savings amounts far into the future is a difficult and risky task for sponsors of prospective projects. Such forecasting requires a great deal of foresight not only from the standpoint of sponsoring companies' long-range plans and objectives that are intended to be achieved through prospective projects but also from the standpoint that such long-range plans and objectives could be counteracted and negated by competitive companies' long-range plans and objectives designed to achieve similar results through prospective projects of their own that they may be sponsoring at some future time. Numerous assumptions may have to be made as to what is likely to take place in the marketplace in the future that will affect prospective projects of companies either favorably or unfavorably. All of these assumptions must be viable and plausible if the streams of prospective projects' future capital outlay, capital recovery, and cash return estimates are to be sound and realistic and produce reliable and dependable financial criteria. Even more important, companies sponsoring prospective projects cannot afford to overlook a single alternative course of action available to them or a single assumption as to what may or may not take place sometime in the future that may affect the projected profitability of prospective projects. The following case history is a good case in point.

Several decades ago, oil companies found themselves in the position of having a huge oversupply of No. 6 heavy fuel oil in their storage tanks. The reason for this huge oversupply of No. 6 heavy fuel oil was that there existed a very limited market for this product at that time. Most industrial firms and particularly utility companies were using coal instead of fuel oil as a fuel at that time. This limited demand for No. 6 heavy fuel oil and its consequent huge oversupply resulted in greatly depressing the price for this product. This situation posed quite a problem for oil companies with respect to the most economic disposition of their huge oversupply of No. 6 heavy fuel oil. On the one hand, they couldn't market this product at a reasonable profit while, on the other hand, they couldn't dispose of it by just dumping it into the ocean.

Since oil companies at that time were receiving substantially less for a 42-gallon barrel of No. 6 heavy fuel oil than they were paying for a 42-gallon barrel of crude oil, their engineers decided to resolve this problem by the installation of cokers in oil companies' refineries. These cokers enabled oil companies to use low-cost No. 6 heavy fuel oil instead of high-cost crude oil as an input material in their refineries, and thus enable oil companies to refine more light products from the No. 6 heavy fuel oil and market them at fair profits.

However, not too many years after the installation of cokers by oil companies, industrial firms—particularly utility companies—found it expedient to convert from coal to No. 6 heavy fuel oil for two reasons: (1) No. 6 heavy fuel oil was much less expensive as a fuel than coal. (2) Burning No. 6 heavy fuel oil was considerably cleaner than burning coal as a fuel. Consequently, as the demand for No. 6 heavy fuel oil increased as more and more industrial firms and particularly utility companies converted from coal to No. 6 heavy fuel oil, the latter's price increased progressively until eventually the price oil companies received for a 42-gallon barrel of No. 6 heavy fuel oil exceeded the price they paid for a 42-gallon barrel of crude oil. For example, in November 1973, before the quadrupling of crude oil prices and the oil embargo, the price oil companies received for a 42-gallon barrel of No. 6 heavy fuel oil (with a 0.3 sulphur content) in New York harbor was $7.88 compared to $4.20 they paid for a 42-gallon barrel of East Texas crude oil at the well head from June to August 1973, and $5.20 in December 1973.

When the cokers were installed by oil companies at capital costs ranging as high as from $15 million to $20 million, these capital costs were justified in terms of the savings that accrued to the oil companies as a result of the substantial spread that existed at that time between the high cost of crude oil and the low-cost No. 6 heavy fuel oil as an input material. As mentioned previously, the installation of these cokers fulfilled two purposes simultaneously: (1) It got rid of the increasing huge oversupply of No. 6 heavy fuel oil. (2) By refining the No. 6 heavy fuel oil further, oil companies obtained more light petroleum products that they could market at more favorable profits.

Since the primary objective for the installation of the cokers at oil companies' refineries was the disposal of the huge oversupply of No. 6 heavy fuel oil, which simply couldn't be disposed of by dumping it into the ocean, it would seem that the capital investments for the installation of these cokers could have been construed as "must" investments. Henceforth, these so-called "must" projects would have required no financial criteria, such as DCF rates of return and payout periods, in order to obtain their approval and acceptance by oil companies' top management. This reasoning would have been logical and would have stood up except for the oversight of one important alternative course of action that was available to the oil companies and that should have been looked into. It may be averred in this situation that hindsight is always better than foresight. Nevertheless, it is reasonable to contend that the following alternative course of action for resolving the above-mentioned No. 6 heavy fuel oil problem was completely overlooked by oil companies' top management. Wasn't it logical to assume that the greatly depressed price of No. 6 heavy fuel oil provided a proper incentive for industrial firms, and for utility companies particularly, to switch from coal to No. 6 heavy fuel oil and in so doing take advantage of the low price for this fuel. As events later proved, this course of action should have been looked into thoroughly and pursued by oil companies' marketing departments. They should have been instructed by their manufacturing departments to create a demand for No. 6 heavy fuel oil by waging a conscientious campaign to induce industrial firms, and particularly utility companies, to convert from coal to No. 6 heavy fuel oil because the latter was not only cheaper to purchase but also cleaner to burn. This marketing campaign would have speeded up the demand for No. 6 heavy fuel oil, and as the demand for this product increased so would its price likewise have increased just as it actually turned out later on.

Obviously, as the price of No. 6 heavy fuel oil continued to advance as the demand for this product continued to increase over the years, so the spread between the price oil companies were receiving for their No. 6 heavy fuel oil and the price they were paying for their crude oil continued to narrow until finally the cost savings that were supposed to justify the capital expenditures of millions of dollars for the installation of cokers completely evaporated. This meant that the oil companies never realized the anticipated cost savings, or the estimated (DCF) rates from the capital investments they made in these cokers. In fact, as the price oil companies eventually were receiving for their No. 6 heavy fuel oil surpassed the price they were paying for their crude oil, it became more economic for them to market this product rather than use it as an input material and refine it further to obtain more light petroleum products from it.

The above example proves that in the sponsor's efforts to estimate streams of future annual cash income or savings amounts of prospective projects, they can ill afford to overlook a single course of action that may be available to them regarding the objectives they are attempting to achieve through the prospective projects.

The differences that exist between repayments of loans plus interest by outside borrowers to banks and repayments of internal loans plus interest (profits) by new projects to treasurer's departments of companies are certainly noteworthy.

In self-amortizing loans made by banks to outside borrowers, the periodic bank loan payment amounts, consisting of the repayment of principal plus interest, are specified in the loan agreements signed by the outside borrowers. These loan agreements, which are legal documents enforceable under the law, obligate the outside borrowers to repay the principal of the loans plus interest during the loan terms. Furthermore, these bank loans generally are secured so that in most instances the risks assumed by the banks in making these loans are fairly limited. If the outside borrowers fail to make the periodic bank loan payments as specified in their loan agreements, the banks can then *(a)* repossess the automobiles, the boats, the furniture, the appliances, or whatever other items were purchased with the monies obtained from the banks; *(b)* foreclose on the houses if the loans were secured by mortgages; or *(c)* sell the stocks, bonds, or other negotiable papers that were put up as security for the loans. In the event that the monies realized by the banks from the repossession, foreclosure, and subsequent sale of the various items that were put up as security for the loans are less than the outstanding balances of the loans owed by the outside borrowers, the banks then have further recourse by taking the outside borrowers to court and sue them for the unpaid amounts of the loans.

Quite a different situation prevails in internal loans made by treasurer's departments of companies to prospective projects. While the industrial companies' annual cash income or savings amounts are comparable to banks' periodic bank loan payment amounts insofar as they both consist of repayments of the principal of the loans plus interest or profit, this, however, is where the analogy between the companies' annual cash income or savings amounts and banks' periodic bank loan payment amounts ends. The reason for this is due to the difference in the nature of the loans.

In the case of the loans made by banks and other lending institutions to outside borrowers, the former merely perform a service by lending money at various interest rates. The outside borrowers, whether they are companies or private individuals, control the use of the money by investing or spending it for the purpose for which it was borrowed, and they assume all the risks in connection with such borrowings.

On the other hand, in the case of internal loans made by treasurer's departments of companies to prospective projects, no second or outside party enters into the picture, controls the use of the money, or assumes all the risks in connection with such borrowings. Companies making internal loans to prospective projects play a dual role, namely, that of the banker, who performs the service of loaning the money, and that of the investor, who controls the use of the money by investing it in prospective projects for the purpose of earning predetermined minimum acceptable DCF rates of return on the projects commensurate with the risks involved. This means that companies' sponsors of prospective projects *(a)* must possess the necessary expertise in their chosen field, *(b)* must exercise great caution in considering all the alternative courses of action available to them, *(c)* must be cognizant of and make top management aware of the imponderables that cannot be reduced to numbers and therefore cannot be included in the economic evaluations, and *(d)* must make certain, to the very best of their ability, that the streams of prospective projects' annual cash income or savings amounts are realistic and attainable and, moreover, that the assumptions on which they are based are plausible and sound.

Projecting the streams of annual cash income or savings amounts during their estimated economic lives, perhaps, is the most difficult and risky task for companies' sponsors of prospective projects to perform for two reasons: (1) Projecting annual cash income or savings amounts far into the future entails many elements of uncertainty as well as many unforeseeable events that could take place in the distant future. This involves the need for making many assumptions and for projecting cash income and savings amounts based on the most sound and most plausible ones. (2) The streams of future annual cash income or savings amounts estimated for prospective projects not only must be sufficient to recover their capital costs plus profits at rates not less than their predetermined minimum acceptable DCF rates of return but they also must be reasonably certain of being attainable.

Pitfalls in Estimating Prospective Projects' Economic Lives

The task of estimating economic lives of prospective projects seems to be nowhere near as difficult as estimating their capital costs or their streams of future cash income or savings amounts. In estimating the economic lives of prospective projects, their sponsors in most instances can resort for guidance to past history and common occurrences as well as to future trends that are available to them as shown in the following three examples:

1. In estimating the economic lives for prospective projects that call for the installation of computers or other electronic devises, the obsolescence factor usually plays a vital part. Rapid new scientific inventions and modifications in the communication field make existing computers and other electronic equipment obsolete, and thus tend to shorten their economic lives. Companies can safeguard against financial losses due to possible shortened economic lives of computers and other electronic equipment, for example, by referring to historical data that show the frequency of their replacement due to obsolescence. This will give them a good indication of their average economic lives. Companies can then proceed to obtain from the manufacturer of the computers and other electronic equipment their approximate salvage values at the end of,

say, three, five, and seven years. With the aid of this information relative to their economic lives and salvage values, companies can then prepare a series of financial criteria (DCF rates of return and payout periods) for the computers and other electronic equipment's three-year, five-year, and seven-year economic lives, and thus determine which estimated economic life shows the most advantageous financial criteria on which to base their investment decision. As mentioned in the Chapter 11 on leasing versus purchasing fixed assets, companies also can consider and if necessary resort to leasing the computers and other electronic equipment providing *(a)* the estimated cost savings warrant the higher cost of lease financing and *(b)* favorable lease terms can be obtained.

2. Another outstanding example is the unexpected shortening of the estimated economic lives of the new projects that called for the installation of cokers at oil companies' refineries for the purpose of resolving the No. 6 fuel oil oversupply problem. This possibility it appears could have been foreseen for this reason. The price of No. 6 heavy fuel oil was so depressed that it would seem that oil companies' top management should have inquired as to *(a)* how the price of No. 6 heavy fuel oil compared with the price of coal, *(b)* whether it wasn't likely that industrial firms and utility companies would take advantage of the considerably lower price of No. 6 heavy fuel oil and switch from coal to No. 6 heavy fuel oil, and *(c)* whether their marketing departments couldn't create a demand for No. 6 heavy fuel oil fast enough to resolve their oversupply problem by inducing industrial firms and utility companies to convert from coal to No. 6 heavy fuel oil by stressing the fuel cost savings that would accrue to them as well as the much cleaner fuel they would be burning as a result of this conversion. The answers to these inquiries more than likely would have resulted in a far different and more economic course of action by the oil companies in resolving the above-mentioned No. 6 heavy fuel oil problem.

3. Still another example is where the estimated economic lives of projects are shortened as a result of imponderables that couldn't possibly be foreseen or reduced to numbers and, therefore, couldn't be included or given effect to in their economic evaluations. Some of these imponderables include the possibility of *(a)* the inauguration of the government controls of companies' prices, *(b)* the expropriation of companies' assets by foreign governments, and *(c)* the nationalization of companies' subsidiaries by foreign governments. Multinational companies that are faced with these problems usually have lobbyists and political analysts on their payrolls who constantly study and observe the political situations, maneuvers, and trends at home and abroad. Moreover, these specialists in domestic and foreign government affairs are pretty much in the know as to the direction in which the domestic and foreign governments are likely to move on matters that are of deep concern to the multinational companies. More often than not the management of

multinational companies is able to work out some form of accommodation that will be agreeable and satisfactory to both parties, providing both parties are reasonable in their demands and are negotiating and acting in good faith. While there undoubtedly is a far greater element of risk involved in operating in foreign countries, multinational companies, nevertheless, appear to be willing to take this risk providing the economic rewards are sufficiently high and the long-range political situations in the foreign countries look promising. The top management of multinational companies does not have to act blindly with regard to the above-mentioned imponderables. It can consult and be guided by their companies' lobbyists and political analysts in making important investment decisions.

Pitfalls Encountered in the Selection of the Most Economic Alternative

In loans made by banks to outside borrowers, the selection of the proper alternative is a relatively simple one because there are only two alternatives to consider in making bank loan decisions. Either the outside borrower's application for a loan is approved or it is disapproved by the bank's top management. If the customary credit investigation authorized by and conducted on behalf of the bank reveals that the outside borrower's credit rating, which indicates his ability to pay back the principal of the loan plus the interest thereon, is found to be satisfactory, the loan under normal circumstances will be approved. On the other hand, if the credit rating is found to be unsatisfactory, then the loan under normal circumstances will be disapproved by the bank's top management. In other words, in bank loan transactions there are only two alternatives involved—banks either approve or they disapprove outside borrowers' applications for bank loans depending upon the outside borrowers' credit ratings.

The problem of making certain that all alternatives are considered and that the most economic alternative is selected by a process of elimination in loans made by the treasurer's departments of companies to prospective projects is a great deal more complicated.

To gain a better understanding as to why there generally are more than just two alternatives to be considered in loans made by the treasurer's departments of companies to prospective projects, it may be helpful to differentiate, as best as possible, between the terms *loan* and *investment* and *interest* and *profit*. Webster's *New American Dictionary* defines these words as follows.

- The word *loan* is defined as "anything borrowed or lent, especially a sum of money put out at interest."
- The word *investment* is defined as "the act of laying out money in expectation of profit, the sum so placed."
- The word *interest* is defined as "money paid for the use of money; money earned by capital loaned or invested."

- The word *profit* is defined as "pecuniary gain; benefit from an act done, business transacted, or investment made."

The definition of the word *loan* is very definitive. It describes a loan as "a sum of money put out at interest." This means that money is loaned to outside borrowers and not invested in them. Furthermore, this definition does not use the words *money put out* in expectation of interest but rather *at interest*. This clearly implies that interest is the accepted and agreed-upon price paid for the use of money. The definition of the word *investment* is equally definitive as it defines investment as "the act of laying out money in expectation of profit." This clearly implies that the investment won't necessarily return a profit. The differentiation that needs to be recognized in the analogy of loans made by the treasurer's departments of companies to prospective projects and loans made by banks to outside borrowers is that in the former case companies play a dual role of *(a)* bankers loaning the necessary funds for and *(b)* investors investing them in prospective projects. In other words, in this dual capacity, the profits expected by companies from capital investments in prospective projects, contrariwise, are considered the interest paid by the prospective projects to the treasurer's departments of companies for the funds loaned to them. However, this conception of interest, which in this analogy represents the prospective project's DCF earnings rate and therefore could be either sky-high or abysmally low, is far different from the more orthodox and accepted meaning of the word *interest* as applied to bank loans.

In this role as investor, a company naturally has to consider and evaluate all alternative courses of action that are available to it regarding a prospective project, and by a process of elimination select the one that promises to maximize the company's return on its capital investment in the prospective project. This is one of the fundamental differences between loans made by banks to outside borrowers and loans made by treasurer's departments of companies that may well spell the difference between earning profits or sustaining losses from prospective projects.

Below is a typical example of a provision company whose management has decided to increase its profits by increasing the manufacture and the sale of its meat products. To accomplish this objective, the provision company has three courses of action open to it as explained below and shown in Table 74. This prospective undertaking shall be called Project E. The four alternative courses of action available to the provision company's management with regard to the prospective Project E are the following:

Alternative I. Increase the provision company's manufacturing facilities at a capital cost of $20,000 and market the additional volume produced through enlargement of the company's present retail outlets at an additional capital cost of $30,000. This $50,000 estimated total capital cost for Project E is estimated to increase the provision company's annual cash income by $8,138 during a 10-year period, as shown in Table 74, Column 1.

TABLE 74

Selection of the Most Economic Alternative for Project E by a Process of Elimination

Year	(1)	(2)	(3)	(4)	(5)	(6)
	Alternatives			Alternatives		
	I	*II*	*III*	*I over II*	*II over III*	*I over III**
0	$(50,000)	$(35,000)	$(20,000)	$(15,000)	$(15,000)	$(30,000)
1	8,138	6,195	3,834	1,943	2,361	4,304
2	8,138	6,195	3,834	1,943	2,361	4,304
3	8,138	6,195	3,834	1,943	2,361	4,304
4	8,138	6,195	3,834	1,943	2,361	4,304
5	8,138	6,195	3,834	1,943	2,361	4,304
6	8,138	6,195	3,834	1,943	2,361	4,304
7	8,138	6,195	3,834	1,943	2,361	4,304
8	8,138	6,195	3,834	1,943	2,361	4,304
9	8,138	6,195	3,834	1,943	2,361	4,304
10	8,138	6,195	3,834	1,943	2,361	4,304
Total	$ 31,380	$ 26,950	$ 18,340	$ 4,430	$ 8,610	$ 13,040
DCF rate of return	10%	12%	14%	5%	9.2%	7.2%

* Memorandum only.

Alternative II.   Increase the provision company's manufacturing facilities at a capital cost of $20,000 and market the additional volume produced through its wholesale department at an additional cost of $15,000 for motor vehicles for its company-employed driver-salesman. This $35,000 estimated total capital cost for Project E is estimated to increase the provision company's annual cash income by $6,195 during a 10-year period, as shown in Table 74, Column 2.

Alternative III.   Increase the provision company's manufacturing facilities at a capital cost of $20,000 and market the additional volume manufactured through its wholesale department at no additional capital cost, as the additional volume manufactured is estimated to be marketed through the company's present distributors, who are self-employed, own, and maintain their own motor vehicles, have their own sales routes and customers, and operate through the provision company's wholesale department. This $20,000 estimated total capital cost is estimated to increase the provision company's annual cash income by $3,834 during a 10-year period, as shown in Table 74, Column 4.

Alternative IV.   Do nothing, that is, do not increase the provision company's manufacturing and marketing facilities in order to increase its profits by increasing the manufacture and the sale of the company's meat products.

It also is assumed that the standard, i.e., the predetermined minimum acceptable DCF rate of return, for prospective Project E is 10 percent.

As shown in Table 74, Columns 1 to 3, the 10 percent, 12 percent, and 14 percent DCF rates of return for Alternatives I, II, and III, respectively, are determined by measuring these alternatives against Alternative IV, i.e., doing nothing. In Table 74, Alternative I earns total profits of $31,380, which is the largest amount of total profits earned compared to the $26,950 and the $18,340 total profits earned by Alternatives II and III, respectively. In other words, Alternative I earns $4,430 or 16.1 percent more total profits than Alternative II and $13,040 or 71.1 percent more total profits than Alternative III. Moreover, since Alternative I's 10 percent DCF rate of return meets the predetermined 10 percent minimum acceptable DCF rate of return for this prospective project and the provision company's top management in all likelihood will be looking for maximum additional profits, it could be inclined to go the Alternative I route.

However, when Alternative I is measured against Alternative II in Column 4, this comparison reveals that the additional $15,000 capital expenditure for Alternative I over Alternative II yields only a 5 percent DCF rate of return, which rate is far below the 10 percent predetermined minimum acceptable DCF rate of return for this project. Consequently, the result of this comparison eliminates Alternative I from any further consideration.

Next, Alternative II must be measured against Alternative III as shown in Column 5. This comparison reveals that the additional $15,000 capital expenditure for Alternative II over Alternative III yields a 9.2 percent DCF rate of return. This gives Alternative III a slight edge over Alternative II because the additional $15,000 capital cost for Alternative II over Alternative III doesn't yield a rate quite high enough to meet the 10 percent predetermined minimum acceptable DCF rate of return for this prospective project. However, since the 9.2 percent DCF rate of return earned on the $15,000 additional capital cost for Alternative II over Alternative III is so close, within eight tenths of 1 percent of the 10 percent predetermined minimum acceptable DCF rate of return for this prospective project; and, moreover, since the provision company's distributors could at any time they find it economically more advantageous change to other suppliers, it seems advisable in this case to go the Alternative II instead of the Alternative III route in order to assure the provision company's market for the additional volume of meat products produced.

The above example proves the importance of selecting the proper alternative in prospective projects that come across the desks of companies' top management if their companies' overall profitability is to be enhanced and maximized.

Pitfalls Encountered in the Consideration of Imponderables

As explained earlier, some of the imponderables that cannot be reduced to numbers and therefore cannot be included in economic evaluations of prospective projects include (a) U.S. government price fixing of American companies' products, (b) expropriation of American companies' assets by foreign governments, and *(c)* nationalization of American companies' subsidiaries by foreign governments. The only safeguard against financial losses accruing from such eventualities is that in accordance with the advice and the guidance obtained from multinational companies' lobbyists and political analysts, a series of financial criteria (DCF rates of return and payout periods) be prepared on the most optimistic, the most pessimistic, and the most likely basis that events pertinent to prospective projects are apt to occur during their economic lives and then let multinational companies' top management make their investment decisions based on this series of financial criteria.

Chapter 15

Post-Completion Audits of New Projects

$\mathbf{B}$roadly speaking, capital investments of companies fall into two major categories. These are "must" investments and *profit-generating* or *cost-saving* investments.

What "Must" Investments Are

"Must" investments are those that are required to be made in compliance with local ordinances and state and federal statutes. These "must" investments may pertain to guaranteeing or improving the safety of employees, the elimination or the reduction of pollution, the conservation of natural resources, etc. These "must" investments are mandatory; and unless they are made, the companies in all likelihood will be enjoined from conducting their normal business activities until such time that they have complied with the local, state, or federal directives. Since these "must" investments are not made for profit-generating or cost-saving purposes, no financial criteria (DCF rates of return and payout periods) must be determined for them to obtain top management's approval. However, if the legal requirements that are to be met by these "must" investments can be achieved by several different methods, then the top management should insist that the capital cost for each method be determined, and that by the process of elimination the least expensive method be selected and submitted for approval.

How to Select the Least Expensive Alternative Method for a "Must" Investment

If some of the alternative methods of achieving the objective and meeting the legal requirement of a "must" investment involve a series of annual cash outlays over a period of years instead of a lump-sum amount immediately, then the discounting procedure should be used to determine the least expensive method. The series of annual cash outlays should be discounted at the company's opportunity cost of money rate, which was discussed in Chapter 7. The alternative method that will show the lowest total present value by this discounting procedure will be the least expensive method that should then be recommended for adoption.

It is assumed below that there are two alternative methods of achieving the objective and meeting the legal requirement of a "must" investment.

Alternative I.   This method involves an immediate $60,000 cash outlay to achieve the "must" investment's objective.

Alternative II.   This method involves a series of annual cash outlays totaling $75,000 over a five-year period to achieve the "must" investment's objective, as shown in Table 75.

TABLE 75

Alternative II—Least Expensive Alternative in Nonprofit-Generating "Must" Investment Selected by NPV Method

Year	Annual Cash Outlays	Present Value Factor at 12%*	Total
1	$ 5,000	.8929	$ 4,465
2	10,000	.7972	7,972
3	15,000	.7118	10,677
4	20,000	.6355	12,710
5	25,000	.5674	14,185
Total	$75,000		$50,009

* Represents company's opportunity cost of money rate.

As indicated in the above alternatives, to achieve the "must" investment's objective it will cost the company $15,000, or 25 percent, more to go the Alternative II route than to go the Alternative I route. However, when effect is given to the timing of the annual cash outlays in Alternative II by discounting them at the company's 12 percent opportunity cost of money rate, we find that Alternative II actually is less costly as proven by the $50,009 present value arrived at by this discounting procedure (see Table 75).

This means that the company instead of having to put up $60,000 at the start of the "must" investment's first year under Alternative I only has to put up $50,009 at that point in time under Alternative II, invest the latter amount in other projects for five years at the company's 12 percent opportunity cost of money rate, and thus generate the $24,991 in profits that represents the balance of the $75,000 capital cost required under Alternative II, as shown in Table 76.

TABLE 76

Proof that Alternative II Is Least Expensive Method for Nonprofit-Generating "Must" Investment

Year	Principal at Start of Year	Cash Savings	Profit at 12%	Amortization of Principal
1	$50,009	$ 5,000	$ 6,001	$ 1,001
2	51,010	10,000	6,121	3,879
3	47,131	15,000	5,656	9,344
4	37,787	20,000	4,534	15,466
5	22,321	25,000	2,679	22,321
Total		$75,000	$24,991	$50,009

By the company having to put up $9,991 ($60,000 − $50,009) less at the start of the "must" investment's first year proves incontrovertably that Alternative II is far (16.7 percent) less costly and therefore is the proper course of action to follow in this "must" investment situation.

Instead of the present value method, the DCF method provides another procedure whereby may be determined that Alternative II is the less costly alternative available to the company for this "must" investment. This procedure requires that the cash flows of Alternative I and Alternative II be laid side by side and that a DCF rate of return be calculated on their net cash flow. As shown in Table 77, if the company should elect to go the Alternative I instead of the Alternative II route, the DCF rate of return on the $15,000 total savings would only be 6.4 percent, which is substantially below the company's 12 percent opportunity cost of money rate. Consequently, in terms of what

TABLE 77

Using DCF Rate of Return to Prove Alternative II Least Expensive Method for Nonprofit-Generating "Must" Investment

Year	Cash Outlays* for Alternative I	Cash Outlays* for Alternative II	Alternative I over Alternative II Cash Outlays* and Cash Savings	Factor at 6%	Present Value Total	Factor at 7%	Present Value Total
0	$(60,000)	—	$(60,000)	1.0000	$(60,000)	1.0000	$(60,000)
1	—	$ (5,000)	5,000	.9434	4,717	.9346	4,673
2	—	$(10,000)	10,000	.8900	8,900	.8734	8,734
3	—	$(15,000)	15,000	.8396	12,594	.8163	12,245
4	—	$(20,000)	20,000	.7921	15,842	.7629	15,258
5	—	$(25,000)	25,000	.7473	18,683	.7130	17,825
Total	$(60,000)	$(75,000)	$ 15,000		$ 736		$ (1,265)

The DCF rate of return is 6.4%.

* Cash outlays are in parentheses.

money is worth to the company, Alternative II is the less costly course of action for the company to take.

As stated earlier, since "must" investments are mandatory and therefore do not require financial criteria (DCF rates of return and payout periods) for their approval, it naturally follows that they also do not require any post-completion audits. Top management only needs to be assured at the time of the approval of "must" investments that in each case the most economical alternative method of achieving their objectives and of meeting their legal requirements has been chosen and submitted for approval.

Post-Completion Audits Required for Profit-Generating and Cost-Saving Prospective Projects

The bulk of the capital investments of companies, of course, falls into the category of investments in *profit-generating* or *cost-saving* projects. These two types of projects require that financial criteria (DCF rates of return and payout periods) be determined for them to assist top management in arriving at sound investment decisions regarding the acceptance or the rejection of these prospective projects.

One of the prerequisites in post-completion audits of new projects is that they should not be undertaken until the capital investments in them have been on the company's books long enough to make the post-completion audit results sufficiently meaningful and conclusive. This will then enable top management to take whatever actions it may deem necessary if the actual performances of new projects fail to compare favorably with their original estimates and the poor performances threaten to lower rather than enhance the company's overall profitability. The reasons for making post-completion audits generally are threefold:

1. Management must know whether the actual performances of new projects measure up to their original estimates, that is, whether from all indications they may be expected to yield the anticipated DCF rates of return and recover their original capital investments as rapidly as forecasted.

2. Management must know whether the additional profits or cost savings anticipated from the new projects are enhancing or diminishing the company's overall profitability. In other words, management must know what impact the additional profits or cost savings from new projects is having on the company's overall profitability.

3. Management must know what steps are required to be taken in the event that actual performances of new projects fail to measure up to their original estimates. If management has sufficient reasons to be concerned about the poor performances of new projects as well as reasonable doubts that their performances will not improve under present conditions, management then can pursue either one of the following two alternative courses of action: *(a)* Management can either

choose to invest additional funds in the new projects in an effort to improve their performances to the point of at least bringing the projects up to their original DCF rate of return and payout period forecasts. *(b)* Or management can elect to scrap the poor performing new projects and channel the funds realized from their disposition into other more lucrative and promising prospective projects.

Principal Obstacles Encountered in Making Post-Completion Audits of New Projects

The source of information for performing post-completion audits, of course, is the company's books of account. This fact immediately poses a number of serious problems. Some of these problems are attributable to present orthodox and widely accepted accounting practices and procedures, while others are attributable to present corporate income tax laws. The principal obstacles encountered in making post-completion audits of new projects include the following.

1. The incomparability of investment and income dollars recorded in the company's books of account. The capital costs of new projects are recorded in expensive prior years' dollars, while the cash income amounts of new projects are recorded in cheap current-year dollars.
2. The DCF rate of return, which is used by many companies to aid their top management in making sound investment decisions involving new projects, is incompatible with the year-to-year rate of return, which is regarded by the management of many companies as the proper financial yardstick to be used for measuring a company's profitability on its total assets as well as on its shareholders' equity. The incompatibility of these two financial yardsticks makes it virtually impossible to gauge with any degree of accuracy the impact that additional profits or cost savings of new projects has on a company's overall profitability.
3. The distortions of the figures in a company's books of account and in their financial statements (balance sheets and profit and loss statements) that cause them to show illusory profits. The distortions of the values of a company's assets, liabilities, and shareholders' equity really must be phenomenal, particularly in the case of multinational companies that have been in business for long periods of time—in many cases as long as from 75 to 100 years or even longer. These multinational companies, no doubt, have owned land for many decades, which in many instances has probably appreciated in value many times its original cost. Yet in accordance with orthodox and accepted accounting practices, the land continues to be shown on the company's books at its original cost. The same holds true for a company's depreciable fixed assets, particularly those that have long useful lives, which likewise continue to be shown on the books at their original costs instead of at their substantially higher replacement costs.

While there are other factors, such as population growth, population shifts, traffic shifts, etc., that are responsible for the appreciation of nondepreciable and depreciable fixed assets of companies, inflation is by far the most predominent one, and the one that creates the most serious and vexing problems in the task of performing post-completion audits for new projects. The seriousness of this problem may be gleaned from excerpts from the following articles on this subject that were published in the 70s.

In an article entitled "The Credibility of Corporations," published in *The Wall Street Journal* on January 17, 1974, Irving Kristol writes in part as follows.

Essentially, as I see it, the problem is one of candor and credibility, not—repeat: not—of public relations. Indeed, one of the reasons the large corporations find it so difficult to persuade the public of anything is that the public always suspects them of engaging in clever public relations, instead of simply telling the truth. And the reason the public is so suspicious is because our large corporations so habitually do engage in clever public relations instead of simply telling the truth.

For instance, what is one to make of a corporation which proudly announces that it has just completed the most profitable year in its history and then simultaneously declares that its return on capital is pitifully inadequate, that it is suffering from a terrible cost-squeeze, etc., etc.? In 1973, most corporations were engaged in precisely this kind of double talk. Is it any wonder they created so enormous a credibility gap?

Now the truth is that 1973 was not so profitable a year for large corporations. One would see this instantly if corporations reported their profits in constant dollars—i.e., corrected for inflation. Trade unions do this when they report their members' earnings to the world at large—they don't want to look like "profiteers" when they sit down at the bargaining table. Corporations, in contrast, do seem to be under a compulsion to look like "profiteers"—even when they are not, in fact, operating at a particularly profitable level.

One of the reasons that the myth of an affluent society became so prevalent—a myth, which in turn, gave birth to all kinds of popular fantasies about the standard of living that Americans are entitled to—is that corporations have helped propagate it by grossly overstating their earnings. They accomplish this by sleazy accounting, shrewd accounting, or technically honest but still misleading accounting.

At a recent conference, attended by some dozen top executives of major corporations, I inquired why they don't take inflation into account when they compare their annual reports. The only answer I got was that, if someone would start doing it, they would be content to follow, but that they were not about to take the lead in dispensing such bitter—if wholesome—medicine.

The New York Times, in an article entitled "Push Made for Accounting Method," reported in the Fort Myers Press on January 11, 1976, as follows:

Inflation causes problems for a lot of people including those in the accounting profession. Proposing to meet the matter head on, Russell E. Palmer, managing partner of Touche Ross & Company, a major accounting firm, began a nationwide campaign for adaption of Current Value Accounting.

"Current Value" Accounting counteracts the distorting effects of inflation. Reporting assets and liabilities at current values reflects true economic profits—

not illusory profits, the kind any number of companies have reported recently, even while heading into bankruptcy.

Various suggestions have been offered in the United States on how financial statements might show the effect of inflation on the financial strength of a company, but no consensus has been reached. Last August the Securities and Exchange Commission proposed that corporate financial statements indicate (in footnotes) that replacement costs would be in current terms for corporate assets and inventories. The Financial Accounting Standards Board has proposed application of a general price level index to historical costs.[1]

The Associated Press, in an article entitled "Business in Fever," reported in the *Daily Herald News* in Punta Gorda, Florida, on January 12, 1976, the following:

How can U.S. corporations be reporting record sales and profits at a time when they are wracked with record problems of liquidity, debt and capital shortage?

Because the profits they are reporting have little relationship to reality.

The dollar figures used are inflated, said Russell E. Palmer, managing partner in launching a campaign this week to experiment with more meaningful accounting. Today's dollar cannot be compared to yesterday's he said.

To illustrate: Nonfinancial corporations reported 1974 after-tax profits of $66 billion compared with $38 billion in 1965, an apparent increase of 74 percent.

Now adjust for inflation: That is use the same dollar to measure both years and thus obtain comparable results. Pick the 1958 dollar as a measure and you learn those earnings didn't rise—they fell, from an adjusted $37 billion in 1965 to around $21 billion in 1974.

One answer to such numerical misrepresentation may be to report a company's financial condition in current or real values rather than current prices, that is, with inflation wrung out. Palmer says we should seek to develop techniques.

Reporting assets and liabilities at current values reflect true economic profits—not illusory profits, the kind any number of companies have reported recently, even while heading into bankruptcy, he said.

Touche Ross isn't the first to make such suggestions, but it seems willing to throw more weight than the others into what it calls "Economic Reality" in Financial Reporting; submitted a Program for Experimentation.

The goals of accounting are to measure, record and communicate reality, the proposal begins, soon illustrating just how these goals are encumbered by persistent inflation.[2]

The above three articles bear out that post-completion audits of new projects are absolutely worthless insofar as measuring their actual performances against their original estimates is concerned unless adjustments for inflation are made. By measuring cheap current-year cash income or savings dollars against expensive prior years' cash outlay dollars, there is a good chance that if cash income or savings and cash outlay dollars of identical purchasing power are compared, the post-completion audits for many new projects will look satisfactory that otherwise will look unsatisfactory. Post-

---

[1] Copyright © 1976 by The New York Times Company. Reprinted by permission.

[2] Used by permission of The Associated Press.

completion audits of new projects also are worthless insofar as measuring their impact on a company's overall profitability is concerned, i.e., whether they are enhancing or diminishing it, unless adjustments for inflation are made first in the company's assets, liabilities, and shareholders' equity.

In addition to the above-mentioned adjustments for inflation that will have to be made, it also will be necessary to develop a year-to-year book rate of return that will be compatible with the DCF rate of return so that companies will be able to determine from post-completion audits what impact or effect additional profits or cost savings from new projects is having on their overall profitability.

New Profit-Generating and Cost-Saving Projects that Warrant Only Limited Post-Completion Audits

Not all new projects require or warrant the time or the expense of making elaborate post-completion audits, even though they may be of a profit-generating or a cost-saving nature. This is especially true in the case of large multinational companies that make huge numbers of investments in new projects annually.

Below are two typical examples of capital investments in large numbers of similar new projects. In the first example, only a separate post-completion audit for several new projects of a large number of similar new projects must be made. In the second example, only a perfunctory post-completion audit for each new project of a large number of similar new projects must be made.

In the first example, it will be assumed that the company converted its entire fleet consisting of several hundred motor vehicles from one type of motor vehicle to a much more modern type that was estimated to be far more efficient and economical to operate, and thus would result in accruing substantial operating savings to the company. It will be assumed further that all the newly acquired motor vehicles in the company's fleet were of similar make and size, and that this conversion occurred during a relatively short period of time of, say, not longer than two years.

It would be extremely foolhardy and wasteful for the company to conduct a separate post-completion audit for each newly acquired motor vehicle under the above circumstances, even though each new motor vehicle may cost as much as $50,000. We are assuming that some of the several hundred motor vehicles are used exclusively for short hauls in dense city traffic, others are used exclusively for long hauls on flat terrain, and the remaining motor vehicles are used exclusively for long hauls on mountainous terrain. In this situation, it would be expedient and sufficient to prepare only three post-completion audits instead of several hundred. One post-completion audit would be prepared for a typical motor vehicle that is used exclusively for short hauls in dense city traffic, a second one for a typical motor vehicle that is used exclusively for long hauls on flat terrain, and a third one for a typical motor vehicle that is used exclusively for long hauls on mountainous terrain. These three post-completion audits would give the company's management a separate post-completion audit for a typical motor vehicle of the three groups of motor vehicles that are used under different operating conditions.

The three post-completion audits for the newly acquired motor vehicles used under three different operating conditions should be conducted not later than one year to two years after they were put into service because of the relatively short serviceable life of these motor vehicles. To enable the company's operating management to assess the actual economic benefits that were estimated to be derived from converting from the old to the more modern motor vehicles, the three post-completion audits should contain the following information.

1. A comparison of the actual versus the estimated purchase price of the newly acquired motor vehicles.
2. A comparison of the actual trade-in value received versus the estimated trade-in value expected to be received from the motor vehicle dealer for the old motor vehicles traded in for the more modern and efficient motor vehicles.
3. A comparison of the actual versus the estimated operating savings accruing to the company as a result of the conversion from the old to the more modern and efficient motor vehicles.
4. A comparison of the actual versus the estimated operating statistics of the newly acquired motor vehicles used under the three different operating conditions. These operating statistics should include the fuel consumption per mile traveled, the annual number of lay ups of the motor vehicles for repairs and maintenance, the average length of time of such lay ups, the actual annual versus the estimated annual cost for repairs and maintenance for the motor vehicles, etc.

For the three separate post-completion audits to be of value to the company's operating management in assessing the economic advantage or disadvantage of having converted from the old to the more modern and efficient motor vehicles, it is essential that the three motor vehicles under review represent average motor vehicles used in each group under the three different operating conditions. The term *average motor vehicles* is used here to mean those motor vehicles that are free from major defects and consequently are not subject to abnormal repair and maintenance expenses.

Now let us assume that the three separate post-completion audits revealed that the newly acquired motor vehicles used for long hauls on both flat and mountainous terrain were as efficient and economical to operate as originally estimated, but that the operating results of the newly acquired motor vehicles used for short hauls in dense city traffic, on the other hand, were most disappointing, i.e., the motor vehicles used in this type of operation were much less efficient and decidedly more costly to operate than originally estimated.

Undoubtedly, this situation would result in a lower DCF rate of return on the total capital cost of converting from the old to the more modern and efficient motor vehicles and could result in an unacceptable DCF rate of return—particularly if a large percentage of the total number of the newly acquired motor vehicles were used for short hauls in dense city traffic.

The unfavorable results of the three post-completion audits naturally poses the obvious question of how should the company best resolve this problem of having invested millions of dollars in converting its entire fleet of motor vehicles from the old to the more modern and efficient motor vehicles, which turned out to be an unprofitable venture because the company failed to realize the operating savings it estimated from the replacement of its entire fleet of motor vehicles.

Investment decisions, particularly those that involve huge sums of money, generally are irreversible. Moreover, if unwise investment decisions are made by companies, they rarely—if ever—are able to escape sizable financial losses as a result of having made such unsound and costly capital investments. In the light of these facts, one may well inquire why post-completion audits of new projects are necessary and important. They are vital and extremely helpful because it is only through them that companies can find out information such as the following: (1) whether or not the capital investments in the new projects are yielding the anticipated DCF rates of return; (2) whether the capital investments in the new projects are in fact enhancing or diminishing companies' overall profitability; (3) what steps are needed to be taken to convert unprofitable new projects to profitable ones by the infusion of additional funds or to minimize financial losses from unprofitable new projects that cannot be scrapped or disposed of; and (4) valuable facts that can be learned from unprofitable new projects to preclude the repetition of similar past mistakes in future capital investments in new projects.

For example, the information developed in the above three post-completion audits brought to light these vital facts:

1. The newly acquired motor vehicles are suitable only for long hauls on both flat and mountainous terrain because only when they are used under these operating conditions are the operating savings, as originally estimated, realized by the company.
2. The newly acquired motor vehicles are unsuitable for short hauls in dense city traffic because when they are used under these operating conditions the operating savings, as originally estimated, are not realized by the company.
3. The estimated DCF rate of return on the total capital cost for the replacement of the company's entire fleet of motor vehicles was not realized because the estimated operating savings for the motor vehicles used for short hauls in dense city traffic did not materialize. The motor vehicles were found to be inefficient and costly to operate in this type of operation.
4. The company's management learned a valuable lesson from the information brought to light by these three post-completion audits, namely, that a thorough study should have been conducted before making this conversion to more modern and efficient motor vehicles to ascertain

what make and model of motor vehicle was most efficient and economical to use under the three widely different operating conditions before millions of dollars were committed for the replacement of the company's entire fleet of motor vehicles. This study should have required the acquisition of only a limited number of the new motor vehicles in order to develop this requisite information. The information obtained from the three post-completion audits is invaluable and should preclude a repetition of similar mistakes in the future acquisition of more modern and efficient motor vehicles to be used under widely different operating conditions.

5. Finally, the facts brought to light by the three post-completion audits should impel the company to take appropriate steps immediately to determine *(a)* what make and model of motor vehicle is most efficient and economical to operate on short hauls in dense city traffic; and *(b)* how soon the newly acquired improper type of motor vehicles, which are now being used in this operation, can be disposed of and replaced by the proper type of motor vehicles for this operation that will produce operating savings that will yield the company an acceptable DCF rate of return on its capital investment.

In the next example involving capital investments in new profit-generating or cost-savings projects that warrant only limited post-completion audits, it is assumed that an oil company built several hundred new service station outlets during a single year.

In this type of situation, assuming that service station outlets have an economic life of 20 years, it is advisable to prepare a separate, simplified post-completion audit for each service station outlet not later than from three to four years after the time that it opened its doors for business. It should be sufficient for these post-completion audits to produce the type of information indicated below. A review by the oil company's management of this simplified type of information should suffice to enable it to take appropriate actions regarding those service stations whose performances are subnormal because their capital costs are substantially higher and/or their cash returns are substantially lower than their original estimates.

1. A comparison of the actual versus the estimated service station's capital cost. If there is a material difference, an explanation should be given showing the reason for this difference and why it wasn't foreseeable.
2. A comparison of the actual versus the estimated service station's annual sales volumes. If the actual sales volumes are substantially lower than their original estimates, explanations should be given showing the reasons for these differences, whether they can be overcome and how they can be overcome.
3. A comparison of the actual versus the estimated service station's annual cash income amounts. If the actual cash income amounts are substantially lower than their original estimates, an explanation should be

given showing why they are lower and whether or not they can be brought up to their original estimates in the not too distant future.

Adjustments for inflation should be made in these simplified post-completion audits only if the inflation rate during this relatively short three- to four-year period under review is significant enough to materially affect the DCF rates of return on the company's investments in these newly constructed service station outlets. How these adjustments for inflation should be made—if they are necessary to be made—will be explained later in this chapter.

Here are just a few of the reasons that may be responsible for the higher actual capital costs of the newly constructed service stations compared to their estimated costs: (1) sudden sharp increases in the rate of inflation, (2) failure to include needed auxillary facilities in the original estimates, (3) thefts of materials and supplies on the building sites, (4) labor disputes and strikes during the construction periods, and (5) lack of expertise in forecasting capital costs. Whatever the reasons are for the substantial increases in the actual capital costs of the service stations, the company's management must take proper steps to determine whether their annual cash income amounts can be increased to a level that will compensate for these increases in their capital costs and thus enable the company to realize the DCF rates of return originally estimated for these newly built service station outlets.

Below are some of the reasons that may be responsible for the actual sales volumes of the newly constructed service stations being substantially below the original estimates: (1) shifts in traffic going passed the newly constructed service stations, which could be a temporary or permanent condition; (2) road construction or repairs that probably would be a temporary condition; (3) the service stations are located on the wrong side of the road; (4) poor and inefficient services rendered by service stations personnel; and (5) poor supervision by service station management.

Some of the reasons that could be responsible for the annual cash income amounts of the newly constructed service stations being substantially lower than the original estimates are: (1) periodic price wars, (2) much lower sales volumes than originally estimated, (3) high write-offs of customers' debts due to their poor credit ratings, and (4) frequent change in management and service station personnel.

In contrast, if the oil company had purchased the several hundred service station outlets from another oil company in a geographical area in which the former was inadequately represented, the post-completion audits for the newly acquired service station outlets would have to be considerably more elaborate and informative for these reasons: (1) In a transaction where an oil company found it expedient to divest itself of several hundred service station outlets in a particular geographical area—for whatever reasons—normally it would be common practice to require that the buying oil company purchase all the service station outlets in that particular geographical area. This would include those that are profitable and meet the buying oil company's predetermined profitability standard for this type of capital investment, those that are marginal, and those that are unprofitable as well as those that are owned and those that are leased by the selling oil company. (2) In this type of investment situation where several hundred service station outlets were acquired and they all were in operation at different stages of their economic lives, it would be necessary to prepare not only a separate post-completion audit for each newly acquired service station outlet but also one post-completion audit for the entire package deal, i.e., for the combined several hundred service station outlets.

The post-completion audits for the individual service station outlets should be prepared from three to four years after their acquisition; and they should reflect the following detailed information:

1. The service station's capital cost for the land, the building, and the other assets at the time of its purchase, even though the service station may have been closed and no longer be in operation, or it may have been completely rehabilitated by demolishing the old service station building and erecting a more modern building that is now operated under more efficient conditions.
2. The capital cost for the modernization or the partial or complete rehabilitation of the service station since its purchase.
3. The future capital outlays for the complete rehabilitation of the service station at the end of its economic life. As pointed out earlier, these capital outlays must include the amount of cash foregone as a result of opting to transfer land or other fixed assets to the service station instead of selling them. The land must be included at its market or resale value and the other fixed assets at their depreciated value (based on the depreciation method used for tax purposes) at the time of their transfer.
4. The capital recoveries from the disposition of the service station's land, building, and other assets if it was closed because its continued operation proved to be unprofitable. If any of the other assets, such as lifts, tools, and other equipment, were transferred to other service stations, then the depreciated value of such other assets must be included in the service station's capital recoveries on the above-mentioned basis.
5. The capital recoveries resulting from the disposition or transfer of assets if the service station was modernized or partially or completely rehabilitated since its purchase.
6. The future capital recoveries from the disposition or the transfer of assets from the service station at the end of its economic life when its building is torn down and a new one is erected in its place.
7. The annual lease rental for the remaining years under the present lease contract as well as those under the new lease contract for the remaining years of the 20-year period under review starting with the

acquisition of the leased service station. These annual lease rentals must be excluded from the service station's operating expenses and thereby from its annual cash income amounts.

8. The investment equivalent for the leased service station must be arrived at by discounting the annual lease rentals, after excluding from them expenses incidental to ownership, by the oil company's direct borrowing rate. This investment equivalent will provide the investment base for calculating the DCF rate of return for the leased service station comparable with the DCF rates of return for the oil company's owned service stations.

9. The residual value of the service station at the end of the 20-year period, which has its start at the time of the service station's acquisition and is equivalent to its 20-year economic life. The economic life of many of the several hundred purchased service stations will not coincide with the above 20-year period, not only because most of them were built at different times but also because many of them were completely rehabilitated (rebuilt) during this 20-year period. Consequently, this large number of newly acquired service stations will have a widely different number of productive years left of their economic lives at the end of this 20-year period; and as a result, they will have substantial residual values that must be reckoned with and given effect to.

10. The service station's actual annual sales volume during the 3- to 4-year period under review as well as its estimated annual sales volume for the remaining years of the 20-year period. The latter is to be based on (a) the pattern of the actual annual sales volume during the three- to four-year period under review and (b) the service station's present facilities and its completely rehabilitated (rebuilt) facilities at the end of its economic life.

11. The service station's actual annual cash income amounts during the 3- to 4-year period under review as well as its estimated annual cash income amounts for the remaining years of the 20-year period. The latter amounts are also to be based on (a) the pattern of the actual annual cash income amounts during the three- or four-year period under review and (b) the service station's present facilities and on its completely rehabilitated (rebuilt) facilities at the end of its economic life.

12. The remaining years of the service station's economic life from the time of its purchase, and also the remaining years of its economic life at the end of the above-mentioned 20-year period during which it was completely rehabilitated (rebuilt).

To make certain that the figures reported in the post-completion audits of the service stations are comparable with those in their applicable economic evaluations, they must be expressed in constant dollars. This means that the capital outlay, capital recovery, and annual cash income amounts in the post-completion audits of the service stations must be expressed in dollars that are equal in purchasing power to those in their applicable economic evaluations. This requires that the actual cash outflows and cash inflows of the service stations that occurred during the three- to four-year period under review be adjusted for inflation to make these dollars equal in purchasing power and comparable to those in their applicable economic evaluations. It further requires that the estimated cash outflows and cash inflows of the service stations that will occur during the remaining years of the 20-year period be expressed in constant dollars of comparable purchasing power or value.

The above information that is recommended to be shown in the post-completion audits of the service stations will make it possible *(a)* to calculate DCF rates of return for them that can be compared with those in their applicable economic evaluations and *(b)* to calculate a DCF rate of return for the post-completion audit that can be compared with that of the economic evaluation for the entire package deal, i.e., for the combined several hundred service stations.

While the preparation of these post-completion audits may appear to be cumbersome, complex, and time-consuming, they are not only worthwhile but essential for these reasons: (1) The huge capital investment in several hundred service station outlets that, undoubtedly, involves many millions of dollars must be justified and proven profitable. (2) The consumer acceptance of one oil company's products versus another oil company's products may be quite different in a particular geographical area. Hence, the performance of the service stations may be quite different when handling the buying oil company's products than when handling the selling oil company's products. This strongly suggests that the past performance of the newly acquired service stations will not be a reliable indicator of how well or how poorly these service stations will perform in the future when they will be handling another oil company's products. (3) These post-completion audits will enable the buying oil company to weed out and dispose of the unprofitable service station outlets and to modernize or completely rehabilitate (rebuild) the marginal ones that show future potential under improved conditions and more efficient management. (4) These post-completion audits also will enable the buying oil company's management to determine whether the total capital investment in the several hundred newly acquired service station outlets will tend to improve or worsen the company's future overall profitability; in other words, whether the buying oil company consumated a profitable or an unprofitable capital investment when it purchased the several hundred service station outlets from another oil company.

It should be noted at this point that the procedure for the preparation of post-completion audits may vary drastically depending upon how the company's capital investments in new projects were made. For example, the post-completion audits would be much shorter, more simple, and far less time-consuming when the several hundred service station outlets are constructed during the same year by the oil company than when they are purchased during the same year from another oil company and most of them are in operation at different stages of their 20-year economic lives at the time of their purchase.

It also should be noted at this point that the basic principles that apply in conducting post-completion audits are much the same whether a company's capital investments in new projects involve the construction, the purchase, or the leasing of service station outlets, grocery stores, haberdashery stores, or any other type of retail outlets.

New Profit-Generating and Cost-Saving Projects that Warrant More Elaborate Post-Completion Audits

Not all capital investments in new projects either require or warrant the time and the expense of having post-completion audits conducted for them. This is particularly true in the case of multinational companies that usually make a large number of capital investments in new projects each year. A line has to be drawn somewhere. Consequently, it seems advisable for companies to pre-determine the type, the nature, and the amount of capital investments in new projects that will require and warrant the expense and the time of conducting post-completion audits for them. It also seems advisable for companies to specify how detailed and extensive post-completion audits should be made for various types of capital investments and various conditions under which they are made.

To decide whether post-completion audits are necessary and warranted for a company's capital investments in new projects, it may be helpful to classify them into three categories: (1) New projects that involve relatively small capital investments normally should not require post-completion audits because they more than likely will not have any perceptible impact on the company's future overall profitability. For example, a $50,000 capital invest-ment in a piece of new equipment by a multinational company that has total assets of $10 billion on its books obviously should not require any post-com-pletion audit because the cost savings the equipment will generate in all prob-ability will not have the slightest impact on the company's future overall profitability. (2) Groups of new projects that are similar in nature and involve only nominal capital investment amounts for the individual new projects but when combined add up to a very sizable capital investment amount may require only a limited number and less detailed post-completion audits, even though the total capital investment for such groups of new projects will in all probability have an appreciable impact on the company's future overall profit-ability. Examples of this type of capital investments are those previously dis-cussed that pertained to *(a)* the replacement of a company's entire fleet con-sisting of several hundred motor vehicles and *(b)* the construction or the purchase of several hundred new service station outlets—both occurring in a group during a single year. In the case of the total capital investment for the replacement of the company's entire fleet of several hundred motor vehicles, only a limited number of post-completion audits were required to be made, namely, one post-completion audit for a motor vehicle used under each one of the three different types of operating conditions, or three altogether instead of several hundred post-completion audits. On the other hand, in the case of the total capital investment for the construction or the purchase of several hundred new service station outlets by an oil company during a single year, only relatively brief post-completion audits were required to be made for the service station outlets to determine their impact on the oil company's future overall profitability. (3) Individual new projects that involve large capital investment amounts will require much more detailed and elaborate post-completion audits because of the far more pronounced impact they will have on the company's future overall profitability. Examples of such new projects include the construction or the purchase of new refineries, chemical plants, manufacturing plants, storage facilities, pipelines, ocean terminals, freighters or tankers, office buildings, hotels, etc., which in all cases involve large capital investments.

The capital investment amounts that will or will not be material in influencing a company's future overall profitability, and therefore determine the type of post-completion audits that should be conducted for the new projects involved will depend to a large extent on the size of the company and the worth of its total assets.

When New Profit-Generating and Cost-Saving Projects Are Ready for Post-Completion Audits

New profit-generating and cost-saving projects will be ready for post-completion audits when the following conditions are prevalent:

1. When the new projects have been in operation sufficiently long to produce meaningful results that will enable top management to take whatever action—if any—that may be deemed to be necessary if the results of the post-completion audits prove to be unfavorable compared to their original estimates and these unfavorable results threaten to lower the company's future overall profitability. The length of time new projects may be considered to have been in operation sufficiently long to produce meaningful results will depend primarily on the length of their economic lives.
2. When top management has reasons to suspect that new projects are not performing as well as anticipated due to internal or external causes and that to rectify these adverse conditions some changes are in order. Good examples of why new projects are not performing as well as anticipated may be due to *(a)* recurring price wars, *(b)* an incomplete line of products handled, *(c)* inadequate facilities, *(d)* poor services rendered, and *(e)* inefficient management, etc.
3. When some unforeseen factors have occurred that are expected to affect the performance of new projects adversely. Examples of such unforeseen factors that could occur and adversely affect the performance of new projects include *(a)* sudden shifts in traffic, *(b)* sudden

shifts in population, *(c)* unforeseeable zoning restrictions, *(d)* unforeseeable scarcity of raw materials and their consequent increased costs, *(e)* unforeseeable price controls instituted by the government, *(f)* additional expenses incurred resulting from unforeseeable governmental regulations imposed on the industry, etc.

Broadly speaking, when new projects will be ready for post-completion audits will depend to a large extent on *(a)* length of the new projects' economic lives, *(b)* type of new projects, *(c)* amount of new projects' capital investment, and *(d)* the internal and external factors that may affect the performance of the new projects and thereby seriously influence the company's future overall profitability either favorably or unfavorably.

Procedure for Conducting Post-Completion Audits for New Profit-Generating and Cost-Saving Projects

How many companies actually conduct post-completion audits of new projects in an effort to determine whether their actual performances measure up favorably or unfavorably with their original estimates and also whether their actual profit or cost-saving performances will enhance or diminish the company's future overall profitability is open to question. However, it seems fairly safe to assert that not enough companies perform post-completion audits and that those that do perform them more or less on a spotty instead of on a regular basis and in a perfunctory rather than in a thorough manner.

The reason for not making any or only spotty and perfunctory post-completion audits appears to be twofold: (1) Many companies appear to be lacking in enough qualified personnel that possess the necessary skills and technical know-how for the proper preparation of post-completion audits. It must be borne in mind that the financial analyst assigned to the task of conducting post-completion audits must be well acquainted with the principles, procedures, and techniques that are customarily employed in the fields of accounting, finance, and economics. For example, he must know how to extract the information required for post-completion audits from the company's books of account. He must understand and know how to apply the discounting and the compounding techniques in cases where capital outlays occurred either before or after the time the projects started generating cash income, and also in cases where their fixed assets were leased instead of purchased and capital investment equivalents at the beginning of the new projects' economic lives had to be determined in lieu of a stream of annual capital outlays or lease rentals. The financial analyst must know how to develop and apply indexes that will enable him to make proper statistical adjustments for inflation and, thereby, convert the investment and income dollars of new projects as well as the total assets, total liabilities, shareholders' equity, and profit dollars of the company from variable and incomparable dollars to constant and comparable dollars, thus precluding the erroneous comparisons of cheap current-year income dollars with expensive prior years' investment dollars. (2) Top management all too frequently will take the mistaken position that because unwise and costly investment decisions have been made, which appear to be irreversible—particularly in the case of long-life new projects—that management is necessarily obliged to live with these unprofitable new projects during their entire lengthy economic lives. While financial losses from such unsound capital investments in new projects can't always be avoided entirely, they frequently can be minimized as the direct result of the facts brought to light by their post-completion audits. Once the reasons for the failure of unsound capital investments in new projects are uncovered and become known, they more often than not will point the way toward minimizing the financial losses from such unsound ventures. After all, this is one of the purposes of making post-completion audits.

The following procedure for conducting post-completion audits for new profit-generating and cost-saving projects is recommended:

1. A duplicate copy of the new projects' economic evaluation on which the company's investment decision for the new project's approval and acceptance was based should be obtained from its sponsor exactly as it was submitted to top management. This economic evaluation should show the new project's estimated capital cost, its estimated capital recoveries, its estimated stream of annual cash income or savings amounts, its estimated DCF rate of return, its estimated payout period, the imponderables that couldn't be reduced to numbers and encompassed in the economic evaluation but that could have a profound effect on the new project's performance and success, and all the sponsor's and the financial analyst's comments who recommended the new project's approval.

2. The original work papers from which the new project's economic evaluation was prepared also should be obtained from the new project's sponsor. These work papers should show how the financial criteria (the DCF rate of return and the payout period) in the new project's economic evaluation were arrived at. They also should show the alternative courses of action that were open to management with respect to the new project, and that the most economic course of action was selected by the process of elimination. They, furthermore, should show the assumptions on which the new project's estimated capital cost, its estimated stream of annual cash income or savings amounts, and its estimated economic life were predicated. Finally, these working papers should show the imponderables that were present and could not be reduced to numbers, but that were brought to the attention of top management along with objective evaluations of their significance and an unbiased recommendation for the acceptance of the new project. Obviously, these work papers should contain important clues as to the prospects for achieving actual performances that will measure up to the new project's original estimates. This indicates that the above-mentioned information is essential and invaluable in the preparation of the post-completion audit.

For the period under review, gather and determine the following information for the post-completion audit of the new project:

1. Extract from the company's books of account the new project's actual capital cost and its actual annual cash income or savings amounts before income taxes.
2. Extract from the company's income tax records or determine the new project's annual depreciation charges calculated by the sum-of-the-years'-digits method on the fixed assets' original cost.
3. Determine the new project's annual taxable income amounts by deducting the above-mentioned annual depreciation charges (used for income tax purposes) from its annual cash income amounts before income taxes.
4. Determine the new project's annual income tax amounts by multiplying the annual taxable income amounts by the 48 percent corporate income tax rate instead of by the company's effective income tax rate because the former (48 percent) corporate income tax rate was used in its economic evaluation.
5. Determine the new project's annual cash income amounts after income taxes by deducting the annual income tax amounts from the annual taxable income amounts and then adding back the annual depreciation amounts.
6. Obtain from the new project's sponsor the annual replacement cost amounts expressed in cheap current-year dollars of the new project's total assets that are comparable in purchasing power to its original capital cost expressed in expensive dollars at the zero reference point, i.e., the point in time just before the new project started generating cash income.
7. Develop the new project's annual capital cost index numbers by dividing its annual replacement cost by its original capital cost, or investment equivalent, at the zero reference point, which represents the new project's capital cost at an index of 100.
8. Adjust the new project's annual cash income or savings amounts expressed in cheap current-year dollars for inflation by dividing them by the annual capital cost index numbers for the corresponding years, and then by multiplying the quotients by the index number of 100. This procedure converts the new project's annual cash income or savings dollars from cheap current-year dollars to constant-level dollars that are comparable in purchasing power to that of the new project's original capital investment dollars at the zero reference point. This adjustment for inflation must be made to preclude measuring cheap current-year annual cash income or cost savings dollars against incomparable expensive capital investment dollars, and thus arrive at a highly distorted and overstated DCF rate of return that will not be comparable to the one arrived at in the new project's economic evaluation.

If the new project's post-completion audit reveals that its actual capital cost and its actual annual cash income or savings amounts during the period under review compare favorably with their original estimates during the same period and consequently the prospect of the new project earning its estimated DCF rate of return and returning its capital cost during its estimated payout period is excellent, then the post-completion audit for the new project should be considered completed, and further work on it should be unnecessary.

On the other hand, if the new project's post-completion audit reveals that its actual performances failed to measure up to its original estimates, then proper steps should be taken to determine whether or not corrective measures can be instituted that will improve its actual performances to a level where the new project will realize its estimated DCF rate of return, or at least its predetermined minimum acceptable DCF rate of return for this type of project.

For example, if the new project's actual capital cost should compare unfavorably with its original estimate and the cost overrun is substantial, it will then be necessary to determine how much the new project's annual cash income or savings amounts will have to increase for the remaining years of its economic life in order for the new project to realize the estimated DCF rate of return and payout period forecasted in its economic evaluation, or at least earn the predetermined minimum acceptable DCF rate of return for this type of project.

This increased constant-level annual cash income amount, which must be generated by the new project for the remaining years of its economic life in order to earn the estimated DCF rate of return shown in its economic evaluation, or at least the predetermined minimum acceptable DCF rate of return for this type of project, is determined by dividing the new project's actual capital cost by the total present value factors for the remaining years of its economic life at its estimated DCF earnings rate, or its predetermined minimum acceptable DCF earnings rate, respectfully. After developing the increased annual cash income or savings amount required to be generated by the new project for the remaining years of its economic life, management must make a determination as whether this future stream of higher cash returns is attainable to yield either the new project's estimated or at least its predetermined minimum acceptable DCF rate of return. If these future higher annual cash returns are not attainable, management is then faced with the decision as to whether it will be more economic to carry on with the new project and earn a lower DCF rate of return than forecasted or normally acceptable, or whether the new project should be scrapped and the proceeds from the disposition of its assets be invested in a more lucrative new project.

Another problem requiring corrective action by management arises even more frequently when post-completion audits disclose that the actual cash income or savings amounts of new projects failed to measure up to their original estimates. This condition may be attributable to a variety of reasons, such as reduced consumer spending, poor quality of products and services, inefficient management, periodic price wars, increased government regulations and controls, overly optimistic original estimates based on implausible and unrealistic assumptions, inflation, etc.

If inflation is the cause, then the problem will be far more deceptive and complex than any other problem most likely would be, because during sustained inflationary periods there is a steady rise in prices along with a steady decline in the value or purchasing power of the dollar. Consequently, the actual cash income or savings amounts of new projects, expressed in cheap current-year dollars, may actually be higher than their original estimates expressed in constant dollars that are equal in purchasing power to that of the new projects' expensive capital investment dollars. However, when proper adjustments for inflation are made in these annual cash income or cost savings amounts, they more often than not will prove to be lower rather than higher than their original estimates. Unfortunately, since conducting post-completion audits and making adjustments for inflation are not common practices engaged in by most companies, it is quite conceivable that many new projects that appear to be profitable and successful are actually unprofitable and unsuccessful, and instead of enhancing are actually worsening a company's future overall profitability.

Top management may well reflect on whether the economic evaluations for prospective projects that come across its desk are prepared with such expertise and accuracy that investment decisions based on them will inevitably lead to channeling a company's available funds into the most profitable channels in most instances, and thus preclude the need for post-completion audits of new projects.

Considering the huge number and the great variety of prospective projects that come across top management's desk each year, the billions of dollars involved in multibillion dollar companies, the numerous alternative courses of action open to management with respect to prospective new projects, the wide range of knowledge, expertise, and know-how required in evaluating the merits of prospective new projects, the need for selecting the most profitable ones in view of the limited supply of available funds, the most advantageous method of financing them—whether they should be equity, debt, or lease financed, etc.,—leaves little doubt that post-completion audits can play an important role in gaining greater expertise and know-how in this vital field of investment analysis, and thus lead to reducing and minimizing unprofitable capital investments in new projects and channeling available company funds into the most profitable ones.

Project D's Economic Evaluation

The financial criteria, i.e., the DCF rate of return and the payout period, for Project D and why they are the true and realistic financial criteria are repeated here only for comparative purposes.

As you will recall, the information contained in Table 72 represents the economic evaluation for Project D prepared for the company's top management to assist it in rendering a sound investment decision regarding the acceptance or the rejection of this prospective project. Table 72 shows that Project D will earn an estimated 15.5 percent DCF rate of return on its $10,000 capital investment and that the latter will be returned to the company during an estimated payout period of 5.9 years.

Since inflation during Project D's estimated 20-year economic life is not injected into the economic evaluation and consequently its estimated capital cost as well as its estimated annual cash income or cost savings amounts are expressed in comparable constant zero reference point dollars, the above-mentioned 15.5 percent DCF rate of return and the estimated 5.9-year payout period are the true and realistic financial criteria for this prospective project.

Project D's Post-Completion Audit which Ignores Proper Adjustment for Inflation

While the preparation of post-completion audits at the end of new projects' economic lives is neither customary nor serves any useful purpose, an exception will be made in this case only for the purpose of highlighting the deleterious effect that inflation and depreciation deficiencies have on new projects' financial criteria, i.e., their DCF rates of return and payout periods, during their entire economic lives.

The information shown in Table 73 serves a twofold purpose: (1) to show that when Project D's annual cash income or cost-savings amounts are estimated to reflect the anticipated rate of inflation during its estimated 20-year economic life, this will result in arriving at grossly distorted and unrealistic financial criteria for this prospective project in its economic evaluation because cheap current-year cash income or cost-savings dollars will be measured against expensive prior years' capital investment dollars; and (2) to show the effect that inflation and depreciation deficiencies under present income tax laws has on the financial criteria arrived at in both the economic evaluation and the post-completion audit for this new project.

The information in Table 73 shows that when inflation at the rate of 8 points annually, from an index of 100 at the zero reference point to an index of 260 in the 20th year, is injected into Project D's annual cash income and cost savings amounts, a grossly distorted and unrealistic 21.7 percent DCF rate of return and 4.9 years' payout period are arrived at in the economic evaluation. These figures are based on annual depreciation charges calculated on Project D's $10,000 original capital cost as permitted under present corporate income laws.

On the other hand, the information in Table 78 shows that this 21.7 percent DCF rate of return would increase to 22.7 percent and the 4.9-year payout period would decrease to 4.7 years if present corporate income tax laws were revised and the annual depreciation charges were permitted to be calculated on Project D's annual current-year replacement cost instead of on its original cost.

Project D's Post-Completion Audit Incorrectly Failing to Adjust Annual Cash Income Amounts For Inflation but Eliminating Depreciation Deficiencies*

	(1)	(2)	(3)	(4)	(5)	(6)
Year	Fixed Asset Cost Index	Original Cost and Replacement Cost	Cash Income before Income Taxes	Sum-of-the-Years'-Digits Depreciation Calculated on Current-Year Replacement Cost	Taxable Income	Income Taxes
0	100	$10,000	—	—	—	—
1	108	10,800	$ 2,700	$ 1,029	$ 1,671	$ 802
2	116	11,600	2,900	1,050	1,850	888
3	124	12,400	3,100	1,063	2,037	978
4	132	13,200	3,300	1,069	2,231	1,071
5	140	14,000	3,500	1,067	2,433	1,168
6	148	14,800	3,700	1,057	2,643	1,269
7	156	15,600	3,900	1,040	2,860	1,373
8	164	16,400	4,100	1,015	3,085	1,481
9	172	17,200	4,300	983	3,317	1,592
10	180	18,000	4,500	943	3,557	1,707
11	188	18,800	4,700	895	3,805	1,826
12	196	19,600	4,900	840	4,060	1,949
13	204	20,400	5,100	777	4,323	2,075
14	212	21,200	5,300	707	4,593	2,205
15	220	22,000	5,500	629	4,871	2,338
16	228	22,800	5,700	543	5,157	2,475
17	236	23,600	5,900	450	5,450	2,616
18	244	24,400	6,100	349	5,751	2,760
19	252	25,200	6,300	240	6,060	2,909
20	260	26,000	6,500	124	6,376	3,060
Total			$92,000	$15,870	$76,130	$36,542

DCF rate of return is 22.7%.

Payout period is 4.7 years.

* This table may also be considered Project D's economic evaluation in which the estimated inflation rate is reflected in its cash income.

Project D's Post-Completion Audit Results versus Its Original Estimates

When the 21.7 percent DCF rate of return based on new Project D's actual performance in Table 73 is compared to the 15.5 percent DCF rate of return based on its original estimates in Table 72, the 6.2 percent difference in these two DCF rates of return is due to the effects of inflation on its annual cash returns and the depreciation deficiency created by calculating its depreciation charges on its fixed assets' original cost as required under present corporate income tax laws. However, when these depreciation charges are calculated on

TABLE 78

(7)	(8)	(9)	(10)	(11)	(12)
Profit after Income Taxes	*Cash Outlay† and Cash Income*	*Present Value*			
		Factor at 22%	*Amount*	*Factor at 23%*	*Amount*
—	$(10,000)‡	1.0000	$(10,000)	1.0000	$(10,000)
$ 869	1,898	.8197	1,556	.8130	1,543
962	2,012	.6719	1,352	.6610	1,330
1,059	2,122	.5507	1,169	.5374	1,140
1,160	2,229	.4514	1,006	.4369	974
1,265	2,332	.3700	863	.3552	828
1,374	2,431	.3033	737	.2888	702
1,487	2,527	.2486	628	.2348	593
1,604	2,619	.2038	534	.1909	500
1,725	2,708	.1670	452	.1552	420
1,850	2,793	.1369	382	.1262	352
1,979	2,874	.1122	322	.1026	295
2,111	2,951	.0920	271	.0834	246
2,248	3,025	.0754	228	.0678	205
2,388	3,095	.0618	191	.0551	171
2,533	3,162	.0507	160	.0448	142
2,682	3,225	.0415	134	.0364	117
2,834	3,284	.0340	112	.0296	97
2,991	3,340	.0279	93	.0241	80
3,151	3,391	.0229	78	.0196	66
3,316	3,440	.0187	64	.0159	55
$39,588	$ 45,458		$ 332		$ (144)

† Cash outlay in parentheses.
‡ Capital outlays are expressed in expensive zero reference point dollars. Annual cash income amounts are expressed in cheap current-year dollars.

the fixed assets' annual replacement cost instead of their original cost, then Project D's depreciation deficiency will be eliminated and its DCF rate of return based on its actual performance will increase from 21.7 percent to 22.7 percent, as shown in Table 78. Furthermore, when Project D's actual annual cash returns, expressed in cheap current-year dollars, in Tables 73 and 78 are properly adjusted for inflation, these two highly distorted and overstated DCF rates of return are reduced to 14.4 percent and 15.5 percent, respectively, as shown in Tables 79 and 80. The 1.1 percent difference between the 14.4 percent DCF rate of return arrived at in the post-completion audit conducted at the end and the 15.5 percent DCF rate of return arrived at in the economic

Project D's Post-Completion Audit Correctly Adjusting the Annual Cash Income Dollars for Inflation and Reflecting the Depreciation Deficiencies

	(1)	(2)	(3)	(4)	(5)	(6)
			Cash Income before Income Taxes		*Sum-of-the Years'-Digits Depreciation Calculated on Original Cost in Constant Dollars*	*Profit after Depreciation but before Income Taxes in Constant Dollars*
Year	*Fixed Asset and Cash Income Price Index*	*Cash Outlay**	*Current-Year Dollars*	*Constant Dollars*		
0	100	$(10,000)	—	—	—	—
1	108	—	$ 2,700	$ 2,500	$ 952	$ 1,548
2	116	—	2,900	2,500	905	1,595
3	124	—	3,100	2,500	857	1,643
4	132	—	3,300	2,500	810	1,690
5	140	—	3,500	2,500	762	1,738
6	148	—	3,700	2,500	714	1,786
7	156	—	3,900	2,500	667	1,833
8	164	—	4,100	2,500	619	1,881
9	172	—	4,300	2,500	571	1,929
10	180	—	4,500	2,500	524	1,976
11	188	—	4,700	2,500	476	2,024
12	196	—	4,900	2,500	429	2,071
13	204	—	5,100	2,500	381	2,119
14	212	—	5,300	2,500	333	2,167
15	220	—	5,500	2,500	286	2,214
16	228	—	5,700	2,500	238	2,262
17	236	—	5,900	2,500	190	2,310
18	244	—	6,100	2,500	143	2,357
19	252	—	6,300	2,500	95	2,405
20	260	—	6,500	2,500	48	2,452
Total		$(10,000)	$92,000	$50,000	$10,000	$40,000

DCF rate of return is 14.4%.

Payout period is 6.2 years.

* Cash outlay in parentheses.

evaluation at the beginning of Project D's 20-year economic life is solely attributable to the depreciation deficiency created under present income tax laws, which provide for calculating depreciation charges on fixed assets original cost instead of their annual replacement costs.

It also should be noted that Project D's 5.9 years' payout period estimated in its economic evaluation decreased erroneously to 4.9 years in its post-completion audit before proper adjustments for inflation were made, as shown in Table 73, but it actually increased to 6.2 years after these adjustments for inflation were made in the post-completion audit figures, as shown in Table 79. This difference of 3/10 of a year in Project D's actual versus its estimated payout period, likewise, was attributable to the depreciation defi-

TABLE 79

(7)	(8)	(9)	(10)	(11)	(12)	(13)	(14)
		Profit after Depreciation and Income Taxes in Constant Dollars	*Cash Outlay* and Cash Income after Income Taxes in Constant Dollars*				
Income Taxes					*Present Value*		
Current-Year Dollars	*Constant Dollars*			*Factor at 14%*	*Amount*	*Factor at 15%*	*Amount*
—	—	—	$(10,000)	1.0000	$(10,000)	1.0000	$(10,000)
$ 839	$ 777	$ 771	1,723	.8772	1,511	.8696	1,498
958	826	769	1,674	.7695	1,288	.7561	1,266
1,077	869	774	1,631	.6750	1,101	.6575	1,072
1,195	905	785	1,595	.5921	944	.5718	912
1,314	939	799	1,561	.5194	811	.4972	776
1,433	968	818	1,532	.4556	698	.4323	662
1,552	995	838	1,505	.3996	601	.3759	566
1,671	1,019	862	1,481	.3506	519	.3269	484
1,790	1,041	888	1,459	.3075	449	.2843	415
1,908	1,060	916	1,440	.2697	307	.2472	356
2,028	1,079	945	1,421	.2366	336	.2149	305
2,146	1,095	975	1,404	.2076	291	.1869	262
2,265	1,110	1,009	1,390	.1821	253	.1625	226
2,384	1,125	1,042	1,375	.1597	220	.1413	194
2,503	1,138	1,076	1,362	.1401	191	.1229	167
2,622	1,150	1,112	1,350	.1229	166	.1069	144
2,741	1,161	1,149	1,334	.1078	144	.0929	124
2,859	1,172	1,185	1,328	.0946	126	.0808	107
2,978	1,182	1,223	1,318	.0829	109	.0703	93
3,097	1,191	1,261	1,309	.0728	95	.0611	80
$39,360	$20,802	$19,197	$ 19,197		$ 160		$ (291)

ciency created by inflation during its economic life and by present income tax laws, which do not allow fixed assets to be depreciated on their annual replacement costs.

Project D's post-completion audit conducted at the close of its 20-year economic life brought to light these significant facts: (1) The increases in its annual cash returns kept pace with the increases in its fixed assets annual replacement costs which increased at an annual rate of 8 points, from an index of 100 at the zero reference point to an index of 260 in the 20th year, as shown in Table 73. (2) Despite this fact, Project D's actual DCF rate of return was 1.1 percent lower and its actual payout period was 3/10 of a year longer than its estimated DCF rate of return and payout period. This was solely

Project D's Post-Completion Audit Correctly Adjusting the Annual Cash Income Amounts For Inflation and Eliminating Depreciation Deficiencies

	(1)	(2)	(3)	(4)	(5)	(6)
			Cash Income before Income Taxes		Sum-of-the-Years'-Digits Depreciation Calculated on Replacement	Profit after Depreciation but before
	Fixed Asset and Cash Income	Cash	Current-Year	Constant	Cost in Constant	Income Taxes in Constant
Year	Price Index	Outlay*	Dollars	Dollars	Dollars	Dollars
0	100	$(10,000)	—	—	—	—
1	108	—	$ 2,700	$ 2,500	$ 952	$ 1,548
2	116	—	2,900	2,500	905	1,595
3	124	—	3,100	2,500	857	1,643
4	132	—	3,300	2,500	810	1,690
5	140	—	3,500	2,500	762	1,738
6	148	—	3,700	2,500	714	1,786
7	156	—	3,900	2,500	667	1,833
8	164	—	4,100	2,500	619	1,881
9	172	—	4,300	2,500	571	1,929
10	180	—	4,500	2,500	524	1.976
11	188	—	4,700	2,500	476	2,024
12	196	—	4,900	2,500	429	2,071
13	204	—	5,100	2,500	381	2,119
14	212	—	5,300	2,500	333	2,167
15	220	—	5,500	2,500	286	2,214
16	228	—	5,700	2,500	238	2,262
17	236	—	5,900	2,500	190	2,310
18	244	—	6,100	2,500	143	2,357
19	252	—	6,300	2,500	95	2,405
20	260	—	6,500	2,500	48	2,452
Total		$(10,000)	$92,000	$50,000	$10,000	$40,000

DCF rate of return is 15.5%.

Payout period is 5.9 years.

* Cash outlay in parentheses.

attributable to the depreciation deficiency created by inflation and by present corporate income tax laws, which fail to permit companies to recover the capital cost of their fixed assets in amounts that are equal in purchasing power to their original capital investments in them. (3) Results from post-completion audits of new projects that operate during inflationary periods are invariably misleading and meaningless unless proper adjustments are made for inflation in their cash outflows and cash inflows. (4) Revision in present corporate income tax laws is requisite in order to permit companies to depreciate fixed assets on their annual replacement costs instead of on their original costs, and thus preclude depreciation deficiencies and resultant lowering of returns from their capital investments in fixed assets.

TABLE 80

(7)	(8)	(9)	(10)	(11)	(12)	(13)	(14)
		Profit after Depreciation and Income	*Cash Outlay* and Cash Income after*		*Present Value*		
Income Taxes		*Taxes in*	*Income Taxes*				
Current-Year Dollars	*Constant Dollars*	*Constant Dollars*	*in Constant Dollars*	*Factor at 15%*	*Amount*	*Factor at 16%*	*Amount*
—	—	—	$(10,000)	1.0000	$(10,000)	1.0000	$(10,000)
$ 802	$ 743	$ 805	1,757	.8696	1,528	.8621	1,515
888	766	829	1,734	.7561	1,311	.7432	1,289
978	789	854	1,711	.6575	1,125	.6407	1,096
1,071	811	879	1,689	.5718	966	.5523	933
1,168	834	904	1,666	.4972	828	.4761	793
1,269	857	929	1,643	.4323	710	.4104	674
1,373	880	953	1,620	.3759	609	.3538	573
1,481	903	978	1,597	.3269	522	.3050	487
1,592	926	1,003	1,574	.2843	447	.2630	414
1,707	948	1,028	1,552	.2474	384	.2267	352
1,826	971	1,053	1,529	.2149	329	.1954	299
1,949	994	1,077	1,506	.1869	281	.1685	254
2,075	1,017	1,102	1,483	.1625	241	.1452	215
2,205	1,040	1,127	1,460	.1413	206	.1252	183
2,338	1,063	1,151	1,437	.1229	177	.1079	155
2,475	1,086	1,176	1,414	.1069	151	.0930	132
2,616	1,108	1,202	1,392	.0929	129	.0802	112
2,760	1,131	1,226	1,369	.0808	111	.0691	95
2,909	1,154	1,251	1,346	.0703	95	.0596	80
3,060	1,177	1,275	1,323	.0611	81	.0514	68
$36,542	$19,198	$20,802	$ 20,802		$ 231		$ (281)

While a 1.1 percent decrease in Project D's DCF rate of return, due solely to the depreciation deficiency, may on the surface appear to be insignificant, it actually is far from being that. This 1.1 percent decrease in its DCF rate of return is equivalent to a $1,603 loss in profits, expressed in constant dollars, which based on Project D's $20,800 total anticipated profits from this project represents a 7.7 percent and based on its $10,000 fixed assets' total capital cost represents a 16.0 percent loss in profits to the company. Obviously, losses in profits attributable to depreciation deficiencies during inflationary periods are apt to be considerable—particularly in the case of multinational companies whose capital investments in depreciable fixed assets run into the billions of dollars annually. For example, based on the inflation rate and the 16.0

percent loss in profits on its fixed assets' capital cost, as shown in Project D's post-completion audit, a $1 billion capital investment in depreciable fixed assets would result in a $160 million loss in profits due to depreciation deficiencies during the fixed assets' 20-year useful lives under similar circumstances. This $160 million loss in profits due to depreciation deficiencies may actually be on the conservative side because it is based on a rise in prices from an index of 100 to an index of 260 during a 20-year period, whereas the actual Consumer Price Index increased from an index of 100 to an index of 272.4 during just a 14-year period from 1967 to 1981.

As the reader may have surmised, the fact that Project D's estimated annual cash returns were assumed to be at a constant level of $2,500, and both its fixed assets' annual replacement costs and its annual cash returns were assumed to increase at the same constant-level rate of eight points, from an index of 100 at the zero reference point to an index of 260 in the 20th year, was done intentionally. It was done for the purpose of simplification as well as for the purpose of demonstrating that when proper adjustments for inflation are made in the project's post-completion audit, comparable constant dollars are arrived at that will be equal in amounts and purchasing power to those in the economic evaluation. Consequently, the DCF rate of return arrived at in the project's post-completion audit will be similar to that arrived at in its economic evaluation, providing the depreciation charges are calculated on the annual replacement costs of the fixed assets. If they are calculated on the fixed asset's original cost, then, of course, the DCF rate of return arrived at in the project's post-completion audit will be lower than that arrived at in its economic evaluation because of the resultant depreciation deficiency.

It may be reasonably safe to aver that in reality the annual cash returns of most new projects more than likely will not be at a constant-level rate; and likewise the annual replacement costs of the fixed assets, as well as their annual cash returns, more than likely will increase neither at a constant-level rate nor at the same rate.

Another Method of Proving Why Present Corporate Income Tax Laws Pertaining to Depreciation Should Be Revised

The information contained in Table 81 shows another method of proving that a revision in present corporate income tax laws is badly needed to permit companies to depreciate their fixed assets on their annual replacement costs instead of on their original costs. This revision will enable companies to recover the full purchasing power of their original capital investments and thus avoid depreciation deficiencies that inevitably will lead to decreases in their future overall profitability.

Table 81 shows three different series of annual rates of return before income taxes and before proper adjustments for inflation are made in the annual cash returns of Project D's post-completion audit. These annual rates of return before income taxes are calculated on Project D's fixed assets' *(a)* original capital cost, *(b)* annual replacement costs, and *(c)* actual replacement cost during the 20th year.

When the annual depreciation charges are calculated on the fixed assets' $10,000 original cost and Project D's annual rates of return before income taxes are also calculated on this original cost, the annual rates of return range from 22.0 percent in the first year to 60.0 percent in the 20th year, as shown in Column 12. This series of annual rates of return before income taxes calculated on Project D's $10,000 original capital cost is unrealistic and grossly overstated because it is based on measuring cheap current-year cash income dollars against incomparable expensive year 0 investment dollars.

Contrariwise, when Project D's annual depreciation charges are calculated on its $26,000 actual replacement cost during the 20th year, and its annual rates of return before income taxes are calculated on this replacement cost, the annual rates of return range from 5.4 percent in the first year to 20.0 percent in the 20th year as shown in Column 14. This series of annual rates of return before income taxes calculated on Project D's $26,000 actual replacement cost is unrealistic and grossly understated because in this case it is based on measuring expensive current-year cash income dollars against incomparable cheap-year 20 investment dollars.

However, when the annual depreciation charges are calculated on the fixed assets' annual replacement costs, and Project D's annual rates of return before income taxes are calculated on these annual replacement costs, ranging from $10,800 in the first year to $26,000 in the 20th year, they will be at a constant-level rate of 20 percent, as shown in Column 13. This series of annual rates of return before income taxes calculated on Project D's annual replacement costs is realistic and true because these rates of return before income taxes are based on measuring cheap current-year cash income dollars against comparable cheap current-year investment dollars.

While depreciation deficiencies created by inflation under present corporate income tax laws affect the actual performances of new projects adversely and therefore justly call for tax reform, they nevertheless represent neither the principal problem in nor the primary objective for making post-completion audits of new projects. The primary objective of companies for making post-completion audits of new projects is to ascertain whether their actual performances measure up to their original estimates and, consequently, determine whether the new projects will yield the DCF rates of return and recover the capital investments as rapidly as estimated in their economic evaluations.

To achieve this objective, the company's financial analysts who are assigned the task of making these post-completion audits generally are confronted with a number of difficult and complex problems that are particularly severe during periods of sustained high inflation rates. These problems include the following: (1) the effects of inflation on new projects' cash flows and how they render the comparability between new projects' actual performance and their original estimates void; (2) the depreciation deficiencies created by inflation under present corporate income tax laws and their effect on new projects' profitability; (3) the incompatability of the DCF rate of return, which is used by companies as the most effective profitability indicator for making

*Comparison of Project D's Rates of Return (a) When Expensive Year 0
Investment Dollars Are Related to Incomparable Cheap Current-Year Income
Dollars (b) When Cheap Current-Year Investment Dollars Are Related to
Comparable Cheap Current-Year Income Dollars, and (c) When Cheap Year
20 Investment Dollars Are Related to Incomparable Expensive Current Year
Income Dollars*

	(1)	(2)	(3)	(4)	(5)	(6)	(7)
			Investment Base End of Year		Straight-Line Depreciation Calculated on		
	Fixed Asset Cost and		Replacement Cost			Replacement Cost	
	Cash Income	Original	Current	Actual	Original	Current	Actual
Year	Price Index	Cost	Year	20th Year	Cost	Year	20th Year
0	100	$10,000	—	—	—	—	—
1	108	—	$10,800	—	$ 500	$ 540	$ 1,300
2	116	—	11,600	—	500	580	1,300
3	124	—	12,400	—	500	620	1,300
4	132	—	13,200	—	500	660	1,300
5	140	—	14,000	—	500	700	1,300
6	148	—	14,800	—	500	740	1,300
7	156	—	15,600	—	500	780	1,300
8	164	—	16,400	—	500	820	1,300
9	172	—	17,200	—	500	860	1,300
10	180	—	18,000	—	500	900	1,300
11	188	—	18,800	—	500	940	1,300
12	196	—	19,600	—	500	980	1,300
13	204	—	20,400	—	500	1,020	1,300
14	212	—	21,200	—	500	1,060	1,300
15	220	—	22,000	—	500	1,100	1,300
16	228	—	22,800	—	500	1,140	1,300
17	236	—	23,600	—	500	1,180	1,300
18	244	—	24,400	—	500	1,220	1,300
19	252	—	25,200	—	500	1,260	1,300
20	260	—	26,000	$26,000	500	1,300	1,300
Total					$10,000	$18,400	$26,000

investment decisions for the acceptance or the rejection of proposed capital
investments in new projects, and the year-to-year book rate of return, which is
used by companies for measuring the effective and economic utilization of
their total assets; (4) the extraction of the necessary data for post-completion
audits from companies' books of account generally poses difficulties because
the data aren't readily available inasmuch as separate accounts are not kept
for individual new projects.

The Effects of Inflation on New Projects' Cash Flows

As prices rise and, conversely, as the value or purchasing power of the dollar
declines proportionately during inflationary periods, the dollar amounts of

TABLE 81

(8)	(9)	(10)	(11)	(12)	(13)	(14)
	Profits before Income Taxes but after Depreciation Based on			*Rates of Return before Income Taxes Based on*		
Profits before Depreciation and Income Taxes		*Replacement Cost*			*Replacement Cost*	
	Original Cost	*Current Year*	*Actual 20th Year*	*Original Cost*	*Current Year*	*Actual 20th Year*
$ 2,500	—	—	—	—	—	—
2,700	$ 2,200	$ 2,160	$ 1,400	22.0%	20.0%	5.4%
2,900	2,400	2,320	1,600	24.0	20.0	6.2
3,100	2,600	2,480	1,800	26.0	20.0	6.9
3,300	2,800	2,640	2,000	28.0	20.0	7.7
3,500	3,000	2,800	2,200	30.0	20.0	8.5
3,700	3,200	2,960	2,400	32.0	20.0	9.2
3,900	3,400	3,120	2,600	34.0	20.0	10.0
4,100	3,600	3,280	2,800	36.0	20.0	10.8
4,300	3,800	3,440	3,000	38.0	20.0	11.5
4,500	4,000	3,600	3,200	40.0	20.0	12.3
4,700	4,200	3,760	3,400	42.0	20.0	13.1
4,900	4,400	3,920	3,600	44.0	20.0	13.8
5,100	4,600	4,080	3,800	46.0	20.0	14.6
5,300	4,800	4,240	4,000	48.0	20.0	15.4
5,500	5,000	4,400	4,200	50.0	20.0	16.2
5,700	5,200	4,560	4,400	52.0	20.0	16.9
5,900	5,400	4,720	4,600	54.0	20.0	17.7
6,100	5,600	4,880	4,800	56.0	20.0	18.5
6,300	5,800	5,040	5,000	58.0	20.0	19.2
6,500	6,000	5,200	5,200	60.0	20.0	20.0
$92,000	$82,000	$73,600	$66,000			

the actual cash flows of new projects will be greater compared to those of their original estimates. Consequently, the DCF rates of return in the post-completion audits of new projects, calculated on the larger dollar amounts of their actual cash returns and expressed in cheap current-year dollars, will tend to be higher than the DCF rates of return in the economic evaluations of new projects, calculated on the smaller dollar amounts of their original estimates and expressed in prior years' expensive dollars. This could be true even when, for example, the dollar amounts of new projects' actual cash returns are much greater, but when adjusted for inflation, the cash returns actually are much smaller than those of their original estimates, yet the DCF rates of return in these new projects' post-completion audits will be deceptively much higher than those in new projects' economic evaluations. As shown in Tables 72, 73, and 79, the DCF rates of return comparing Project D's actual performance versus its original estimates is a good case in point.

As shown in Tables 72 and 73, as prices rise at the constant-level rate of 8 points annually, from an index of 100 at the zero reference point to an index of 260 in the 20th year and, conversely, the value or purchasing power of the dollar declines from 100.0 cents to 38.5 cents during this 20-year period, Project D's actual annual cash returns increase in dollar amounts, ranging from $2,700 in the first year to $6,500 in the 20th year, and to a total of $92,000 compared to its original estimates of a constant-level annual amount of $2,500, and a total of $50,000. Consequently, the DCF rate of return based on Project D's actual performance shows an illusory 21.7 percent in its post-completion audit compared to the 15.5 percent DCF rate of return based on its original estimates shown in its economic evaluation.

As shown in Tables 73 and 79, when Project D's actual cash returns totaling $52,640, and expressed in cheap current-year dollars, are adjusted for inflation and expressed in comparable constant dollars, they are equivalent to only $29,197 compared to its $30,800 original estimates. This proves that Project D's DCF rate of return based on its actual performance is only 14.4 percent compared to the 15.5 percent based on its original estimates. This shows that Project D's actual performance measured in real dollars is actually $1,603 less in its total cash returns, and 1.1 percent lower in its DCF rate of return, than originally estimated in its economic evaluation. This difference is entirely due to the depreciation deficiency created under present corporate income tax laws. It should be pointed out here that the examples in Tables 72, 73, 78, and 79 are based on the assumptions that all, or 100 percent, of Project D's fixed assets' annual replacement costs increase at the same rate and, furthermore, that the increases in its annual cash returns keep pace with those of its fixed assets' annual replacement costs, i.e., they both increase at an annual rate of 8 points, from an index of 100 at the zero reference point to an index of 260 in the 20th year.

It should be pointed out further that these assumptions aren't typical or based on common occurrences. It is far more likely that the annual replacement costs of various types or classes of new projects' total fixed assets increase at different rates instead of at the same rate and, moreover, that their annual cash returns increase at a different rate—either higher or lower—than their fixed assets' annual replacement costs. This brings us to the problems encountered in the task of adjusting new projects' cash flows for inflation. These problems entail what index to use for this purpose, how to develop it, and who should develop it.

The Proper Index to Use for Adjusting New Projects' Cash Flows for Inflation

The first problem to resolve is what index to use for this purpose. This must be an index that reflects the increases in the annual replacement costs of new projects' fixed assets. This contention is based on the rationale that except for so-called "must" projects, proposed capital expenditures for new projects' fixed assets normally are justified on the basis of their estimated cash returns, which must be sufficiently large to recover such capital expenditures in addition to yielding profits at rates equal to or exceeding their predetermined minimum acceptable DCF rates of return. In other words, new projects' cash returns as well as their profitability are intrinsically related to and contingent upon the capital costs of the fixed assets. Consequently, when the annual replacement costs of new projects' fixed assets increase due to inflation, as the value or purchasing power of the dollar declines steadily, the annual cash returns of the new projects must increase at the same rate dollar-wise if the new projects are to yield DCF rates of return equal to those estimated in their economic evaluations. If their annual cash returns increase at either slower or faster rates than their fixed assets' annual replacement costs, then the new projects will yield either lower or higher DCF rates of return respectively than those estimated in their economic evaluations. This proves that in order to obtain meaningful and realistic DCF rates of return in the post-completion audits of new projects, their annual cash returns, expressed in cheap current-year dollars, must be adjusted for inflation by an index that reflects the increases in their fixed assets' annual replacement costs. This, of course, is equally true for capital outlays, expressed in cheap current-year dollars, which occur subsequent to the time new projects start generating cash returns.

The second problem to resolve is how this index is to be developed, since the prices, construction costs, or lease rentals for various types or classes of new projects' component fixed assets generally increase at different rates during inflationary periods. The method for resolving this problem is shown in Table 82. It is assumed in Table 82 that the annual replacement cost of 40 percent, or $4,000, of Project D's total fixed assets increases at the rate of 12 points, from an index of 100 at the zero reference point to an index of 340 in the 20th year and that the remaining 60 percent, or $6,000, of its total fixed assets increases at the rate of 10 points, from an index of 100 at the zero reference point to an index of 300 in the 20th year. When these two series of index numbers, representing the annual replacement cost increases for 40 percent and 60 percent of Project D's total fixed assets, are multiplied by these percentages, respectively, and the resultant products are added, the composite annual replacement cost index for Project D's total fixed assets is arrived at. This type of composite annual replacement cost index can be developed for new projects' component fixed assets during inflationary periods whether the increases in the annual replacement costs of the fixed assets vary due to the differences in their types or classes, their methods of acquisition, the geographic areas, etc.

As indicated previously, when annual cash returns of new projects increase either less or more rapidly than their fixed assets' annual replacement costs during inflationary periods, then the DCF rates of return in their post-completion audits—after proper adjustments for inflation have been made—will be either lower or higher respectively than those estimated in their eco-

Effect on Project D's Profitability and Liquidity When Its Annual Cash Returns Are Increasing at a Slower Rate than Its Fixed Assets' Annual Replacement Costs

Year	(1) Fixed Asset and Cash Income Price Index	(2) Cash Income before Taxes	(3) Sum-of-the-Years'-Digits Depreciation Charges	(4) Taxable Income	(5) Income Taxes	(6) Profit after Income Taxes
0	100.0	—	—	—	—	—
1	110.8	$ 2,700	$ 952	$ 1,748	$ 839	$ 909
2	121.6	2,900	905	1,995	958	1,037
3	132.4	3,100	857	2,243	1,077	1,166
4	143.2	3,300	810	2,490	1,195	1,295
5	154.0	3,500	762	2,738	1,314	1,424
6	164.8	3,700	714	2,986	1,433	1,553
7	175.6	3,900	667	3,233	1,552	1,681
8	186.4	4,100	619	3,481	1,671	1,810
9	197.2	4,300	571	3,729	1,790	1,939
10	208.0	4,500	524	3,976	1,908	2,068
11	218.8	4,700	476	4,224	2,028	2,196
12	229.6	4,900	429	4,471	2,146	2,325
13	240.4	5,100	381	4,719	2,265	2,454
14	251.2	5,300	333	4,967	2,384	2,583
15	262.0	5,500	286	5,214	2,503	2,711
16	272.8	5,700	238	5,462	2,622	2,840
17	283.6	5,900	190	5,710	2,741	2,969
18	294.4	6,100	143	5,957	2,859	3,098
19	305.2	6,300	95	6,205	2,978	3,227
20	316.0	6,500	48	6,452	3,097	3,355
Total		$92,000	$10,000	$82,000	$39,360	$42,640

DCF rate of return . . . .
Payout period . . . .

nomic evaluations. This type of situation is illustrated in Table 82, in which it is assumed that Project D's annual cash returns increase at a slower rate of 8 points, from an index of 100 at the zero reference point to an index of 260 in the 20th year, while its fixed assets annual replacement costs increase at a rate of 10.8 points, from an index of 100 at the zero reference point to an index of 316.0 in the 20th year. Under these conditions, the DCF rate of return in Project D's post-completion audit—after proper adjustments for inflation are made—is only 12.7 percent compared to 14.2 percent when the increases in its annual cash returns keep pace with those of its fixed assets' annual replacement costs at the rate of 10.8 points, as shown in Tables 83 and 84.

The reverse, of course, would be true if Project D's annual cash returns were to increase at a more rapid rate than its fixed assets' annual replacement costs of 10.8 points, in which case the DCF rate of return in its post-comple-

TABLE 82

	(7)	(8)	(9)	(10)	(11)	(12)	(13)
		Net Cash Flow		Present Value		Present Value	
	Depreciation	Current-Year Dollars	Constant Dollars	Factor at 12%	Amount	Factor at 13%	Amount
	—	$(10,000)	$(10,000)	1.0000	$(10,000)	1.0000	$(10,000)
$	952	1,861	1,680	.8929	1,500	.8850	1,487
	905	1,942	1,597	.7972	1,273	.7831	1,251
	857	2,023	1,528	.7118	1,088	.6930	1,059
	810	2,105	1,470	.6355	934	.6133	902
	762	2,186	1,419	.5674	805	.5428	770
	714	2,267	1,376	.5066	697	.4803	661
	667	2,348	1,337	.4523	605	.4251	568
	619	2,429	1,303	.4039	526	.3762	490
	571	2,510	1,273	.3606	459	.3329	424
	524	2,592	1,246	.3220	401	.2946	367
	476	2,672	1,221	.2875	351	.2607	318
	429	2,754	1,199	.2567	308	.2307	277
	381	2,835	1,179	.2292	270	.2042	241
	333	2,916	1,161	.2046	238	.1807	210
	286	2,997	1,144	.1827	209	.1599	183
	238	3,078	1,128	.1631	184	.1415	160
	190	3,159	1,114	.1456	162	.1252	139
	143	3,241	1,101	.1300	143	.1108	122
	95	3,322	1,088	.1161	126	.0981	107
	48	3,403	1,077	.1037	112	.0868	93
	$10,000	$ 42,640	$ 15,641		$ 391		$ (171)
	....	21.7%	12.7%				
	....	4.9 years	6.7 years				

tion audit—after proper adjustments for inflation were made—would be higher instead of lower than 14.2 percent.

Finally, the third problem to resolve is who is best suited to provide the requisite data for developing annual replacement cost indexes of fixed assets, which are required by companies in the performance of post-completion audits of new projects. It appears to be wasteful and costly for individual companies to perform this task of gathering and keeping records pertaining to prices, lease rentals, construction costs, etc., for various types and classes of fixed assets in numerous geographic areas in the United States as well as abroad in the case of multinational companies. Most industries have an industry institute, such as the American Petroleum Institute (API) for example, which provides data and various other services for American Oil companies. It would be far more efficient and certainly much less costly for such industry

TABLE 83

Effects on Project D's Profitability and Liquidity When Its Annual Cash Returns Increase at the Same Rate as Its Fixed Assets' Annual Replacement Costs

	(1)	(2)	(3)	(4)	(5)	(6)	(7)	(8) Net Cash Flow	(9) Net Cash Flow
Year	Fixed Asset and Cash Income Price Index	Cash Income before Taxes	Sum-of-the Years'-Digits Depreciation Charges	Taxable Income	Income Taxes	Profit after Income Taxes	Depreciation	Current-Year Dollars	Constant Dollars
0	100.0							$(10,000)	$(10,000)
1	110.8	$ 2,770	$ 952	$ 1,818	$ 873	$ 945	$ 952	1,897	1,712
2	121.6	3,040	905	2,135	1,025	1,110	905	2,015	1,657
3	132.4	3,310	857	2,453	1,177	1,276	857	2,133	1,611
4	143.2	3,580	810	2,770	1,330	1,440	810	2,250	1,571
5	154.0	3,850	762	3,088	1,482	1,606	762	2,368	1,538
6	164.8	4,120	714	3,406	1,635	1,771	714	2,485	1,508
7	175.6	4,390	667	3,723	1,787	1,936	667	2,603	1,482
8	186.4	4,660	619	4,041	1,940	2,101	619	2,720	1,459
9	197.2	4,930	571	4,359	2,092	2,267	571	2,838	1,439
10	208.0	5,200	524	4,676	2,244	2,432	524	2,956	1,421
11	218.8	5,470	476	4,994	2,397	2,597	476	3,073	1,404
12	229.6	5,740	429	5,311	2,549	2,762	429	3,191	1,390
13	240.4	6,010	381	5,629	2,702	2,927	381	3,308	1,376
14	251.2	6,280	333	5,947	2,855	3,092	333	3,425	1,363
15	262.0	6,550	286	6,264	3,007	3,257	286	3,543	1,352
16	272.8	6,820	238	6,582	3,159	3,423	238	3,661	1,342
17	283.6	7,090	190	6,900	3,312	3,588	190	3,778	1,332
18	294.4	7,360	143	7,217	3,464	3,753	143	3,896	1,323
19	305.2	7,630	95	7,535	3,617	3,918	95	4,013	1,315
20	316.0	7,900	48	7,852	3,769	4,083	48	4,131	1,307
Total		$106,700	$10,000	$96,700	$46,416	$50,284	$10,000	$ 50,284	$18,902
DCF rate of return								23.3%	14.2%
Payout period								4.7 years	6.3 years

Method For Developing Composite Replacement Cost Index for Project D's Total Fixed Assets

TABLE 84

	(1)	(2)	(3)	(4)	(5)	(6)	(7)	(8)	(9)
	40% of Fixed Assets' Replacement Cost		60% of Fixed Assets' Replacement Cost		Total Fixed Assets' Replacement Cost	Fixed Assets Composite Replacement Cost Index			Total Fixed Assets' Replacement Cost
Year	Index	Amount	Index	Amount		40% of Fixed Assets	60% of Fixed Assets	100% of Fixed Assets	
0	100	$ 4,000	100	$ 6,000	$10,000	40.0	60.0	100.0	$10,000
1	112	4,480	110	6,600	11,080	44.8	66.0	110.8	11,080
2	124	4,960	120	7,200	12,160	49.6	72.0	121.6	12,160
3	136	5,440	130	7,800	13,240	54.4	78.0	132.4	13,240
4	148	5,920	140	8,400	14,320	59.2	84.0	143.2	14,320
5	160	6,400	150	9,000	15,400	64.0	90.0	154.0	15,400
6	172	6,880	160	9,600	16,480	68.8	96.0	164.8	16,480
7	184	7,360	170	10,200	17,560	73.6	102.0	175.6	17,560
8	196	7,840	180	10,800	18,640	78.4	108.0	186.4	18,640
9	208	8,320	190	11,400	19,720	83.2	114.0	197.2	19,720
10	220	8,800	200	12,000	20,800	88.0	120.0	208.0	20,800
11	232	9,280	210	12,600	21,880	92.8	126.0	218.8	21,880
12	244	9,760	220	13,200	22,960	97.6	132.0	229.6	22,960
13	256	10,240	230	13,800	24,040	102.4	138.0	240.4	24,040
14	268	10,720	240	14,400	25,120	107.2	144.0	251.2	25,120
15	280	11,200	250	15,000	26,200	112.0	150.0	262.0	26,200
16	292	11,680	260	15,600	27,280	116.8	156.0	272.8	27,280
17	304	12,160	270	16,200	28,360	121.6	162.0	283.6	28,360
18	316	12,640	280	16,800	29,440	126.4	168.0	294.4	29,440
19	328	13,120	290	17,400	30,520	131.2	174.0	305.2	30,520
20	340	13,600	300	18,000	31,600	136.0	180.0	316.0	31,600

institutes to gather, maintain, and furnish this type of information to companies within their industry.

The Problem of Depreciation Deficiencies—What Can Be Done about It

As discussed in great detail in a previous chapter, depreciation deficiencies pose a definite problem to companies insofar as they have an adverse effect on the profitability of new projects. It is unlikely that this problem will be resolved in the foreseeable future inasmuch as this would require a revision in present corporate income tax laws by the U.S. Congress to permit companies to calculate depreciation allowances on their fixed assets' annual replacement costs instead of on their original cost. Until such a corporate income tax revision materializes, the only alternative open to companies to offset losses in profits sustained as a result of depreciation deficiencies appears to be through increased sales volumes, sales prices, and cost savings—if the marketplace makes this possible.

Chapter 16

Incompatibility of DCF Rate of Return and Year-to-Year Book Rate of Return and How to Resolve This Problem

By far the most baffling problem in connection with post-completion audits is the incompatibility of the DCF rate of return and the year-to-year book rate of return. What makes this such an agonizing problem is that the objective of companies in making capital investments in new projects is to enhance their future overall profitability, and this problem, unfortunately, makes it impossible to determine whether this objective has been achieved. The reason for this problem is fourfold: (1) One rate, the DCF rate of return, is used as a profitability indicator in assessing the acceptance or the rejection of proposed capital investments in new projects; while another rate, the year-to-year book rate of return, is used as a profitability indicator in assessing the effective and efficient utilization of companies' total assets, including those of new projects. (2) The DCF rate of return is incompatible with the year-to-year book rate because these two rates are diametrically opposed to one another. In the DCF rate of return calculation, the profit is calculated first on the unrecovered portion of the capital investment while the remainder represents the capital recovery; contrariwise, in the year-to-year book rate of return calculation, the capital recovery (depreciation) is calculated first on the fixed asset's original cost, while the remainder represents the profit. (3) The DCF rate of return is a true and realistic profitability indicator because, similar to the compound interest rate, it is calculated on the unrecovered (unpaid) balance of the capital investment (principal); whereas the year-to-year book rate of return can be anything companies want it to be depending upon the depreciation method chosen for book purposes and the investment base chosen as a divisor. The latter could be the company's total assets *(a)* at the beginning of the year, *(b)* at the end of the year, or *(c)* averaged during the year.

Since the present year-to-year book rate of return is neither a true nor a meaningful profitability indicator for the above-mentioned reasons, a rate must be devised that will be compatible with the DCF rate of return used in the decision-making process involving the acceptability of prospective projects. Obviously, this type of a rate can be devised only by an application of the discounted cash flow (DCF) concept to a method that will produce a year-to-year book rate of return that will be compatible with the DCF rate of return. (4) Even when a year-to-year book rate of return has been devised that promises to be compatible with the DCF rate of return, this problem still will not be fully resolved. The reason for this is that profits or losses of companies are expressed in cheap current-year dollars, while their assets, liabilities, and shareholders' equity are expressed in incomparable expensive prior years' dollars. This leads to grossly distorted, unrealistic, and illusory year-to-year book rates of return—a condition that will persist until companies decide to make proper upward adjustments statistically for inflation as well as for other factors that have caused assets and shareholders' equity to appreciate in value. The failure of companies to make these adjustments statistically is just another important reason present year-to-year book rates of return not only are grossly misleading but also of little value—if any.

This brings us to the subject of year-to-year book rates of return and of how to devise a method that will produce a year-to-year book rate of return that will be compatible with the DCF rates of return used in the economic evaluations of new projects and in their subsequent post-completion audits.

Project D's Year-to-Year Book Rates of Return

Theoretically, year-to-year rates of return are presumed to measure the effective and efficient utilization of a company's total assets and thus indicate its overall profitability. Normally, year-to-year book rates of return are calculated on the average of the total assets employed by them during the year. However, in the three series of year-to-year book rates of return computed for Project D's total assets in Tables 85, 86, and 87, these rates are computed on the assets' depreciated book value at the start of the year by the conventional bookkeeping method. The reason for computing the present year-to-year book rates of return for Project D's total assets on the start of the year basis is for comparative purposes because the newly devised year-to-year book rates of return determined by an application of the DCF concept are calculated on the unrecovered portion of the assets' capital cost at the start of each year. While it is recognized that year-to-year book rates of return usually are not computed for individual new project's total assets, nevertheless the conclusions that can be drawn from these year-to-year book rates of return are equally as valid as those computed for companies' total assets.

The purpose of the three series of year-to-year book rates of return for Project D's total assets in Tables 85, 86, and 87 is to prove that year-to-year book rates of return computed on a company's total assets are unrealistic, misleading, and illusory, and above all they are the direct antipode of and,

TABLE 85

Project D's Year-to-Year Book Rates of Return Calculated on the Fixed Assets Depreciated Book Value at the Start of the Year and the Capital Investment and the Income Dollars are Expressed in Comparable (Expensive) Zero Reference Point Dollars*

Year	(1) Fixed Assets' Original Cost	(2) Depreciated Book Value Start of Year	(3) Cash Income before Income Taxes	(4) Straight-Line Depreciation	(5) Profit after Depreciation but before Income Taxes	(6) Income Taxes	(7) Net Book Income	(8) Year-to-Year Book Rate of Return	(9) Reserve for Depreciation
0	$10,000	—	—	—	—	—	—	—	—
1		$10,000	$ 2,500	$ 500	$ 2,000	$ 743	$ 1,257	12.6%	$ 500
2		9,500	2,500	500	2,000	766	1,234	13.0	1,000
3		9,000	2,500	500	2,000	789	1,211	13.5	1,500
4		8,500	2,500	500	2,000	811	1,189	14.0	2,000
5		8,000	2,500	500	2,000	834	1,166	14.6	2,500
6		7,500	2,500	500	2,000	857	1,143	15.2	3,000
7		7,000	2,500	500	2,000	880	1,120	16.0	3,500
8		6,500	2,500	500	2,000	903	1,097	16.9	4,000
9		6,000	2,500	500	2,000	926	1,074	17.9	4,500
10		5,500	2,500	500	2,000	948	1,052	19.1	5,000
11		5,000	2,500	500	2,000	972	1,028	20.6	5,500
12		4,500	2,500	500	2,000	994	1,006	22.4	6,000
13		4,000	2,500	500	2,000	1,017	983	24.6	6,500
14		3,500	2,500	500	2,000	1,040	960	27.4	7,000
15		3,000	2,500	500	2,000	1,063	937	31.2	7,500
16		2,500	2,500	500	2,000	1,086	914	36.6	8,000
17		2,000	2,500	500	2,000	1,109	891	44.6	8,500
18		1,500	2,500	500	2,000	1,131	869	57.9	9,000
19		1,000	2,500	500	2,000	1,154	846	84.6	9,500
20		500	2,500	500	2,000	1,177	823	164.6	10,000
Total	$10,000	$ –0–	$50,000	$10,000	$40,000	$19,200	$20,800		

* Assumes that no inflation will occur.

Project D's Year-to-Year Book Rates of Return Calculated on the Fixed Asset's Depreciated Book Value at the Start of the Year and Expensive Investment Dollars Are Related to Cheap Current-Year Income Dollars*

	(1)	(2)	(3)	(4)	(5)	(6)	(7)	(8)
Year	Original Cost	Depreciated Book Value Start of Year	Cash Income before Income Taxes	Straight-Line Depreciation*	Profit after Depreciation but before Income Taxes	Income Taxes*	Net Book Income	Year-to-Year Book Rate of Return
0	$10,000		—	—	—	—	—	—
1		$10,000	$2,700	$ 500	$2,200	$ 839	$1,361	13.6%
2		9,500	2,900	500	2,400	958	1,442	15.2
3		9,000	3,100	500	2,600	1,077	1,523	16.9
4		8,500	3,300	500	2,800	1,195	1,605	18.9
5		8,000	3,500	500	3,000	1,314	1,686	20.5
6		7,500	3,700	500	3,200	1,433	1,767	23.6
7		7,000	3,900	500	3,400	1,552	1,848	26.4
8		6,500	4,100	500	3,600	1,671	1,929	29.7
9		6,000	4,300	500	3,800	1,790	2,010	33.5
10		5,500	4,500	500	4,000	1,908	2,092	38.0
11		5,000	4,700	500	4,200	2,028	2,172	43.4
12		4,500	4,900	500	4,400	2,146	2,254	50.1
13		4,000	5,100	500	4,600	2,265	2,335	58.4
14		3,500	5,300	500	4,800	2,384	2,416	69.0
15		3,000	5,500	500	5,000	2,503	2,497	83.2
16		2,500	5,700	500	5,200	2,622	2,578	103.1
17		2,000	5,900	500	5,400	2,741	2,659	133.0
18		1,500	6,100	500	5,600	2,859	2,741	182.7
19		1,000	6,300	500	5,800	2,978	2,822	282.2
20		500	6,500	500	6,000	3,097	2,903	580.6
Total	$10,000		$92,000	$10,000	$82,000	$39,360	$42,640	

* Depreciation for book and income tax purposes as allowed under present tax laws.

TABLE 86

therefore, completely incompatible with the DCF rates of return used in the economic evaluations of new projects and their subsequent post-completion audits.

The first series of year-to-year book rates of return for Project D's fixed assets shown in Table 85, ranging from 12.6 percent in the first year to 164.6 percent in the 20th year, is based on the same financial factors its 15.5 percent DCF rate of return is based on in this project's economic evaluation shown in Table 72. Both this series of year-to-year book rates of return and its DCF rate of return are calculated on Project D's estimated capital cost and cash returns, which are both expressed in comparable constant zero reference point dollars.

Project D's annual depreciation charges used for income tax purposes are calculated by the sum-of-the-years'-digits method, while those used for book purposes are calculated by the straight-line method. Both series of depreciation charges are calculated on the original cost of the fixed assets.

This series of year-to-year book rates of return for Project D's $10,000 capital investment in fixed assets is calculated by dividing its annual book income, ranging from $1,257 in the 1st year to $823 in the 20th year, by its fixed assets' depreciated book value at the start of the year, ranging from $10,000 in the 1st year to $500 in the 20th year. These would be the actual year-to-year book rates of return for Project D's $10,000 capital investment in its fixed assets providing the value or purchasing power of the dollar would remain constant, i.e., if there would be no inflation throughout Project D's 20-year economic life. Unfortunately, this didn't turn out to be the case as assumed in Table 73.

The series of year-to-year book rates of return for Project D's fixed assets shown in Table 86 is calculated on the same financial factors that its 21.7 percent DCF rate of return is based on in its post-completion audit shown in Table 73. Table 73 shows that Project D's annual cash income amounts increased from $2,700 in the first year to $6,500 in the 20th year, which represents an 8-point annual increase, from an index of 108 in the first year to an index of 260 in the 20th year. Although the replacement cost of Project D's fixed assets, likewise, increased at the same rate during its 20-year economic life—from $10,800 in the first year to $26,000 in the 20th year—this fact is purposely omitted from Tables 73 and 86 in order to avoid confusion and possible misunderstandings. However, the primary reason for the exclusion of this information is that according to conventional and orthodox accounting principles and practices, no adjustments for the appreciation in value of assets due to inflation or other factors are made in a company's books of account until such time that the assets are disposed of at a profit or a loss. Furthermore, companies apparently are not as yet ready to make proper statistical adjustments in their financial statements for the appreciation in value of their assets due to either inflation or other factors. Consequently, Project D's $10,000 original capital cost for its fixed assets will be shown in expensive zero reference point dollars during its entire economic life, while its annual net

Project D's Year-to-Year Book Rates of Return after Adjustments for Inflation Are Made and the Fixed Asset's Depreciated Book Values Expressed in Cheap Current-Year Dollars Are Related to Comparable Cheap Current-Year Book Income Dollars*

Year	(1) Fixed Asset and Cash Income Price Index	(2) Original Cost and Replacement Cost End of Year	(3) Depreciated Book Value Adjusted for Inflation Start of Year	(4) Cash Income before Income Taxes	(5) Straight-Line Depreciation Adjusted for Inflation
0	100	$10,000	—	—	—
1	108	10,800	$10,800	$ 2,700	$ 540
2	116	11,600	11,020	2,900	580
3	124	12,400	11,160	3,100	620
4	132	13,200	11,220	3,300	660
5	140	14,000	11,200	3,500	700
6	148	14,800	11,100	3,700	740
7	156	15,600	10,920	3,900	780
8	164	16,400	10,660	4,100	820
9	172	17,200	10,320	4,300	860
10	180	18,000	9,900	4,500	900
11	188	18,800	9,400	4,700	940
12	196	19,600	8,820	4,900	980
13	204	20,400	8,160	5,100	1,020
14	212	21,200	7,420	5,300	1,060
15	220	22,000	6,600	5,500	1,100
16	228	22,800	5,700	5,700	1,140
17	236	23,600	4,720	5,900	1,180
18	244	24,400	3,660	6,100	1,220
19	252	25,200	2,520	6,300	1,260
20	260	26,000	1,300	6,500	1,300
Total				$92,000	$18,400

* Depreciation for book and income tax purposes calculated on annual replacement costs instead of on original cost as required under present tax laws.

income (profit) will be shown in incomparable cheap current-year dollars on the company's books and in its financial statements.

In Table 86, Project D's annual depreciation charges used for income tax purposes, similar to those in Table 85, are calculated by the sum-of-the-years'-digits method, while annual depreciation charges used for book purposes are calculated by the straight-line method, and both series of depreciation charges are calculated on the original cost of the fixed assets.

This series of year-to-year book rates of return for Project D's $10,000 capital investment in fixed assets is calculated by dividing the annual book income (profit), expressed in cheap current-year dollars, by the fixed assets' depreciated book value at the start of the year expressed in expensive zero reference point dollars. This results in an incredible series of year-to-year

TABLE 87

(6)	(7)	(8)	(9)	(10)	(11)
	Income			*Depreciated Book Value Start of Year*	
Profit after Depreciation but before Income Taxes	*Taxes Adjusted for Inflation*	*Net Book Income*	*Year-to-Year Book rate of Return*	*Unadjusted for Inflation*	*Adjusted for Inflation*
$ 2,160	$ 802	$ 1,358	12.6%	$10,000	$10,800
2,320	888	1,432	13.0	9,500	11,020
2,480	978	1,502	13.5	9,000	11,160
2,640	1,071	1,569	14.0	8,500	11,220
2,800	1,168	1,632	14.6	8,000	11,200
2,960	1,269	1,691	15.2	7,500	11,100
3,120	1,373	1,747	16.0	7,000	10,920
3,280	1,481	1,799	16.9	6,500	10,660
3,440	1,592	1,848	17.9	6,000	10,320
3,600	1,707	1,893	19.1	5,500	9,900
3,760	1,826	1,934	20.6	5,000	9,400
3,920	1,949	1,971	22.4	4,500	8,820
4,080	2,075	2,005	24.6	4,000	8,160
4,240	2,205	2,035	27.4	3,500	7,420
4,400	2,338	2,062	31.3	3,000	6,600
4,560	2,475	2,085	36.6	2,500	5,700
4,720	2,616	2,104	44.6	2,000	4,720
4,880	2,760	2,120	57.9	1,500	3,660
5,040	2,909	2,131	84.6	1,000	2,520
5,200	3,060	2,140	164.6	500	1,300
$73,600	$36,542	$37,058			

book rates of return ranging from 13.6 percent in the first year to 580.6 percent in the 20th year. These year-to-year book rates of return obviously are grossly overstated and unrealistic as well as illusory and misleading due to measuring cheap current-year income dollars against expensive investment dollars.

This is precisely how year-to-year book rates of return on the capital investments in companies' total assets are calculated by the conventional bookkeeping method, which provides neither for proper statistical adjustments for the appreciation in value of companies' assets due to inflation or some other factors nor permits the annual depreciation charges to be calculated on fixed assets' current-year replacement costs instead of on their original cost as required under present corporate income tax laws.

This final series of year-to-year book rates of return for Project D's fixed assets shown in Table 87 is based on the same financial factors on which its 22.7 percent DCF rate of return is based on in Table 78. The principal differences between this series and the series of year-to-year book rates of return shown in Table 86 are *(a)* that Project D's capital investment in its fixed assets is adjusted for inflation and is shown to appreciate in value at the rate of $800 annually, from $10,000 at the zero reference point to $26,000 in the 20th year, and *(b)* that Project D's annual depreciation charges are calculated by the sum-of-the-years'-digits method for tax purposes and by the straight-line method for book purposes, but that in this case both series of depreciation charges are calculated on the annual replacement costs of fixed assets instead of on their original cost as required under present corporate income tax laws.

This series of year-to-year book rates of return for Project D's capital investment in fixed assets is calculated by dividing the annual book income (profit), expressed in cheap current-year dollars, by the fixed assets' depreciated book value at the start of the year, also expressed in cheap current-year dollars. This, it should be noted, results in year-to-year book rates of return, ranging from 12.6 percent in the first year to 164.6 percent in the 20th year, that are identical with those that are based on the same financial factors Project D's 15.5 percent DCF rate of return is based on, as shown in Tables 72 and 86.

Project D's year-to-year book rates of return are identical whether they are based on comparable constant expensive zero reference point dollars, as shown in Table 85, or comparable variable cheap current-year dollars, as shown in Table 87, providing the purchasing power of the total depreciation charges for income tax and book purposes is equal to that of the fixed asset's original cost.

The comparability of Project D's year-to-year book rates of return in Tables 85 and 87 once again points up both the need as well as the justification for a revision in present corporate income tax laws that would permit companies to calculate depreciation charges on their fixed assets' current replacement costs instead of on their original cost, and thus preclude depreciation deficiencies with the resultant losses in profits and decreases in companies' overall profitability during inflation periods.

A closer scrutiny of Project D's DCF rate of return and year-to-year book rates of return is warranted as they are used in assessing Project D's acceptability as a sound capital investment, its actual performance versus its original estimates, and its impact on the company's future overall profitability. This closer look at these two financial criteria, and how they are used, leads to these conclusions:

1. As the DCF rate of return is used in the economic evaluations of new projects, it is a true and realistic profitability indicator and a reliable project selection device, providing the projects' cash flows are expressed in constant dollars and the inflation factor is excluded from them.

2. As the DCF rate of return is used in post-completion audits of new projects, it likewise is a true and realistic profitability indicator, providing proper adjustments for inflation are made in their annual cash returns as well as in their cash outlays in the event of any delayed capital spending subsequent to the time the new projects started generating cash returns.

3. These adjustments for inflation in the annual cash returns and delayed capital outlays of new projects must be made by means of an index that reflects the increases in the fixed assets' annual replacement costs.

4. Failure to make these adjustments for inflation will result in overstated, illusory, and misleading DCF rates of return in new projects' post-completion audits that are incomparable with those estimated in their economic evaluations.

5. Even when the increases in their annual cash returns keep pace with the increases in their fixed assets' annual replacement costs, new projects, nevertheless, will show lower DCF rates of return in their post-completion audits compared to those estimated in their economic evaluations. This, of course, will be due to the depreciation deficiencies created by inflation under present corporate income tax laws.

6. If new projects' depreciation charges were calculated on their fixed assets' annual replacement costs instead of on their original cost, as required under present corporate income tax laws, then in their post-completion audits the DCF rates of return would be identical with, higher, or lower compared to those estimated in their economic evaluations, depending on whether the increases in their cash returns kept pace with, were faster or slower, respectively, than the increases in their fixed assets' annual replacement costs.

7. In the banking community, the term *interest,* in accordance with the compound interest principle, represents the sum of money paid by the borrower and, conversely, earned by the lender for the use of money. It is calculated by the compound interest rate on the unpaid balance of the loan principal. The remainder of the periodic loan payment amount represents amortization, or repayment of the loan principal. Similarly, in the business community, the term *profit,* in accordance with the DCF concept, represents the sum of money paid by the new project (the borrower) and, conversely, earned by the company (the lender) for the use of money. It is calculated by the DCF rate on the unrecovered (unpaid) balance of the capital investment (loan principal). The remainder of the periodic cash return (loan payment) amount represents capital recovery (repayment of principal).

8. However, in accordance with orthodox and accepted accounting prin-

ciples and practices, the term *profit* has a much different connotation because, in compliance with present corporate income tax laws, fixed assets' depreciation charges are calculated first at a fixed rate, and the remainder of new projects' cash returns represents their book income, or profit.

9. This procedure, of course, results in variable year-to-year book rates of return, which in the case of new Project D, for example, range from 20.0 percent in the first year to 400.0 percent in the 20th year, as shown in Table 88.

TABLE 88

Project D's Year-to-Year Book Rate of Return Based on Profits before Income Taxes

Year	(1) Fixed Assets Original Cost	(2) Depreciated Book Value Start of Year	(3) Cash Income before Income Taxes	(4) Straight-Line Depreciation	(5) Net Income before Income Taxes	(6) Year-to-Year Book Rate of Return
0	$10,000	—	—	—	—	—
1		$10,000	$ 2,500	$ 500	$ 2,000	20.0%
2		9,500	2,500	500	2,000	21.1
3		9,000	2,500	500	2,000	22.2
4		8,500	2,500	500	2,000	23.5
5		8,000	2,500	500	2,000	25.0
6		7,500	2,500	500	2,000	26.7
7		7,000	2,500	500	2,000	28.6
8		6,500	2,500	500	2,000	30.8
9		6,000	2,500	500	2,000	33.3
10		5,500	2,500	500	2,000	36.4
11		5,000	2,500	500	2,000	40.0
12		4,500	2,500	500	2,000	44.4
13		4,000	2,500	500	2,000	50.0
14		3,500	2,500	500	2,000	57.1
15		3,000	2,500	500	2,000	66.7
16		2,500	2,500	500	2,000	80.0
17		2,000	2,500	500	2,000	100.0
18		1,500	2,500	500	2,000	133.3
19		1,000	2,500	500	2,000	200.0
20		500	2,500	500	2,000	400.0
Total			$50,000	$10,000	$40,000	

10. In a similar situation, but one in which the loan is made by a lending institution to an outside borrower, it would be unthinkable that the lending institution would ever consider that the outside borrower is paying and, conversely, that the lender is earning interest at year-to-year interest rates, ranging from 20.0 percent in the first year to 400.0 percent in the 20th year on a $10,000 self-amortizing loan that calls for a 24.7 percent specified interest rate for a 20-year term. These year-to-year interest rates would be arrived at (if they were prepared)

by the lending institution arbitrarily assigning a 5 percent, or $500, fixed rate for the repayment of the loan principal and considering the $2,000 remainder of the $2,500 annual loan payment amounts interest when in reality the annual interest amounts calculated at the 24.7 percent specified interest rate on the unpaid balance of the loan principal at the beginning of the year range from $2,470 in the first year to $404 in the 20th year, and the remainder of the $2,500 annual loan payment amounts, which represents repayment of the principal, range from $30 in the first year to $2,096 in the 20-year. Obviously, the true interest rate for this $10,000 loan is the 24.7 percent specified interest rate, while the year-to-year interest rates reflect neither the outside borrower's true interest cost nor the lender's true interest income.

TABLE 89

Project D's DCF Rate of Return Calculation before Income Taxes

	(1)	(2)	(3)	(4)	(5)
		Present Value		Present Value	
Year	Net Cash Flow	Factor at 25%	Amount	Factor at 24%	Amount
0	$(10,000)	1.0000	$(10,000)	1.0000	$(10,000)
1	2,500	.8000	2,000	.8065	2,016
2	2,500	.6400	1,600	.6504	1,626
3	2,500	.5120	1,280	.5245	1,311
4	2,500	.4096	1,024	.4230	1,058
5	2,500	.3277	819	.3411	853
6	2,500	.2621	655	.2751	688
7	2,500	.2097	524	.2218	555
8	2,500	.1678	420	.1789	447
9	2,500	.1342	336	.1443	361
10	2,500	.1074	268	.1164	291
11	2,500	.0859	215	.0938	235
12	2,500	.0687	172	.0757	189
13	2,500	.0550	138	.0610	153
14	2,500	.0440	110	.0492	123
15	2,500	.0352	88	.0397	99
16	2,500	.0281	70	.0320	80
17	2,500	.0225	56	.0258	65
18	2,500	.0180	45	.0208	52
19	2,500	.0144	36	.0168	42
20	2,500	.0115	29	.0135	34
Total	$ 40,000		$ (115)		278

DCF rate of return is 24.7%.

11. The same rationale that applies to these hypothetical year-to-year interest rates (were such rates prepared in the banking community) applies to the year-to-year book rates of return used in the business community. In other words, the year-to-year book rates of return are

TABLE 90

Proof that Project D's DCF Rate of Return is 24.7 Percent before Income Taxes

Year	(1) Investment Balance Beginning Year	(2) Annual Cash Income	(3) Gross Profit at 24.7%	(4) Capital Recovery
1	$10,000	$ 2,500	$ 2,470	$ 30
2	9,970	2,500	2,463	37
3	9,933	2,500	2,453	47
4	9,886	2,500	2,442	58
5	9,828	2,500	2,428	72
6	9,756	2,500	2,410	90
7	9,666	2,500	2,388	112
8	9,554	2,500	2,360	140
9	9,414	2,500	2,325	175
10	9,239	2,500	2,282	218
11	9,021	2,500	2,228	272
12	8,749	2,500	2,161	339
13	8,410	2,500	2,077	423
14	7,987	2,500	1,973	527
15	7,460	2,500	1,843	657
16	6,803	2,500	1,680	820
17	5,983	2,500	1,478	1,022
18	4,961	2,500	1,225	1,275
19	3,686	2,500	910	1,590
20	2,096	2,500	404	2,096
Total		$50,000	$40,000	$10,000

as unrealistic, meaningless, and misleading as the hypothetical year-to-year interest rates.

12. Just as the specified compound interest rate is the true interest rate for self-amortizing loans made by lending institutions to outside borrowers, so the DCF rate of return is the true rate of return for internal loans (capital investments) made by treasurer's department of companies to new projects.

13. There appears to be considerable confusion regarding the DCF rate of return and the year-to-year book rate of return, which are diametrically opposed to one another, and the problem this poses in determining the impact that the profits generated by new projects has on a company's future overall profitability. The best way to clear up this confusion is by a thorough understanding of the so-called financial, or investment profit as opposed to the book, or operating profit, because these two rates are irreconcilable not just for procedural but for even more deep-seated reasons.

14. The financial, or investment, profit in accordance with the DCF concept deals strictly with cash flows. The excess of the total cash inflow over the total cash outflow represents the new project's total profit.

The DCF rate of return that this total profit represents is determined by discounting the new project's stream of cash returns at various rates until a rate is found that discounts it down to a total present value equal to that of the new project's total cash outlays at the zero reference point. The rate that does this is the new project's DCF rate of return. Its annual profit amounts are then determined by calculating the unrecovered portion of its capital investment at the beginning of each year by its DCF rate, and the remainder of its annual cash returns represents capital recovery.

One of the accelerated depreciation methods—either the sum-of-the-years'-digits method or the double-declining-balance method—is used exclusively for income tax purposes.

Furthermore, new projects' financial, or investment, profits tend to vary widely from their book, or operating, profits when some of their fixed assets, which are already owned by the sponsoring companies, are transferred to new projects instead of purchased from outside sources. For example, when land—already owned by the sponsoring company for an extended period of time during which it appreciated considerably in market value—is transferred to a new project, it is done at the land's current market value instead of at its original cost as recorded on the company's books and reported in its financial statements. As explained earlier, the reason for considering its current market value the new project's capital cost for the land is that by transferring it to the new project the company is forfeiting its option of selling the land and, thereby, is foregoing an amount of cash equal to the land's prevailing market value. Consequently, by transferring the land at the substantially higher current market value, the new project is required to generate a larger amount of profit than it would have to generate if the land were transferred at its original cost as recorded on the company's books. This accounts for the difference in the new project's financial, or investment, profit shown in its economic evaluation as opposed to its book, or operating, profit as it will appear on the company's books and in its financial statements.

Another example that proves that financial, or investment, profits of new projects tend to vary widely from their book, or operating, profits is when some or all of their fixed assets are leased instead of purchased. You will recall that according to sound and realistic investment principles, leasing is treated in a prospective project's economic evaluation as a method of financing the acquisition of its fixed assets, and that an investment equivalent is determined by discounting the fixed assets' annual lease rentals at the company's direct borrowing rate. The resultant present value represents the investment equivalent at the start of the fixed assets' useful lives. Based on this investment equivalent, the fixed assets are then required to generate a stream of cash income or savings during their useful lives that would be sufficient to recover a sum equal to the investment equivalent in addition to a financial or investment, profit at least equal to the proposed new project's predetermined minimum acceptable DCF rate of return.

On the other hand, according to orthodox and accepted accounting principles and practices, lease rentals for the use of leased fixed assets are treated as operating expenses on the company's books, and since the fixed assets are not owned by the company, no capital investments for them are recorded on its books or reported in its financial statements. Consequently, any excess of the cash income or savings generated by the leased fixed assets over their lease rentals represents the book, or operating, profit realized from the leased fixed assets.

This difference in the treatment of lease rentals in proposed new projects' economic evaluations and that on a company's books of account is normally responsible for the marked difference between the financial, or investment, profit and the book, or operating, profit expected to be realized from leased fixed assets.

To Determine the Impact New Projects Have on Companies' Overall Profitability Poses a Twofold Problem

Companies primary objective in making capital investments in new projects is to enhance their future overall profitability. To determine whether they have achieved this objective entails a twofold problem: (1) The assets of companies shown in their balance sheets must be adjusted for inflation as well for other factors that are responsible for the appreciation in their values, which means the assets must be expressed in cheap current-year dollars comparable to those shown in the companies' profit and loss statements. (2) By an application of the DCF concept, a method must be devised that will produce year-to-year book rates of return to be used for measuring companies' overall profitability, which will be compatible with the DCF rates of return that are used for measuring individual new projects' profitability.

The need for these upward adjustments in the value of companies' assets is spelled out graphically in excerpts from three articles referred to earlier titled "The Credibility of Corporations," published in *The Wall Street Journal;* "Push Made in Accounting," published in the *New York Times;* and "Business in Fever," reported by the *Associated Press.* All three publications deal with the serious distortions in the financial reporting of companies brought on principally by inflation. Some of the factors other than inflation that are responsible for the appreciation of assets over extended periods of time, which apply principally to nondepreciable assets such as land, include population growth, population shifts, zoning changes, traffic changes, scarcity, etc. It doesn't require a great deal of ingenuity to be able to visualize to what extent capital assets of multinational companies, which may run into tens of billions of dollars, must be understated, after these companies have been in business for many decades, because the conventional and accepted accounting practice decrees that capital assets must be recorded and kept on the company's books and reported in its financial statements at the capital assets' original cost and not at their current appreciated market value or replacement cost. How serious this problem has become over the years may be gleaned from excerpts from the following article titled "The Cash-Flow Takeover Formula," which appeared in *Business Week* on December 18, 1978.

> Like many of the amount being paid in big acquisitions of the last year, the $350 million that Eaton Corporation will have paid this January to acquire Cutler Hammer Inc. appears to be a stiff price. That sum amounts to a seemingly high 14 times Cutler's 1977 earnings—compared with the five times earnings Eaton currently sells at—and an 85% premium over Cutler's market price of about $30 per share before news of a possible takeover broke early this year.
>
> Eaton is justifying the price in large part by using an old but increasingly popular financial tool: discounted cash flow (DCF). To set the price, Eaton projected the future cash flows it expected from Cutler over the next 5 to 10 years and then discounted them, using a rate that reflects the risks involved in the investment and the time value of the money used. Eaton figures that based on DCF, Cutler will return at least 12% on its $350 million outlay.
>
> While other methods base a company's value on earnings history or market price, "discounted cash flow is a powerful method of viewing future performance and returns," contends Robert G. Brown, Eaton's executive vice president of corporate development. "We are putting it to use more and more."
>
> Increased use. Eaton is not alone. Financial experts estimate that as many as half of the big companies now active in making acquisitions are relying heavily on DCF, compared with only a handful during the merger wave of the late 1960s when purchase prices were commonly figured on earnings per share.
>
> Companies traditionally use DCF to gauge the returns they expect from internal capital investments in such things as plant and equipment. Until recently DCF has been commonly used, however, in evaluating the worth of an entire company to be acquired and in fixing a purchase price.
>
> The reason for the sharply increased use of DCF now is that managers are finding it more meaningful than simpler methods that are based on net income, book value, and price-earnings multiples. As a result of high rates of inflation, they reason, a company's book value may seriously understate the worth of its assets in current dollars. And with depressed stock prices, they increasingly find themselves disagreeing with the value the market places on their companies as well as on those they might acquire. The traditional measures also fail to take into account the cost of capital, economic uncertainty, and the crucial timing of cash flows.[1]

The above excerpts make it abundantly clear that assets of companies are so seriously understated, principally as a result of inflation, that the traditional bookkeeping criteria, including book value, net income, earnings per share, year-to-year book rates of return, and price-earnings ratios, have become unreliable and ineffective financial yardsticks for determining a company's true worth. This has led financial experts in recent years to resort more and more to the use of discounted cash flow (DCF) in an effort to determine meaningful purchase prices for companies to be acquired.

---

[1] Reprinted from the December 18, 1978 issue of Business Week by special permission, © 1978 by McGraw-Hill, Inc.

These substantial understatements of the value of assets of companies on their books of account and in their financial reports present a serious problem to management not only determining the true worth of their companies as well as that of companies to be acquired but also in determining the impact their capital investments in new projects is having on their companies overall profitability.

How to Make Adjustments for Inflation and for Factors Other than Inflation in Companies' Financial Reports

It should be made clear at this point that adjustments for inflation and other factors responsible for the appreciation in value of companies' assets over the years are suggested to be made only in companies' financial statements and not in their books of account. And, furthermore, these adjustments should be made by means of a supplementary column in their balance sheets in which companies' assets should be shown at their current market value or replacement cost. This supplementary column should be alongside the traditional column in which they will be shown at their original cost. The appreciation in companies' assets, i.e., the difference between their current market value or replacement cost and their original cost should then be reflected in the shareholders equity in the supplementary column. In other words, handling these upward adjustments for inflation and for other factors in this manner will preclude tampering with the orthodox and accepted accounting principle and practice of recording and carrying companies' assets on the books of account at their original cost.

However, there should be two separate and distinct methods for making these upward adjustments in the value of companies' assets—one method for nondepreciable assets such as land, and another method for depreciable assets such as plants, machinery, and equipment. The reason for this is that nondepreciable assets such as land, for example, are inclined to appreciate in value more dramatically as a result of factors such as population growth, population shifts, zoning changes, traffic changes, site location, etc., rather than as a result of inflation. Consequently, to obtain the most realistic and meaningful results qualified appraisers should be assigned the task of determining the current market value of nondepreciable assets such as land, leaseholds, etc.

On the other hand, the adjustments in the value of depreciable assets, which tend to appreciate principally as a result of inflation, are best achieved by means of indexes representing their cost increases. However, past history has proven that increases in depreciable assets' current market value or replacement cost are inclined to vary widely over the years depending on their type, their function, the industry they are used in, and the geographic area they are acquired in. Consequently, one might reasonably suspect that multinational companies—particularly those that are integrated both vertically and horizontally and which operate in both domestic and foreign markets—would find it cumbersome, time-consuming, and costly to develop appropriate cost indexes that would enable them to make the necessary adjustments for inflation on a worldwide basis. However, this isn't necessarily true for two good reasons.

First, similar to the American Petroleum Institute (API), which serves companies in the petroleum industry, most other major industries in the United States likewise have institutes that serve the companies in their respective industries. Therefore, it would be most advantageous for American companies who financially support these institutes to direct them to expand their services to include developing indexes that would reflect the cost increases due to inflation for various types and classes of depreciable assets used by companies in their respective industries.

Second, the same highly sophisticated computers, electronic devices, and modern equipment used by scientists, engineers, and researchers in their highly technical fields are also at the disposal of industry institutes and large companies. Hence, it should be possible for them to make the complex and numerous mathematical calculations that will be necessary to develop indexes to reflect the cost increases of depreciable assets by types and classes, functions, and geographical areas.

To have the industry institutes develop the basic cost indexes by types and classes of depreciable assets and by geographical areas, and then from these basic cost indexes as a basis have the companies within the respective industries develop their composite cost indexes, based on the structure or pattern of their total depreciable assets as well as on the functions and the geographical areas in which they are used, has these advantages: (1) It would be far less costly and time-consuming to have the industry institutes develop these basic cost indexes than to have each company within the respective industries develop them in addition to its own composite cost indexes. (2) It would make for uniformity and standardization insofar as all companies within the respective industries would be using the same basic cost indexes instead of each company using its own which, more than likely, would tend to vary widely between companies within the same industry. (3) It would result in more realistic adjustments for inflation on an industrywide basis and thereby improve the comparability of companies' financial reports within industries. (4) It would lend added credibility to needed revisions in present corporate income tax laws to prevent depreciation deficiencies occasioned by inflation.

Using the petroleum industry as an example, the basic cost indexes for the depreciable assets used in various functions by petroleum companies could look as shown in Table 91.

These basic cost indexes, of course, could be further refined by subfunctions and geographical areas if annual cost increases by subfunctions and in geographical areas varied widely and, therefore, warranted such refinements. For example, for the exploration function there could be separate cost indexes for exploration *(a)* on land, *(b)* off shore, *(c)* for crude oil, and *(d)* for natural gas. For the marketing function there could be separate cost indexes for retail marketing and for wholesale marketing. For the transportation function there could be separate cost indexes for marine transportation, pipe-

TABLE 91

Basic Cost Indexes for Depreciable Assets by Functions Developed by the American Petroleum Institute

	Depreciable Asset Cost Index		
Functions	Year 1*	Year 2	Year 3
Exploration	100	120	135
Producing	100	115	125
Refining	100	118	128
Marketing	100	112	120
Transportation	100	115	125

* Represents the base year.

line transportation, and motor vehicle transportation. For different geographical areas there could be different cost indexes for petroleum companies located in various parts of the country such as in states east of the Rocky Mountains and in those west of the Rocky Mountains as well as in states in the northern part and those in the southern part of the United States. For multinational petroleum companies there could be separate basic cost indexes developed by the American Petroleum Institute by individual foreign countries in which multinational American petroleum companies are operating.

While these basic cost indexes prepared by the American Petroleum Institute would be identical for all petroleum companies, the end result, i.e., the effect that inflation would have on the different petroleum companies' total depreciable assets, could still differ widely for these reasons: (1) Some petroleum companies aren't integrated at all; they are either 100 percent marketing, refining, or producing companies. Other petroleum companies are integrated vertically; but some of them are more marketing oriented, while others are more refining or producing oriented. Still other petroleum companies are integrated both vertically and horizontally, which means they also are engaged in business activities outside of the petroleum industry. This diverse concentration of depreciable assets could result in widely different effects inflation could have on petroleum companies if the cost increases in depreciable assets used in the different operations were to vary widely. (2) Similarly, there could be marked differences in the effect inflation could have on petroleum companies because they operate in different markets at home and abroad and at different operating levels in these marketplaces if the cost increases of the depreciable assets used in these geographical areas at home and abroad were to vary widely.

How the composite replacement cost index numbers of companies' depreciable assets are developed is shown by functions for two petroleum companies, A and B, in Table 92.

As shown in Table 92, the composite cost index number for Company A and Company B in year 3 is 124.60 and 125.85, respectively, which means that the replacement cost of Company A's and Company B's total depreciable

TABLE 92

Composite Cost Indexes by Function Developed by Company A and Company B for Year 3

		Total Depreciable Assets*				Calculation of Composite Cost Index	
		Company A		Company B			
	Basic						
	Cost	Original	Percent of	Original	Percent of	Company	Company
Functions	Index	Cost	Total	Cost	Total	A	B
Exploration	135	$ 1,000	10	$ 1,750	17.5	13.500	23.625
Producing	125	1,000	10	1,750	17.5	12.500	21.875
Refining	128	2,000	20	2,000	20.0	25.600	25.600
Marketing	120	4,000	40	3,000	30.0	48.000	36.000
Transportation	125	2,000	20	1,500	15.0	25.000	18.750
Total		$10,000	100	$10,000	100	124.600	125.850
Composite cost index number		× 124.60		× 125.85			
Current year's replacement cost		$12,460		$12,585			

* Original cost expressed in (base) year 1 dollars.

assets increased from $10,000 in base year 1 to $12,460 and $12,585 in year 3. Obviously, Company B is more severely affected by inflation during this two-year period because larger amounts of its total depreciable assets are concentrated in functions in which the replacement cost of depreciable assets increased more rapidly than that of depreciable assets in other functions. In developing composite cost index numbers it is important to bear in mind that the original cost of companies' depreciable assets must be expressed in base year dollars and not in dollars of the years in which they were acquired.

To prove that the 124.60 and 125.85 composite index numbers for Company A's and Company B's total depreciable assets, respectively, are reliable, the original cost of the depreciable assets used in the various functions are multiplied by the applicable basic cost index numbers, as shown in Table 93. The resultant $12,460 and $12,585 replacement cost for Company A's and Company B's total depreciable assets are identical with those arrived by using the composite cost index numbers developed in Table 92 and multiplying them by Company A's and Company B's $10,000 original cost in base year 1.

Similarly, just as increases in the replacement cost for depreciable assets in various functions may vary widely, so may those for depreciable assets in various geographic areas vary widely, as shown in Table 94. When this occurs, the same procedure used for developing composite cost index numbers for depreciable assets in various functions may be used just as effectively for developing composite index numbers for depreciable assets in various geographic areas. This requires multiplying the area percentages of the depreciable assets' total original cost by the applicable basic cost index numbers and then adding the products. The resultant total represents the composite cost

TABLE 93

Proof that the Composite Index Numbers for Company A's and Company B's Total Depreciable Assets Are Reliable

		Company A		Company B	
Functions	Basic Cost Index	Original Cost Base Year 1	Replacement Cost Year 3	Original Cost Base Year 1	Replacement Cost Year 3
Exploration	135	$ 1,000	$1,350	$ 1,750	$ 2,363
Producing	125	1,000	1,250	1,750	2,187
Refining	128	2,000	2,560	2,000	2,560
Marketing	120	4,000	4,800	3,000	3,600
Transportation	125	2,000	2,500	1,500	1,875
Total		$10,000	$12,460	$10,000	$12,585

TABLE 94

Calculation of Composite Cost Index Number for Company A's Depreciable Assets Five Marketing Areas for Year 3

Marketing Areas	Basic Cost Index	Depreciable Assets Original Cost Dollars	Percent of Total	Composite Cost Index
Area 1	115	$ 525	13.123	15.094
Area 2	120	700	17.500	21.000
Area 3	125	1,125	28.125	35.156
Area 4	130	1,300	32.500	42.250
Area 5	110	350	8.750	9.625
Total		$4,000	100.000	123.125

Composite cost index number is 123.125.

Replacement cost in year 3 is $4,925.

index number for the depreciable assets in the combined five marketing areas. As shown in Table 94 when the 123.125 composite index number is multiplied by the $4,000 original cost of the total depreciable assets in the combined five marketing areas, it shows their replacement cost to have increased to $4,925 in the year 3, which represents a 23.1 percent increase.

To prove that the 123.125 composite cost index number for Company A's depreciable assets in the combined five marketing areas is reliable, their original costs by individual marketing areas are multiplied by their applicable basic cost index numbers. The resultant products represent the depreciable assets' replacement cost in the five marketing area in year 3. The $4,925 total represents Company A's replacement cost in year 3 for its total depreciable assets in the combined five marketing areas and this amount, you will note, is identical with the $4,925 replacement cost arrived at in Table 94 by multiplying the $4,000 original cost of Company A's total depreciable assets in the five marketing areas by the 123.125 composite cost index number. This proves that this composite cost index number is reliable.

The same method that is used for determining composite cost index numbers for depreciable assets used in various functions and in various geographical areas, as shown in Tables 91 to 95, is adaptable and can be used for

TABLE 95

Proof that the Composite Cost Index Number for Company A's Depreciable Assets in Five Marketing Areas Is Reliable

Marketing Areas	Basic Cost Index	Depreciable Assets	
		Original Cost	*Replacement Cost*
Area 1	115	$ 525	$ 604
Area 2	120	700	840
Area 3	125	1,125	1,406
Area 4	130	1,300	1,690
Area 5	110	350	385
Total		$4,000	$4,925

determining composite cost index numbers for depreciable assets used by multinational companies operating on a worldwide basis.

Statistical Adjustments for Inflation Are Practical, Needed, and Worthwhile

Since the task of making adjustments for inflation in companies' post-completion audits and financial reports appears to be a cumbersome, time-consuming, and costly one, these questions invariabley arise. Are these adjustments for inflation practical? Are they necessary? Are they worthwhile? The answers to these questions are all in the affirmative.

With the help of industry institutes to develop the basic cost indexes for companies within their respective industries, which probably would account for a large share of the work and moreover with the aid of sophisticated computers, electronic devices, and other modern equipment, there are good reasons to believe that it would be feasible and practical for companies to make these adjustments for inflation in their post-completion audits as well as in their financial reports.

There are a number of undeniable reasons why adjustments for inflation are not only desirable but actually necessary to obtain meaningful and realistic results. Some of these reasons include the following:

1. Post-completion audits of new projects are a total waste of time and money unless they encompass proper adjustments for inflation to preclude measuring cheap current-year income dollars against expensive prior-year investment dollars, and thus arrive at highly overstated and unrealistic DCF rates of return and payout periods. For example, as shown in Tables 73 and 79, respectively, Project D's post-completion audit shows a highly overstated and unrealistic 21.7 percent DCF rate of return and 4.9-year payout period before proper adjustments for inflation are made, and a true and realistic 14.4 percent DCF rate of return and 6.2 payout period after they are made.

2. The development of a year-to-year book rate of return, by an application of the DCF concept, that will be compatible with the DCF rate of return will be absolutely useless for assessing the impact capital investments in new projects is having on the overall profitability of companies unless proper adjustments for inflation are made in the post-completion audits of new projects as well as in the company's financial reports.

3. The conventional year-to-year book rate of return, in addition to being incompatible with the DCF rate of return, will continue to be an extremely ineffective financial tool for assessing the impact capital investments in new projects is having on overall profitability of companies as well as for measuring the effective utilization of their total assets, until proper adjustments for inflation are made in companies' post-completion audits of new projects and in their financial reports.

4. The true worth of companies will continue to be seriously understated and their overall profitability highly overstated as a result of the orthodox and accepted accounting practice of reporting companies' total assets in expensive prior years' dollars and their income in cheap current-year dollars, until such time that the accounting profession agrees to the need of making proper statistical adjustments for inflation and other factors in financial reports. Until this is done, there isn't much point in making post-completion audits of new projects.

It has been established that adjustments for inflation and for other factors that tend to appreciate the value of companies' assets are necessary as well as feasible and practical to make. The next step is to decide whether they are worth the time, the effort, and the expense of making them. This shouldn't be too difficult a decision to make in view of what is involved. Management needs only to ask itself this question. Can it afford not to make these statistical adjustments for inflation and other factors? The answer to this question is quite self-evident.

The primary purpose of financial reports is to inform the shareholders of the true worth of the company's total assets and the current value of its equity in these total assets, and also to inform them of the company's realistic overall profitability based on the effective utilization of its total assets. This purpose, of course, cannot be realized unless proper adjustments for inflation and for other factors are made in the company's financial reports.

When standing alone, the annual profits of companies often appear to be large to the American public, which repeatedly has referred to them as obscene—particularly in the case of multinational companies. In reality, a company's annual profits, expressed in cheap current-year dollars due to inflation, are not only highly overstated and illusory when compared to previous years' annual profits, expressed in expensive dollars of much greater purchasing power, but also when they are related to the seriously understated values of a company's total assets. To put a company's annual profits, expressed in cheap current-year dollars, in proper perspective, they must be measured and viewed in terms of the company's total assets, expressed in comparable cheap current-year dollars. This correct comparison will put a company's annual profits in proper perspective and show them as being reasonable and justifiable and not as being subject to suspicion and criticism by the American people.

The present method of financial reporting used by companies, which compares grossly inflated profits to seriously understated total asset values and thus arrives at highly overstated and unrealistic year-to-year book rates of return, is not conducive to improving the company's image or its credibility, which have deteriorated and suffered badly in recent years.

The reluctance of companies to discontinue reporting highly inflated and unrealistic profits and rates of return as well as seriously understated total asset values year after year in their financial reports isn't helpful in ever getting the federal government to consider revising present corporate income tax laws to prevent depreciation deficiencies, and thus enable companies to recover the full purchasing power of their original capital investments.

The addition of a supplementary column in financial reports that would reflect the statistical adjustments for inflation and for other factors that tend to appreciate the value of assets would show both the profits and asset values of companies in comparable cheap current-year dollars and thereby show their profits and rates of return in proper perspective. This type of financial reporting not only would remove the onus of companies appearing like profiteers but also would be helpful in minimizing government regulations and controls of American business.

In view of the above, there should be little doubt that statistical adjustments for inflation and for other factors in financial reports of companies are well worth the time, the effort, and the expense of making them.

How to Determine Year-to-Year Book Rates of Return that Will Be Compatible with DCF Rates of Return

As mentioned previously, normally the bulk of the funds in the annual capital budgets of companies is allocated for investment in profit-generating or cost-saving new projects. These annual capital investments in new projects are made primarily for the purpose of improving the company's overall profitability. However, since a company's overall profitability ordinarily is measured in terms of its year-to-year book rates of return calculated on the annual average of the total assets employed in its business operations, this poses a somewhat complex problem insofar as the year-to-year book rate of return determined by the conventional bookkeeping method is incompatible with the DCF rate of return determined by the DCF method. This incompatibility makes it virtually impossible to measure or assess the impact that profits or cost savings generated by new projects has on a company's overall profitability inasmuch as the latter is measured in terms of year-to-year book rates of return determined by the conventional bookkeeping method, while the investment decisions for the approval and the acceptance or the disapproval and the rejection of new projects are predicated on their estimated DCF rates of return determined by the DCF method.

However, the DCF concept can be applied just as readily *(a)* in determining the annual profit amounts companies are required to generate in order to earn predetermined year-to-year book rates of return on their total assets in future years and *(b)* in determining the year-to-year book rates of return companies have earned on their total assets in prior years as the DCF concept is now applied *(a)* in determining the annual cash income amounts new projects are required to generate in order to earn predetermined DCF rates of return during their economic lives and *(b)* in determining the DCF rates of return new projects are estimated to earn based on the estimates of their capital outlays, annual cash income amounts, and economic lives.

The rationale, however, varies quite extensively in the application of the DCF concept when the above-mentioned financial factors are determined for business operations of companies as a whole as opposed to when they are determined for individual new projects of companies.

As explained earlier, the application of the DCF concept in the economic evaluations of new projects is based on the rationale that treasurer's departments of companies loan the necessary funds to new projects for their acquisition and that the new projects in turn are expected to generate sufficient cash income or cost savings during their economic lives to repay the principal of these internal loans in addition to earning profits that will yield DCF rates of return at least equal to or higher than the standards predetermined for them.

On the other hand, the application of the DCF concept in measuring a company's overall profitability during specific time periods is based on the rationale that companies must generate sufficient profits on their total assets that will yield year-to-year book rates of return during these time periods that at least are equal to the standards predetermined by top management.

The methodology used in determining various financial criteria in the proposed acquisition of companies, such as their worth, or the price to pay for them, the cash income they are expected to generate, and the rate of return they are estimated to yield, is equally effective in determining similar financial criteria for companies that are in business regardless whether they are expected to purchase, or be purchased by, another company.

First, let us consider that Company A is a company that is expected to be purchased by another company, that the buying company's opportunity cost of money rate is 15 percent, and, finally, that it expects Company A to yield a rate of return equal to its 15 percent opportunity cost of money rate.

Now let us assume that Company A's asking price for the company is $100,000. This means that Company A will have to generate an annual cash income of $15,000 during the five-year period, providing the capital recovery at the end of the fifth year is equal to the $100,000 capital investment at the start of the first year of this five-year period. The $15,000 annual cash income required to be generated during this five-year period is arrived at by subtracting the $49,720 present value of the $100,000 capital recovery from the $100,000 proposed capital investment, and then dividing the $50,280 remainder, which represents the capital cost for tieing up $100,000 for five years, by the 3.3522 total present value factors at the 15 percent rate. The $15,000 quotient, as shown in Table 96, represents the annual cash income amount

TABLE 96

Determine Company A's Year-to-Year Book Rates of Return over a Five-Year Period by an Application of the DCF Concept and Illustrate Principle Involved in This Method

	(1)	(2)	(3)	(4)	(5)
	Capital Investment			Present Value	
	and Capital	Cash	Net Cash	Factor	
Year	Recovery	Income	Flow	at 15%	Amount
0	$(100,000)		$(100,000)	1.0000	$(100,000)
1		$15,000	15,000	.8696	13,043
2		15,000	15,000	.7561	11,341
3		15,000	15,000	.6575	9,862
4		15,000	15,000	.5718	8,576
5		15,000	15,000	.4972	7,458
	$ 100,000		100,000	.4972	49,720
Total	$ −0−	$75,000	$ 75,000		$ −0−

DCF rate of return is 15%.

Capital investment at start of 5-year period	$100,000
Less: Present value of $100,000 capital recovery	49,720
Capital cost of tieing up funds in total assets	$ 50,280
$50,280 capital cost ÷ 3.3522 total present value factors at 15% is equal to annual cash volume	$ 15,000

required to be generated by Company A to yield the buying company at 15 percent DCF rate of return on its $100,000 proposed capital investment in the acquisition of Company A.

To prove that the $15,000 annual cash income amount will yield the buying company a 15 percent DCF rate of return as well as a 15 percent year-to-year book rate of return on its proposed capital investment in Company A may be done *(a)* by discounting Company A's net cash flow at the 15 percent rate which should discount down to a total present value equal to zero, which it does as shown in Table 96, and *(b)* by multiplying the $100,000 unrecovered capital investment balance at the start of each year by the 15 percent year-to-year book rate of return which should be equal to the $15,000 profit amount each year, which it is as shown in Table 97.

TABLE 97

Proof that Company A's Year-to-Year Book Rate of Return Is 15 Percent as Determined in Table 96

Year	(1) Capital Investment Balance Start of Year	(2) Profit at Year-to-Year Rate of Return of 15%	(3) Cash Income	(4) Write-Offs	(5) Capital Recovery
1	$100,000	$15,000	$15,000	–0–	
2	100,000	15,000	15,000	–0–	
3	100,000	15,000	15,000	–0–	
4	100,000	15,000	15,000	–0–	
5	100,000	15,000	15,000	–0–	
	100,000	—	—	—	$100,000
	–0–				
Total	$ –0–	$75,000	$75,000		$100,000

Year-to-year book rate of return is <u>15%</u>.

Next, let us consider Company A any company engaged in business that is neither expected to purchase, nor expected to be purchased by, another company.

In this financial situation let us assume that Company A's $100,000 capital investment at the beginning and its $100,000 capital recovery at the end of its five-year period represents the current resale value or replacement cost of its total assets after proper adjustments for inflation and other factors responsible for their appreciation have been made. Let us assume further that Company A's capital investment and capital recovery dollars as well as its annual cash income dollars are all expressed in comparable cheap current-year 5 dollars. When Company A's net cash flow, expressed in these cheap current-year 5 dollars, is discounted at various rates, it is found that it will discount down to a total present value equal to zero at the 15 percent rate, as shown in Table 96. This rate represents not only Company A's 15 percent DCF rate of return on the current resale value or replacement cost of its total assets but it also represents its 15 percent year-to-year book rate of return on the $100,000 unrecovered balance of the current resale value or replacement cost of its total assets at the start of each year, as shown in Table 97. This type of constant-level year-to-year book rate of return, arrived at by an application of the DCF concept, isn't only compatible but actually is identical with the DCF rate of return used in economic evaluations of proposed new projects. Hence, by using this type of constant-level year-to-year book rate of return, which is comparable and compatible with the DCF rate of return, companies will be able to assess the impact cash income or savings generated by new projects is having on their overall profitability.

Now let us assume Company A's capital recovery at the end of the five-year period is only $95,000 instead of $100,000. To earn a 15 percent DCF rate of return and a 15 percent year-to-year book rate of return in this situation, Company A will be required to generate an annual cash income of $15,740 instead of $15,000 because the capital cost for the use of its total assets during the five-year period has increased from $50,280 to $52,766.

Company A's net cash flow, when discounted at the 15 percent rate, discounts down to a total present value equal to zero. This indicates that 15 percent is its DCF rate of return in this situation on the current resale value or replacement cost of its total assets during this five-year period, as shown in Table 98.

TABLE 98

Determine Company A's Year-to-Year Book Rate of Return When Its Total Assets Are Worth $100,000 at the Start and $95,000 at End of the Five-Year Period, the Capital Additions Are Zero, the Write-Offs Are $5,000 and the Annual Cash Income Is $15,740 During the Five-Year Period

	(1)	(2)	(3)	(4)	(5)
	Capital Investment				*Present Value*
	and Capital	*Cash*	*Net Cash*	*Factor*	
Year	*Recovery*	*Income*	*Flow*	*at 15%*	*Amount*
0	$(100,000)		$(100,000)	1.0000	$(100,000)
1		$15,740	15,740	.8696	13,688
2		15,740	15,740	.7561	11,902
3		15,740	15,740	.6575	10,349
4		15,740	15,740	.5718	9,000
5		15,740	15,740	.4972	7,827
	95,000		95,000		47,234
Total	$ (5,000)	$78,700	$ 73,700		$ —0—

DCF rate of return is 15%.

Capital investment start of five-year period	$100,000
Less: Present value of $95,000 capital recovery	47,234
Capital cost of tieing up funds in total assets	$ 52,766
$52,766 capital cost ÷ 3.3522 total present value factors at 15% is equal to annual cash income	$ 15,740

Company A's $78,700 total cash income is made up of profits totaling $73,700 and write-offs totaling $5,000. The latter amount reflects the company's $5,000 lower capital recovery at the end of the five-year period. Company A's annual profits range from $15,000 in the first year, to $14,886 in the second year, to $14,444 in the fifth year, and they are computed at the 15 percent year-to-year book rate of return on capital investment balances of $100,000 at the start of the first year, $99,260 at the start of the second year, and $96,296 at the start of the fifth year, respectively; while the annual write-offs, which constitute the remainder of the annual cash income amounts, range from $740 in the first year, to $854 in the second year, to $1,296 in the fifth year.

For the purpose of showing (a) the techniques whereby year-to-year book rates of return that are compatible with DCF rates of return are calculated and (b) the rationale on which it is based, the cash flows of the previous two Company A examples shown in Tables 96 and 97 and Tables 98 and 99 are

TABLE 99

Proof that Company A's Year-to-Year Book Rate of Return Is 15 Percent as Determined in Table 93

Year	(1) Capital Investment Balance Start of Year	(2) Profit at Year-to-Year Rate of Return of 15%	(3) Cash Income	(4) Write-Offs	(5) Capital Recovery
1	$100,000	$15,000	$15,740	$ 740	
2	99,260	14,886	15,740	854	
3	98,406	14,758	15,740	982	
4	97,424	14,612	15,740	1,128	
5	96,296	14,444	15,740	1,296	
	95,000				$95,000
Total	$ –0–	$73,700	$78,700	$5,000	$95,000

Year-to-year book rate of return is 15%.

oversimplified and atypical because they exclude annual capital additions and show annual cash income amounts at constant-level rates.

This is not the case in the next two Company A examples, shown in Tables 100 and 101 and Tables 102 and 103, which are included primarily for the purpose of showing the impact the $7,000 capital addition, the $1,500 increased cash income, and the $2,000 higher write-offs in the sixth year is having on Company A's overall profitability for that period, as measured by a comparison of Company A's 14.93 percent year-to-year book rate of return for the five-year period ending with the fifth year and its 14.90 percent year-to-year book rate of return for the six-year period ending with the sixth year. Obviously, Company A's overall profitability shows only a slight, three hundredth of 1 percent, reduction for the six-year period compared to the previous five-year period.

To make this comparison it is assumed that company A's capital investment in total assets is $100,000 at the start of the five-year period, its capital additions total $28,000 during that period, its capital recovery is $120,000 at the end of that period, and its annual cash income ranges from $17,000 in year 1 to $18,000 in year 5 and totals $87,500 during this five-year period, as shown in Table 100. It is assumed further that Company A's $100,000 capital investment at the start of the five-year period, its $28,000 capital additions

TABLE 100

Determine Company A's Year-to-Year Book Rate of Return during Same Five-Year Period When Its Total Assets Are Worth $100,000 at Start and $120,000 at End of Five-Year Period, Its Total Capital Additions Are $28,000, Its Total Write-Offs Are $8,000, and Its Annual Cash Income ranges from $17,000 in First Year to $18,000 in Fifth Year during Five-Year Period

	(1)	(2)	(3)	(4)	(5)	(6)	(7)
	Capital Investments and	Cash	Net Cash		Present Value		
				Factor		Factor	
Year	Capital Recovery	Income	Flow	at 14%	Amount	at 15%	Amount
0	$(100,000)	—	$(100,000)	1.0000	$(100,000)	1.0000	$(100,000)
1	(5,000)	$17,000	12,000	.8772	10,526	.8696	10,435
2	(6,000)	17,250	11,250	.7695	8,657	.7501	8,439
3	(4,000)	17,500	13,500	.6750	9,112	.6575	8,876
4	(5,000)	17,750	12,750	.5921	7,549	.5718	7,290
5	(8,000)	18,000	10,000	.5194	5,194	.4972	4,972
	120,000		120,000	.5194	62,328	.4972	59,664
Total	$ (8,000)	$87,500	$ 79,500		$ 3,366		$ (324)

DCF rate of return is <u>14.93%</u>.

during that period, and its $120,000 capital recovery at the end of that period represent the assets' current resale value or replacement cost, after proper adjustments for inflation and other factors have been made, and that along with its annual cash income dollars they are all expressed in comparable cheap current-year five dollars.

When Company A's net cash flow for this five-year period is discounted at various rates, it is found to discount down to a total present value equal to zero at the 14.93 percent rate, which indicates that this is Company A's 14.93 percent DCF rate of return on the current resale value or replacement cost of its total assets during this five-year period, as shown in Table 100.

This rate also is Company A's 14.93 percent year-to-year book rate of return as shown in Table 101 where Company A's annual profits range from $14,930 in the first year to $16,866 in the fifth year computed at its 14.93 percent year-to-year book rate of return on the $100,000 and the $113,134 current resale value or replacement cost of its total assets at the start of the first year and the fifth year, respectively.

To complete this comparison it is assumed that Company A's capital addition is $7,000 and its cash income is $19,500 during the sixth year, and its capital recovery is $125,000 at the end of the sixth year. This means that

TABLE 101

Proof that Company A's Year-to-Year Book Rate of Return Is 14.93 Percent as Determined in Table 95

Year	(1) Capital Investment Start of Year	(2) Profit at Year-to-Year Rate of Return at 14.93%	(3) Cash Income	(4) Write-Offs	(5) Net Capital Additions	(6) Capital Investment End of Year	(7) Capital Recovery
1	$100,000	$14,930	$17,000	$2,070	$ 5,000	$102,930	
2	102,930	15,367	17,250	1,883	6,000	107,047	
3	107,047	15,982	17,500	1,518	4,000	109,529	
4	109,529	16,355	17,750	1,395	5,000	113,134	
5	113,134	16,866	18,000	1,134	8,000	120,000	
	120,000	—	—	—	—	—	$120,000
Total	$ –0–	$79,500	$87,500	$8,000	$28,000		$120,000

Year-to-year book rate of return is 14.93%.

Company A's capital investment at the start of the six-year period is $100,000, its total capital additions are $35,000, and its total cash income is $107,000 during that period, and its capital recovery is $125,000 at the end of that period. It is assumed further that there is no inflation during year 6, i.e., no change in the purchasing power of the dollar from the end of year 5 to the end of year 6, and that the $100,000 capital investment at the start of the six-year period, the $35,000 capital additions during that period and the $125,000 capital recovery at the end of that period represent the current resale value or replacement cost of the assets, and that along with Company A's annual cash income amounts they are all expressed in comparable cheap current-year 6 dollars which are equal in purchasing to the year 5 dollars.

When Company A's net cash flow for this six-year period is discounted at various rates, it is found to discount down to a total present value equal to zero at the 14.90 percent rate, which indicates that this is Company A's 14.90 percent DCF rate of return on the current resale value or replacement cost of its total assets during this six-year period.

This rate, as we have seen, is also Company A's 14.90 percent year-to-year book rate of return during this six-year period as shown in Table 103 where its annual profits range from $14,900 in the first year to $17,691 in the fifth year computed at its 14.90 percent year-to-year book rate of return on the $100,000 and the $119,809 current resale value or replacement cost of its total assets at the start of the first year and the fifth year, respectively.

A comparison of Company A's 14.93 percent and 14.90 percent year-to-year book rates of return for the years 1 to 5 and 1 to 6, respectively, reveals only a slight three hundredths of 1 percent decrease as a result of its $7,000 capital addition, its $1,500 increase in cash income, and its $2,000 higher write-offs in year 6—everything else being equal.

TABLE 102

Determine Impact Company A's $35,000 Total Capital Additions and $10,000 Total Write-Offs during Six-Year Period and $1,500 Increase in Its Annual Cash Income in the Sixth Year Is Having on Company A's Year-to-Year Book Return from Five-Year to Six-Year Period

	(1)	(2)	(3)	(4)	(5)	(6)	(7)
	Capital Investments and	Cash	Net	Factor	Present Value	Factor	
Year	Capital Recovery	Income	Cash Flow	at 14%	Amount	at 15%	Amount
0	$(100,000)	—	$(100,000)	1.0000	$(100,000)	1.0000	$(100,000)
1	(5,000)	$ 17,000	12,000	.8772	10,526	.8696	10,435
2	(6,000)	17,250	11,250	.7695	8,657	.7561	8,506
3	(4,000)	17,500	13,500	.6750	9,113	.6575	8,876
4	(5,000)	17,750	12,750	.5921	7,549	.5718	7,250
5	(8,000)	18,000	10,000	.5194	5,194	.4972	4,972
6	(7,000)	19,500	12,500	.4556	5,695	.4323	5,404
	125,000	—	125,000	.4556	56,950	.4323	54,038
Total	$ (10,000)	$107,000	$ 97,000		$ 3,684		$ (479)

DCF rate of return is 14.90%.

TABLE 103

Proof that Company A's Year-to-Year Book Rate of Return Is 14.90 Percent as Determined in Table 102

	(1)	(2)	(3)	(4)	(5)	(6)	(7)
	Capital Investment	Profit at Year-to-Year Rate of Return	Cash		Net Capital	Capital Investment	Capital
Year	Start of Year	at 14.90%	Income	Write-Offs	Additions	End of Year	Recovery
1	$100,000	$14,900	$ 17,000	$ 2,100	$ 5,000	$102,900	
2	102,900	15,332	17,250	1,918	6,000	106,982	
3	106,982	15,940	17,500	1,560	4,000	107,422	
4	109,422	16,304	17,750	1,446	5,000	112,976	
5	112,976	16,833	18,000	1,167	8,000	119,809	
6	119,809	17,691	19,500	1,809	7,000	125,000	
	125,000	—	—	—	—	—	$125,000
Total	$ –0–	$97,000	$107,000	$10,000	$35,000		$125,000

One of the principal prerequisites before determining year-to-year book rates of return by this DCF technique, which are compatible with DCF rates of return, is to properly adjust the book value of companies' total assets, as they are recorded on their books and reported in their financial statements, for inflation. This is accomplished by the use of index numbers. In the following example, the Producer Price Index is used for this purpose.

It is assumed in this example that the capital cost of a company going into business in 1974 is $160,100 and that its capital additions total $28,000 from 1975 to 1979 and $7,000 in 1980, which adds up to a grand total capital investment of $195,100 as of the end of 1980. The first step in making this adjustment for inflation is to convert the book values of the company's assets expressed in variable current-year dollars to constant base year 1967 dollars. This is done by dividing them by the applicable index numbers and then multiplying the quotients by 100, which represents the index number for base year 1967. Next, these book values, now expressed in constant base year 1967 dollars are then multiplied by the index number of the final year of the time period for which the year-to-year book rate of return is computed. As shown in Table 104, the book value of the company's total assets, as recorded on its

TABLE 104

How to Adjust the Book Value of a Company's Assets for Inflation
Book Value of Company's Assets Expressed in

Year	Producer Price Index	Variable Current-Year Dollars	Constant Base Year 1967 Dollars	Constant Current-Year 1979 Dollars	Constant Current-Year 1980 Dollars
1967	100	—	—	—	—
1974	160.1	$160,100	$100,000	$235,600	$274,100
1975	174.9	5,000	2,859	6,735	7,836
1976	183.0	6,000	3,279	7,725	8,987
1977	194.2	4,000	2,060	4,853	5,634
1978	209.3	5,000	2,389	5,628	6,548
1979	235.6	8,000	2,396	8,000	9,307
Total	—	188,100	113,983	$268,541	—
1980	274.1	7,000	2,554		7,000
Total	—	$195,100	$116,537		$319,407

books and reported in its financial statements in variable current-year dollars, is $188,100 and $195,100 at the end of 1979 and 1980, respectively; expressed in constant base year 1967 dollars, it is $113,983 and $116,537 at the end of 1979 and 1980, respectively; and adjusted for inflation and expressed in constant year 1979 and 1980 dollars, it is $268,541 and $319,407 at the end of 1979 and 1980, respectively.

The company's annual cash income amounts also have to be adjusted for inflation in the same manner and expressed in constant current-year dollars representing those of the final year of the time period for which the year-to-year book rate of return is computed.

The year-to-year book rate of return determined by an application of the DCF concept, as shown in Tables 96–103, is compatible with the DCF rate of return used in prospective projects' economic evaluations because, like the DCF rate of return, it calls for calculating the profit first and the remainder of the cash income amount represents capital recovery; whereas the present year-to-year book rate of return determined by the orthodox bookkeeping method calls for calculating the depreciation, or capital recovery, first and the remainder of the cash income amount represents profit and, therefore, it is incompatible with and diametrically opposed to the DCF rate of return used for evaluating proposed new projects.

This year-to-year book rate of return determined by the DCF technique will make it possible for companies to assess the impact cash income or cost savings generated by new projects is having on their overall profitability.

Chapter 17

Conclusion —————————————————————————

$\mathbf{T}$he field of investment analysis is broad and shows that capital investments of companies pass through numerous phases from the time they are first contemplated until they are fully recovered. Their successful handling, while passing through these different phases, depends to a large extent on the financial tools chosen to perform these different tasks. To perform them efficiently and successfully, the financial tools must be realistic, dependable, and effective. A thorough study of the various financial tools, or financial criteria, available to corporate management reveals that those determined by the use of discounted cash flow pass these tests most adequately and favorably.

Consequently, this study reveals that discounted cash flow can be used most effectively by companies in determining (1) the viability of prospective projects in feasibility studies, (2) their acceptability in economic evaluations, (3) their actual performances versus their original estimates in post-completion audits, and (4) their impact on a company's overall profitability in periodic profitability studies.

More specifically, discounted cash flow also can be used most effectively in determining (1) how much companies can afford to invest in prospective projects, (2) how much cash income or savings they have to generate, (3) how long they have to be productive, (4) what rate of return they will earn, (5) whether their capital assets should be leased or purchased and debt financed if outside financing is contemplated, and (6) how much companies to be acquired are worth and what price to pay for them.

This study reveals also that there is nothing intrinsically wrong with the financial criteria determined by discounted cash flow techniques; and that quite to the contrary, these techniques are actually far more meaningful, realistic, and reliable compared to those determined by other, more orthodox methods.

For example, the DCF rate of return, unquestionably is far superior to the average annual earnings rate of return, both as a profitability indicator and as a project selection device, because it reflects both the capital recovery of prospective projects and the timing of their cash flows, which the average annual earnings rate does not reflect.

Furthermore, how can anyone possibly doubt that the DCF rate of return, which is comparable with the compound interest rate and is determined by the same discounting technique, isn't as true and realistic a rate as the compound interest rate—a rate used by banks and other lending institutions for calculating interest charges for the use of money loaned to outside borrowers.

Another example of the effective use of discounted cash flow is in determining the worth of companies to be acquired which indicates the price to pay for them. This financial criterion is far superior to the price-earnings ratios, year-to-year book rates of return, book values, earnings per share, etc., determined by the more orthodox bookkeeping methods, because the latter invariably are grossly distorted due to the deleterious effects of inflation and accepted accounting and financial reporting principles and practices that cause cheap income dollars to be measured against expensive investment dollars.

This study further reveals that when financial criteria determined by discounted cash flow techniques are found to be distorted and unrealistic, this invariably is attributable to one or both of the following two reasons: (1) poorly prepared estimates of prospective projects' capital cost, cash returns, and economic life, which may be woefully unrealistic for a wide variety of reasons; and (2) improper application of the discounted cash flow concept by compounding and/or discounting prospective projects' cash flows at an improper rate.

Another important fact brought to light by this study is that depreciation deficiencies, or failure to recover the full purchasing power of companies' capital investments in depreciable fixed assets has an adverse effect not only on the profitability of new projects but also on the companies' overall profitability. This condition could be remedied by a revision in present corporate income tax laws that would permit companies to depreciate fixed assets on their current-year replacement costs instead of on their original cost.

Finally, this study reveals that the DCF rate of return, which is used in the decision-making process for the acceptance or the rejection of prospective projects, and the year-to-year book rate of return, which is used to assess the efficient utilization of companies' total assets, are incompatible. This incompatibility makes it virtually impossible to assess the impact profits generated by new projects are having on companies' overall profitability. However, this problem, which has caused considerable confusion and consternation among executives of companies that use the DCF rate of return for evaluating prospective projects, can be resolved successfully by determining year-to-year book rates of return by the use of discounted cash flow, which will be comparable and compatible with the DCF rate of return.

Index